D0919454

East Meadow Public Library
1886 Front Street, East Meadow, NY 11554
(516) 794-2570
www.eastmeadow.info

ALL ■ IN ■ ONE

CompTIA Server+® Certification

EXAM GUIDE

(Exam SK0-004)

Daniel Lachance

New York Chicago San Francisco
Athens London Madrid Mexico City
Milan New Delhi Singapore Sydney Toronto

Cataloging-in-Publication Data is on file with the Library of Congress

McGraw-Hill Education books are available at special quantity discounts to use as premiums and sales promotions, or for use in corporate training programs. To contact a representative, please visit the Contact Us pages at www.mhprofessional.com.

CompTIA Server+® Certification All-in-One Exam Guide (Exam SK0-004)

1 2 3 4 5 6 7 8 9 LCR 21 20 19 18 17 16

ISBN: Book p/n 978-1-25-983800-2 and CD p/n 978-1-25-983801-9
of set 978-1-25-983803-3

MHID: Book p/n 1-25-983800-5 and CD p/n 1-25-983801-3
of set 1-25-983803-X

Sponsoring Editor
Hilary Flood

Editorial Supervisor
Jody McKenzie

Project Manager
Poonam Bisht, MPS Limited

Acquisitions Coordinator
Claire Yee

Technical Editor
S. Russell Christy

Copy Editor
Lisa Theobald

Proofreader
Paul Tyler

Indexer
James Minkin

Production Supervisor
James Kussow

Composition
MPS Limited

Illustration
MPS Limited

Art Director, Cover
Jeff Weeks

Becoming a CompTIA Certified IT Professional Is Easy

It's also the best way to reach greater professional opportunities and rewards.

Why Get CompTIA Certified?

Growing Demand

Labor estimates predict some technology fields will experience growth of more than 20% by the year 2020. (Source: CompTIA 9th Annual Information Security Trends study: 500 U.S. IT and Business Executives Responsible for Security.) CompTIA certification qualifies the skills required to join this workforce.

Higher Salaries

IT professionals with certifications on their resume command better jobs, earn higher salaries, and have more doors open to new multi-industry opportunities.

Verified Strengths

91% of hiring managers indicate CompTIA certifications are valuable in validating IT expertise, making certification the best way to demonstrate your competency and knowledge to employers. (Source: CompTIA Employer Perceptions of IT Training and Certification.)

Universal Skills

CompTIA certifications are vendor neutral—which means that certified professionals can proficiently work with an extensive variety of hardware and software found in most organizations.

ABOUT THE AUTHOR

Daniel Lachance, CompTIA Security+™, CompTIA A+®, CompTIA Network+®, CompTIA Server+, CompTIA Cloud Essentials, MCITP, MCTS, MCSA, is the owner of Lachance IT Consulting Inc. He is the author of *CompTIA Cloud Essentials Certification Study Guide* and co-author of *CompTIA Security+ Certification Practice Exams*.

Dan is an experienced trainer, having delivered IT training in Canada and the Caribbean since the 1990s on topics ranging from various Microsoft products, including Visual Basic, Hyper-V, and System Center Configuration Manager, to other products, including UNIX, Linux, Novell, and IBM Notes and Domino.

Dan has recorded numerous tech support videos for products such as Microsoft Azure, Amazon Web Services, Microsoft System Center Configuration Manager, various cybersecurity and mobility topics, and Linux.

He enjoys spending time with his spouse, Stacey; children, Roman, Trinity, Raylee, Anastasia, and Zoey; and the family dogs, Dori and Bailey. He is also a member of Clusterfunk, a Halifax, Nova Scotia–based cover band.

About the Technical Editor

S. Russell Christy is a trainer for New Horizons Computer Learning Center of Memphis, Tennessee, where he delivers traditional and online classroom learning for adults, covering a wide variety of products. He specializes in web and print design, Microsoft Office applications, and computer maintenance, network, and security. For nearly 20 years, he has deployed new desktops and operating systems, servers, and network hardware and software, while simultaneously troubleshooting various hardware and software issues.

Russ holds a bachelor's degree in business administration from the University of Memphis. He has also gained industry certifications in CompTIA A+, CompTIA Network+, CompTIA Security+, CompTIA Server+, MTA Windows Server Administration Fundamentals, Network Fundamentals, Security Fundamentals, Windows OS Fundamentals, Microsoft Office Specialist 2007 Master, Microsoft Office Specialist 2013 Master, Adobe Certified Expert Dreamweaver CS6, and Adobe Education Trainer.

Learn	Certify	Work
Learn more about what the exam covers by reviewing the following: • Exam objectives for key study points. • Sample questions for a general overview of what to expect on the exam and examples of question format. • Visit online forums, like LinkedIn, to see what other IT professionals say about CompTIA exams.	Purchase a voucher at a Pearson VUE testing center or at CompTIAstore.com. • Register for your exam at a Pearson VUE testing center. • Visit pearsonvue.com/CompTIA to find the closest testing center to you. • Schedule the exam online. You will be required to enter your voucher number or provide payment information at registration. • Take your certification exam.	Congratulations on your CompTIA certification! • Make sure to add your certification to your resume. • Check out the CompTIA Certification Roadmap to plan your next career move.

Learn More: Certification.CompTIA.org/aplus

CompTIA Disclaimer

CONTENTS AT A GLANCE

CONTENTS

PREFACE

Welcome to *CompTIA Server+ Certification All-in-One Exam Guide (Exam SK0-004)*! By reading and understanding each chapter including the questions, completing the included lab exercises, and taking the included master exams, you will greatly increase your likelihood of passing the CompTIA SK0-004 exam.

This book maps to the official CompTIA SK0-004 exam objectives to help you prepare for the exam, but it also goes beyond the objectives to provide insight that will prove valuable when you are working in server-related environments.

ACKNOWLEDGMENTS

With each book project, I am always amazed at the collection of talented people required to make it all happen. I would like to thank Hilary Flood for providing the opportunity to create this book. Claire Yee, Jody McKenzie, and Poonam Bisht were the guiding lights as to what I should be doing, and when I should be doing it. I would also like to thank the rest of the wonderful team at McGraw-Hill Education for making this project a great experience, resulting in a solid and fun book.

This book is chock-full of technical goodies, but credit must be given to S. Russell Christy for keeping the technical content consistent, accurate, and relevant—thanks, Russ! Feedback about ideas and content from other parties always improves a product: thank you to Roman Lachance for invaluable feedback and great ideas that helped shape this book.

I would like to say a special thank you to my family for enduring the many hours I spent preparing for and creating this book, as well as the endless techno-rambling I tend to fall prey to—love you guys!

INTRODUCTION

The CompTIA Server+ certification exam is becoming increasingly popular and showing up in IT job listings as a desired certification. Topics formerly included in the discontinued CompTIA Storage+ certification are now included with Server+. This change makes sense because of the close relationship servers have with storage, especially network storage.

Certified CompTIA Server+ candidates demonstrate a solid understanding of topics ranging from server hardware to server operating systems, networking and security, storage, and cloud-based solutions. Today's server administrators are responsible for remote administration of potentially hundreds of physical and virtualized servers, whether in a small server room or in a large data center.

The true skill required by CompTIA Server+ technicians is effective troubleshooting. Yes, it's important to understand concepts and the sequence of steps required to yield a desired result, but what about when things going wrong? The timely and efficient resolution of server-related issues is what distinguishes a casual server technician from an outstanding server technician. This book includes entire chapters dedicated to troubleshooting and disaster recovery.

Exam Details

You can book your Chinese Simplified, English, or Japanese CompTIA Server+ SK0-004 exam online at www.pearsonvue.com/comptia/ or by phone with your local Pearson Vue testing center. Consult the web site to find the testing center nearest you, including directions to the center.

You can use an exam voucher if you have one; otherwise, the cost is USD $285. Payment methods include various debit or credit cards.

Preparing for the Exam

People learn in different ways. Reading and comprehension is important, especially when it comes to end-of-chapter and master exam questions included with this book. Some folks learn best by doing; that's why you'll find hands-on exercises using both Windows and Linux at the end of each chapter. Doing can sometimes sear concepts or configuration steps into our brains.

It's been proven that doing something related to a discussed topic helps our brains to understand how the topic is relevant and thus aids in retention. For more on this, be sure to read up on the CompTIA Brain+ certification. (Actually, this is just a techie's attempt at humor [fail?]; Brain+ does not exist!)

The following list provides some general test-taking tips:

- Have a positive attitude.
- Learn the material in earnest; it is interesting and it can help your career.
- Get a full night's sleep for a few days prior to taking the exam.
- Eat properly before taking the exam.
- Don't cram right before the exam.
- Arrive at the testing center 15 minutes early.
- Read questions and *all answers* thoroughly.
- With complex questions, ask yourself, "What is the question really asking?"

At the Testing Center

After booking your exam, take the time to ensure that you know how to get to the center, including any buses you might take, and find out where you can park if you plan on driving.

You will need two pieces of ID at the testing center, including one bearing your picture. The testing center will also take a picture of you for your exam score report, so make sure you look your best! Smartphones, books, or notes are not allowed in the testing room with you.

Making the Grade

The required passing score for the CompTIA SK0-004 exam is 750, and the exam consists of 100 multiple-choice questions that you must answer within 90 minutes. The exam is scored between 100 and 900, and some questions included on the exam may not count toward your score. CompTIA does this occasionally to test out new content or question formats, but you won't know which question(s) this applies to.

Table 1 lists the exam domains and their weight against the overall exam. Notice the emphasis on server administration and troubleshooting. For a detailed

Table 1 CompTIA Server+ SK0-004 Exam Domains

Exam Domain	Percentage of the Exam
1.0 Server Architecture	12%
2.0 Server Administration	24%
3.0 Storage	12%
4.0 Security	13%
5.0 Networking	10%
6.0 Disaster Recovery	9%
7.0 Troubleshooting	20%

breakdown of CompTIA Server+ SK0-004 exam objectives, visit certification.comptia.org/certifications/server and click the Get Sample Questions And Exam Objectives button.

During the exam, you can use a marker and laminated paper to write notes and calculate values, such as valid subnet ranges. Each question has a Prev (previous) and Next button you can click to allow navigation throughout the entire exam. You can also flag certain questions for review; an item review screen will appear after the last question, where you can review some or all of your answers before ending the exam.

The exam contains multiple-choice questions in which you will be asked to choose one or more correct answers.

When studying for this exam, always keep the following in mind:

- What is the most efficient way of completing an IT configuration task?
- What sequence of steps must be followed to achieve a goal?
- What is the first step in troubleshooting a specific issue?
- What can be done to improve the performance or security of an IT system?

You will know right away whether you've passed the exam. CompTIA does not require a waiting period for your first or second attempts at the exam, but you will have to wait 14 calendar days if you want to make a third attempt. Using this book properly should not require a second exam attempt.

Objective Map

The following objective map has been constructed to enable you to cross-reference the official exam objectives with the objectives as they are presented and covered in this book. References have been provided for the objective exactly as the exam vendor presents it, the section of the exam guide that covers that objective, and a chapter reference.

CompTIA Server+ Certification Exam SK0-004

Official Exam Objective	All-in-One Coverage	Chapter No.
1.0 Server Architecture		
1.1 Explain the purpose and function of server form factors	Server Form Factors	2
	Tower Servers	2
	Rack-mounted Servers	2
	Blade Servers	2
1.2 Given a scenario, install, configure and maintain server components	Server Components	2
	CPUs	2
	Memory	2
	Buses	2
	NICs	2
	RAID Controllers	2

(continued)

Official Exam Objective	All-in-One Coverage	Chapter No.
1.3 Compare and contrast power and cooling components	Power Environmental Controls	2 2
2.0 Server Administration		
2.1 Install and configure server operating systems	Server Installation Local vs. PXE BIOS UEFI File Systems Configuring IPv4 Configuring IPv6	3 3 2 2 4 5 5
2.2 Compare and contrast server roles and requirements for each	Server Roles DHCP DNS WINS NTP Directory Services Web Server Application Server File Server Print Server Mail Server RRAS Server Virtualization Server	3 3 3 3 3 3 3 3 3 3 3 3 3
2.3 Given a scenario, use access and control methods to administer a server	Server Administration Methods KVM iLO and iDRAC SSH RDP	3 3 3 3 3
2.4 Given a scenario, perform proper server maintenance techniques	Maintaining Servers Patch Management Optimization Storage Problems and Solutions	3 3 7 7
2.5 Explain the importance of asset management and documentation	Server Documentation Service-Level Agreements Asset Inventory	3 3 3
2.6 Explain the purpose and operation of virtualization components	Virtualization Servers Hypervisor Types Hypervisor Host Configuration Virtual Machine Guest Configuration	3 3 3 3

Official Exam Objective	All-in-One Coverage	Chapter No.
3.0 Storage		
3.1 Given a scenario, install and deploy primary storage devices based on given specifications and interfaces	Storage Technologies Magnetic Hard Disks Solid-State Drives Storage Device Installation	4 4 4 4
3.2 Given a scenario, configure RAID using best practices	RAID Configuration RAID 0 RAID 1 RAID 5 RAID 6 RAID 10	4 4 4 4 4 4
3.3 Summarize hardware and features of various storage technologies	Storage Technologies Optical Drives Direct-Attached Storage Network-Attached Storage Storage Area Networks	4 4 4 4 4
3.4 Given a scenario, calculate appropriate storage capacity and plan for future growth	Base 2 vs. Base 10 Storage Capacity and Future Growth Where Did All the Disk Space Go? Using Less Disk Space Compression	4 4 4 4
4.0 Security		
4.1 Compare and contrast physical security methods and concepts	Physical Security	6
4.2 Given a scenario, apply server hardening techniques	Operating System Hardening Hardware Hardening Application Hardening	6 6 6
4.3 Explain basic network security systems and protocols	Data Security Authentication	6 6
4.4 Implement logical access control methods based on company policy	Windows NTFS Permissions Network-based Firewalls	6 6
4.5 Implement data security methods and secure storage disposal techniques	Encrypting Data at Rest Secure Media Disposal	6 6
4.6 Given a scenario, implement proper environmental controls and techniques	UPS Racks Electrostatic Discharge Humidity Fire Suppression	2 2 2 2 2

(continued)

Official Exam Objective	All-in-One Coverage	Chapter No.
5.0 Networking		
5.1 Given a scenario, configure servers to use IP addressing and network infrastructure services	Configuring IPv4	5
	Configuring IPv6	5
	Default Gateway	5
	DNS Servers	5
	WINS Servers	5
	DNS	5
	DHCP	5
5.2 Compare and contrast various ports and protocols	TCP and UDP	5
	SNMP	5
	SMTP	5
	FTP	5
	SFTP	5
	SSH	5
	SCP	5
	NTP	5
	HTTP	5
	HTTPS	5
	TELNET	5
	IMAP	5
	POP3	5
	RDP	5
	FTPS	5
	LDAP	5
	DNS	5
	DHCP	5
5.3 Given a scenario, install cables and implement proper cable management procedures	Copper Cables	5
	Copper Cable Connectors	5
	Fiber-optic Cables	5
	Fiber-optic Connectors	5
6.0 Disaster Recovery		
6.1 Explain the importance of disaster recovery principles	Alternate Sites	8
	Data Replication	8
	Disaster Recovery Plan	8
	Business Continuity	8
6.2 Given a scenario, implement appropriate backup techniques	Backup Types	8
	Backup Media	8
	On-premises Backup	8
	Cloud Backup	8
	Backup and Restore Best Practices	8

Official Exam Objective	All-in-One Coverage	Chapter No.
7.0 Troubleshooting		
7.1 Explain troubleshooting theory and methodologies	Troubleshooting Methodology	7
7.2 Given a scenario, effectively troubleshoot hardware problems, selecting the appropriate tools and methods	Hardware Problems and Solutions	7
7.3 Given a scenario, effectively troubleshoot software problems, selecting the appropriate tools and methods	Software Problems and Solutions	7
7.4 Given a scenario, effectively diagnose network problems, selecting the appropriate tools and methods	Network Problems and Solutions	7
7.5 Given a scenario, effectively troubleshoot storage problems, selecting the appropriate tools and methods	Storage Problems and Solutions	7
7.6 Given a scenario, effectively diagnose security issues, selecting the appropriate tools and methods	Security Problems and Solutions	7

CHAPTER 1

Introduction to CompTIA Server+ Essentials

In this chapter, you will

- Learn about server hardware components
- Learn how storage systems can be configured and provisioned
- Review basic network concepts
- Review the basics of monitoring and maintaining server operating systems
- Review basic security concepts
- Learn about troubleshooting and optimizing performance
- Learn about disaster recovery

This chapter provides an overview of topics (all of the gory details follow in Chapters 2–8) that you're sure to see on the CompTIA Server+ SK0-004 exam. We'll also cover these juicy topics in such a way that you'll be well armed working in the IT field, whether you're discussing network storage for cloud-based virtualized servers, determining specific server hardware that must be ordered, or working in a data center.

Data centers are neat—these big facilities host a wide array of IT services that are consumed by clients located hundreds, even thousands, of miles away! You can bet that, among others, CompTIA Server+ certification is often preferred for data center jobs. (And, by the way, if you're just starting at a data center, be prepared for the 7 P.M. to 7 A.M. shift!)

Why This Book Is Relevant

Because you're reading this book, you probably already see the value in learning about the CompTIA Server+ SK0-004 exam. CompTIA is respected globally in the IT industry for its certifications for A+, Network+, Server+, Linux+, and many others. If you check out IT job listings on your favorite job-hunting site or ask people working at IT academic institutions, you'll learn that many jobs require CompTIA certification in one form or another.

Being a server expert is much different today from what it was in the 1990s, and that's going back only 20 or so years! If you've been working in IT for a while, you might agree that there was a time when

- We could know everything about a server operating system.
- Arguably, overall server support was *simpler* because the software wasn't doing as many things.

- Arguably, overall server support was *harder* because we didn't have great Internet search engines and video tutorials.
- Applying patches didn't occupy nearly as much of our time.
- Malware infections weren't nearly as ubiquitous.
- Storage was contained physically inside the server case.
- TCP/IPv4 was groundbreaking.
- "The cloud" meant it was going to rain.
- "Fiber" meant nothing more than bread and cereal.
- What's a data center anyway?

The CompTIA SK0-004 exam makes sure that candidates really know what they're talking about, and that includes much more than just servers themselves. You need to be familiar with server types and components, virtualization, IPv4 and IPv6 networking, cloud computing, operating systems, network storage, security, and troubleshooting. If all this interests you (and you need this certification to get a job!), then you are in the right place.

What kinds of jobs relate to the CompTIA Server+ certification? Countless, but let's list a few general categories:

- Data center IT technician
- Server administrator
- Network technician
- Help desk technician

Remember that an understanding of the body of knowledge presented in this book is crucial for IT server and network technicians working for companies in any industry.

Server Hardware Basics

Everybody uses servers in one way or another, even if they don't realize it—from teenagers posting content to social media from their smartphones, to shoppers making online purchases, companies backing data up to the cloud, and all the way up to Wall Street executives making decisions based on server-supplied data. Although the role of a server (the centralized serving of content and services to concurrent users over a network) hasn't changed much over the decades, the scale of clients demanding quick and reliable access, the amount of data processed, as well as how servers are implemented, *have changed*. It's not enough to know about servers themselves; there is an entire ecosystem we need to be aware of.

Servers offer some kind of a service to clients over the network, such as a web server offering a web site to a client's web browser. The server role and number of clients it will serve dictate how much horsepower is needed. The interesting part is that this is true whether you're working with physical or virtual servers.

The CompTIA SK0-004 exam will test your knowledge on the best hardware configuration given a specific server scenario.

Server Form Factors

Physical servers come in different sizes and shapes, as you'll see in Chapter 2. For instance, tower servers take up more space than their slimmer cousins, blade and rack-mount servers. Blade servers take the least amount of space.

Arranging physical servers requires knowledge of server racks with sliding rails for equipment, including, but not limited to, servers. This is a much better use of space than tower servers arranged on the floor. Blade enclosures make even better use of space. A blade enclosure is mounted into a rack, and blade servers slide into the enclosure for the utmost in space savings (what techies like to call "increasing data center server density").

Server CPUs

While a single CPU chip may suffice for a desktop, servers often have multiple physical CPU chips plugged into CPU sockets on the server motherboard. Each CPU chip consists of one or more cores. A CPU core has the same functionally as a physical CPU and multiple cores can be embedded on a single CPU chip.

CPUs use high-speed L1, L2, and L3 cache memory for data and instructions to speed up processing. A 4 GHz CPU slows down when data needs to get on a bus to get to a different component in the server—for example, down to 600 MHz.

Where desktops and servers commonly use the more powerful Complex Instruction Set Computing (CISC) processors, mobile and consumer electronic devices need less power, which means less heat and cooling required, so they tend to user Reduced Instruction Set Computing (RISC) processors.

Server Memory

Scaling a database server to support larger datasets means adding memory (RAM). Virtual servers can be configured to use more RAM as needed. The extra RAM becomes available from other virtual servers on the same underlying physical host that have RAM to spare at the time.

Memory is either static (SRAM) or dynamic (DRAM). SRAM is used in smaller amounts and is faster than DRAM, which requires a constant refresh of electricity. SRAM is used for L1, L2, and L3 CPU cache memory and *not* the main system memory in your server—that would be DRAM.

You need to know about the various types of RAM chips and which ones will work in your specific hardware. Some servers will accept only double data rate 3 (DDR3) memory, others use DDR4, and so on. Memory chips might also have to be added in pairs for efficient use by server motherboards with multiple CPU sockets. Modern motherboards color-code memory chip sockets to facilitate pairing.

Many servers use memory chips that can detect and fix memory corruption errors; this is known as Error Correcting Code (ECC) memory. That's why memory chips from a desktop, even though they might physically fit on a server motherboard, may not work correctly; they're usually non-ECC chips.

Buses and Slots

Then there are expansion slots. Let's say you need to add a 10Gb Ethernet card in your physical server. All slots are not created equally; an older PCI Express (PCIe) x2 card will fit and work in a PCIe x16 slot, for example, but it won't work the other way around!

Cards have their own form factor, and you might even have run into this at home; some expansion cards might fit into a slot on the motherboard, but the card is too tall and the case won't fit back on. Expansion cards need a bus to move data into and out of the card; servers use a variety of buses to move data around the system.

Thinner servers such as rack-mount and blades won't accommodate standard height expansion cards, but some rack-mount models will allow a daughter card to plug in, which in turn has slots oriented in such a way that standard-size cards can be used.

Blades get their additional capabilities such as storage and networking from other components plugged into the blade enclosure; you won't find a blade server with PCI network cards plugged in.

Virtualization

Virtual servers run as guests on a host (physical) computer, but they are still configured with virtual hardware. Some hypervisors (virtualization software) allow virtual guests to access physical hardware components directly, whereas others emulate hardware for the guest. Consider, for instance, how many virtual CPUs (vCPUs) a virtual machine is configured with. Each vCPU maps to a CPU core and not a physical CPU chip.

A physical multiprocessor system enables each virtual machine to be configured with multiple vCPUs, but more vCPUs doesn't necessarily mean better performance. This is because the hypervisor can get bogged down finding physical CPU time slots for all of the vCPUs; it really depends on what is running within the virtual machine, but sometimes less is more.

Bumping up the number of vCPUs can also cause another problem: licensing. Many software vendors license their server-based products based on the number of physical or logical processors; talk to your software vendor to ensure your compliance with their license rules. Ideally, you'll have an automated way to periodically inventory both hardware and software in use on servers; this is especially useful in a data center.

Environmental Factors

Adding virtual servers to a hypervisor host doesn't make as much difference to power consumption and heat as does adding physical server hardware to a server room or data center. Careful arrangement of equipment can allow for optimal airflow, and ensuring adequate temperature and humidity control goes a long way toward ensuring that hardware runs at peak efficiency and has the longest life possible.

Heat and Air Flow

Imagine cramming dozens of physical servers into a tiny closet with no airflow—excessive heat and servers do not get along well. In Chapter 2 we will explore how to determine that you have sufficient heating/ventilation/air conditioning (HVAC) for your hardware.

The more equipment you have, the greater the power draw, which means more heat is generated, which means more cooling is required. Using blade enclosures and server virtualization are two ways to reduce power consumption and heat.

When you're working with a lot of equipment, it's important to ensure that cool air is fed into devices and that the warmer resulting air is exhausted elsewhere and properly taken out of the room or cooled down again. Data centers normally send cool air from the floor up to rack components. Arranging racks of equipment in rows facilitates the creation of hot and cold aisles.

CPUs generate a lot of heat the faster they run. Heat sinks are placed over the CPU chip to dissipate heat away from the chip, and this can be accelerated with a fan to suck the warm air away from the chip.

Liquid cooling is another server cooling option that uses cool water brought into the server. The heated water then leaves the server and is cooled externally.

Static Charges

An often overlooked aspect of environmental control includes electrostatic discharge (ESD) and fire suppression. Of course, large server rooms and data centers are designed with these things in mind, but smaller environments might simply convert the janitor's closet into a server/wiring closet.

ESD is the frenzied rush of electrons between differently charged objects; this is bad news because it can damage sensitive electronic components. There are ways to reduce the possibility of ESD—basically, taking steps to ensure that objects coming into contact with each other are equally charged.

Fire Suppression

In the event of an electrical fire, we do *not* want to use water as a fire suppressant. Server room and data center designs call for special construction and fire-suppression mechanisms not only to extinguish fires, but also to minimize damage to electrical equipment. Chapter 2 will dive into proper ESD and fire suppression practices.

Storage

Most individuals and business like to keep data around for a while. Servers can play the role of a centralized file repository. You need to know the variations on how disk subsystems can be configured and provisioned. This topic in all its glory was formerly a separate CompTIA certification (Storage+) that no longer exists; instead, all of the storage details are now a part of the CompTIA Server+ certification.

Traditionally, servers housed local disks within their physical enclosures, otherwise known as direct-attached storage (DAS). This has evolved to the point where server storage needs are addressed by accessing storage over a storage area network (SAN) and in some cases in the cloud. A server might boot the operating system from DAS and store data on the SAN. Various SAN standards will be covered in Chapter 4.

There are various types of storage media, including traditional magnetic hard disks and the much sought-after solid-state drives (SSDs). SSDs have no moving parts, and as such are quieter, consume less power, and are pretty quick; the downside is price. But as with many other things, all storage media are not alike. Disk interfaces such as universal serial bus (USB), serial-attached SCSI (SAS), and fiber channel are an important consideration when working with servers, as are disk characteristics such as input/output operations per second (IOPS) and storage capacity.

Redundant array of independent disks, or, depending on who you ask, redundant array of *inexpensive* disks (RAID) groups multiple physical disks together for two potential purposes: better performance and fault tolerance. If your hardware supports RAID, you can configure it at the firmware level; alternatively, software RAID organizes disks to work as a logical unit within the supported operating system. You need to understand RAID levels so that you can configure disks to best suit a particular server need. For instance, RAID level 1 (disk mirroring) increases the resilience to failure, but RAID level 0 (disk striping) improves performance. We'll talk about how this works in Chapter 4.

EXAM TIP Rest assured that successful CompTIA Server+ candidates are expected to know when to apply specific RAID configurations given a particular scenario. It's not enough to know just the theory; make sure you have experience configuring and using various RAID configurations, even at the software level. A hands-on exercise in Chapter 4 can help guide you.

Once a server connects to storage of any kind, it's business as usual—partitioning, formatting, and setting user permissions. In some cases, disk or file encryption might be needed to secure data further.

Network Concepts

Ah, networking. This is what make computing devices extremely useful—the immediate accessing of services and the sharing of data. You may remember a time (the 1980s) when sharing data involved copying files to tape cassettes or floppy disks. In the early 1990s, we had modems with dial-up bulletin boards at nonscreaming, painfully slow transmission rates. How things have changed over the decades!

Cables and Connectors

A solid understanding of computer networks includes network hardware as well as network software. Ask yourself how many miles of cables or wireless transmissions are involved when you check the local news web site each morning—it really is amazing how it works, since there are so many different technologies actually talking to each other.

Cables and connectors matter as much to the average home Internet user as they do to IT pros installing cabling in office buildings, data centers, and provider networks. Chapter 5 will provide the nitty-gritty for copper- and fiber optic–based transmission media.

IP

On top of correctly configured network hardware, we have what most of us will configure and troubleshoot during our IT careers—Transmission Control Protocol/Internet

Protocol (TCP/IP), usually referred to simply as IP. IPv4 and the newer IPv6 are collections of protocols that make things work on a network, but only if we've configured things correctly such as the IP address, subnet mask, default gateway, and DNS server, among other settings.

NOTE There is no IPv5; IPv6 is newer than the 1970s-era IPv4, although IPv6 has yet to be widely adopted within the enterprise.

IPv6 uses a 128-bit address space compared to IPv4's 32-bit address space. This means IPv6 has many more unique IP addresses compared to IPv4. IPv6 also includes built-in mechanisms that improve network quality of service (QoS) as well as security. IPv4 is used everywhere on the Internet, but IPv6 is not ubiquitous yet, so currently we can use tunneling technologies to get IPv6 traffic routed through the Internet.

It is only with a clear understanding of IP addressing and protocols in a multisubnet environment that you can properly support TCP/IP. For example, for a client workstation unable to connect to a server on a remote subnet, you might verify that name resolution and the default gateway (router) are configured correctly and reachable by the client.

Ports and Protocols

The application layer of the TCP/IP model contains protocols that allow direct interaction with users over the network, and they depend on lower layer transport protocols such as User Datagram Protocol (UDP) and Transmission Control Protocol (TCP). Think of a web server listening for requests from client web browsers. HyperText Transfer Protocol (HTTP) is an application protocol that listens for client requests on TCP port 80. You can think of a port as a listening channel that uniquely identifies a network service.

Port numbers are 16-bit values tied either to TCP or UDP. There are 65,535 possible port numbers (2^{16}). The first 1024 are called *well-known ports* and are reserved for common network services such as HTTP.

Other application protocols such as Simple Mail Transfer Protocol (SMTP) and Domain Name Service (DNS) use different port numbers—TCP 25 and UDP 53, respectively. Some network software will allow you to specify the port number that it listens on while others will not.

EXAM TIP Know the application layer protocols and their port numbers. Scenario-based questions may indirectly test your knowledge in this area. A much more exhaustive list will be presented in Chapter 5.

Server Operating Systems

When it comes to servers, a myriad of questions need answers. What is the server's purpose? How many users will be connecting at once? How critical is it that the server stay up and running no matter what? Planning servers before jumping into the fun stuff is paramount.

Chapter 3 will address these questions and more:

- Will the server operating system be installed onto physical hardware or in a virtual machine?
- Does the server support BIOS or UEFI?
- Are we installing the Windows, UNIX, or Linux operating system?
- What type of disk partitioning and file systems should we use?
- How will we remotely connect to the server?
- How will patches be applied?
- How will we secure the server?

Servers provide services and content to users. Companies often have their own servers running on their own equipment (on premises), but installing, configuring, and running various server roles in the cloud is becoming more and more common. The great thing about provisioning virtual server roles in the public cloud (on provider equipment) is how quickly you can get servers up and running without an investment in hardware. And, generally, you pay only for the time the virtual server is running—no wonder its popularity has soared!

NOTE Throughout this book you will learn about not only Windows Server operating systems, but also Red Hat Enterprise Linux, in both physical and virtual environments. This includes hands-on exercises and troubleshooting tips as well.

Server Roles

Infrastructure services such as Network Time Protocol (NTP), DNS, and Dynamic Host Configuration Protocol (DHCP) must be in place before anything else will work on the network. NTP assures that network devices agree on the time. DHCP delivers a valid IP configuration to hosts where DNS is used to resolve friendly names (such as www.mheducation.com) to an IP address.

Directory servers provide a central network database of configuration objects, such as user accounts used for authentication. In a Microsoft Active Directory Domain Services (AD DS) environment, DNS must be functional for AD to be functional. In Chapter 3, we will install an AD domain and then explore the various ways that computers can be joined to the domain for centralized administration.

Application servers and web servers—how are they different? Traditionally, application servers run a server-side application that clients can access over the network in various ways. These days, the connection often uses HTTP or its secure counterpart, HTTPS. This means a web server needs to be on the server to handle these requests. The application server comes into play when developers build a business-specific solution on the web server—in other words, business logic, such as a payment processing service for e-commerce transactions. Planning for and configuring a web or application server have different requirements than an internal file server would.

File servers are file repositories in the enterprise. As IT administrators, we grant user permissions and set quotas on disk space usage. Having enough fast disks is a primary concern here, as is the network speed for file access. These days, cloud storage is all the rage; individuals and enterprises can provision storage as needed on provider equipment and pay only for the amount of disk space used. There are also hybrid solutions where enterprise file servers can synchronize and even do backups to the cloud.

Maintenance

Once servers are humming along, we want to keep them going. A service level agreement (SLA) is a contract between a provider and consumer stating expected levels of service, including details such as uptime and response time. Maintenance tasks, such as applying patches and firmware updates and ensuring that the server complies with organizational configuration settings and security policy, require continual attention, so just because the server is installed and configured, it doesn't mean our work is complete. Your approach to these tasks will differ in a small company with a handful of servers compared to a large data center with thousands of servers. You'll also need a way to connect remotely to servers through either a software or a hardware solution.

One way to ensure server uptime is to configure failover clustering. This involves at least two server nodes working together to provide the same service. If one cluster node fails, users are automatically switched over to the service running on a remaining node. Network load balancing (NLB) can be used to achieve optimal network performance, such as for a busy web site. It does this by distributing incoming traffic to the least busy back-end server hosting the web site. In the case of public cloud computing, failover and load balancing is often enabled with minimal effort, and in some cases it is automatically enabled!

Server Management

Long gone are the days of logging in directly at the physical server console. Instead, administrators connect remotely over the network to manage servers. This can be done using software or hardware solutions.

Software remote management solutions such as Secure Shell (SSH) depend on the server operating system functioning properly. But what if the server hangs and doesn't respond? Then what?

Hardware remote management solutions such as Intelligent Platform Management Interface (IPMI) and Integrated Dell Remote Access (iDRAC) run independently of the operating system—so a server that hangs isn't a problem. Hardware management solutions require a valid IP configuration so that the server can be accessed remotely.

Monitoring

Monitoring the performance of servers is an ongoing task. You'll normally monitor some aspect of CPU, memory, disk, and network use. You might even enable alerts based on configured thresholds ("We're almost out of RAM—do something!"). In a virtualization (and certainly a data center) environment, monitoring can be complex and must be configured carefully. Not only should we monitor aspects of physical virtualization hosts (hypervisors) but also the virtual machine guests that run on them.

Service Level Agreements

Data centers hosting IT services for numerous customers must diligently monitor server performance and network availability to ensure adherence to SLAs. An SLA is a contract between the provider and consumer of a service that details expected levels of service—for IT, that includes the response time over the network and uptime (expressed as a percentage) of a network service.

Security Considerations

Servers can run on networks that are completely isolated from the Internet (air-gapped), or they can in some way be connected. Either way, servers need to be secured and the effectiveness of security controls continuously evaluated. In fact, a large percentage of security breaches actually occur from *within* the network.

Hardening

Hardening is an all-encompassing term used to describe how we lock down or tighten security. For servers this includes, but is not limited to,

- Placing servers in locked rooms/racks
- Disabling unnecessary services
- Applying patches
- Running antimalware software
- Adhering to the principle of least privilege
- Enabling multifactor authenticating
- Auditing the use of sensitive data
- Encrypting data in motion (network)
- Encrypting data at rest (storage)

In a larger network, instead of hardening each server manually, we can apply security settings from a central configuration. Many tools can accomplish this for Windows, UNIX, and Linux servers, such as Microsoft PowerShell Desired State Configuration (DSC) and System Center Configuration Manager (SCCM).

Larger networks need an easy way to determine which servers are not compliant with organizational security policies. They also need an easy way to bring these devices into compliance. Enterprise tools such as SCCM have these problems covered.

EXAM TIP Knowing how to harden a handful of servers is very important. The CompTIA Server+ certification also applies to server management in large environments (such as data centers), so always keep in mind how you can apply configurations on a large scale.

Network Security

Everything would be so much more secure if computers didn't connect to a network, but this is not reality. There are plenty of hardware and software security solutions to address network security.

The first step in protecting a network is being very selective about which users and devices connect to the network. The IEEE 802.1x security standard controls access to a network. The idea is that network edge devices (VPN concentrators, wireless access points, and Ethernet switches) do not perform authentication of connecting devices, but instead forward those requests to a central authentication server on a protected network.

In the case of a LAN device not supporting IEEE 802.1x, it can be disabled at the switch port level.

Authentication

Authentication is the proving of one's identity. This applies to users as well as computing devices. For instance, a smartphone might be required to authenticate itself to a VPN before allowing user credentials.

Multifactor authentication combines at least two different categories of authentication, such as *something you know* (such as a PIN) and *something you have* (such as a smartcard). Combined with firewalls that control the flow of traffic into and out of a network, this is a good first step to securing your network.

PKI

Public Key Infrastructure (PKI) is a hierarchy of trusted digital certificates used for security. Certificates are issued from a trusted authority to users, devices, or services, and they can exist as files on a disk or settings located in a secured storage location (such as the Windows Certificate Store), or they might be written to a smartcard.

Certificates can be used in many ways:

- Authenticate a smartphone to a VPN appliance
- Digitally sign an app before it is published to an app store
- Encrypt sensitive e-mail messages before transmission

You can get certificates from a trusted third party on the Internet, or you can create self-signed certificates for internal use. Chapter 6 will demonstrate how to install and configure a PKI using Windows Certificate Services.

Access Control

After successful authentication, authorization to use a network resource is granted based on access control lists (ACLs). There are many types of ACLs, such as those allowing access to a network and those that allow or deny access to a specific resource such as a file or a web site, often through the use of groups.

In the real world and on the CompTIA Server+ exam, you have to be able to determine which permissions must be set to accomplish a specific goal, and you must also understand permission *inheritance* and *precedence*. The principle of least privilege states that only the permissions required to complete a tasks should be granted and this must always be followed. We'll go through this in detail, including a hands-on exercise, in Chapter 6.

Data at Rest

Securing transmissions to and from servers is always a good idea, but what about data once it reaches a destination and is stored on media? We keep hearing media reports about how millions of customers' personal data has been compromised, and in some cases this involves a malicious user gaining physical access to a storage device.

Encrypting entire disk volumes or individual files and folders adds another layer of security. In the case of a stolen physical storage device, if encryption has been implemented properly, you needn't worry—the device could serve as a lovely paperweight. Encryption of data at rest is very useful with public cloud computing, where data center administrators are prevented from accessing cloud tenant data.

You can use tools to encrypt specific files and folders, or you might choose to encrypt entire disk volumes. Data backups should also be encrypted for additional protection.

When data reaches the end of its useful life, it needs to be disposed of in a secure manner, which might be required for regulatory compliance. This includes the remote wiping of mobile devices, soft and hard wiping of data, and the physical destruction of storage media.

Troubleshooting and Optimizing Performance

Solid troubleshooting stems from truly understanding the underlying technologies and the proper application of a troubleshooting methodology. The ability to reproduce a problem and determine its scope are just a few considerations in quickly resolving issues.

Optimizing Performance

Optimizing the performance of servers and their surrounding ecosystem can prevent negative incidents from occurring in the first place. In the enterprise, troubleshooting can involve poor performance. A server running out of disk space will slow the system to a crawl and could cause services to freeze, yet this could be caused by a lack of memory (RAM). Chapter 7 deals with both performance and troubleshooting, since often they are related.

Troubleshooting

We can apply the CompTIA troubleshooting methodology to real-world situations as well as to scenario-based CompTIA Server+ exam questions. For instance, change only one thing at a time and observe the results of that change. Organizations use a variety of tools to document problems and their eventual resolutions, from recording this information in a spreadsheet to a full-fledged enterprise help desk ticketing system. Over time, this type of knowledge base can prove very valuable.

Hardware and Software Troubleshooting

One area you must be able to troubleshoot is hardware. All hardware eventually fails, in some cases prematurely due to excessive heat or perhaps ESD. Think of the dreaded "Operating system not found" message on a server. Is that a hardware problem, or is it a software problem such as a corrupt file? You have to ask yourself, "Self, what has changed since this last worked correctly?"

You're more than likely going to encounter software rather than hardware issues in your IT career. Consider software misconfigurations. A specific server configuration may work well in one environment for a particular use, but it may fail spectacularly under different circumstances—it's all about meeting business needs.

Other software problems can be much more difficult to troubleshoot—take random freezes, for example. You can still successfully troubleshoot unresponsive systems by viewing log files over time to determine whether or not a pattern exists, or to see what else on the system might have caused the problem.

Network Troubleshooting

Problems with server network communications can be a real pain in the neck; in some cases, such as with physical servers, we may need to be physically present to solve a problem. Hardware and software remote control solutions do nothing if we can't remotely communicate with the server in the first place.

An enterprise IPv4 or IPv6 environment can be tricky to troubleshoot because the problem is specific to that implementation. Technical knowledge and network documentation (or details about network configurations including infrastructure) is central to snuffing out issues quickly when they arise. As always, we need to determine who (or what) is experiencing network communication issues. If it's a single user or station, we know our infrastructure is good, so that allows us to focus our attention on the most likely problem sources.

Just because we can't connect a network resource by name doesn't mean the Internet is broken. Chapter 7 is chock-full of tips and tools at our disposal.

EXAM TIP One way to ensure your success in passing the CompTIA SK0-004 exam is to know *when* to use a particular network troubleshooting tool or command. Of course, you are also expected to know *how* to use a tool to solve a specific problem. Naturally, this will make you valuable in the real world!

Storage Troubleshooting

Because the former CompTIA Storage+ certification body of knowledge is now included in the CompTIA Server+ certification, not only do you have to understand the subject of storage, but you also have an obligation to know how to fix it when it's broken or performing badly.

Equaling the other troubleshooting topics in Chapter 7, here you are required to know how to use the correct tools to solve storage problems that are interwoven with hardware (inappropriate RAID configurations), software and network issues (inability to connect to network storage), as well as matters of security (most often permissions).

Security Troubleshooting

This topic is interweaved with some form of hardware, software, or network troubleshooting. Think of an expired PKI certificate on a laptop that prevents that laptop from connecting to a VPN—sounds like a network issue, right? Well, it is, sort of, but it's not the *source* of the problem.

The CompTIA Server+ exam could include questions related to users being unable to access some type of network resource because of misconfigured permissions. Again, it *sounds* like it could be a network issue, but if other users can access that same resource, we know that's not the case.

Security-related hardware and software have log files that we can peruse to determine problem causes. But really, you can't solve problems with silo thinking—in other words, you need to know about surrounding configurations (hardware, software, and network) and business processes to solve security problems effectively.

Chapter 7 will dive into malware and firewall issues, group policy configurations, and many other problems (and resolutions) associated with security.

Preparing for the Worst

Bad things happen. We can't always predict how or when, but we *can* plan in advance for potential future negative incidents. This is the theme in Chapter 8.

Disaster recovery (DR) and business continuity relate to matters such as

- Determining the impact of interruptions
- Duplication (removing single points of failure)
- Data replication
- Data backup
- Alternate locations to resume business operations

You can't prevent all adverse situations, but you can minimize the unfavorable impacts against servers and business operations. This can succeed only with up-front planning and ensuring that technicians know their roles when it comes to incident response handling.

Chapter Review

This chapter provided insight into what the rest of this book offers. The body of knowledge covered for the CompTIA Server+ certification exam is valuable for any IT-related job.

Questions

1. Which server form factor occupies the most space?
   - A. Blade
   - B. Virtual
   - C. Rack-mount
   - D. Tower

2. What term is used to describe a virtualized operating system?
   - A. Host
   - B. Guest
   - C. Hypervisor
   - D. Load balancer

3. Which two of the following items are related to HVAC?
   - A. Perimeter fencing
   - B. Ventilation
   - C. Dual power supplies
   - D. Temperature control

4. How can ESD be reduced?
   - A. Storing hardware components in a freezer
   - B. Ensuring that objects coming into contact with one another have different charges
   - C. Ensuring that objects coming into contact with one another have equal charges
   - D. Storing hardware components in plastic bags

5. What is the difference between DAS and a SAN?
   - A. DAS allows the server to use network storage as if it were local. SAN storage is local to the server.
   - B. DAS is local storage, and SAN is network storage.
   - C. DAS is local storage specifically for virtual servers. SAN refers to cloud storage.
   - D. DAS and SAN are separate terms that refer to exactly the same thing.

6. What benefits do SSDs provide over magnetic hard disks? Choose two.
   A. Stronger encryption
   B. Increased file integrity
   C. Less power consumption
   D. Quicker file access

7. You would like to improve disk I/O performance for data residing on a physical server. In accordance with your organizational policy, a server must remain running even if an operating system disk fails. The server is currently configured with RAID 1 for the operating system and data. What should you configure?
   A. Nothing. RAID 1 already offers the best performance.
   B. Remove the existing RAID configuration and enable RAID 0.
   C. Add disks to the server. Configure RAID 0 and create a file system. Move the existing data to the newly created filesystem.
   D. Add disks to the server. Configure RAID 0 and create a file system. Move the existing operating system file to the newly created file system.

8. What role does a default gateway perform in an IPv4/IPv6 environment?
   A. It prevents local area network broadcasts from reaching other subnets.
   B. It is a router that allows traffic into and out of a network.
   C. It prevents multicasts from reaching other subnets.
   D. It is a router that performs domain name–to–IP address resolution.

9. Roman is the server administrator for an international insurance company. The London office currently has Active Directory domain controller servers configured with IPv6. The Toronto office domain controllers are also configured with IPv6, yet replication over the Internet is failing between Toronto and London. What should Roman do to enable domain controller replication between the two sites?
   A. Enable IPv6 replication through group policy.
   B. Configure an IPv6 tunneling solution.
   C. Make sure the server PKI certificates allow domain controller replication.
   D. Ensure that servers at both locations are configured with the same default gateway.

10. While capturing network traffic, you notice an excessive amount of traffic destined to a particular host on TCP port 25. What is one possible explanation for this?
    - A. A mail server is being flooded with spam.
    - B. A network broadcast attack is taking place.
    - C. Users' devices on the network happen to be issuing DNS queries at the same time.
    - D. A web server is experiencing a large volume of concurrent visitors.

11. Which of the following demonstrates an advantage of cloud computing? Choose two.
    - A. Web servers can be scaled to handle heavy volumes of traffic.
    - B. SLAs provide fault tolerance.
    - C. Virtual machines and storage can be rapidly provisioned.
    - D. SLAs provide guaranteed uptime.

12. Your company's e-commerce site is experiencing excessive traffic during the holiday shopping season. Being the server specialist, you have been directed to configure the site to improve user response time during peak loads. What should you configure?
    - A. Network load balancing
    - B. Failover clustering
    - C. VPN
    - D. Operating system virtualization

13. Industry regulations require multifactor authentication to be used for sensitive server systems. Currently users authenticate to these systems using a username and password. What should be done to ensure regulatory compliance?
    - A. Nothing. Multifactor authentication is already in use.
    - B. Configure a PIN requirement in addition to current authentication settings.
    - C. Use PKI certificates to secure authentication further.
    - D. Enforce periodic password changes.

14. What category of processor do mobile devices use?
    - A. CISC
    - B. BISC
    - C. RISC
    - D. DISC

15. You plan to use extra DDR3 memory chips for your server, which currently supports DDR4. What should you consider?

    A. DDR3 chips can be plugged into DDR4 sockets.

    B. DDR3 chips cannot be plugged into DDR4 sockets.

    C. The server BIOS will have to be updated.

    D. The server must use UEFI.

Questions and Answers

1. Which server form factor occupies the most space?

    A. Blade

    B. Virtual

    C. Rack-mount

    D. Tower

    D. Tower servers take up the most space. A, B, and C are incorrect. Blade servers are essentially circuit boards that plug into a single server chassis. Virtual is not a server form factor. Rack-mount servers are installed in a tall metal rack along with other rack-mount servers.

2. What term is used to describe a virtualized operating system?

    A. Host

    B. Guest

    C. Hypervisor

    D. Load balancer

    B. Virtualized operating systems are known as guests. A, C, and D are incorrect. Hosts are the physical machines on which guests run, and this is the same with hypervisor. Load balancers distribute incoming network traffic destined for a network service (such as a web site) to increase network performance.

3. Which two of the following items are related to HVAC?

    A. Perimeter fencing

    B. Ventilation

    C. Dual power supplies

    D. Temperature control

B, D. HVAC means heating, ventilation, and air conditioning, which encompasses ventilation and temperature control. A and C are incorrect. Perimeter fencing is a physical security measure, and dual power supplies provide hardware redundancy.

4. How can ESD be reduced?

A. Storing hardware components in a freezer

B. Ensuring that objects coming into contact with one another have different charges

C. Ensuring that objects coming into contact with one another have equal charges

D. Storing hardware components in plastic bags

C. Equalizing the charge between objects that will come into contact reduces the flow of electrons, which can damage sensitive electronic components. A, B, and D are incorrect. ESD is not reduced by storing components in plastic bags or freezers.

5. What is the difference between DAS and a SAN?

A. DAS allows the server to use network storage as if it were local. SAN storage is local to the server.

B. DAS is local storage, and SAN is network storage.

C. DAS is local storage specifically for virtual servers. SAN refers to cloud storage.

D. DAS and SAN are separate terms that refer to exactly the same thing.

B. Direct-attached storage (DAS) means storage local to the server. Storage area network (SAN) is network storage, not the other way around; they are not the same thing. A, C, and D are incorrect. DAS can be used by physical or virtual servers. SANs are not specifically related to cloud computing.

6. What benefits do SSDs provide over magnetic hard disks? Choose two.

A. Stronger encryption

B. Increased file integrity

C. Less power consumption

D. Quicker file access

C, D. Solid-state drives (SSDs) have no moving parts and thus consume less power and generally provide quicker file access than magnetic hard disks. A and B are incorrect. Encryption and file integrity are normally configured at the software level and are not specific to SSDs.

7. You would like to improve disk I/O performance for data residing on a physical server. In accordance with your organizational policy, a server must remain running even if an operating system disk fails. The server is currently configured with RAID 1 for the operating system and data. What should you configure?
   - **A.** Nothing. RAID 1 already offers the best performance.
   - **B.** Remove the existing RAID configuration and enable RAID 0.
   - **C.** Add disks to the server. Configure RAID 0 and create a file system. Move the existing data to the newly created filesystem.
   - **D.** Add disks to the server. Configure RAID 0 and create a file system. Move the existing operating system file to the newly created file system.

   C. RAID 0 is disk striping. A, B, and D are incorrect. The existing RAID 1 mirror does not provide a performance benefit, and it should be left alone for operating system file fault tolerance, but data should be moved to the new file system on the RAID 0 array.

8. What role does a default gateway perform in an IPv4/IPv6 environment?
   - **A.** It prevents local area network broadcasts from reaching other subnets.
   - **B.** It is a router that allows traffic into and out of a network.
   - **C.** It prevents multicasts from reaching other subnets.
   - **D.** It is a router that performs domain name–to–IP address resolution.

   B. The default gateway is a router that allows traffic into and out of a network, in some cases based on conditions. A, C, and D are incorrect. Although routers do not forward broadcasts, that is not the role of the IP default gateway from an IP perspective. Multicast (group) traffic can normally traverse routers. Domain name–to–IP address resolution is a function of a DNS server.

9. Roman is the server administrator for an international insurance company. The London office currently has Active Directory domain controller servers configured with IPv6. The Toronto office domain controllers are also configured with IPv6, yet replication over the Internet is failing between Toronto and London. What should Roman do to enable domain controller replication between the two sites?
   - **A.** Enable IPv6 replication through group policy.
   - **B.** Configure an IPv6 tunneling solution.
   - **C.** Make sure the server PKI certificates allow domain controller replication.
   - **D.** Ensure that servers at both locations are configured with the same default gateway.

   B. Roman should configure an IPv6 tunneling solution that will enable the IPv6 packets to traverse the Internet (an IPv4 network). A, C and D are incorrect. There is no such thing as IPv6 replication. PKI will not enable replication; it is used for security purposes. Servers at each site should point to their local default gateway, not the same default gateway overall.

10. While capturing network traffic, you notice an excessive amount of traffic destined to a particular host on TCP port 25. What is one possible explanation for this?

A. A mail server is being flooded with spam.

B. A network broadcast attack is taking place.

C. Users' devices on the network happen to be issuing DNS queries at the same time.

D. A web server is experiencing a large volume of concurrent visitors.

A. TCP port 25 is normally reserved for SMTP mail servers. Excessive traffic destined for the mail server could indicate spamming is taking place. B, C, and D are incorrect. Packets destined for port 25 are not broadcast packets, nor are they DNS queries, which use UDP port 53, or web server requests, which would use TCP port 80 or 443.

11. Which of the following demonstrates an advantage of cloud computing? Choose two.

A. Web servers can be scaled to handle heavy volumes of traffic.

B. SLAs provide fault tolerance.

C. Virtual machines and storage can be rapidly provisioned.

D. SLAs provide guaranteed uptime.

C, D. Although virtual machines can be provisioned without a cloud environment, one characteristic of cloud computing is the rapid deployment of services by users. Service Level Agreements (SLAs) can guarantee uptime among other details; it is a contract between a provider and a consumer. A and B are incorrect. Web servers can be configured to handle heavy traffic volumes without cloud computing. SLAs themselves do not provide fault tolerance.

12. Your company's e-commerce site is experiencing excessive traffic during the holiday shopping season. Being the server specialist, you have been directed to configure the site to improve user response time during peak loads. What should you configure?

A. Network load balancing

B. Failover clustering

C. VPN

D. Operating system virtualization

A. Network load balancing (NLB) distributes incoming traffic to the least busy of multiple back-end servers offering the same service. B, C, and D are incorrect. Failover clustering enables network services to continue even if servers fail, as long as at least one cluster node remains running. VPNs enable encrypted connectivity to a private network over an untrusted network. Operating system virtualization enables multiple OSs to run in their own virtual environments on the same physical host.

13. Industry regulations require multifactor authentication to be used for sensitive server systems. Currently users authenticate to these systems using a username and password. What should be done to ensure regulatory compliance?

A. Nothing. Multifactor authentication is already in use.

B. Configure a PIN requirement in addition to current authentication settings.

C. Use PKI certificates to secure authentication further.

D. Enforce periodic password changes.

C. Multifactor authentication requires multiple authentication "categories"; in this case, something you know (username and password) and something you have (PKI certificate). A, B, and D are incorrect. Multifactor authentication is not in place when only the *something you know* category is in use, which is also true even if you enable PINs or enable periodic password changes.

14. What category of processor do mobile devices use?

A. CISC

B. BISC

C. RISC

D. DISC

C. Reduced Instruction Set Computing (RISC) processors are often used by mobile devices because of their low power requirements. A, B, and D are incorrect. Complex Instruction Set Computing (CISC) processors tend to be used in desktops and servers where more complex processing is required. BISC and DISC are fictitious terms.

15. You plan to use extra DDR3 memory chips for your server, which currently supports DDR4. What should you consider?

A. DDR3 chips can be plugged into DDR4 sockets.

B. DDR3 chips cannot be plugged into DDR4 sockets.

C. The server BIOS will have to be updated.

D. The server must use UEFI.

B. DDR memory chips are not interchangeable with other DDR version standards. A, C, and D are incorrect. DDR3 chips cannot be physically plugged into DDR4 sockets. The BIOS and UEIF are irrelevant to whether DDR3 chips can be used in DDR4 slots.

CHAPTER 2

Server Hardware

In this chapter, you will

- Learn about server form factors: tower servers, rack-mounted servers, and blade servers
- Learn how BIOS works
- Learn how UEFI works
- Review the basics of CPUs and how they handle data
- Review the different types of memory
- Learn about bus types
- Learn about NICs
- Review storage types
- Learn about power and environmental controls

Server hardware isn't just about the components inside the server—it's also about the size of the server case and components as well. This chapter will cover what you need to know when ordering and replacing server components.

Server Form Factors

Physical servers and their parts come in a variety of shapes and sizes, or *form factors*. Not all components will fit into any server. For example, adapter cards that fit well within a server tower will not fit into a blade server, and a tower server can't be rack-mounted in a server room rack.

Form factors also apply to computer cases, power supplies, motherboards, expansion cards, and so on. The dimensions of these pieces determine which ones fit together properly. Data centers need to fit as many servers as possible within a finite amount of space, so increasing server density is possible using smaller server form factors.

Other components such as PCI Express (PCIe) expansion cards adhere to industry-standard form factors. Perhaps we want to add a 10 GBps (gigabits per second) Ethernet network card to our rack-mounted server. This could be a problem, because a standard PCIe card won't fit within most rack-mounted servers, which are are much thinner and smaller than tower servers.

Server technicians need to know all the details related to the type of servers they are responsible for. Let's say it's the first day on the job for a Server+ certified tech. How can this person know what servers are in place? Clearly one way is to inventory servers physically in server rooms or data centers, but larger enterprises will have automated solutions that inventory physical and virtual servers and store the results in a database that be queried and reported on. Virtual servers, of course, don't have form factors.

Tower Servers

Tower servers have been around for a long time, and the tower is what most people think of when they hear the word "server." Powerful desktop computers (such as those used by gamers) are often towers. This server form factor isn't screwed into any type of mounting device; it is a stand-alone computer that can be easily moved without removing screws or sliding it out of a rack.

This server form factor has all server components housed within a single case that can sit directly on the floor or on a desk. Server components are easy to find, because this is a tried-and-true hardware technology.

Adding components such as disk storage dedicated to the server is easy, because there is plenty of physical space inside a tower server. This isn't the case with other server form factors such as blade servers, however, although blades can use rack-mounted storage devices; the storage just isn't physically installed inside the blade. Imagine trying to accommodate hundreds or thousands of these servers in a server room or data center: the cost of real estate alone would be tremendous! Suffice it to say that tower servers don't scale well. They take up a lot of space and they can't be rack-mounted, as you can see in Figure 2-1.

Tower servers are often used in smaller offices. If IT budgets are stretched, towers might be an attractive option, because even a standard desktop PC could be configured with a server operating system—but, of course, this isn't designed for large-scale use.

Figure 2-1 Tower T620 server, courtesy of Dell Inc.

Another possibility is a central IT office that preconfigures servers to be used in branch offices. Perhaps only a single server is needed at a branch office to localize user access to server services, so it might make sense to ship a tower server to that location instead of purchasing expensive server racks and a single-rack mounted device.

When it comes to component redundancy, most tower servers fall short. They can accommodate standard hardware components, but they don't often come with redundant power supplies. There's also the issue of power and data cables. If your server room contains only towers, you may find it tricky to organize all of the cables. Server racks have conduits into which cables are easily and neatly arranged, which makes labeling and troubleshooting easier. (Just make sure you label both ends of each cable!)

Rack-mounted Equipment

The 1990s produced the server rack form factor courtesy of Compaq, which was acquired by Hewlett-Packard in 2002. Computing and the Internet were taking off, and many companies realized they needed servers on premises. Nowadays that has shifted to running servers in the public cloud on somebody else's equipment.

Rack-mounting increases the potential server density in a server room or a data center, and using this equipment can increase security, because most racks have front and back doors that can be locked. In a large data center that accommodates multiple customers or tenants, controlling physical access to rack-mounted servers and equipment is important. The size of your enterprise and its data requirements, and the size of the data center, determine how many racks you can use.

Special cases and rails are used so that rack-mounted equipment can be easily inserted and removed from racks. Rack-mounted servers ship this way out of the box, and sometimes they also include rails and the screws needed to secure the rails on the rack.

Rack-mounted Servers

Rack-mounted servers will appeal to those who prefer tidiness and organization; they are essentially thin computers (from 2 to 12 inches wide) that are designed to be stacked vertically in a metal framework, or rack. This keeps things tidy and uses a minimum of space, so this form factor is definitely scalable. Rack-mounted equipment can be blocky, with sharp edges, however.

To assist in removing single points of failure, rack-mounted servers normally have dual power supplies. There are normally at least two network cards and in some cases management ports, and all of these connections are on the back of the device. Figure 2-2 shows ports on the front of the server; these allow a keyboard, mouse, video display, or a KVM (keyboard, video, mouse) switch to be connected.

Racks

Full metal racks can be heavy. Server room and data center construction must account for how much weight the floors can safely support. Not only that, but we don't want racks tipping over, so bolting them to the floor is recommended.

Most racks are 19 inches wide (they do come wider), and they often use metal sliding rails that the servers and other types of appliances (such as network firewalls, storage enclosures, and so on) neatly fit into. Racks may not come with rails, so you might

Figure 2-2 Dell PowerEdge R515 rack server, courtesy of Dell Inc.

have to acquire rail kits. Rack-mounted equipment such as servers usually comes with a rail kit. (Be careful not to get pinched when inserting or removing equipment on these sliding rails.)

Not all racks are equal. They are available in different widths and heights. You might use one rack to accommodate servers and another to accommodate storage arrays. Rack-mountable devices use their own units of measurement for height, called rack units (U)—1U is 1 3/4 inches, 2U is 3 1/2 inches, 4U is 7 inches, and so on. This measurement is a standard that refers to the vertical distance between the holes in the rack to which rails and rack-mounted equipment are secured. A single rack-mounted device might be 1U or up to 7U in height. Most racks have a maximum of 42U (see Figure 2-3). When ordering rack-mountable servers, the specs will detail how many Us the enclosure is so you can plan placement within the rack.

Now, because we can place many servers together in a rack, it just makes sense to place server storage appliances, power sources (including UPSs), and network cables in the rack, too. Too many times I've seen messy racks with cables hanging everywhere, both in front of and behind the rack—not only is this a safety hazard, but tracing cables when troubleshooting will be next to impossible!

Power distribution units (PDUs) provide power outlets to racks in server rooms and data centers. To eliminate a single point of failure, redundant PDUs should be plugged into separate circuits. To extend this point, redundant server power supplies should each plug into separate PDUs.

Because many different types of items can draw power from PDUs, you should check your PDU's rating to ensure your equipment isn't above the load capacity.

Cable Management Arm

A *cable management arm* is a metal or plastic folding component that is attached to the back of a rack-mounted device. All cables from the device (power, network, and so on) are fitted into the arm, which serves as a conduit or trench in which the cables are placed.

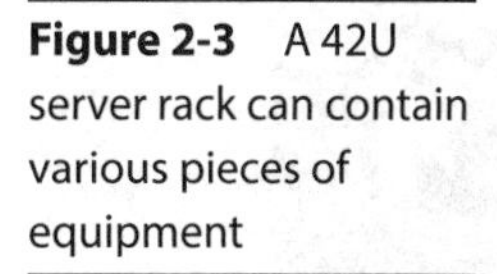
Figure 2-3 A 42U server rack can contain various pieces of equipment

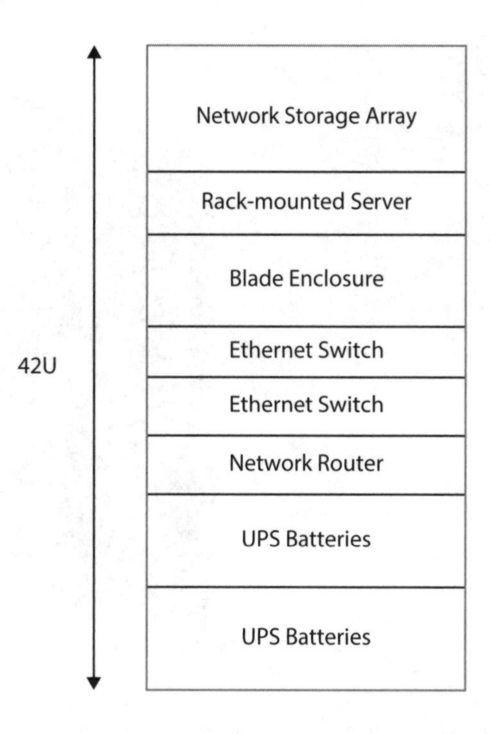

You would also normally use cable zip ties to bundle together cables from a device. (A standard rack-mounted server has dual power supplies and at least two network cards, so that's four cables right away for a single device.) When you pull out a rack-mounted device (on the sliding rails), the cable arm expands so that you don't pull the cables out.

After your rack-mounted devices and cabling are in place, use rack fillers (blanking panels) to cover empty spaces in the rack. These, in addition to cable management arms, ensure that fan intake vents are not blocked. This can improve airflow, which can also save money by saving energy in the long run. Rack fillers are also measured using the U system and are available with venting holes.

Blade Servers

Blade servers make me think of *Star Trek*: a technician inserts a highly sophisticated card into a slot to prevent the destruction of the *USS Enterprise*. And that's essentially what the blade server form factor is—a circuit board containing its own processors, memory, and network capabilities, and, in some cases, a small amount of storage, but no power supply or cooling mechanisms. Blade servers cannot run on their own. Most blades have a USB connector on the front in case you want to connect external components such as a DVD drive.

This small server form factor (Figure 2-4) will most likely replace rack-mounted servers at some point. Large data centers can increase their server density using blades, so scalability is not a problem. Like everything in IT, it's a tradeoff—sure, we can fit more

Figure 2-4 Dell PowerEdge M520 blade server, courtesy of Dell Inc.

blades than towers in a fixed amount of space, but towers are cheaper and easier to expand if you need expansion cards or additional storage.

Blade Enclosure

A blade enclosure is a proprietary chassis that can house several blade servers from the same vendor, and it can measure from 6U to 12U. Blade servers slide into the blade enclosure. The enclosure provides

- Temperature control mechanisms, including fans
- Power
- Network connectivity
- Storage connectivity
- Server remote management connections

Within the enclosure, the *backplane* connects server and I/O blades. I/O blades (or cards) can provide faster network connectivity, storage for blade servers, management capabilities, and other things. The *midplane* is a printed circuit board (PCB) with server blades that connect on one side (the front) and other components accessible on the other side (the back). If, for example, 10 Gb network switching is required, you would have to use a specific midplane with this support.

Note that some manufacturers provide backplane and midplane redundancy to reduce single points of failure. Blanking panels are used where there are empty slots in the enclosure for better cooling and airflow.

Server Components

Whether we are working with tower, rack-mounted, or blade servers, they all have components that give them specific functionality:

- Multiple processors (each with multiple cores)
- Memory (RAM)
- Storage (local and/or network accessible)
- Network connectivity (servers often have multiple cards)
- Management capabilities (for blade systems or hardware-level remote control)

Firmware is essentially software stored in a chip, and it's used all over the place—a server's motherboard BIOS, smartphones, and expansion cards, to name a few. Like operating system or application software, firmware comes in different versions with different capabilities and needs to be updated periodically.

Hardware problems can sometimes masquerade as software issues. For instance, flawed firmware code could cause server operating system instability. The solution is sometimes as simple as downloading and applying a firmware update from the manufacturer's web site.

Most manufacturers supply an MD5 hash value on the download web page that you can recompute after downloading, to verify that the file hasn't been changed. Plus, you need to be sure you're applying the correct version of the update. The big guys (Dell, HP, IBM) often offer rollback options if you don't like the applied firmware update.

BIOS

The *basic input-output system (BIOS)* is firmware built into a circuit board such as a motherboard or a RAID disk controller. BIOS has been around for decades. This is the magic that kicks in the moment you turn on the power for your server or when a card initializes.

When starting up, the server BIOS checks critical hardware components such as power, CPU, RAM, and video to make sure they are in place and functional. If the components are not functional, you'll get various beep codes or error numbers and messages, provided video is working. This is called the power on self test (POST). Assuming things are working, the BIOS then checks the master boot record (MBR) to hand control over to an installed operating system.

The complementary metal oxide semi-conductor (CMOS) is essentially your specific configuration of hardware settings supported by the BIOS. For example, you might change the boot order on your server to first boot from USB (requiring a password of course!), and then local hard disk. The BIOS has the capabilities, and the CMOS retains your configuration of those capabilities. Figure 2-5 shows a basic BIOS configuration screen.

But how can you configure CMOS settings? In other words, how can you configure the BIOS? It depends on the BIOS manufacturer. The following list shows a few common BIOS manufacturers:

- ASUS
- Phoenix

```
                        PhoenixBIOS Setup Utility
  Main    Advanced    Security    Boot    Exit

                                                  Item Specific Help
  System Time:                  [10:28:34]
  System Date:                  [06/03/2016]
                                                  <Tab>, <Shift-Tab>, or
  Legacy Diskette A:            [1.44/1.25 MB 3½"] <Enter> selects field.
  Legacy Diskette B:            [Disabled]

▶ Primary Master                [None]
▶ Primary Slave                 [None]
▶ Secondary Master              [None]
▶ Secondary Slave               [None]

▶ Keyboard Features

  System Memory:                640 KB
  Extended Memory:              2096128 KB
  Boot-time Diagnostic Screen:  [Disabled]

F1  Help  ↑↓ Select Item  -/+   Change Values       F9  Setup Defaults
Esc Exit  ↔  Select Menu  Enter Select ▶ Sub-Menu  F10 Save and Exit
```

Figure 2-5 Phoenix BIOS screen

- IBM
- Dell
- HP

If we're using a Dell system, for example, when the system is first powering up, we can press the F2 key on the keyboard to enter the BIOS settings. Some BIOS firmware will briefly display a message telling you what to press. Properly configured servers will require a password before these settings can be viewed or changed.

NOTE Not only do motherboards have BIOS settings, but expansion cards, such as disk RAID controllers, have BIOS settings, too. Refer to the manufacturer's documentation to determine how to enter specific BIOS settings. Documenting BIOS configurations is an important part of proper server management and facilitates troubleshooting. Make your life easier!

UEFI

Unified extensible firmware interface (UEFI) is the new BIOS: BIOS is old, and UEFI is new. On PCs, UEFI has become common over the last few years, but Apple Mac computers have used UEFI for a long time.

Here's a list of a few UEFI features that *most* BIOS firmware does not support:

- Graphical interface with mouse support
- GPT hard-disk support
- IPv6 support during boot
- Secure Boot
- Support for new modules for additional functionality

Let's zoom in to the UEFI Secure Boot feature for a moment. If malware can inject itself into the pre–operating system (OS) boot environment, then even the most secure OSs can be compromised. Think about it: Code that is in place before the OS boots and then has direct access to hardware. It sounds nasty, and it is. Secure Boot prevents *untrusted* executable code from running before the OS initializes. Digital signatures are used to validate trusted code.

EXAM TIP Some Linux distributions do not support Secure Boot. To install those Linux operating systems, you first have to disable UEFI Secure Boot by entering UEFI settings on your server.

CPUs

The *central processing unit (CPU)* is the brain of the server and comes on a chip. Of course, to handle more intense workloads, having more brains helps. The first version of a CPU is referred to as step 0. As the manufacturer releases the same CPU with improvements, the step value increases—for example, from 0 to 1. Adding more horsepower to a server is called *scaling up*, while adding additional servers to handle a workload is called *scaling out*.

CPU Architecture

Although most modern CPUs have a 64-bit data path, you might also come across 32-bit. Newer server operating systems, however, such as Microsoft Windows Server 2012 R2, support only 64-bit. The 32-bit machines have a maximum addressable memory limit of 4 GB, while 64-bit machines have a limit of 16 EB (exabytes).

Modern mobile devices use Advanced RISC Machine (ARM) processors. A few examples include Apple iPod, iPad, and iPhone products; Raspberry Pi devices; and Microsoft Surface tablets. ARM processors come in both x86 (32-bit) and x64 (64-bit) flavors.

If you plan on running a hypervisor (such as Microsoft Hyper-V or VMware), your CPUs must support hardware virtualization. AMD processors must support AMD Virtualization (AMD-V) and Intel processors must support Intel Virtualization Technology (Intel VT).

When planning server hardware, you should also consider the CPU speed. Naturally, a 4 GHz processor gets things done more quickly than a 2 GHz processor. But this speed refers to how fast instructions are processed internally; you have to ask yourself, "How quickly can data get to and from the CPU on the motherboard?" The following illustration shows a CPU in its motherboard socket.

Waiting for the Bus

Buses move data between various components within a computing device, so there isn't just a single bus on a server motherboard. Consider the fact that there is a front side bus (FSB), a PCIe bus, and others. Collectively, some technicians will refer to all of the buses as simply "the bus." The bus speed (usually expressed in megahertz, or MHz) is different from the internal CPU speed, and it does determine how quickly data gets to and from certain areas of the system.

The front side bus (FSB) moves data directly between the CPU and the *Northbridge* chipset, which includes system memory (RAM) and, on some motherboards, video controllers. The *Southbridge* chipset isn't directly connected to the CPU, but is indirectly connected via the Northbridge. It handles slower data transfers such as USB and PCI Express (PCIe) expansion card slots.

There is a value involving the FSB and CPU called the *clock multiplier*, which defines a relationship between the external CPU bus speed (MHz) and the internal CPU speed (GHz). For example, a FSB speed of 400 MHz with a multiplier of 10 would result in an internal CPU speed of approximately 4 GHz. Some motherboard manufacturers allow this value to be adjusted within defined ranges.

CPU Cache

CPUs have small amounts of high-speed memory, or *caches*, to speed up the execution of anticipated CPU instructions—or, said differently, to increase the *hit rate*. The hit rate indicates that when the CPU needed instructions or data, it was retrieved from cache (a hit) instead of from another slower location (such as finding data in L1 cache instead of L2). L1, L2, and L3 caches are common in today's server hardware: L1 is the fastest and L4 is the slowest (and largest).

The L1, L2, and L3 caches are typically built into the processor, while L4 uses main system memory. The reason L1 cache, for example, is faster than normal system memory is because it uses static RAM (SRAM) as opposed to dynamic RAM (DRAM) or synchronous DRAM (SDRAM). SRAM uses transistors to retain data, which speeds up data access. Table 2-1 shows common CPU cache sizes, which will vary between CPUs and motherboards. Bear in mind that L3 and L4 cache memory is used by all CPU cores for CPU chips in a socket.

A server can have multiple identical physical CPUs working together via *symmetric multiprocessing (SMP)*, but of course the server motherboard must have sockets to accommodate the CPUs. So by distributing work among a group of CPUs, we reduce the amount of time it takes to complete the work. *Reduced Instruction Set Computing (RISC)* refers to processors that are very efficient, in that they are designed to work with simpler and smaller instruction sets; today, this type of processor is often found in mobile devices.

On the server side of things, Table 2-2 outlines common CPU sockets and processors. You can't just plug any CPU into any socket; they have to match!

Taking the discussion a step further, each physical CPU chip can have multiple cores—essentially, multiple CPUs within the same chip plug into a single motherboard socket. This means more computing power while using less space than an SMP system. Figure 2-6 shows a single CPU socket Windows host with four internal cores and with L1 and L2 caches.

Table 2-1 CPU Cache Sizes

Cache	Size
L1	96 KB
L2	2 MB
L3	8 MB
L4	16 MB

Table 2-2 CPU Sockets and Processors

Socket Type	CPU Type
LGA 1248	Intel Itanium 9300
LGA 1567	Intel Xeon 6500/7500
LGA 2011 (Socket R)	Intel Core i7, Intel Xeon E5
LGA 1155 (Socket H2)	Intel Xeon E3

Figure 2-6 Multicore CPU and cache listing

Utilization	Speed		Maximum speed:	1.86 GHz
38%	1.97 GHz		Sockets:	1
			Cores:	4
Processes	Threads	Handles	Logical processors:	4
85	1540	56710	Virtualization:	Enabled
			L1 cache:	224 KB
Up time			L2 cache:	2.0 MB
7:00:28:03				

NOTE When you're working in the field, SMP and multicore systems present the CPUs in the exact same way to operating system monitoring tools such as the Windows Task Manager.

Memory

Random access memory (RAM) is the electronic volatile memory used by running programs; it needs electricity to retain data, unlike disk storage devices. Servers can accommodate different amounts and types of RAM, and motherboards can have specific memory module placement rules.

Server motherboards normally require memory chips to be installed in pairs for efficient use by CPU sockets. Pairing, along with other memory requirements, can differ from one motherboard to the next, so be sure to read the motherboard documentation.

Memory Timing

Schemes such as double pumping can transmit data on the rise *and* fall of a clocking, or timing, signal. This means your data transfer rate is effectively doubled. You can think of electronic memory being organized into rows and columns.

The trick is getting data into or out of memory addresses as quickly as possible. Factors influencing memory speed include

- How long it takes to select a memory column
- How long it takes to select a memory row
- How long it takes to read data when a memory row is selected

ECC

Most server motherboards can accommodate *error correcting code (ECC)* memory. This type of memory chip has the added capability of detecting and fixing memory errors at the bit (0 or 1) level. It does this by using an extra bit of information (the *parity bit*) for each group of memory bits. Physically, today's server motherboards accept Dual Inline Memory Module (DIMM) chips.

Although most non-ECC modules can detect memory errors, they don't do anything about it. You'll find this often in consumer-grade computing equipment as opposed to servers. Non-ECC memory is cheaper than ECC memory. Your motherboard documentation will specify what type of memory chip can be used and how to enable ECC. The following illustration shows how ECC can be enabled in the BIOS.

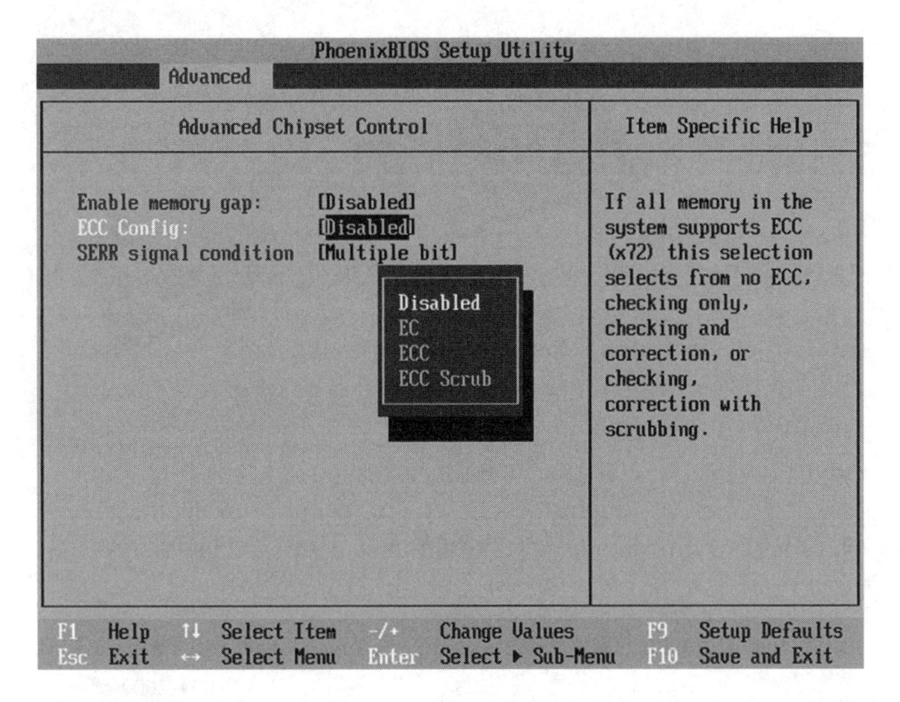

EXAM TIP If your server allows the use of both ECC and non-ECC memory and you plan to use both, make sure you pair ECC chips together and non-ECC chips together. If you don't do this, memory error correction will be disabled.

DDR

Double data rate (DDR) memory increases data transfer rates to and from memory, compared to single data rate (SDR); it's all based on timing. As any musician will tell you, timing is crucial, and the same is true in the world of computing. There are different DDR standards, or versions, and they are not compatible with one another. This means DDR3 chip sockets on a motherboard will accept only DDR3 memory chips.

DDR2 supersedes DDR1, DDR3 supersedes DDR2, and so on. So if your server motherboard supports DDR2 through DDR4 RAM chips, you should choose DDR4 for the best performance. DDR3 memory is shown in Figure 2-7. The column access strobe (CAS) latency defines how long it takes for requested memory contents to leave the actual memory chip on their way to the bus. Table 2-3 shows DDR memory details.

Buses

Motherboards and expansion cards need a way to move data around, and this is where the bus comes in. Think of computers buses like you think of real buses, which move people around using roads; a computer moves data bits around the system using buses.

Figure 2-7 DDR3 240-pin memory module

Table 2-3 DDR Memory Details

Type	Number of Physical Pins	Approximate Bus Speed (MHz)
DDR2	240	200–500
DDR3	240	400–1000
DDR4	288	1000–2000

There are many different types of buses, and some motherboards accommodate multiple buses. The buses we discuss here are for expansion cards plugged into expansion slots and include the PCI, PCI-X, and PCIe standards. Using additional buses not supported by the motherboard is possible by using host bus adapter (HBA) cards, such as those used for SAN connectivity. Slimmer server form factors (such as rack-mounted servers) benefit from riser circuit boards that plug into the motherboard and enable expansion cards that otherwise wouldn't fit to be plugged in.

PCI

Peripheral Component Interconnect (PCI) is a 32- and 64-bit bus and expansion slot card standard, but you won't find it on many of today's server motherboards. Back in the 1990s, PCI was a big deal, since it really was plug-and-play (PnP). This meant we didn't have to fiddle around with jumpers and dip switches to configure the card. As long as the BIOS and operating system supported PnP, all was good.

Interestingly, 64-bit PCI cards could be plugged into 32-bit PCI expansion slots and would still function, although at a slower rate. Another consideration was the card height, and this is an issue affecting more than just PCI cards. PCI full-height cards take more space than the related lower profile cards, and depending on the server case and motherboard form factors, a full-height card might not fit properly. PCI is rated between 133 and 800 MBps, depending on 32- or 64-bit and the frequency used.

PCI-X

PCI eXtended supersedes PCI by improving transfer rates up to four times to and from slots with bit transfer rates between 2 and 4 GBps. This 64-bit parallel transmission standard runs at various frequencies (often the case with expansion slots and cards), which influences the data transmission speed.

PCI Express

The serial transmission-based PCIe standard supersedes both PCI and PCI-X, with more bandwidth, which is especially useful with video, storage, and network cards. The bandwidth will vary depending upon the specific version of PCIe and how many lanes (channels of communication) are used. Table 2-4 shows examples of PCIe speeds in megabytes per second (MBps) as well as gigabytes per second (GBps).

If your PCIe slots can accommodate x16, like the example shown in Figure 2-8, then of course you should opt for that type of card if you have the option, since it has the highest transmission rate. Direct memory access (DMA) is supported by some devices and enables access to system memory without involving the CPU.

PCIe cards are not as tall as PCI cards, and most modern servers support PCIe cards. In some cases, the PCIe card might be hot-pluggable. The great thing about PCIe is that you can, for example, plug an x8 card into an x16 slot.

NICs

Most physical servers have at least two integrated network interface cards (NICs), but it's pretty easy to find them with four or more interfaces in some cases. Virtual servers can have as many virtual NICs (vNICs) as required for the server role. For instance, a VPN server should have at least two interfaces.

Table 2-4 PCI Express Speed Examples

PCIe Standard	Number of Channels	Data Transfer Rate
PCIe 1.0	x1	250 MBps
	x2	500 MBps
	x16	4 GBps
PCIe 2.0	x1	500 MBps
	x16	8 GBps
PCIe 3.0	x8	8 GBps
	x16	15 GBps

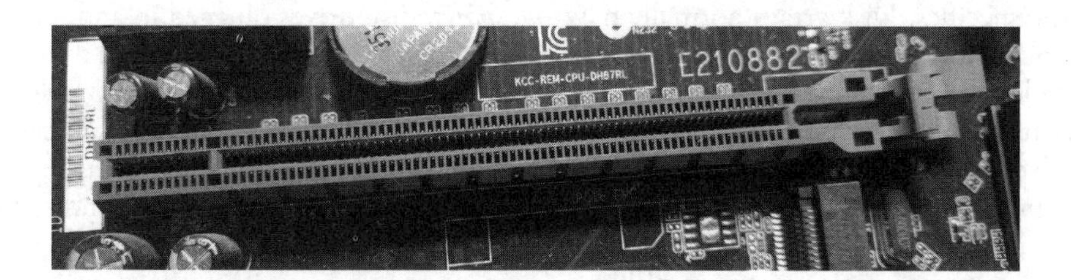

Figure 2-8 A PCIe x16 motherboard slot

If you're adding NICs to a physical server, you need to know which type of unused expansion slots your motherboard has (PCI, PCI-X, or PCIe). The network transmission speed is a big deal; your network infrastructure might support 10 Gbps, so you want to get the fastest NIC possible that will work in your environment.

Each NIC needs to be configured with the appropriate IPv4 or IPv6 settings, more of which will be detailed in Chapter 5. Even though the NIC is specific to the server, you should consider what it is plugging into. For example, a multihomed server (one with more than one NIC) might have each NIC plugged into different network switches or a specific switch VLAN port. Then there's NIC teaming—grouping NICs together for load balancing or better throughput; this applies both to physical and virtual machine NICs. Virtual machine NICs can be tied to specific underlying physical NICs.

Storage

Storage is sometimes embedded on a server motherboard, such as with some blade servers. Other times, servers have local disks available; yet another possibility is reaching out over a network to use disk space. Storage attached to a local server is known as *direct-attached storage (DAS)*, whereas network storage can come in the form of *network-attached storage (NAS)* or *storage area networks (SANs)*. Chapter 4 covers storage in greater detail.

Virtual machines running server operating systems have a variety of options, including these:

- Using a physical disk partition available from the underlying hypervisor
- Using storage accessible over a SAN through the underlying hypervisor
- Using a virtual hard disk (VHD) file

VHD files might be stored on a local disk on the underlying physical server or on a network storage location. For physical servers, you may also have to add an expansion card that connects the server to additional storage.

RAID Controllers

RAID groups physical disks together as a logical unit to increase disk performance and/or to provide disk-level fault tolerance. You can set this up at the software level (within the server OS) or at the hardware level using a RAID controller. RAID levels will be discussed in Chapter 4.

Most server motherboards include an integrated RAID controller that connects to multiple physical disks. RAID controllers have their own firmware configuration utility to set up the specifics. Disk arrays normally have *hot spares*, disk drives plugged in and ready to take over if disks currently active in the array fail. Now if this happens, you need to remove the failed disk itself and replace it with a functional one—this is called *hot-swapping*.

Battery-backed write caching is used for disk array controllers for a number of reasons. On occasion, you may find yourself reconfiguring or migrating disk stripe settings and data and this feature proves useful; however, a common use is when stopping and restarting a disk array. Upon restart, data not yet written is cached (so it is not lost during a power cycle), so it gets written to disk.

Consider these items when working with hardware RAID:

- Don't worry about whether your server OS supports hardware RAID; this is a non-issue. The hardware will present what appears to be a single disk to the server OS.
- Ensure that you have access to two or more disks either locally or over a storage network. This could involve asking your storage administrator to "carve out" a LUN (a number identifying a chunk of disk space) for you.
- Decide which level of RAID makes sense for your situation. Are you concerned with fault tolerance, performance, or both? Check out Chapter 4 for details on RAID levels.
- Keep performing server backups! Some RAID levels duplicate data, but this doesn't mean you shouldn't continue server backup procedures.

USB

The fastest transmission technologies are serial, not parallel, and that includes universal serial bus, or USB. USB creators weren't kidding when they selected the word "Universal"—you can plug just about anything into a USB port:

- Keyboard
- Storage device (see Figure 2-9)
- Smartphone

Figure 2-9 An external USB solid-state drive

Table 2-5 USB Standards and Transfer Rates

USB Standard	Data Transfer Rate
USB 1.0	12 Mbps
USB 2.0	480 Mbps
USB 3.0	5 Gbps

- Tablet
- USB hub
- Coffee mug warmer
- Lamp
- Cute mechanical puppy

Servers commonly use USB for keyboards and mice, which are referred to as *human interface devices (HIDs)*. Storage is usually connected to a RAID controller. A few USB versions have evolved over the years, from USB 1.*x* all the way up to 3.*x*. You'll find these details in Table 2-5. (Mbps means megabits per second.)

NOTE Server rooms and data centers use KVM switches, which link numerous servers to a single keyboard, display, and mouse. These connections are made using a USB or IP addresses on a network.

USB 3 is backward-compatible, so you can plug a USB 3 device into a non-USB 3 port. USB hubs enable you to plug in more devices than your machine could otherwise accommodate, but watch out for power draw for USB devices that don't have their own external power source. Also watch out for the appropriate use of USB cables—for example, one cable may be used only to charge a smartphone, while a similar looking cable may be used for both charging and data transfer.

Power

From the smallest server in the enthusiast's basement to thousands of servers in a data center, power is essential. Server virtualization reduces power consumption by consolidating multiple physical servers into virtual machines, but virtual machines must run on physical server hardware, and it needs to be powered.

Power connections (plugs and sockets) come in a variety of standards. The standard two-prong (or three-prong with ground) plug used in North America, the NEMA connector (National Electronic Manufacturers Association), is shown in Figure 2-10. Edison plugs are more rounded than NEMA plugs, but like NEMA, Edisons have three prongs. Industrial-grade equipment uses a twist-lock mechanism to prevent the accidental disconnection from the socket.

Figure 2-10 NEMA three-prong socket and plug

Voltage

When two points in a circuit have differing potential electrical charges, they are said to differ in voltage. This difference encourages the flow of electrons, so, with a higher voltage (difference in charge), we have a stronger flow of electrons being forced through a circuit. This is a good thing when we want to power electrical components in a controlled manner, but it's bad when we (humans) come into contact with components.

Different parts of the world provide electricity at different voltages using alternating current (AC) as opposed to direct current (DC), which is provided by batteries. In North America, the standard is 110–120 volts (V), but in Jamaica and most of Europe, 220–240 volts is the norm. Some equipment (notably telecommunications) reduces voltage (–48 volts) for the proper functioning of integrated circuits (ICs).

CPUs don't need as much power as is often fed from power supplies in the form of +5 or +12V, so the voltage regulator module (VRM) ensures that the CPU gets only the voltage it needs. This is normally built into the server motherboard.

Industrial environments using specialized equipment such as robotic machinery, motors, hydraulics and the like will have different power requirements, such as 208, 440, 460, or even 480 volts. Transformers are used to supply the correct voltage. Most power companies around the world deliver 1-phase and 3-phase power. One-phase power is designed for moderate power requirements, and it's what you'll find being used in most households. Industrial environments use 3-phase power.

Electrostatic Discharge

In a perfect world, our bodies (and clothing, jewelry, and so on) would have the exact same charge as the electrical components that we touch, which would prevent the flow of electrons. In reality, the stronger flow of electrons is of concern for personal safety and to prevent damage to equipment, but the good news is there are preventative measures we can take! ESD can be controlled in a number of ways:

- **ESD strap (bracelet)** Connect the alligator clip to the computer chassis.
- **ESD mat** Stand on this while servicing hardware.
- **ESD footwear** Seriously, this exists—footwear containing resistors.
- **Touch the computer chassis** Do this *as often as possible* to dissipate any built-up static charge.

NOTE About touching the computer chassis: ideally you will be touching an unpainted part of the case. Should the machine be plugged into a wall outlet? No, because it presents an electrocution risk and isn't needed.

The ideal way to minimize ESD would be to ensure that everything is at the voltage as earth ground, but not if it means we might get electrocuted! What's more important is that you, the chassis, and the components are at the *same electrical potential* in terms of voltage.

Our bodies and clothing can build up a static charge, especially in a low-humidity environment. (We'll take about environment controls later in this chapter.) Sensitive electronic components, when not in use, should be stored entirely in ESD bags (those shiny metal–looking bags). So when we are working with electronic components, including customer replaceable units (CRUs) provided under warranty by a vendor, we must take care. Certified technicians, such as those from a reputable vendor, will follow proper procedures when working with field replaceable units (FRUs).

CAUTION You can destroy sensitive components without even knowing it. Your body builds up a static charge naturally as you move about, and as little as 5 volts could fry a component. Always take precautions to minimize ESD.

Wattage

Server components draw power from the power supply unit (PSU), and most server-class hardware has redundant PSUs in case one fails. It's important that you calculate the sum of power required for all internal components and to make sure the PSU form factor matches the server chassis form factor.

The more CPUs and RAM in a system, the greater the power draw. The more disks you have connected to a RAID controller, the more power that is drawn. Bear in mind that SSDs draw less power than traditional spinning hard disks. Most servers these days use network storage, so the power consumption in this case would apply to the storage enclosure itself and not the server.

PSUs have total wattage listings, such as 500W, 1400W, and so on. Some equipment will sometimes specify the power draw in volt-amps (VA) instead of watts. When planning server capacity, make sure you think about all components and their power requirements.

CAUTION Never, ever open up a PSU unless you are a qualified technician. It's not just the voltage that can harm humans, but the voltage and amperage, or the flow of current. For example, as little as 10 mill amps (thousandths of an ampere) at 110V alternating current (AC) can stop your heart.

UPS

UPS batteries are constantly charged from standard power wall outlets, so that in the event of a power outage, servers plugged into the UPS can at least shut down gracefully. UPS devices are normally rack-mounted in server rooms or data centers, and you should make sure the floor can handle their weight. But how can you make sure the UPS batteries can supply enough power to devices? Kilowatts (kW), or thousands of watts, are usually used for UPS power ratings, although sometimes the rating is in volt-amperes (VA). You should total the draw for a UPS to ensure there's enough power to go around.

CAUTION Uninterruptible power supplies (UPS) are heavy! As with other heavy items, use proper lifting techniques to avoid injury: lift with legs, not your back. Try not to turn around at the waist while carrying a UPS; instead, turn your entire body around.

The UPS runtime capacity specifies how long UPS batteries can support a specific wattage load when the power goes out. For example, a UPS with a certain number of batteries might supply 900 W of power for 9 minutes, whereas with a draw of only 300 W, it might supply power for 50 minutes.

Conduct UPS battery testing periodically to ensure that the batteries will provide power when needed. There are battery testers you can use that work even when the batteries are in use, but some of these can be expensive. When maintenance of the UPS or its batteries is required, you can use bypass devices to ensure the UPS power load is not interrupted.

TIP Don't plug nonessential devices into the UPS. For example, laser printers draw a lot of power and really don't need power to shut down gracefully if the power goes out. Similarly, it might not make sense to plug a router into the UPS if network switches are not also plugged into it.

As a Server+ technician, once servers are up and running, you might not find yourself physically near them for day-to-day management, and this also includes UPS devices. Here are a few UPS remote management considerations:

- The UPS can be connected to the server via a USB cable.
- The UPS can be plugged into the network.
- Remote monitoring and management is possible using protocols such as Simple Network Management Protocol (SNMP).
- Most vendors offer a mobile device app for UPS monitoring.

Environmental Controls

Too much heat is bad for electrical equipment and shortens its life, and not enough humidity increases the likelihood of ESD. HVAC (heating, ventilation, air conditioning) is a big deal for server rooms and data centers.

Temperature

Some CPUs will throttle their throughput if the temperature is too high. Some have pointy thermal dissipation (heat sinks) on the chip; more surface area helps quickly dissipate heat. But if the CPU gets too hot, it will run much slower than it normally does (faster CPU speeds means more heat), and it's not just CPUs you should be concerned with; it's all electronic equipment. Generally speaking, server rooms and data centers should fall somewhere in the 65° to 80°F range; for metric system people, that's 18° to 27°C.

HVAC can control room temperature, but internal server temperature is more directly controlled with fans or liquid cooling systems, in which pipes carry cool liquid throughout the system to cool the surrounding air. Computer case fans are designed to take in cooler room air to pass over internal components and then expel the warmed air out to the room.

NOTE British thermal units (BTUs) are a standard way to measure the heat output of computing equipment. You can use this value to calculate HVAC requirements to accommodate the heat generated by equipment.

Air Flow

Larger server rooms and data centers have racks of heat-generating equipment. Cool air needs to be fed into the rooms for cooling, and the expelled warmer air needs to be kept separate—but how?

Hot and Cold Air Separation

Separating hot and cold air is achieved using hot and cold aisles. Racks of equipment are arranged in rows, or aisles, for optimal airflow. Baffles are used to control the flow of cooler air into rack-mounted equipment intake fans and to make sure the resulting warmer air is kept separate. So, stated simply, cool air should be channeled using baffles and fed to the front of equipment (assuming intake fans are on the front), and baffles or shrouds should channel the resulting warm air from the back away from the cooler air.

Server room racks might not be fully populated with devices, and remember that vented rack blanking panels can be used to control airflow. The added benefit of properly designed airflow systems is that they are less wasteful of energy and thus save money.

Humidity

Controlling the amount of moisture in the air is crucial for the proper functioning of equipment and to prevent ESD. Too little humidity increases the likelihood of ESD; too much humidity results in water condensation on equipment.

Temperature and humidity sensors are a must in server rooms and data centers. More sophisticated HVAC systems will provide a way to configure threshold and alert notifications when values are unacceptable, or they can automatically make adjustments. As a rule of thumb, relative humidity levels should fall somewhere within 40 to 60 percent. The longer temperature and humidity levels are out of range, the more likely equipment will fail.

Fire Suppression

The problem with baffles and shrouds being used to funnel airflow is that they are bulky. In the event of a server room or data center fire, this can impede fire extinction. Of course, the safe evacuation of personnel always takes priority over replaceable equipment. Periodic fire drills are a must!

Smoke detectors can alert technicians to impending fire issues, but the detectors used in data centers are much more sensitive than those you would use in the home. Clean-agent fire suppression systems remove heat to extinguish fires, whereas inert-gas solutions remove oxygen from the fire. Halon systems were used in the past but are no longer the norm because of their negative environmental effects.

Water sprinkler systems should be avoided, unless they are a secondary system when primary fire suppression systems fail. Water will certainly damage electronic equipment, and it can increase the possibility of electrocution (water conducts electricity). As if that isn't scary enough, pooling and running water can spread fires throughout a facility. There are variations of water "misting" solutions that can help with these problems.

Fire suppression systems, including fire extinguishers (Figure 2-11), can help minimize equipment damage including smoke damage, but no system is perfect.

Figure 2-11 A Class C fire extinguisher is capable of putting out electrical fires.

Table 2-6 Classes of Fire Extinguishers

Class	Fire Source
A	Paper, wood, cloth
B	Solvents, propane, gasoline
C	Electrical equipment
D	Combustible metals
E	Cooking oils

Table 2-6 lists common fire extinguisher classes and when they should be used. As with any crucial system, testing, monitoring, and periodic drills can make all the difference when a fire incident actually occurs.

Hands-on Exercises

Exercise 2-1: Calculate Rack Space

A server room rack measures 42U. Currently the rack contains

- Three rows of 7U UPS batteries
- A 10U blade enclosure

How many additional 7U UPS batteries can be mounted in the rack?

The answer

Since the server room rack totals 42U, and 31U are currently used, that leaves us with 11U (42–31). Therefore, only one row of 7U UPS batteries can be mounted in the rack.

Exercise 2-2: Create a Windows Server 2012 R2 Virtual Machine Configuration

Make sure the lab setup instructions in Appendix A have been completed before attempting this exercise. This exercise does not actually install the Windows Server operating system; it just gets the virtual hardware configured for use in a later exercise.

1. Start VMware Workstation 10.*x*. Choose File | New Virtual Machine.
2. Accept the default of Typical and click Next.
3. Choose I Will Install The Operating System Later, and then click Next.
4. From the Guest Operating System list, ensure that Microsoft Windows is selected, and from the Version drop-down list, ensure that Windows Server 2012 is selected. Click Next.

5. Name the virtual machine **Srv2012-1** and specify a location that has sufficient free hard disk space. Click Next.

   Note that this name applies only to VMware. The name configured within the operating system can be something completely different, although in further exercises it will be set to the same value.

6. On the Specify Disk Capacity wizard page, accept the defaults and click Next. Then, on the final wizard page, click Finish.

7. We want our server to have four hard disks in total so that we can configure software RAID later. In VMware workstation, click Edit Virtual Machine Settings on the left side of the screen. Notify the existing single virtual hard SCSI hard disk of 60 GB.

8. Click the Add button, select Hard Disk, and click Next.

9. Select SCSI, click Next. Choose Create A New Virtual Disk and click Next.

10. Notice the default size is 60 GB. Click Next.

11. On the Specify Disk File page, click Finish. Notice the new 60 GB hard disk that is now listed.

12. Repeat steps 8 through 11 two more times to add more disk space. Your virtual machine settings will then list four virtual hard disks as shown in the following illustration. Click OK.

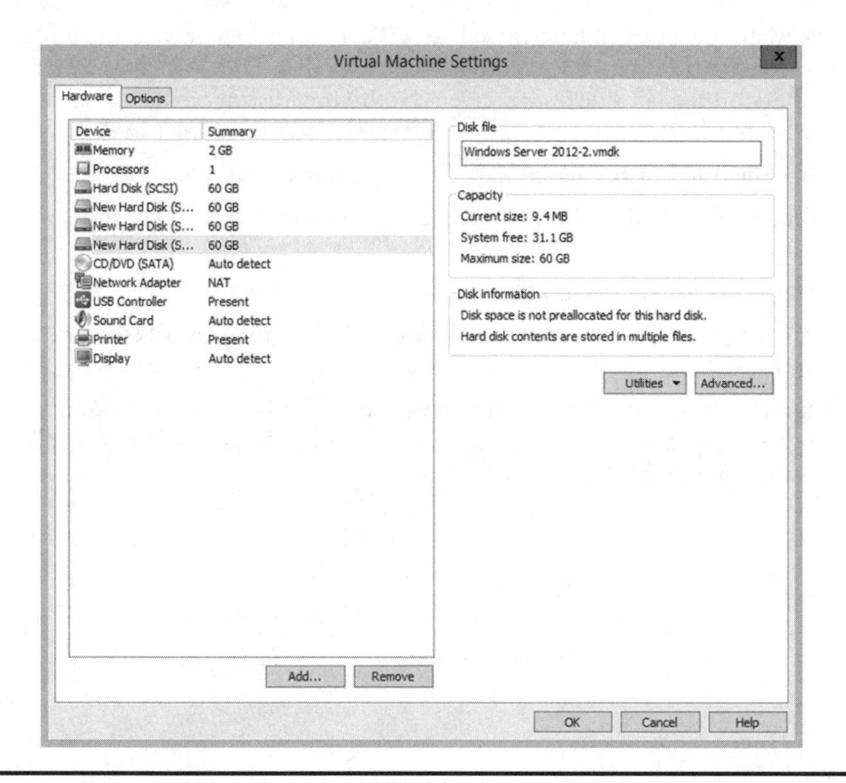

Exercise 2-3: Create a Red Hat Enterprise Linux 7 Virtual Machine Configuration

Make sure the lab setup instructions in Appendix A have been completed before attempting this exercise. This exercise does not actually install the Linux operating system; it just gets the virtual hardware configured for use in later exercise.

1. Start VMware Workstation 10.*x*. Choose File | New Virtual Machine.
2. Accept the default of Typical and click Next.
3. Choose I Will Install The Operating System Later, then click Next.
4. From the Guest Operating System list, ensure that Linux is selected, and from the Version drop-down list, ensure that Red Hat Enterprise Linux 6 64-Bit is selected. Click Next.
5. Name the virtual machine **RHEL7-1** and specify a location that has sufficient free hard disk space. Click Next.

   Note that this name applies only to VMware. The name configured within the operating system can be something completely different, although in further exercises it will be set to the same value.
6. On the Specify Disk Capacity wizard page, accept the defaults and click Next. On the final wizard page, click Finish.
7. We want our server to have three hard disks in total so that we can configure software RAID later. In VMware workstation, click Edit Virtual Machine Settings on the left side of the screen. Notify the existing single virtual hard SCSI hard disk of 20 GB.
8. Click the Add button, select Hard Disk, and click Next.
9. Select SCSI and click Next. Choose Create A New Virtual Disk, and click Next.
10. Change the size to 10 GB and click Next.
11. On the Specify Disk File page, click Finish. Notice the new 10 GB hard disk is now listed.
12. Repeat steps 8 through 11 one more time to add more disk space. Your virtual machine settings will then list three virtual hard disks as shown in the following illustration. Click OK.

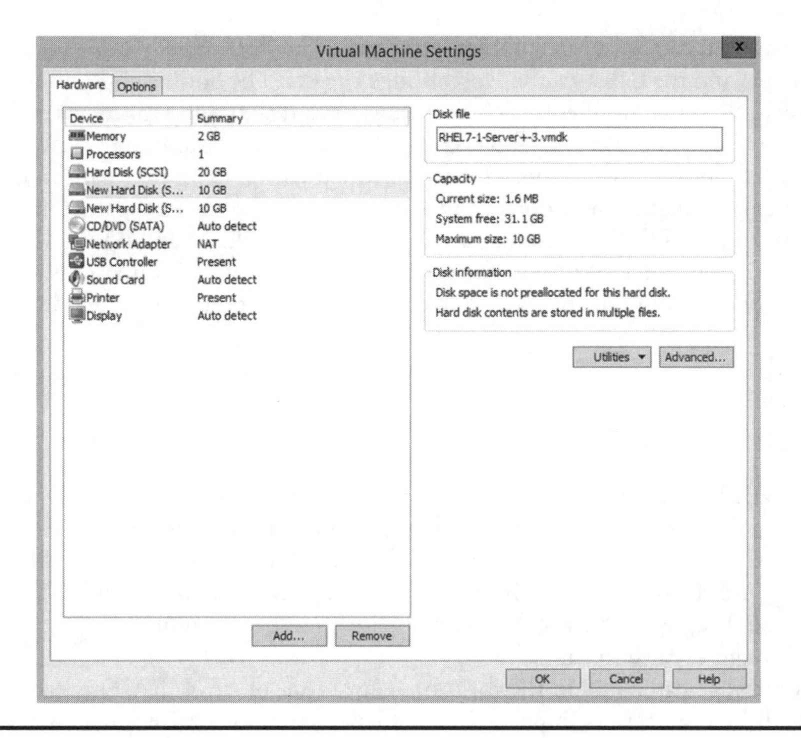

Chapter Review

In this chapter, you learned that servers consist of various hardware components that must be carefully selected to meet functionality needs. This is true of both physical and virtual server computing environments.

Server Form Factors

The most common form factors are tower, rack-mounted, and blade servers. Blade servers take the least amount of space because they are essentially circuit boards. Racks and rack-mounted equipment are measured in Us, where 1U is 1 3/4 inches in height. Server components such as disks and PSUs as well as rack components such as PDUs are often duplicated to eliminate single points of hardware failure.

Server Components

Server motherboards use either the older BIOS or the newer UEFI firmware standard. UEFI supports enhanced features such as IPv6 boot support and Secure Boot. Modern motherboards have many components built-in or integrated, such as NICs, RAID controllers, and video. CPUs are mostly 64-bit. SMP server motherboards have multiple CPU sockets, and each CPU chip can contain multiple cores, which speeds up processing.

Buses move data around in a computer system. The FSB quickly moves data between system RAM and the CPU via the Northbridge chipset. The Southbridge chipset controls data flow to slower components such as expansion card slots and USB devices. CPU processing can be sped up using L1–L3 caches, where L1 is the fastest (and most expensive).

Servers often use ECC memory modules, which use an extra parity bit to detect and correct memory corruption problems. ECC chips should be paired together in the correct motherboard slots. DDR4 modules transfer data more quickly than DDR2. Motherboard documentation will detail support for types of memory and denominations.

The most common type of expansion card slots on motherboards include

- PCI
- PCI-X
- PCIe

PCI is an older standard, and newer motherboards do not have PCI slots. PCI-X and PCIe are newer card types. PCIe uses lanes to transmit and receive data. An x16 PCIe card transfers data much more quickly than an x4 or x8 PCIe card. Servers, either directly (tower) or indirectly (blade via backplane or midplane), often use PCIe NICs. Blade systems could require a backplane/midplane upgrade before supporting faster network speeds through expansion cards.

Server storage can come in the form of DAS, NAS, or SAN. RAID is used to group physical disks together to improve disk I/O performance (striping) or for disk fault tolerance. Server hardware normally supports RAID integrated on the motherboard; otherwise software RAID within the operating system can be used.

Servers can use USB for input devices such as keyboards. USB standards and speeds are as follows:

- USB 1: 12 Mbps
- USB 2: 480 Mbps
- USB 3: 5 Gbps

Power

The main types of power connectors are NEMA, Edison, and twist-lock. Wattage refers to a unit of power. Voltage refers to the potential electrical charge difference between two points in a circuit. Kilowatts (kW) and volt-amperes (VA) are units of measurement used with UPS power ratings. To prevent ESD, which can ruin electronics, ESD straps or mats should be used.

Environmental Controls

Properly designed HVAC systems provide the correct temperature and humidity for the optimal operations of electronic equipment. Airflow in server rooms and data centers is crucial to keep incoming cool air separated from outgoing warmer air.

Hot and cold aisles, baffles, and shrouds are used to control airflow. Water should not be used as the primary fire suppressant when electronics are involved. Modern solutions aim to remove heat or oxygen from the fire.

Questions

1. Data center equipment racks are normally how wide?
   - A. 16 inches
   - B. 19 inches
   - C. 24 inches
   - D. 32 inches

2. Which unit of measurement is used for racks and rack-mounted devices?
   - A. W
   - B. Inches
   - C. Centimeters
   - D. U measure

3. Which term describes the chassis housing multiple blade servers?
   - A. Blade house
   - B. Blade enclosure
   - C. Blade box
   - D. Blade baffle

4. Which firmware standard supports the Secure Boot feature?
   - A. UEFI
   - B. Northbridge
   - C. BIOS
   - D. Southbridge

5. Larry, a server technician, is attempting to start the Linux operating system on a blade server but keeps getting "Access Denied" messages. What should Larry do?
   - A. Reinstall Linux.
   - B. Update the motherboard firmware.
   - C. Disable UEFI Secure Boot.
   - D. Enable UEFI Secure Boot.

6. You are ordering server hardware that will run mathematically intensive engineering applications. Which server component can help the most in speeding up processing time?
   A. RAM
   B. Greater disk storage capacity
   C. L1 cache
   D. L4 cache

7. A newly installed tower server will function as a packet-filtering firewall. Currently, the server has three NICs, each connected to separated VLANs. A fourth NIC is required for connectivity to a perimeter network. When choosing a new NIC, what factor should be considered?
   A. PCIe versus PCI
   B. RAID 0 versus RAID 1
   C. IPv4 versus IPv6
   D. BIOS versus UEFI

8. Which USB standard supports transmission rates up to 480 Mbps?
   A. USB 1
   B. USB 2
   C. USB 3
   D. USB 4

9. Which term identifies the flow of electrons between two differently charged endpoints in a circuit?
   A. Volts
   B. Watts
   C. PSD
   D. ESD

10. You are planning to upgrade your existing UPS system. How can you ensure device power needs will be met?
    A. Determine UPS kW or VA rating, calculate power draw sum of devices.
    B. Determine UPS V or W rating, calculate power draw sum of devices.
    C. Determine UPS kW or VA rating, calculate power draw average of devices.
    D. Determine UPS V or W rating, calculate power draw average of devices.

11. Which two items are critical when planning server room racks? Choose two.
    A. Length of network cables
    B. Total amount of CPU computing power
    C. Rack weight
    D. Airflow

12. A line-of-business database application is regularly accessed by many users concurrently. After monitoring server performance metrics, you conclude that disk I/O is the bottleneck. What can you do to optimize application performance?
    A. Configure RAID disk striping.
    B. Configure BIOS disk striping.
    C. Configure RAID disk fault tolerance.
    D. Configure BIOS disk fault tolerance.

13. What can be used to prevent server interruptions when disks fail?
    A. Hot-swappable disks
    B. RAID fault tolerance
    C. RAID disk striping
    D. UEFI

14. In which type of environment is 1-phase power most often used?
    A. Industrial
    B. Data center
    C. Manufacturing
    D. Residential

15. What purpose does a UPS serve?
    A. Enables servers to perform graceful shutdowns
    B. Keeps servers running when the power goes out
    C. Increases wattage for components requiring it
    D. Protects server from malicious attacks

16. Which items are affected by server form factors? Choose two.

A. Type of expansion card

B. Amount of supported RAM

C. Rack mount ability

D. Disk space capacity

17. Which server rack item prevents cables from pulling out when you slide out a server for servicing?

A. Rack cable arm

B. Cable management arm

C. Rack cable extender

D. Cable management extender

18. Which statement regarding blade servers is true?

A. The server is a stand-alone piece of equipment.

B. The server is mounted into rails on a server rack.

C. The server has its own power supply.

D. The server slides into an enclosure.

19. How is data transmitted throughout a computer system?

A. PCI

B. Bus

C. PCIe

D. Northbridge

20. You want to ensure that your RAID controller caches disk writes. Which option must the controller support?

A. Write-back caching

B. Read-write caching

C. Restart-enabled write caching

D. Battery-backed write caching

21. What is a KVM switch used for?

    A. Network device interconnect

    B. Server management

    C. Redundancy

    D. RAID controllers

22. Why are server racks arranged in rows?

    A. To optimize airflow

    B. To allow access to servicing panels

    C. To reduce the impact of fire

    D. To increase security

23. Which class of fire extinguisher is used to extinguish cooking fires?

    A. A

    B. C

    C. D

    D. E

24. You are the server technician for a Caribbean telecommunications provider. Power on the island is unreliable and you want to prevent servers from abruptly shutting down. What should you acquire?

    A. ABS

    B. UPS

    C. RDP

    D. ESD

25. One of your clients, FakeRUs Inc., needs a new physical server to store files and run a small customer database application. The IT budget is very small and the company wants to reuse any existing hardware components, such as network cards, that they have on hand. Which server form factor should you recommend to FakeRUs Inc.?

    A. Tower

    B. Rack-mounted

    C. Blade

    D. Virtual

Questions and Answers

1. Data center equipment racks are normally how wide?
   - A. 16 inches
   - B. 19 inches
   - C. 24 inches
   - D. 32 inches

   B. Most rack systems are 19 inches wide, although they are available in wider formats such as 23 inches. A, C, and D are incorrect. These values are not used for rack widths.

2. Which unit of measurement is used for racks and rack-mounted devices?
   - A. W
   - B. Inches
   - C. Centimeters
   - D. U measure

   D. A U is 1 3/4 inches. This is used to measure racks and the devices that fit into them. A, B, and C are incorrect. These units of measurement are not used in rack-mounted systems.

3. Which term describes the chassis housing multiple blade servers?
   - A. Blade house
   - B. Blade enclosure
   - C. Blade box
   - D. Blade baffle

   B. A blade enclosure contains multiple blade servers. A, C, and D are incorrect. The other blade terms are fictitious.

4. Which firmware standard supports the Secure Boot feature?
   - A. UEFI
   - B. Northbridge
   - C. BIOS
   - D. Southbridge

   A. UEFI supersedes the older BIOS standard and supports the Secure Boot feature, which ensures that only trusted (digitally signed) operating systems are allowed to start. B, C, and D are incorrect. The Northbridge is a chipset that connects the CPU to memory via the memory controller. BIOS is a firmware motherboard standard that predates UEFI. The Southbridge firmware connects slower hardware such as hard disk controllers, the USB bus, PCI slots, and so on.

5. Larry, a server technician, is attempting to start the Linux operating system on a blade server but keeps getting "Access Denied" messages. What should Larry do?

   A. Reinstall Linux.

   B. Update the motherboard firmware.

   C. Disable UEFI Secure Boot.

   D. Enable UEFI Secure Boot.

   C. Some operating systems cannot be used with the UEFI Secure Boot feature because they are not digitally signed. This lack of a trusted signature can result in error messages when the system boots if the Secure Boot feature is enabled, so one solution is to disable UEFI Secure Boot. A, B, and D are incorrect. Reinstalling Linux, updating motherboard firmware, and enabling UEFI Secure Boot will not solve the problem. Linux is already installed (it had to have worked somehow at some point for the installation to complete); the quick and simple solutions is to disable UEFI Secure Boot.

6. You are ordering server hardware that will run mathematically intensive engineering applications. Which server component can help the most in speeding up processing time?

   A. RAM

   B. Greater disk storage capacity

   C. L1 cache

   D. L4 cache

   C. L1 cache is high-speed memory that is used by the CPU to fetch instructions and/or data quickly that has already been accessed. A, B, and D are incorrect. Adding RAM enables more programs and services to run simultaneously, but it doesn't help with the requirements in this scenario. More disk space will not speed up programs that are mathematically intensive, and L4 cache is not accessed as quickly by the CPU as L1 cache is.

7. A newly installed tower server will function as a packet-filtering firewall. Currently, the server has three NICs, each connected to separated VLANs. A fourth NIC is required for connectivity to a perimeter network. When choosing a new NIC, what factor should be considered?

   A. PCIe versus PCI

   B. RAID 0 versus RAID 1

   C. IPv4 versus IPv6

   D. BIOS versus UEFI

A. Tower server motherboards will most likely accommodate PCIe cards, but older ones might support PCI. B, C, and D are incorrect. RAID is related to multidisk configuration and not networking. IPv4 and IPv6 are software protocols that are not directly impacted when choosing a server NIC. Whether the older BIOS or newer UEFI firmware standard is used has no impact on the NIC selection, as long as the selected NIC can be accommodated by the motherboard slots.

8. Which USB standard supports transmission rates up to 480 Mbps?

A. USB 1

B. USB 2

C. USB 3

D. USB 4

B. In theory, the USB 2 standard can transfer data at approximately 480 Mbps. A, C, and D are incorrect. The USB 1 maximum speed is 12 Mbps, USB 3 is 5 Gbps, and as of this writing the USB 4 standard does not exist.

9. Which term identifies the flow of electrons between two differently charged endpoints in a circuit?

A. Volts

B. Watts

C. PSD

D. ESD

D. ESD, or electronic static discharge, is the transfer of electronic between two differently charged points in a circuit. This can damage sensitive electronic components, so precautions such as ESD wrist straps or ESD mats should be used. A, B, and C are incorrect. Volts are a unit of measurement related to expressing the difference in electrical potential. Watts are used to measure units of power. PSD is not a valid acronym in this context.

10. You are planning to upgrade your existing UPS system. How can you ensure device power needs will be met?

A. Determine UPS kW or VA rating, calculate power draw sum of devices.

B. Determine UPS V or W rating, calculate power draw sum of devices.

C. Determine UPS kW or VA rating, calculate power draw average of devices.

D. Determine UPS V or W rating, calculate power draw average of devices.

A. Most UPSs express their power ratings in either kilowatts (kW) or volt-amperes (VA). The power draw for all devices that will be plugged into the UPS system should be totaled to ensure that enough power will be supplied in the event of a power failure. B, C, and D are incorrect. Volts and watts are not used to rate power supplied from a UPS system. When determining whether the UPS can support devices, the total power draw of those devices must be compared to the UPS rating.

11. Which two items are critical when planning server room racks? Choose two.

A. Length of network cables

B. Total amount of CPU computing power

C. Rack weight

D. Airflow

C, D. A full rack can weigh hundreds of pounds; floors must be able to support these loads properly. Airflow can be controlled around racks using baffles, shrouds, and vented filler panels. A and B are incorrect. Although recommended network cable lengths should not be exceeded, this is not as important as rack weight and airflow. CPU computing power is a server planning consideration, not a rack planning consideration.

12. A line-of-business database application is regularly accessed by many users concurrently. After monitoring server performance metrics, you conclude that disk I/O is the bottleneck. What can you do to optimize application performance?

A. Configure RAID disk striping.

B. Configure BIOS disk striping.

C. Configure RAID disk fault tolerance.

D. Configure BIOS disk fault tolerance.

A. RAID disk striping arranges multiple disks to work as a single unit to optimize disk reads and writes. B, C, and D are incorrect. There is no such thing as BIOS disk striping. Disk fault tolerance will not improve application performance.

13. What can be used to prevent server interruptions when disks fail?

A. Hot-swappable disks

B. RAID fault tolerance

C. RAID disk striping

D. UEFI

A. Hot-swapping enables the exchanging of hardware components while the server is running. B, C, and D are incorrect. Even though there are types of RAID configurations that can ensure that things keep running when disks fail, it depends on the implementation; hot-swapping is a better answer. UEFI is a firmware standard that replaces the BIOS standard; it is not related to disk failures.

14. In which type of environment is 1-phase power most often used?

A. Industrial

B. Data center

C. Manufacturing

D. Residential

D. One-phase power is used for small power draw needs such as heating systems and lighting. A, B, and C are incorrect. Industrial and manufacturing environments, along with data centers, often use 3-phase power because of the larger power draw.

15. What purpose does a UPS serve?

A. Enables servers to perform graceful shutdowns

B. Keeps servers running when the power goes out

C. Increases wattage for components requiring it

D. Protects server from malicious attacks

A. UPS systems enables servers to shut down properly instead of abruptly, which can corrupt open files. B, C, and D are incorrect. UPS systems are not designed to keep servers running other than for very short periods, nor do they increase wattage or protect from attacks.

16. Which items are affected by server form factors? Choose two.

A. Type of expansion card

B. Amount of supported RAM

C. Rack mount ability

D. Disk space capacity

A, C. Expansion cards, such as PCI, may not fit into slimmer server profiles such as rack-mounted servers. Tower servers cannot be rack-mounted, so rack mount ability is another item affected by server form factors. B and D are incorrect. The amount or RAM or disk space is not affected by server form factors.

17. Which server rack item prevents cables from pulling out when you slide out a server for servicing?

A. Rack cable arm

B. Cable management arm

C. Rack cable extender

D. Cable management extender

B. Cable management arms contain server cables and fold out when the server is slid out on rails. A, C, and D are incorrect. Rack cable arm, rack cable extender, and cable management extender are not proper terms.

18. Which statement regarding blade servers is true?

A. The server is a stand-alone piece of equipment.

B. The server is mounted into rails on a server rack.

C. The server has its own power supply.

D. The server slides into an enclosure.

D. A blade enclosure can contain many blade servers that slide in to make a connection to the midplane. A, B, and C are incorrect. Blade servers cannot run on their own; they must be placed in a blade enclosure. Blades themselves are not rack-mounted, although blade enclosures are. Blades do not have on-board power sources; this comes from the enclosure.

19. How is data transmitted throughout a computer system?

A. PCI

B. Bus

C. PCIe

D. Northbridge

B. Computers contain multiple buses that transmit data throughout the system. A, C, and D are incorrect. PCI and PCIe are expansion card standards that have their own buses for moving data into and out of card slots. The Northbridge connects the CPU to memory and the PCI bus and some other components, but not all of them.

20. You want to ensure that your RAID controller caches disk writes. Which option must the controller support?

A. Write-back caching

B. Read-write caching

C. Restart-enabled write caching

D. Battery-backed write caching

D. Battery-backed caching uses a battery to supply power to cached data writes. A, B, and C are incorrect. Write-back caching, read-write caching, and restart-enabled write caching are incorrect terms in this context.

21. What is a KVM switch used for?

A. Network device interconnect

B. Server management

C. Redundancy

D. RAID controllers

B. KVM switches have a keyboard, video display, and mouse attached along with these cables plugged into numerous servers; the servers can be managed locally without each needing a keyboard, video, and mouse. A, C, and D are incorrect. KVM switches do not interconnect network devices, nor do they provide redundancy or RAID controller features.

22. Why are server racks arranged in rows?

A. To optimize airflow

B. To allow access to servicing panels

C. To reduce the impact of fire

D. To increase security

A. Rows of racks allow cool air to be taken into devices and warm air to be exhausted out the back; these are called hot and cold aisles. B, C, and D are incorrect. Rack rows do not facilitate servicing, nor do they reduce fire impact or increase security.

23. Which class of fire extinguisher is used to extinguish cooking fires?

A. A

B. C

C. D

D. E

D. Class E fire extinguishers are designed to put out cooking fires. A, B, and C are incorrect. Class A extinguishers are for paper, wood, or cloth fires. Class C is for electrical equipment, and class D is for combustible metal fires.

24. You are the server technician for a Caribbean telecommunications provider. Power on the island is unreliable and you want to prevent servers from abruptly shutting down. What should you acquire?

A. ABS

B. UPS

C. RDP

D. ESD

B. UPS systems enable servers to shut down properly instead of abruptly, which can corrupt open files. A, C, and D are incorrect. ABS is not a valid term in this context. RDP is the Remote Desktop Protocol used to manage a computer remotely over the network. ESD is electrostatic discharge; this occurs when two devices in close proximity have varying electrical charges.

25. One of your clients, FakeRUs Inc., needs a new physical server to store files and run a small customer database application. The IT budget is very small and the company wants to reuse any existing hardware components, such as network cards, that they have on hand. Which server form factor should you recommend to FakeRUs Inc.?

A. Tower

B. Rack-mounted

C. Blade

D. Virtual

A. Tower servers are generally cheaper than blade or rack-mounted servers, and since they contain standard hardware, reusing components is not a problem. B, C, and D are incorrect. Rack-mounted and blade servers can get expensive and are not the best choices for a small shop. A virtual server is not an option since the question states a physical server is required.

CHAPTER 3

Server Operating Systems

In this chapter, you will
- Learn about server roles
- Understand the benefits of virtual servers
- Install Windows Server 2012 R2
- Install Red Hat Enterprise Linux 7.1
- Know when to use various server administration methods
- Understand the importance of server documentation
- Learn about patch management

Servers are the core of network services. UNIX, Linux, and Windows can be used for most standard uses such as file servers, mail servers, and Directory servers, but in some cases a line of business application will require a specific platform.

Server Roles

Servers are deployed to offer services that provide some kind of business value to an organization. For example, Domain Name Service (DNS) servers provide a name-to–IP address lookup service, mail servers enable communication through e-mail messages, and so on. Planning these roles includes determining whether multiple roles will be co-located on the same server or spread out among multiple servers—and those servers can be physical or virtual.

In the cloud, customers can quickly provision and deprovision virtual servers as needs dictate. Cloud providers such as Microsoft Azure, shown in Figure 3-1, offer virtual machines templates that customers can use to deploy not only the server OS, but also additional services, such as a MySQL database server virtual machine.

Cloud virtual machines can offer services not only to other devices running in the cloud, but also to Internet consumers and on-premises devices. Connectivity with on-premises devices can be accomplished with the following:

- Site-to-site virtual private network (VPN) connections
- Dedicated connection from on-premises to cloud provider, bypassing the Internet

Figure 3-1 Virtual machines templates available in the Microsoft Azure cloud

After server roles are installed and configured, these services must be enabled to ensure that the service is running when the server comes up. The installation, configuration, and management of server roles vary depending on the specific server OS version. Figure 3-2 shows the Add Roles and Features Wizard that is used to add roles to a Windows server.

Infrastructure Roles

The network infrastructure enables devices to communicate with one another. This begins with hardware such as network cables, connectors, routers, switches, network cards, wireless access points, and so on. Then there are the software components that provide network infrastructure services, and this is where our discussion becomes more in-depth.

DHCP

TCP/IP v4 is the standard software communication protocol suite used by modern network devices, although IPv6 is gaining traction. With both IPv4 and IPv6, the Dynamic Host Configuration Protocol (DHCP) is used to provide central IP settings that are delivered to network nodes. This saves technicians from having to configure IP settings manually on each and every device.

Chapter 5 dives into the DHCP packet exchange between DHCP clients and servers. A DHCP server can run on a server OS, or it might run as a service on a router, including a wireless router. DHCP listens for client connections on UDP port 67, so firewalls between DHCP clients and servers must allow this traffic to the DHCP server. Traffic to

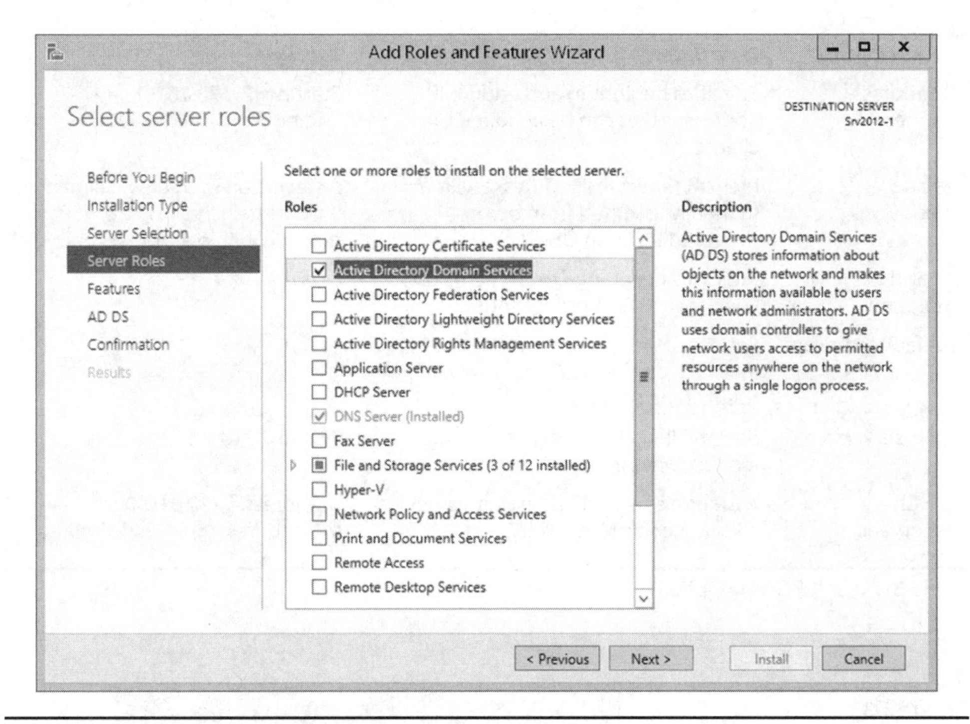

Figure 3-2 Installing a Windows Server 2012 R2 role using Server Manager

the DHCP client is addressed to UDP port 68. After the DHCP server role is installed on a server, it must be configured to support the needs of the network, as discussed in the following sections.

DHCP Scopes The first thing that gets configured with DHCP is the scope. Scopes are IP settings grouped together into a manageable unit; they must be activated before they can be used in the DHCP process. Table 3-1 shows common scope settings.

DHCP Vendor Classes When communicating with a DHCP server, a network device sends information regarding what type of device it is. For example, a Cisco or Nortel IP phone, an Apple iPhone, Android phone, and HP network printer can all be easily identified. But how is this useful?

DHCP vendor classes, as shown in Figure 3-3, let you apply specific IP settings to certain types of network devices. For instance, you could assign an IP address range, default gateway, and DNS server, specifically to Cisco IP phones. This way, your IP phone traffic could be on an isolated network.

You must first determine what specific vendor class data is included in the network transmission. You can find this information by searching the Internet, by visiting the vendor's web site, or by capturing network traffic related to a specific device type during DHCP transmissions.

Scope Option	Description	Example
IP address ranges	Specifies beginning and ending IP addresses that can be acquired by clients	Starting IP: 172.16.0.1 Ending IP: 172.16.0.100
IP address exclusions	Prevents specific IP addresses already manually assigned from being delivered through DHCP	A server configured with a manual IP address such as 172.16.0.50 that falls within a DHCP scope
IP address lease duration	Indicates how long DHCP clients can keep their IP address settings	8 days
Default gateway	Sets the IP address(es) of the router(s) interface on the local network; enables traffic to be sent outside of the LAN	172.16.0.253
DNS servers	Sets the IP address(es) of the name lookup server(s)	172.16.0.210
DHCP reservation	Assigns a specific IP address to a device with a specific MAC address	IP address: 172.16.0.60 MAC address: 00-50-56-C0-00-01

Table 3-1 DHCP Scope Options

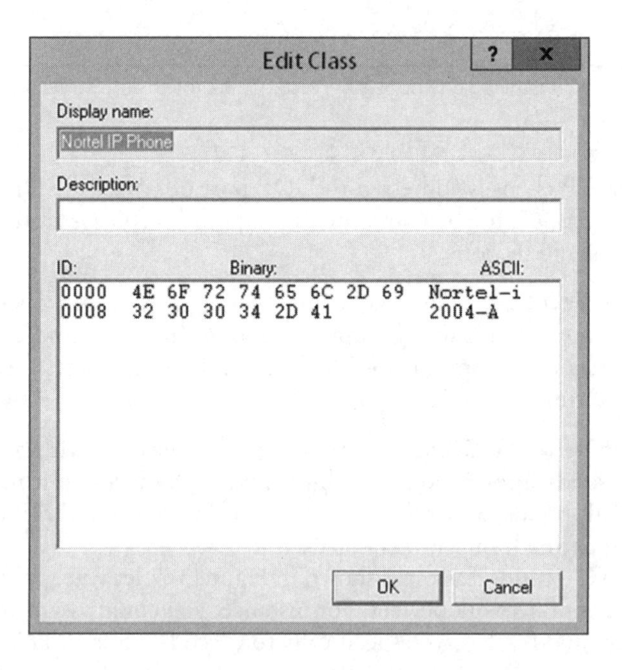

Figure 3-3 DHCP vendor classes for Nortel IP phones

APIPA DHCP is a critical infrastructure service, and without it device communication can be a problem. When DHCP clients can't reach a DHCP server, they autoconfigure themselves with an Automatic Private IP Address (APIPA).

APIPAs fall in the 169.254.0.1 to 169.254.255.254 range, where 169.254.255.255 is the broadcast address for this network. The client device assigns itself a unique address on the LAN—but the device will not be able to communicate outside of the LAN, and within the LAN it can communicate only with other APIPA hosts. Once DHCP is reachable, the APIPA is no longer used on the network interface.

From the command prompt on a Windows computer, you use the `ipconfig` command to work with DHCP. The `ipconfig /all` command shows network details, including whether DHCP is being used, and, if so, the IP address of the DHCP server along with lease information. You'll find more detail about this in Chapter 5.

IPv6 does something similar, but not exactly the same. A link-local IPv6 address is a unique self-assigned address, but it is always bound to the network interface whether or not DHCP is reachable. Actually, it is used even if you manually configure IPv6 on a host. This type of address has an FE80 network prefix, and it's used by IPv6 to discover network devices and router network prefixes using multicast transmissions.

When determining the best configuration options for your DHCP scopes, consider the following:

- Talk to the network infrastructure team to determine which valid IPv4 or IPv6 address ranges can be used.
- Environments where clients are connected for short periods of time should have short lease durations to maximize IP address reuse.
- Try to specify at least two default gateways for remote network connectivity in case one router becomes unavailable.
- Try to specify at least two DNS servers in case one becomes unavailable.
- For multihomed (multiple network card) DHCP servers, configure DHCP bindings for the correct network interface.
- Think high availability: What happens if your single DHCP host crashes? Windows servers allow two DHCP hosts to replicate DHCP configuration and lease data between each other.

DNS

DNS is a lookup service, and, much like DHCP, without it, most network communication grinds to a halt. It is most often used to look up an IP address when given a fully qualified domain name (FQDN). Let's say, for example, that ServerA needs to download updates from windowsupdate.microsoft.com. A DNS query will be sent from ServerA destined for UDP port 53 on ServerA's configured DNS server. The DNS server will return the IP address for windowsupdate.microsoft.com to ServerA. This is a DNS *forward lookup*.

Reverse lookups do the opposite: given an IP address in a DNS query, the DNS server looks up and returns the FQDN. This can be useful if you're looking through firewall logs and notice suspicious activity from a certain IP address. Back in the day, client systems each had (and still have!) a HOSTS file containing FQDN names and IP addresses.

DNS Domains DNS is a hierarchy that begins at the top with the root domain. Under the root domain are top-level domains (TLDs) that we've all heard of—.com, .org, .net, .mil, .gov, .beer, .uk, and so on—that are maintained by DNS root servers. Figure 3-4 shows the default root hints configured on a Windows DNS server that enable the Windows DNS server to resolve Internet names.

Companies and individuals can register a unique DNS domain name through a DNS authority such as FreeDNS, GoDaddy, and others. The DNS domain for a company reflects its Internet presence, such as mheducation.com. The internal network for a company might use a different DNS domain name such as mheducation.local. Some services such as Microsoft Active Directory Domain Services require and create a DNS domain in order to function.

A domain, such as mheducation.local, can have subdomains. Examples include sales.mheducation.local and hr.mheducation.local, which could each have data stored on a different DNS server. In this case, a DNS server controlling the data for only mheducation.local is said to be *authoritative* over the mheducation.local zone. Another DNS server would be authoritative over the sales.mheducation.local zone, and so on.

DNS Resource Records DNS domains contain resource records (RRs), as shown in the DNS Manager screen in Figure 3-5. Different types of RRs are used for different purposes—for example, DNS *A records* are used to look up IPv4 addresses when a FQDN is provided, and *mail exchange (MX) records* are used to find Simple Mail Transfer Protocol (SMTP) mail servers. Table 3-2 lists common RR types and their uses.

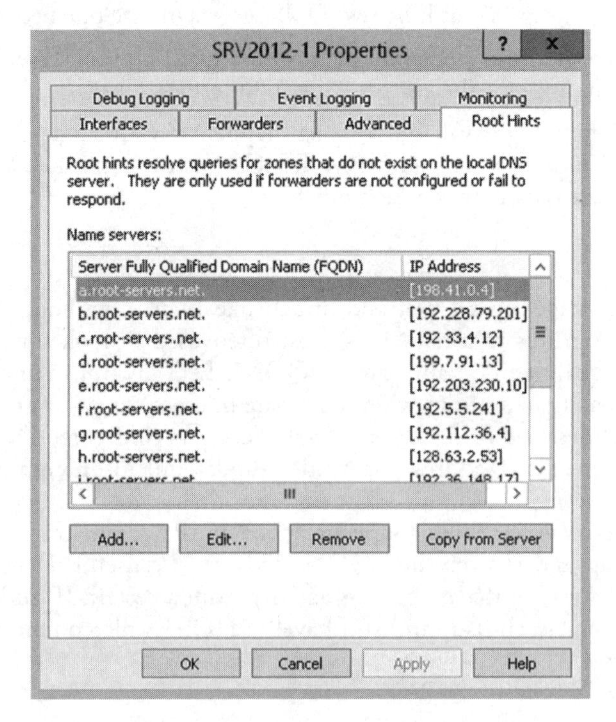

Figure 3-4 Setting Windows DNS server root hints

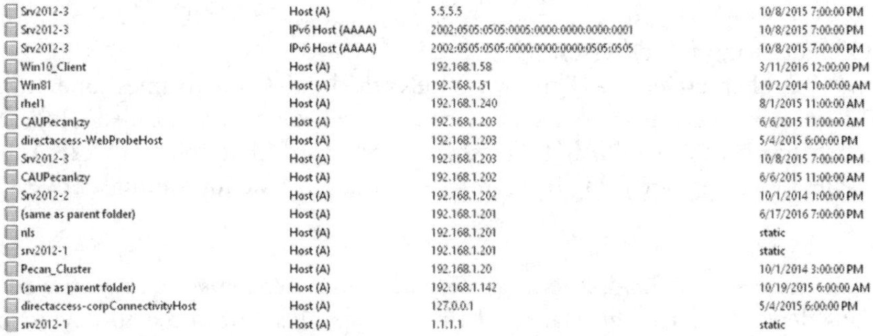

Srv2012-3	Host (A)	5.5.5.5	10/8/2015 7:00:00 PM
Srv2012-3	IPv6 Host (AAAA)	2002:0505:0505:0005:0000:0000:0000:0001	10/8/2015 7:00:00 PM
Srv2012-3	IPv6 Host (AAAA)	2002:0505:0505:0000:0000:0000:0505:0505	10/8/2015 7:00:00 PM
Win10_Client	Host (A)	192.168.1.58	3/11/2016 12:00:00 PM
Win81	Host (A)	192.168.1.51	10/2/2014 10:00:00 AM
rhel1	Host (A)	192.168.1.240	8/1/2015 11:00:00 AM
CAUPecankzy	Host (A)	192.168.1.203	6/6/2015 11:00:00 AM
directaccess-WebProbeHost	Host (A)	192.168.1.203	5/4/2015 6:00:00 PM
Srv2012-3	Host (A)	192.168.1.203	10/8/2015 7:00:00 PM
CAUPecankzy	Host (A)	192.168.1.202	6/6/2015 11:00:00 AM
Srv2012-2	Host (A)	192.168.1.202	10/1/2014 1:00:00 PM
(same as parent folder)	Host (A)	192.168.1.201	6/17/2016 7:00:00 PM
nls	Host (A)	192.168.1.201	static
srv2012-1	Host (A)	192.168.1.201	static
Pecan_Cluster	Host (A)	192.168.1.20	10/1/2014 3:00:00 PM
(same as parent folder)	Host (A)	192.168.1.142	10/19/2015 6:00:00 AM
directaccess-corpConnectivityHost	Host (A)	127.0.0.1	5/4/2015 6:00:00 PM
srv2012-1	Host (A)	1.1.1.1	static

Figure 3-5 DNS resource records

RR Type	How It Is Used
SOA	Start of authority SOA contains zone details such as serial number and refresh interval.
A	Forward lookup record FQDN is included in the query and an IPv4 address is returned.
AAAA	Forward lookup record FQDN is included in the query and an IPv6 address is returned.
CNAME	Canonical name record or alias record Used as an additional name for an existing name. Points to an A record.
MX	Mail exchanger Used for e-mail domain suffixes to locate an SMTP mail server. Points to an A record that has the IP address of an SMTP mail server.
SVR	Service record Used to locate a network service such as Microsoft Active Directory. Includes the TCP or UDP port numbers for the service. Clients query DNS SVR records to locate services.
PTR	Pointer record Used in DNS reverse lookup zones. Client queries include the IP address and seek the FQDN.

Table 3-2 DNS Resource Record Types

WINS

Prior to Windows 2000, Microsoft TCP/IP networks relied on the Windows Internet Name Service (WINS) to resolve NetBIOS computer names (maximum 15 characters) to their respective IP addresses. Legacy software might still require this on modern networks, but let's face it, that would be the exception and not the rule!

WINS is a centralized and replicated database of NetBIOS computer names and their IP addresses; there is no naming hierarchy as there is with DNS. It is installed as a "feature" (as opposed to a "role") on Windows Server 2012 for backward compatibility. Like DNS, client devices needing WINS must point to the IP address of one or more

WINS servers. In the past, client systems each had an LMHOSTS file containing NetBIOS names and IP addresses.

An available alternative since Windows 2008 is the DNS GlobalNames zone. Instead of WINS, client devices can point to a DNS server, where a zone literally called GlobalNames exists. DNS admins create CNAME (alias) resource records that point to DNS A records. This enables older software using flat computer names to function through DNS.

NTP

Time is of the essence; this is so very true with computer networks, because so many operations depend on accurate date and time stamps. It's crucial for all devices on the network to agree on the date and the time—log file entries, Microsoft Active Directory user logon time stamps, and many other activities depend on it!

Network Time Protocol (NTP) is a service that runs on a network host, whether it is UNIX, Linux, Windows, or a Juniper Networks router; it can run on anything, and there are thousands of NTP servers on the Internet. Pool.ntp.org is widely used to provide time synchronization for Internet devices.

NTP Tiers NTP is a network service that listens on UDP port 123 for time requests, and there can certainly be more than one NTP server on a network! Different tiers, or stratums, of NTP hosts exist:

- **Stratum 0** Time source, or reference clock
- **Stratum 1** NTP server connected to Stratum 0 device
- **Stratum 2** NTP server gets time over the network from a Stratum 1 host

These stratums imply the delays involved with getting time packets sent over the network in the first place. A Stratum 2 NTP server might be off from UTC time by 10 milliseconds, for example, where a Stratum 1 NTP server might be off by only 1/2 millisecond. Figure 3-6 shows the NTP status on the Windows operating system.

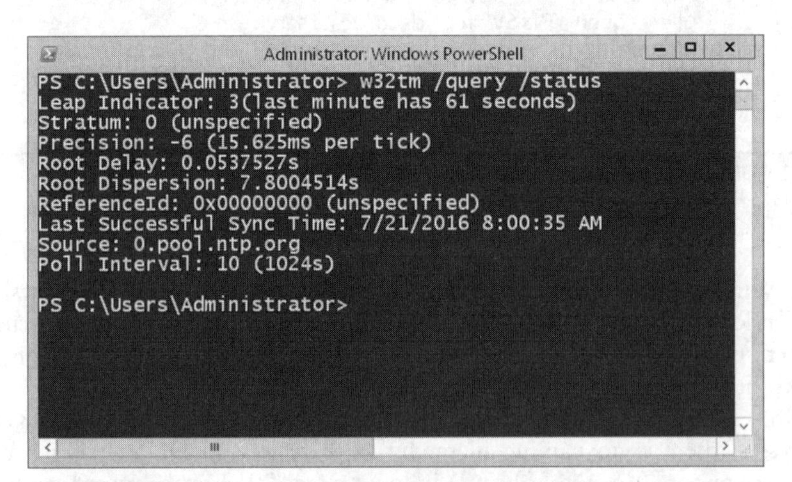

Figure 3-6 Viewing NTP status on Windows Server 2012 R2

Directory Services

A directory service (DS) is a centralized network database containing objects such as the following:

- Users
- Groups
- Computers
- Network service locators
- Shared folders
- Shared printers
- Software licenses

In the enterprise, this normally means replicating the DS data among servers for redundancy and performance benefits. If one server fails and you're using DS for user authentication, other remaining servers can handle the authentication. Of course, these DS servers need to be locatable on the network, normally via DNS.

Microsoft network environments tend to use Microsoft Active Directory Domain Services (AD DS), but there are many other options including OpenLDAP, Oracle Directory Services, and Novell (now a part of Micro Focus) eDirectory. These solutions are all based on essentially the same LDAP standards.

Microsoft Active Directory The Lightweight Directory Access Protocol (LDAP) provides access over an IP network to a central network database. It listens on TCP ports 389 and 636 (clear text and encrypted, respectively). Microsoft AD DS, or simply AD, is LDAP-compliant.

AD is a replicated network database that is synchronized between domain controllers (DCs). A DC is a server that is configured to hold a replica of the AD database, which by default lives on the DC under C:\Windows\Ntds\Ntds.dit.

Windows enterprise environments join computers (Windows clients and servers, Linux hosts, and so on) to the AD domain for the purposes of centralized administration (through group policies) and centralized authentication. Users with accounts in AD can log on using that account on any domain-joined computer—in other words, we don't have to create an account for user Bob on every computer with the same password; creating it once in AD suffices.

NOTE Only a small subset of Group Policy options are used by certain Linux distributions. Consult the documentation for your specific variant of Linux.

DCs are discovered by clients through DNS queries. The creation of a DC also creates DNS service location records, which clients use to find the nearest DC. Clients need the DC not only for authentication, but also to periodically pull down Group Policy settings configured by the Windows administrator. So in other words, AD needs DNS.

AD is a Windows Server role and can be installed and managed using the following:

- **Windows PowerShell cmdlets** Commands that enable automation
- **Server Manager** GUI tool on the server or the client

Other Server Roles

We have jobs in IT because we use technology to solve business problems. There are other server roles beyond the basic infrastructure role mentioned so far that you need to understand. Some roles might be on their own server, but you can also co-locate multiple roles on a single server; it depends on the role and the scale of work it will be performing.

Web Server

Web servers use the HyperText Transfer Protocol (HTTP) or its secured variant (HTTPS) to present content to a web browser. The following ports are normally used on a web server:

- **TCP 80** Not encrypted
- **TCP 443** Encrypted with Secure Sockets Layer (SSL) or the newer Transport Layer Security (TLS)

Administrators can choose a different port if they want. The web server transmits data to clients on a higher numbered port such as 45,000. If SSL or TLS will be used, a Public Key Infrastructure (PKI) certificate is required for the web server (not clients). Check out Chapter 6 to learn more about crypto and PKI.

Client web browsers normally use DNS to resolve FQDNs to IP addresses; this is so much easier than typing in a difficult-to-remember IP address in the browser's address bar.

Common web server products include these:

- Microsoft Internet Information Services (IIS), shown in Figure 3-7
- Apache
- NGINX (engine X)

Simply stated, a web server listens for HTTP connections and delivers data back to client web browsers. It can become more involved than that, however.

Developers can build static HTML web pages that sit on the web server and are transmitted to clients upon request. Developers can also use server- or client-side scripting languages such as Python (server-side) or JavaScript (client-side) that can dynamically generate page content or take specific actions based on conditions. Client-side scripting is used less often where possible because of the security implications of running that code locally on a client computer.

Web server authentication to protected web sites is often performed by an underlying DS, whether the web site is on-premises or in the cloud. Using web Single Sign-On (SSO) means using a single identity store, even between different companies: this is called *identity federation*.

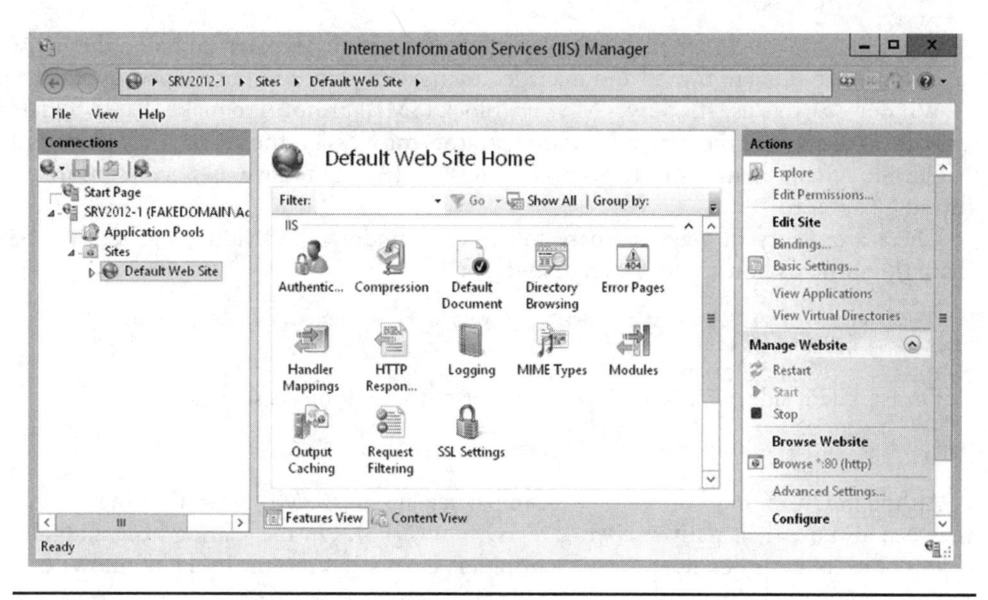

Figure 3-7 Microsoft IIS web server management tool

Application Server

Most of us probably think of database servers when we hear the term "application server." Although this is partially true, there's more to application servers than that.

Many people confuse web, database, and application servers. The web server is basically an HTTP engine; it doesn't address a specific business solution. A database server is essentially a container that could be used for storage and retrieval of relevant data. Now, if our company's developers build a travel expense application available on the HTTP web server that stores data in a back-end database, we can say we now have an *application server*: it serves a specific business need.

Common application server database engines include these:

- Microsoft SQL Server
- MySQL
- Oracle Database

If you are building and testing a web application, the cloud comes in quite nicely. It takes very little time to spin up a bunch of virtual machines, some of which are HTTP or database servers. Then once development ceases, you can deprovision these virtual machines so you no longer get charged for them—sounds like a great idea!

File Server

Despite the popularity of cloud storage, file servers are still very important in the enterprise. It's safe to say that accessing your enterprise network probably performs better than accessing files over the Internet. Sometimes laws or regulations leave us no choice; files must be stored on equipment owned and managed by the company and not a cloud provider.

Windows servers use the Server Message Block (SMB) protocol to make shared folders available to users over the network. Administrators must assign the appropriate share and NTFS file system permissions to access control lists (ACLs) to give user access; more on this in Chapter 6.

There are plenty of ways to share folders in Windows (individual files cannot be shared), but here's how to do it using PowerShell:

```
New-smbshare -name "Projects" -Path d:\projects -readaccess
"fakedomain\authenticated users"
```

On the client side, we could map a drive letter to the Projects share as follows:

```
Net use g: \\server1\projects
```

Although UNIX and Linux systems can participate in an SMB network using Samba, they can also use their native network file system (NFS). On the sharing host, the /etc/exports file contains details about which folders clients can mount (only Windows uses drive letters) over the network.

These days, many organizations such as legal firms have turned to document management systems such as Microsoft SharePoint Server or Hummingbird DOCS Open, where it is easy to work with multiple file versions, metadata, and many other document actions.

Print Server

As the name implies, a print server manages the printers on a network. Print servers also spool print jobs from clients using server disk space. Depending on your environment, you may not need or use a print server; instead, client devices can be configured to print directly to network-based printers, but this lack of centralized management control can prove challenging on a larger network.

Print servers act as an intermediary between clients that want to print and the physical printer devices; security and printer settings for many printers can be managed using a centralized administrative tool. Windows shared printers can of course be configured in the GUI by right-clicking a printer, and they can also be shared using PowerShell as follows:

```
Set-Printer -Name fakeprinter -Shared $True -ShareName fakeprintershare
```

CUPS Common UNIX Printing System (CUPS) has been around for decades. It's the standard UNIX and Linux print server solution. Just like a Windows print server, CUPS manages printers and queues.

UNIX and Linux hosts in a Windows environment can also use Samba to print to Windows shared printers.

Cloud Printing The idea of cloud printing is to remove any printing dependencies such as operating system versions, print drivers, printing devices, and so on. In addition, cloud printing can be used with mobile devices, which do not offer great printing support—certainly not for a large variety of printing devices.

Many mobile device users save files that they want to print to a cloud storage account that they then access from a laptop or desktop that supports printing. But there's a better way—cloud printing to the rescue! If your mobile device apps don't support cloud printing, don't worry, because there are helper apps for Android, Windows, and iOS devices.

Mail Server

You can run several different types of mail solutions on your server, whether on-premises or in the cloud. They all run as services (or daemons) that enable connections on specific ports, as listed in Table 3-3. Always remember that most network services allow the port number to be changed, and that using an encrypted connection means using a different port number.

With so many people in the workforce using mobile devices, our mail server will have to accommodate mobile device connections. Of course, the appropriate mobile device e-mail apps will have to be installed and configured correctly.

With bring your own device (BYOD), where employees can use their personal mobile devices for work, mobile device partitioning solutions enable the use of a single mail app for both personal and work e-mail. Most modern mobile device management (MDM) tools support this. Additionally, configurations might, for instance, restrict file attachments to corporate e-mail messages from being stored on personal cloud storage locations. MDM tools can run on the on-premises server in the cloud.

Routing and Remote Access Service

This server role normally uses at least two network interfaces connected to different networks. Servers with more than one interface are said to be *multihomed.* Windows server administrators use Routing and Remote Access Service (RRAS) to configure the following:

- IPv4 and IPv6 routing
- Network address translation (NAT)
- Virtual private networks as seen in Figure 3-8

Mail Protocol	Nonencrypted Port	Description
Simple Mail Transfer Protocol (SMTP)	25	Used to transfer e-mail between SMTP hosts
Post Office Protocol (POP)	110	Enables clients to download e-mail messages from the POP server
Internet Message Access Protocol (IMAP)	143	Enables clients to use different e-mail clients running on different devices to access their mail; the mail is synchronized between devices

Table 3-3 Common Mail Protocols

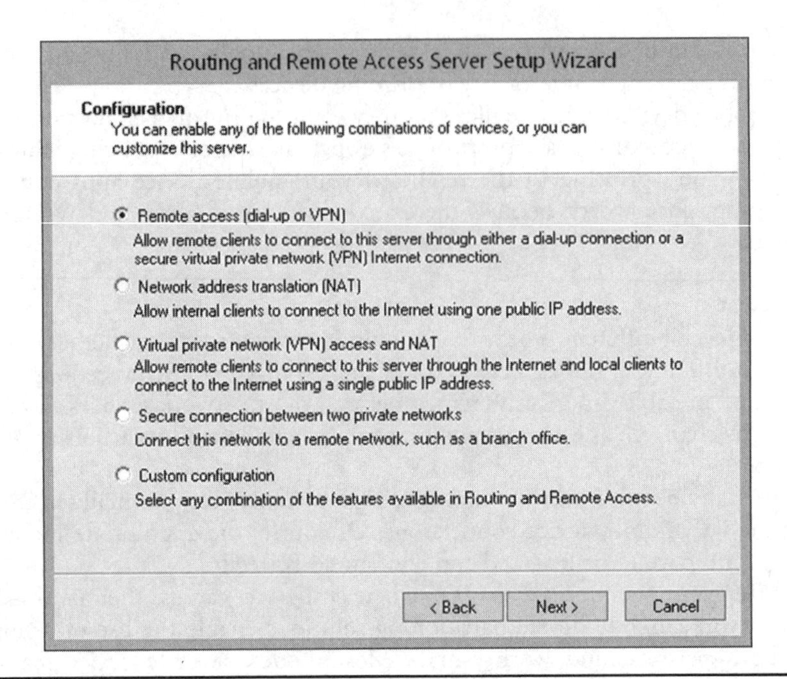

Figure 3-8 RRAS configuration wizard

Say, for example, that you want to configure a NAT router to enable multiple internal stations to access the Internet through a single public IP address. This requires both a public and private network interface connected to the appropriate networks. Clients simply point to the internal NAT router interface as their default gateway. (For more on IP and default gateways, be sure to devour Chapter 5.) IP routing is used to send network traffic between different subnets. Configuring this requires at least two interfaces in the host.

VPNs allow clients to connect securely to a private destination network over an untrusted network such as the Internet. VPN client software on a device establishes an encrypted tunnel with a VPN host on the work network (must be reachable by clients over the Internet). Anything sent through the tunnel is encrypted. The VPN host then decrypts the traffic and sends it on its way to the Internet network.

Plenty of UNIX and Linux solutions provide RRAS services, including the following:

- IP routing using the `ip` command
- NAT configuration using the `iptables` command
- OpenVPN

Virtualization Servers

Virtualization is hot these days, but it's not new technology. Mainframes have long decoupled applications and user environments from the underlying hardware to enable multiple concurrent isolated computing sessions.

We must also consider the different types of virtualization, including operating system virtualization (this is what most techies think of), user desktop virtualization, application virtualization, and so on. Our focus will be on operating system virtualization.

Common modern virtualization solutions include these:

- VMware
- Microsoft Hyper-V
- Citrix XenServer
- Oracle VM VirtualBox

The combination of slim-profile physical servers (blades) along with running virtual server operating systems maximizes the possible server density in a small server room or a large data center facility. If you monitor hardware use over time for a physical server, in many cases you'll find that, overall, the hardware isn't being fully utilized—you aren't getting the biggest bang for your buck.

Virtualization is a better use of hardware resources, where multiple virtual machines (VMs) are running simultaneously and sharing the underlying hardware, but each VM doesn't manage hardware access: that's the job of the hypervisor.

Hypervisor Types

There are a few types of hypervisors, and each has its place in certain computing environments. One hypervisor might work well on a developer's laptop, while a different type of hypervisor is best for mission-critical applications. Many companies often use a hybrid of hypervisor solutions. When discussing virtualization, the hypervisor is often called the "host" and each virtual machine is called a "guest."

Some hypervisors require specific hardware capabilities such as Intel Virtualization Technology (Intel VT) or AMD Virtualization (AMD-V—hardware virtualization support built into the BIOS or UEFI). If you plan on creating a cluster of multiple hypervisor nodes for VM high availability, moving VMs from one cluster node to another could require physical CPUs to be similar or exactly the same on each node; consult your specific hypervisor documentation to see if this is the case.

Type 1

This type of hypervisor is used for more serious virtualization environments. The hypervisor itself has direct access to physical hardware, and it controls hardware resource access between VMs. You'll hear this sometimes referred to as a *bare-metal hypervisor*.

The less stuff running, the quicker it is to patch, and the more secure your system is. Because Type 1 hypervisors don't rely on another operating system, they have the benefit of increased security over Type 2 hypervisors.

Examples include

- Microsoft Hyper-V Server
- VMware ESXi

Type 2

This type of hypervisor is an application that runs on top of an existing operating system. This means the hypervisor does *not* have direct access to hardware; the underlying operating system does.

Examples include

- VMware Workstation (Figure 3-9)
- Oracle VM VirtualBox

Hypervisor Host Configuration

Running a bunch of VMs at the same time on one set of hardware requires careful planning. It's not really about the number of VMs (VM density), but rather what type of IT workloads will be running inside those VMs. An SMB file server used by 50 people, for example, won't need as much horsepower as a Microsoft SharePoint Server used by 5000 people.

Let's take a look at planning physical hardware for a Type 1 hypervisor in Table 3-4. Remember to read the documentation for your specific solution to see what is and is not supported. For further hardware details refer back to Chapter 2.

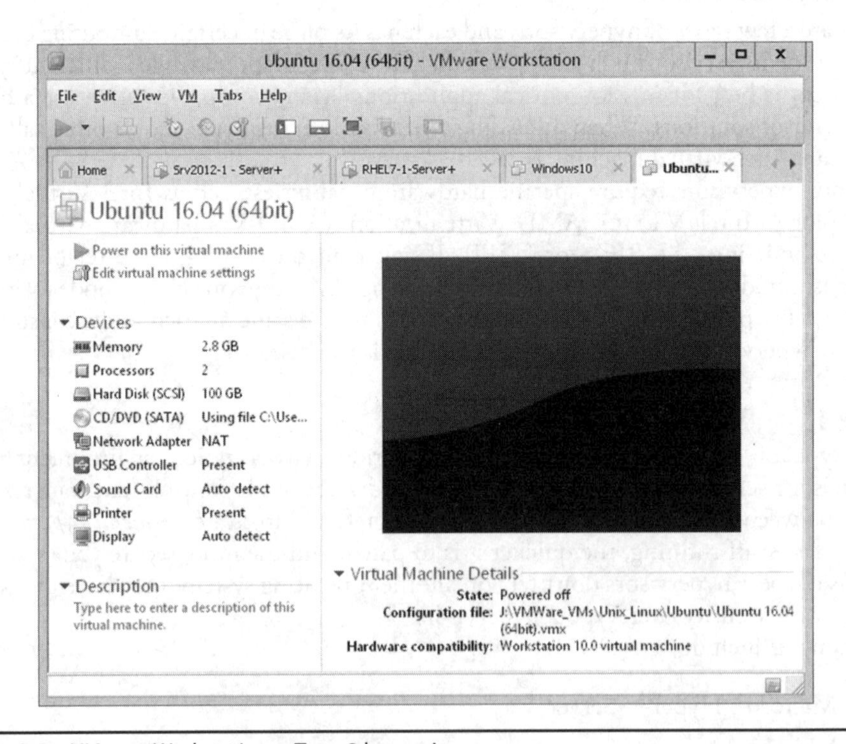

Figure 3-9 VMware Workstation, a Type 2 hypervisor

Resource	Considerations
CPU	• SMP or multicore CPUs are a must. • Faster CPU cores are, of course, preferred. • VMs can be configured with multiple virtual CPUs (vCPUs), but this does not necessarily mean better performance, • If you plan to migrate or fail over VMs within a cluster, you may need the same or similar CPUs in each cluster node; refer to your hypervisor documentation.
Memory	• More is better, and faster is better. • VMs can be configured with dynamic memory; VMs needing RAM can get it from other VMs not needing it at the time. • Some VM workloads such as database servers with millions of records will need more RAM than a file-sharing host serving a small number of users. • If you plan to migrate or fail over VMs within a cluster, consider the memory impact of running additional VMs.
Storage	• Get the fastest storage possible (ideally SSD). • Consider using RAID configurations that optimize performance. • VMs can use virtual hard disk files that can be stored on a local hypervisor disk volume or on a SAN. • VMs can use raw disk space on the hypervisor. • VMs can talk through the hypervisor's Fibre Channel host bus adapter to access SAN storage directly.
Networking	• Virtual network switches are used to enable connectivity to the physical network, or they can be used for VM communication within the hypervisor host, and hybrids of the two. • Some hypervisors enable the replication of virtual network switch configuration among hypervisor cluster nodes. • VM virtual NICs are assigned to a virtual switch. • A VM's virtual network adapter can be linked to a specific physical network adapter through a virtual network switch. • Consider VMs that need to be plugged into specific physical network components such as specific switch ports for port-based VLANs; think about failover and migration of VMs to other hypervisor hosts. • Some Type 1 hypervisors require a dedicated NIC for management purposes.

Table 3-4 Type 1 Hypervisor Hardware

Virtual Machine Guest Configuration

Creating a VM (not installing the OS) is like planning the physical hardware for a new server. How much memory, CPU, disk, and network capacity do you need? The answer, of course, depends on the IT workload the server will be running.

VM settings, as seen in Figure 3-10, include the following:

- Amount of startup, minimum and maximum memory, dynamic memory
- Number of vCPUs and compatibility settings
- Storage such as virtual hard disk files, raw disk space, and SAN storage
- Virtual network adapters and their connected virtual switches, virtual MAC address, network bandwidth throttling, and VLAN tag settings:
  - **Bridging** Connects to the physical network
  - **NAT** Uses the hypervisor host IP address to access the network
  - **VM to VM** Enables communication only between VMs
  - **VM and host** Enables communications between VMs and the hypervisor host
- Display settings for number of monitors, accelerated graphics
- Integration tools with the host hypervisor for time synchronization, backup services, and so on
- Snapshot/checkpoint settings

Some virtualization solutions provide an integration tools installer that optimizes VM display settings, keyboard and mouse movement, time synchronization with the host,

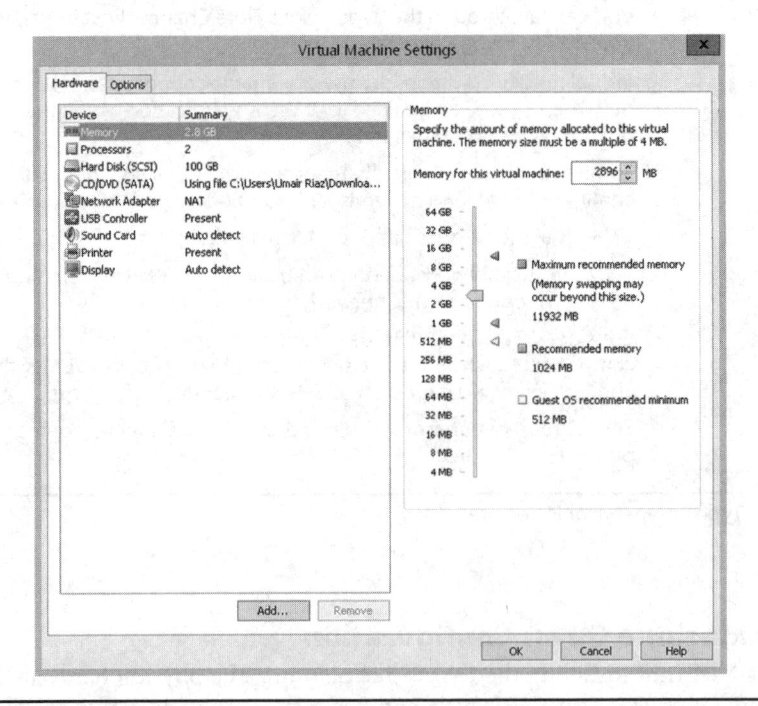

Figure 3-10 Virtual machine settings

and other settings. Check your hypervisor's details to make sure you're getting the most out of your VMs.

Server Installation

Hardware compatibility lists (HCLs) provide details about which specific hardware is supported by a given server OS. You also have to consider the requirements for specific drivers and applications. You might have to supply device drivers during installation if they aren't detected by the installation program.

Installing a Type 1 Hypervisor

Before installation, do your homework and make sure you have supported hardware. Trying to cut corners here will take more time later down the road.

Most modern Type 1 hypervisor require 64-bit architecture as well as hardware virtualization support. If you're using true server-class hardware, this won't be an issue. If you're testing the hypervisor using standard desktop hardware, you need to be extra careful.

Firmware updates (such as BIOS or the unified extensible firmware interface [UEFI]) may be required prior to installation, even for indirect reasons, such as network Preboot Execution Environment (PXE) boot, USB device boot support, and so on. If you plan on installing the hypervisor from a DVD or USB you may also have to change the boot order configuration on your machine.

Installing a Server Operating System

Whether you want to end up with a physical or virtual server OS, there isn't much difference in the actual OS installation itself.

Common server operating systems include

- Microsoft Windows Server
- UNIX variants such as BSD, AIX, Solaris
- Linux variants such as Red Hat, Ubuntu, SuSe Linux

Interestingly, the Apple Mac OS X is based on BSD UNIX. Of course, OS X has plenty of APIs beyond BSD. If you like UNIX-style shells and scripts, you'll feel right at home in OS X at a terminal prompt.

Keep in mind that many modern operating systems have just the bare minimum available with a default installation. You may have to install and enable additional services such as file sharing and web servers.

Server Installation Methods

You can begin the server OS installation from CD, DVD, USB, or a shared folder over the network—one way or another, you need access to the installation files. Many on-premises and cloud environments use VM images to create new VMs, but there are many legitimate cases for which you'll be installing the OS on physical hardware. This chapter includes lab exercises that step through the installation of both a Windows and a Linux server.

Server OS images might have been already created so that you can apply the image to your new physical or virtual server instead of running the installer from the installation media. You can capture and apply server OS images using tools such as these:

- Symantec Ghost Solution Suite
- Microsoft System Center Configuration Manager
- Microsoft Deployment Toolkit
- Microsoft DISM.exe command line tool

For example, we can capture a server OS image by booting from alternative media and using DISM:

```
dism /Capture-Image /ImageFile:e:\Images\win2012.wim /CaptureDir:c:\
/Name:"Vanilla Server 2012 R2"
```

In this example, we are capturing an image of c:\ and storing it on drive e: (presumably an external USB drive). We can apply an image by booting from alternative media, including booting over the network using the following:

```
dism /Apply-Image /Imagefile:e:\Images\win2012.wim /index:1 /ApplyDir:c:\
```

Because multiple images can be stored using the Windows Imaging Format (WIM), we specify the image with the `/index` parameter. WIM requires the disk to be partitioned and formatted prior to the application of an image.

Whether you are applying an image or installing from source media, you can also create an answer file to automate some or all of the OS installation. Windows Server installations can be automated using an XML answer file created with the Windows System Image Manager (SIM) tool. Red Hat Enterprise Linux 7, for example, uses Kickstart files to automate installations.

Local vs. PXE

In addition to performing the server OS installation from local media (setup.exe for Windows server installations) or a locally stored image, we can also boot over the network—this is referred to as Preboot Execution Environment (PXE). Figure 3-11 shows a PXE boot screen.

PXE must be supported by the physical or virtual machine's BIOS or UEFI settings, the NIC itself, and we need a PXE boot server listening on the network. Microsoft's Remote Installation Service (RIS) and the newer Windows Deployment Services (WDS) provide this functionality, although there are many vendor solutions out there.

The great thing about PXE installation/imaging is that technicians don't have to carry around storage devices containing installation files or OS images. The downside is that you're pulling the OS down to the machine over the network, so network bandwidth use goes up.

```
Network boot from Intel E1000
Copyright (C) 2003-2008  VMware, Inc.
Copyright (C) 1997-2000  Intel Corporation

CLIENT MAC ADDR: 00 0C 29 FD 90 11  GUID: 564D4883-869E-471D-73CF-16551
CLIENT IP: 192.168.1.51  MASK: 255.255.255.0  DHCP IP: 192.168.1.200
GATEWAY IP: 192.168.1.200

Downloaded WDSNBP from 192.168.1.200 Srv2012-1.fakedomain.local

Press F12 for network service boot

Windows Deployment Services: PXE Boot Aborted.

PXE-M0F: Exiting Intel PXE ROM.
_
```

Figure 3-11 PXE boot screen

PXE boot relies on DHCP to assign IP settings to PXE clients, and it also uses Trivial File Transfer Protocol (TFTP) to download a small boot image OS used for installation and imaging.

Installation Details

When you are actually installing a server OS, if it's not an automated installation you may be asked for the following:

- Disk layout, including disk partitioning, file system formats, swap file/partition
- Server name
- IP configuration settings
- Administrative user credentials
- Product key or subscription details used to activate the installation and receive updates
- Additional software that should be installed

Server Administration Methods

According to Microsoft, these days, servers shouldn't have a GUI. A default Windows Server 2012 R2 installation is a Server Core installation (no GUI). The same thing is true with a default installation of Red Hat Enterprise Linux Server 7—no GUI.

Windows servers and clients with a GUI can use the Microsoft Management Console (MMC), which is a general tool that enables you to add snap-ins for specific management capabilities. For example, you might run mmc.exe and add the snap-in for Group Policy and certificate management.

You can use GUI tools installed on a client workstation to administer servers remotely over the network. In the case of Windows servers, administrators can download the Remote

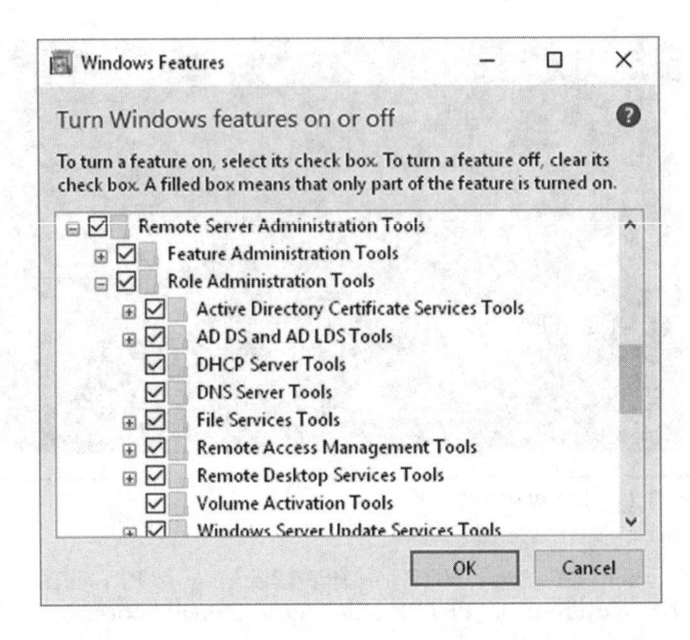

Figure 3-12 Enabling RSAT tools on a Windows client machine

Server Administration Tools (RSAT) to accomplish this. Figure 3-12 shows RSAT tools on a client being enabled. Windows Server 2016 has a Nano Server installation option that doesn't even have a local command line interface, so remote management is a big deal!

KVM

With KVM—keyboard, video, mouse—instead of having a separate display, keyboard, and mouse for each individual physical server, KMV switches connect the servers to a single display, keyboard, and mouse. You switch to different servers to manage them locally.

Keyboards and mice have different interfaces; modern devices use USB, but older input devices use PS/2 or serial connectors. For video, older displays use Video Graphics Array (VGA) connectors, while newer displays use High-Definition Multimedia Interface (HDMI) for both video and audio. Make sure your KVM solution matches the connectors for your devices, or you'll have to buy adapters to get everything plugged in.

Out-of-band Remote Administration

Physical and virtual servers must be accessible over the network for management purposes. Although there are plenty of software-based remote management solutions, hardware-based solutions provide more security and reliability.

Web-based Enterprise Management (WBEM) is a standardized way of managing and monitoring services and devices from different vendors. Of course, many vendors have their own proprietary management and monitoring tools.

The monitoring of server components such as CPU use, temperature, OS health, and so on, falls under the umbrella of lights-out management (LOM) and is supported by most vendor management solutions.

KVM over IP

These days, KVM also works over IP. This enables remote server access even over the Internet, and it can enable hardware-level (out-of-band) remote access if that is supported by your server hardware.

KVM-over-IP switches are hardware appliances with centralized management and auditing tools. For instance, KVM can require its own authentication in addition to whatever is required by servers themselves.

Traditional software-based remote management solutions such as VNC, Remote Desktop Protocol, and SSH all depend on the operating system function. But what if the system crashes? KVM over IP can overcome this, but, again, physical servers must support this out-of-band type of hardware remote management. It also means TCP/IP settings must be configured at the hardware level to enable remote access across WANs.

IPMI

The Intelligent Platform Management Interface (IPMI) is a remote server management solution commonly used with various vendor blade enclosures. IPMI also provides server monitoring and inventory functionality.

A *baseboard management controller* (BMC) is the interface between server management tools and the physical server hardware being managed. Server administrators can connect to IPMI management systems locally or over a network.

iLO and iDRAC

The Hewlett-Packard–specific out-of-band solution is Integrated Lights Out (iLO) management. The iLO solution offers not only secure remote management capabilities but also includes server monitoring and alert capabilities.

For hardware-based out-of-band management, Dell servers support Integrated Dell Remote Access (iDRAC). Administrators can connect to remote servers at the hardware level, even using a friendly web browser interface.

In-band Remote Administration

This type of remote management relies on software running within the OS. If the OS hangs, remote management of this type no longer works. Although each OS has its own remote management solutions, you can also use the cross-platform VNC remote control tool.

Many tools use the Simple Network Management Protocol (SNMP) to query management information bases (MIBs) on devices. MIBs are used to gather inventory and statistic data about network devices.

SSH

Secure Shell (SSH) has long been the standard and secure way of remotely managing not only UNIX and Linux hosts but also network devices such as switches and routers. It supersedes the insecure Telnet protocol, which sends credentials in clear text.

SSH needs a server-side listener for clients to be able to connect; the standard listening port is TCP 22. Although SSH is normally used for command-line remote management,

X-forwarding can be enabled within SSH to redirect graphical UNIX and Linux applications to show up on the client computer. In other words, you can interact with UNIX and Linux GUI apps on your Windows client station.

Besides the standard username and password authentication, SSH can also use public-key authentication. An administrator's public key is stored on the SSH host. The mathematically related private key is stored on the administrator's workstation. The keys are used to authenticate the admin to the SSH host.

You can download and configure the free PuTTY tool to make SSH connections to network devices including UNIX and Linux hosts from within a Windows environment, as shown in Figure 3-13.

RDP

Windows hosts normally use the Remote Desktop Protocol (RDP) for remote management of both Windows clients and servers. RDP listens on UDP and TCP port 3389 by default.

Newer versions of the Windows Server OSs support Network Level Authentication (NLA) for RDP sessions. NLA improves on older versions of RDP in the following ways:

- Entering the username and password uses client resources, not server resources.
- RDP sessions are encrypted with an SSL certificate.

RDP, as seen in Figure 3-14, gives admins the ability to access a Windows server remotely to run GUI management tools, but what if the server is installed as Server Core?

Figure 3-13 Configuring PuTTY for SSH remote administration

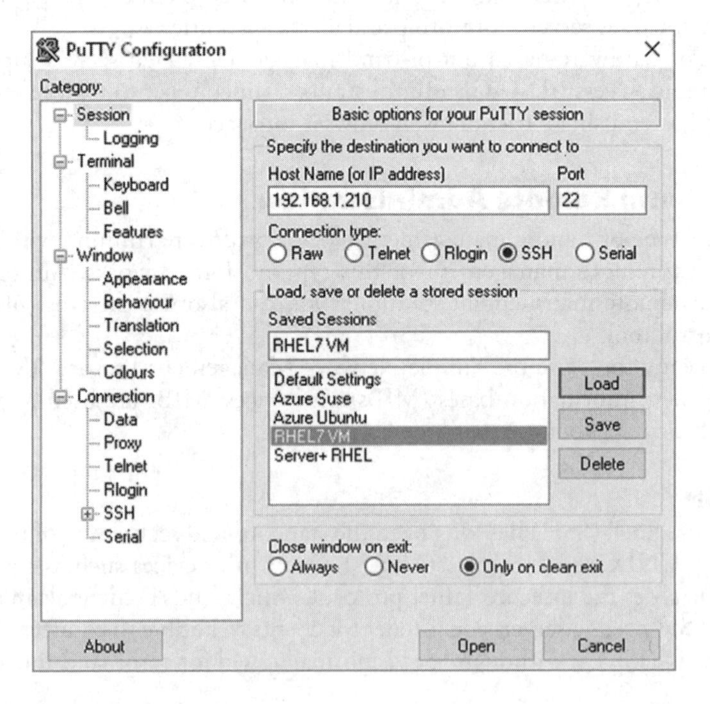

Figure 3-14 Connecting to a Windows host using RDP for remote management

Server Core is a Windows server option that does not include the GUI. When admins RDP into Server Core, they simply get a command prompt. Note that Server 2016's Nano Server doesn't even provide a command prompt; it's designed to be managed remotely using tools such as PowerShell.

WinRM and PowerShell

Windows admins can also use PowerShell to manage Windows servers remotely at the command line. PowerShell depends on the Windows Remote Management (WinRM) service to be configured, to run, and to be accessible through firewalls. Newer versions of WinRM use TCP port 5985/5986 for unencrypted and encrypted connections, respectively.

Outside of PowerShell, you can use the Windows `winrs` command to execute commands remotely on a Windows host, but you need to ensure that WinRM has been enabled. This can be done via a Group Policy or by using the `winrm qc` command. You might use `winrs` with `-r` to specify the remote host as follows:

```
Winrs -r:Server1 dir c:\
```

The preceding example lists items on c:\ on Server1. Consider the three PowerShell remote management examples in Table 3-5.

Command	Description
`Get-Service -computername Server1, Server2, Server3`	Some PowerShell cmdlets have a `-computername` parameter.
`Enter-PsSession -computername Server1` `Get-Service`	You can interactively start a remote PowerShell session on a remote host.
`Invoke-Command (Get-WmiObject win32_bios) - computername Server1, Server2, Server3`	For cmdlets without a `-computername` parameter, you can use `invoke-command`.

Table 3-5 PowerShell Remote Management Examples

Additionally, PowerShell Desired State Configuration (DSC) enables administrators to configure and manage Window and Linux hosts centrally using a declarative syntax, as shown in the following example:

```
configuration IISInstall
{
    node ("localhost")
    {
        WindowsFeature IIS
        {
            Ensure = "Present"
            Name = "Web-Server"
        }
    }
}
```

This would be placed in a PowerShell script. It ensures that the Windows IIS web server is installed, and if not, it will be. PowerShell DSC can even be used to manage cloud virtual machines.

Server Documentation

If you've ever done IT consulting, you know that accurate and readily available documentation saves everybody time and money. Troubleshooting a server that isn't performing well takes much longer when you know nothing about how the server is configured.

Each server needs documentation and a change log, and, ideally, this is all automated and inventoried in a database somewhere that is easily searched. Aside from OEM hardware and software service manuals, we need to know *how* these technological solutions have been put in place in a specific environment.

How companies implement technology is sensitive information. This is a big part of reconnaissance when malicious users try to learn about a network to identify vulnerabilities. Keep this documentation under lock and key, and encrypt any files containing this stuff.

Asset Life Cycle

On-premises servers, and even cloud servers running critical IT systems, are assets in the sense that we must apply a risk-management framework to them to protect them throughout their useful life. Here's an example of a server life cycle:

1. Provision servers and their IT workloads.
    - Procurement of servers on-premises or the cloud
2. Configure servers and their IT workloads.
    - Manually or automatic
3. Manage servers and their IT workloads.
    - Security
    - Patching

- Compliance with laws/regulations
- Change management policy and forms

4. Monitor servers and their IT workloads.
    - Ensure peak performance
    - Provide centralized monitoring and logging
5. Decommission servers.
    - Proper disposal techniques
        - Physical destruction
        - Sanitize/wipe media
6. Upgrade or functionally replace IT workloads.

Asset Inventory

Until the 1990s, there weren't many automated asset inventory options available for IT environments. Long were the days spent crouching under desks and behind server racks to inventory equipment physically and to document configuration settings.

These days, all of this can be automated and is readily accessible for small, medium, and large enterprises. Even so, physical equipment still needs to be labeled or inscribed for tracking purposes. Inventorying servers falls into two categories: hardware and software.

Hardware Inventory

We can't troubleshoot or optimize something if we don't know what we have to begin with—we have no reference point! Even virtual machines have "virtual hardware." This can be very useful when optimizing and troubleshooting, both of which are covered later in the book.

Server items that might be inventoried include the following:

- Make and model
- Motherboard and device serial numbers
- Physical or digital asset tag (a sticker or stored in the BIOS)
- RAM
- Storage
- Network interfaces
- Other peripherals
    - Printers
    - USB devices other than storage
    - Monitor displays

Here are some reasons for creating a detailed and accurate hardware inventory:

- Inventory audits
- Asset tracking
- Determine asset use
- Asset repair and warranty
- Asset recall
- Asset security

Solutions provided by Spiceworks, Altiris, or Microsoft System Center Configuration Manager (SCCM) (see Figure 3-15), for example, provide ways to inventory devices on a large scale, such as in a data center. Inventory solutions may or may not have a software agent running within the OS; more detail is available when an agent is used, since it knows everything about that specific server. Inventory scanning schedules determine whether inventory data is up to date. Running queries or reports against inventory data stored in a database makes managing server assets easier.

In a data center with thousands of pieces of IT equipment, inventorying and monitoring is easier when radio-frequency identification (RFID) tags are used. RFID mobile reading devices scan items with RFID tags in close proximity, so, for instance,

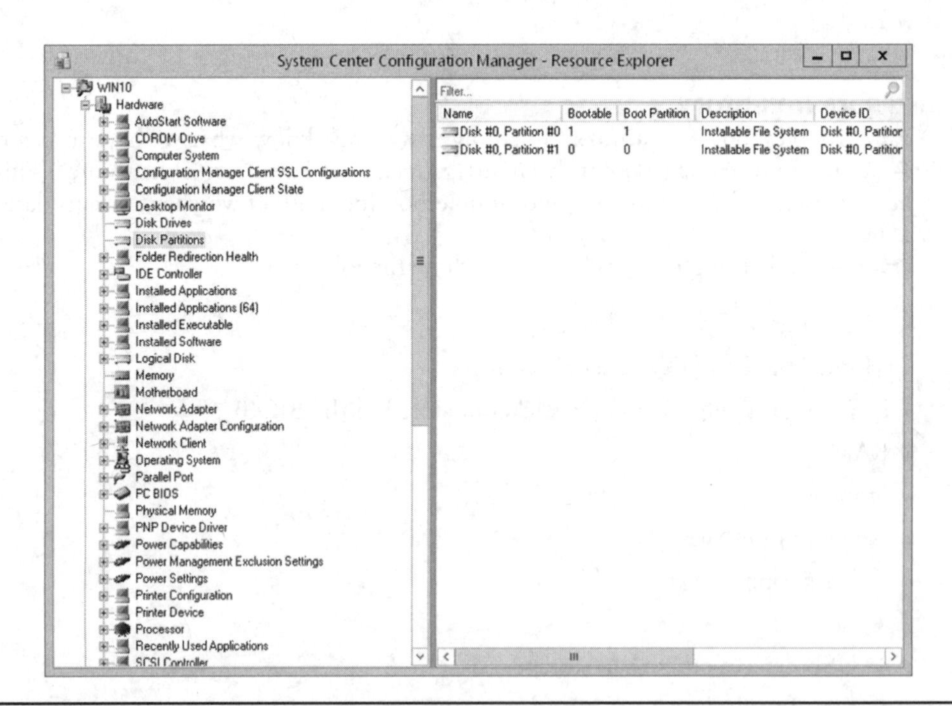

Figure 3-15 SCCM hardware inventory for a Windows computer

rack-mounted servers could have RFID tags adhered to the front of the server for ease in scanning.

Software Inventory

Knowing the specific versions of operating systems, drivers, and application software in use is critical. Let's say, for example, that a software vendor has released a critical security update that needs to be applied immediately. If you don't know how many servers are running the affected software, you can't even determine the scope of the work required!

Similar to hardware inventory, software inventory can and should be automated on a scheduled basis. Using the same type of enterprise tools used for hardware inventory (Spiceworks, Altiris, and SCCM, to name a few) allows for automation. You can then run queries and reports against inventoried software. As another example, you may want to know how many instances of a version of a certain server OS are running on your network to ensure license compliance.

Service Level Agreements

A service level agreement (SLA) is a contract outlining expected service from a service provider to a service consumer. This could exist between your company and a public cloud provider, or you might use SLAs within an organization between business units and the services offered by the IT department. When things go wrong, the SLA can be very valuable.

The two most common items found in SLAs are

- Uptime
  - This specifies expected availability for IT services.
  - Providers are usually obligated to notify clients of scheduled maintenance and downtime.
- Response time
  - This specifies how quickly IT services respond when they are needed.
  - This can also specify how quickly the provider responds when you need support.
    - How long will it take for a problem to be *resolved*?
    - Is support available only during business hours?

When providers fail to meet SLA expectations, they may offer credits of some kind, and you should determine whether there is a maximum number associated with this. It's a good idea to ensure that the SLA includes a clause for leaving a provider if it chronically fails to meet thresholds documented in the SLA.

All of the responsibility, however, isn't just on the provider. As an IT service consumer, you may have to adhere to certain rules, such as how servers are used or what updates and software are allowed on servers.

Other Documentation

Documentation goes beyond just servers. Servers live in a technological ecosystem that affects them, so there are other factors to consider:

- **Network diagrams** Server placement
- **Dataflow diagrams** Server involvement in dataflow
- **Baseline documentation** Normal operating conditions and troubleshooting (see Chapter 7)
- **Recovery documentation** Procedures to return server to an operational state as quickly as possible (see Chapter 8)

Much can be learned about server and IT workload configurations by checking log files. Most UNIX and Linux variants store log files in the /var directory. Windows logs are accessible using the GUI event viewer tool or PowerShell cmdlets such as `get-eventlog`.

If Group Policy is used heavily in your environment, it can be helpful to get a complete report of all Group Policy Objects (GPOs) and their settings. One quick way of achieving this is as follows:

```
Get-gporeport -all -reporttype html c:\gpo_report.html
```

This example retrieves all GPOs and settings and puts them into a nicely formatted HTML document.

Maintaining Servers

With inventory in place, server maintenance becomes easier through automated inventory and documentation. Proactive management also includes ensuring that firmware and software patches are delivered in a timely fashion. Then we need reports that can confirm that patches have been successfully applied. Of course, we'll also know all of this because of frequent software inventory scans on our servers.

Patch Management

UNIX and Linux variants sometimes require a subscription before updates can be applied, just like Windows Server OSs require activation before *all* updates are available.

There are different types of updates. Some are critical security updates that must be applied right away, while others add additional functionality to software. This also holds true for firmware updates for motherboard BIOS/UEFI, printer firmware, router firmware, and so on.

Imagine a data center with 1000 hypervisor operating systems, which, of course, will need updates on a continuous basis. Instead of each of those 1000 systems downloading the same updates, we can configure centralized update management and then run reports on update compliance.

Windows Server Update Services (WSUS) is a free Microsoft patch management tool that has been available for years. Microsoft SCCM uses WSUS to manage and deploy patches using the SSCM infrastructure (see Figure 3-16). Updated metadata is synchronized from either Microsoft update servers online or from another WSUS server. Updates can be applied manually or on a scheduled basis to a group of computers.

Deploying and managing non-Microsoft updates in a Windows environment can be done using tools such as Microsoft System Center Updates Publisher (SCUP) or other vendor-specific solutions.

It's wise to test updates in a controlled environment before pushing them out to production machines; sometimes updates cause problems.

Proactive Maintenance

At this point, you know that hardware and software inventory, patching, and various types of documentation can help ease server management over time, but there are other factors to consider as well.

Sometimes the simplest physical issues can make a big difference with IT computing. Servers need to be kept clear of dust, with no obstructions near intake fans. And they must be kept cool; overheating servers could cause performance degradation (CPU throttling to slow down speed, which reduces heat), or worse—server power-downs.

Speaking of server power-downs, servers should be plugged into uninterruptible power supplies (UPSs) to ensure the graceful shutdown of servers when the power goes out. You'll find more about UPSs in Chapter 8.

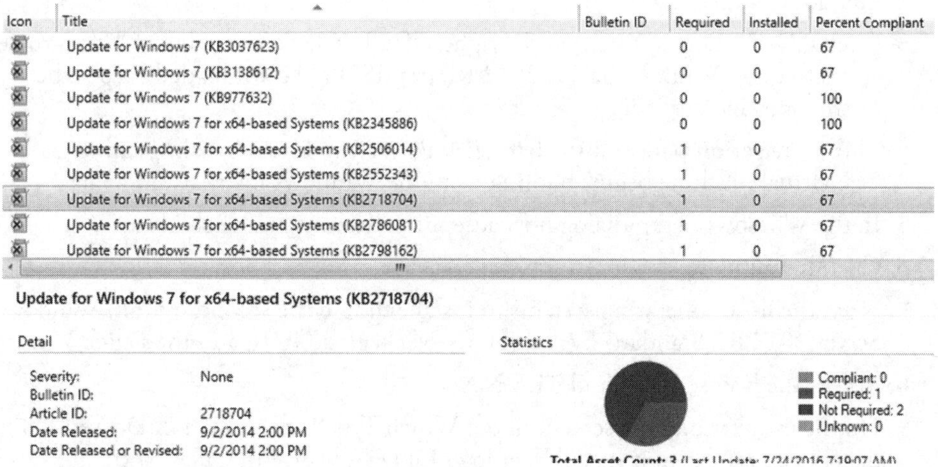

Icon	Title	Bulletin ID	Required	Installed	Percent Compliant
	Update for Windows 7 (KB3037623)		0	0	67
	Update for Windows 7 (KB3138612)		0	0	67
	Update for Windows 7 (KB977632)		0	0	100
	Update for Windows 7 for x64-based Systems (KB2345886)		0	0	100
	Update for Windows 7 for x64-based Systems (KB2506014)		1	0	67
	Update for Windows 7 for x64-based Systems (KB2552343)		1	0	67
	Update for Windows 7 for x64-based Systems (KB2718704)		1	0	67
	Update for Windows 7 for x64-based Systems (KB2786081)		1	0	67
	Update for Windows 7 for x64-based Systems (KB2798162)		1	0	67

Update for Windows 7 for x64-based Systems (KB2718704)

Detail

Severity: None
Bulletin ID:
Article ID: 2718704
Date Released: 9/2/2014 2:00 PM
Date Released or Revised: 9/2/2014 2:00 PM

Statistics

Compliant: 0
Required: 1
Not Required: 2
Unknown: 0

Total Asset Count: 3 (Last Update: 7/24/2016 7:19:07 AM)

Figure 3-16 Software updates in SCCM

Reactive Maintenance

Despite the best-laid proactive plans, sometimes we have to react quickly to certain events when managing servers. Chapter 8 provides details, but there are few everyday things you should keep in mind:

- LED indicators on equipment such as servers, UPS systems, and storage arrays
    - Indicates problems as well as normal status messages
    - Failing disk arrays, RAM errors, problems with batteries or backplanes, and so on
- Error and beep codes
    - Vendor equipment has specific error and beep codes
    - Warning of some kind, such as imminent drive failure

Hands-on Exercises

Exercise 3-1: Install the Microsoft Windows Server 2012 R2 Operating System

1. Start VMware Workstation and ensure that the Srv2012-1 virtual machine you created in Chapter 2 is open.
2. In the navigation panel on the left, click Edit Virtual Machine Settings. On the left side of the screen, notice that the Network Adapter is configured for NAT. This allows the virtual machine to communicate on your network (and potentially the Internet if you have an Internet connection) while using its own unique IP addressing scheme.
3. Click CD/DVD, and then, on the right, click Use ISO Image File. Click Browse and select the Windows Server 2012 R2 trial ISO file downloaded, as per the instructions in Appendix A. Click OK.
4. In the navigation panel on the left, click Power On This Virtual Machine. The virtual machine begins booting from the Windows installation media.
5. In the Windows Setup dialog box, accept the defaults and click Next.
6. Click Install Now.
7. From the list of operating systems to install, choose the second option, Windows Server 2012 R2 Standard Evaluation (Server with a GUI), and then click Next.
8. Accept the license terms and click Next.
9. On the installation type screen, in the Which Type Of Installation Do You Want? dialog, choose Custom:Install Windows Only (Advanced). Click Next.
10. You will see the four virtual hard disks you created in an earlier lab. Ensure that Disk 0 Unallocated Space is selected. Click Next.

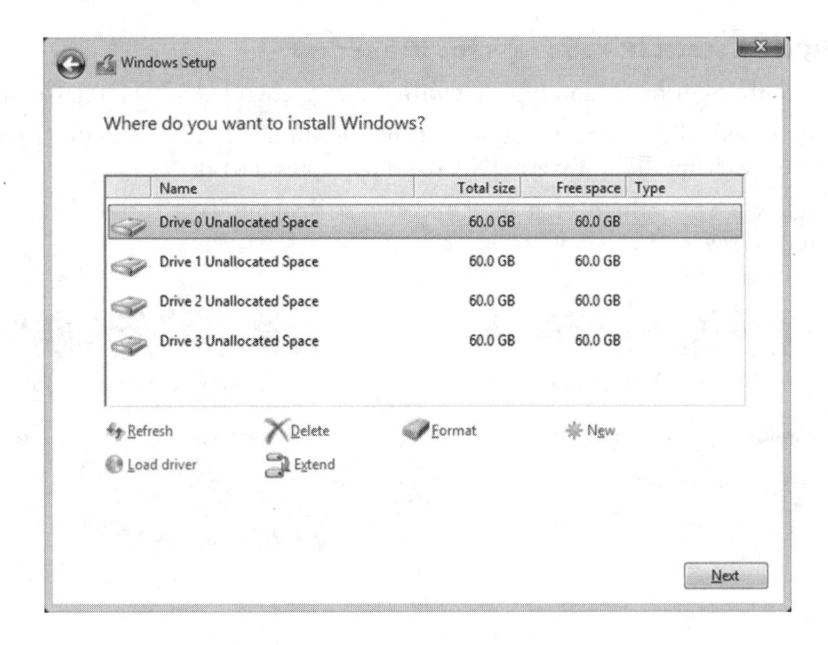

11. Windows begins copying files. This is a good time to get a cup of coffee, but be quick! Depending on your machine, this part of the install may take only 2 or 3 minutes.
12. The installation will reboot your virtual machine automatically and continue the installation. You will be prompted to specify the administrator password. Enter **Pa$$w0rd** and click Finish.
13. After a moment the server login screen is displayed. From the VMware VM menu, choose Send Ctrl+Alt+Del and enter the Administrator password, **Pa$$w0rd**. Then press ENTER. The server desktop is displayed and the Server Manager tool automatically launches. If you get a Network message about finding PCs, devices, and so on, click Yes.
14. Configure Server Manager *not* to start automatically: In Server Manager, choose Manage | Server Manager Properties. Check the box that says Do Not Start Server Manager Automatically At Logon. Click OK, and then close Server Manager.

Add a second network adapter for the server

15. From the VMware VM menu, choose Settings.
16. Click Add at the bottom of the screen, choose Network Adapter, and then click Next.
17. Choose Custom: Specific Virtual Network and choose VMnet5 from the drop-down list. Click Finish and OK. Your virtual machine screen may be blank for a few seconds as the change is put into effect.

Configure a static IP4 address for the server

18. Click the Start menu and type **network**. Click Network And Sharing Center.
19. On the left, click Change Adapter Settings. Right-click the Ethernet0 adapter and choose Rename. Type **ExternalNAT** and then press ENTER.
20. Right-click the Ethernet1 adapter and choose Rename. Type **Internal** and then press ENTER.

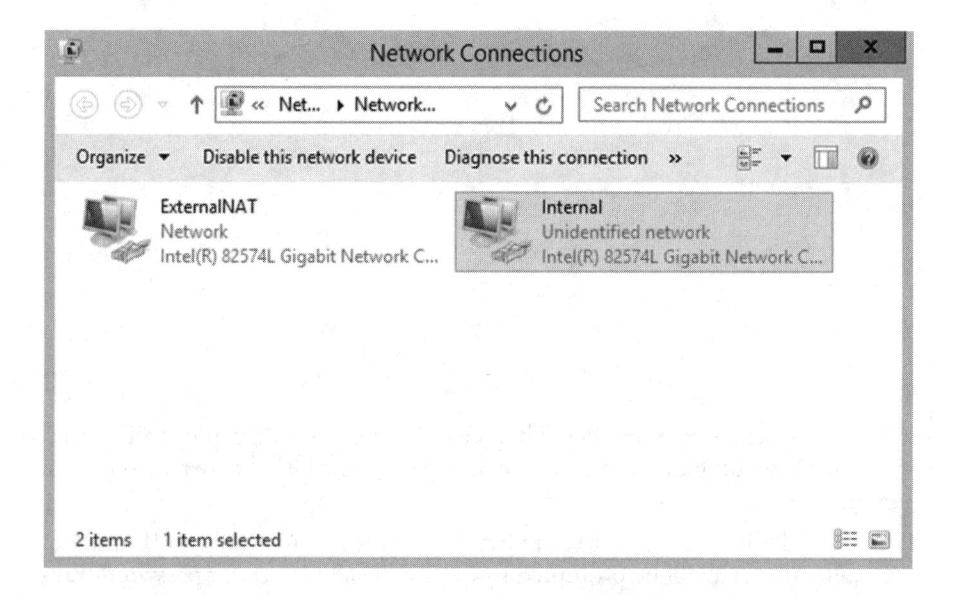

21. Right-click the Internal adapter and choose Properties. Select Internet Protocol Version 4, and then click the Properties button.
22. Choose Use The Following IP Address and enter the following values:
    IP address: **192.168.1.200**
    Subnet mask: **255.255.255.0**
23. Click OK and then Close.
24. Click the Start menu and type **cmd**, and at the command prompt, press ENTER.
25. Enlarge the command prompt screen, and then type **`ipconfig`** and press ENTER. Notice the IP address information listed for the Internal and ExternalNAT network adapters.

Name the server

26. Click the Start menu, right-click This PC Tile, and choose Properties.
27. On the right, click Change Settings, and then click the Change button.

28. For the computer name, type **Srv2012-1** and click OK.
29. On the restart prompt, click OK, and then click Close. Choose Restart Now.

Create a snapshot of the installation after the computer has restarted, in case you need to revert to this configuration in the future

30. From the VMware VM menu, choose Snapshot, Take Snapshot.
31. Type **Fresh Installation** for the name, and then click Take Snapshot. You may have to wait a few minutes as the snapshot is created.

Create a second virtual machine by cloning the one we just created

32. Shut down your Srv2012-1 virtual machine: from the VM menu, choose Power, and then choose Shut Down Guest.
33. From the VM menu, choose Manage, Clone. Click Next twice.
34. On the Clone Type screen, choose Create A Full Clone. Click Next.
35. Name the clone **Srv2012-2** and choose a location that has plenty of free disk space. Click Finish and then close the dialog box when completed.
36. Start the Srv2012-1 virtual machine.
37. Ensure that the *new* virtual machine is selected, and from the VM menu, choose Settings. Remove the Network Adapter configured with NAT. Click OK and then start the virtual machine.
38. Log in to Srv2012-2 and change the following:
    - Configure IPv4 to obtain the IP address and DNS server address automatically.
    - Type the computer name: **Srv2012-2**.
39. When prompted, restart Srv2012-2.
40. After the server Srv2012-2 has restarted, from the VM menu, choose Snapshot, Take Snapshot. Type **Fresh Installation – Server2** for the name and then click Take Snapshot. You may have to wait a few minutes as the snapshot is created.

Exercise 3-2: Install the DNS Server Role in Windows Server 2012 R2

1. Make sure you are logged into your Srv2012-1 virtual machine with the Administrator account.
2. Start PowerShell from the taskbar and type
   `install-windowsfeature dns -includemanagementtools`
   (Note that there should be no space between the – symbol and the `includemanagementtools` parameter.)

3. After the DNS server role is installed, type **`get-windowsfeature *dns*`** to ensure that it shows up as being installed (X in the box). The asterisks are wildcard symbols that will show any features containing the text *dns*.
4. Configure the internal server network interface to use itself for DNS name resolution by typing
   `set-dnsclientserveraddress -interfacealias internal -serveraddress 127.0.0.1`
5. Configure the external server network interface to use itself for DNS name resolution by typing
   `set-dnsclientserveraddress -interfacealias externalnat -serveraddress 127.0.0.1`
6. Type **`ipconfig /all`** to verify the DNS server being used by the interfaces is 127.0.0.1, as shown in the following illustration.

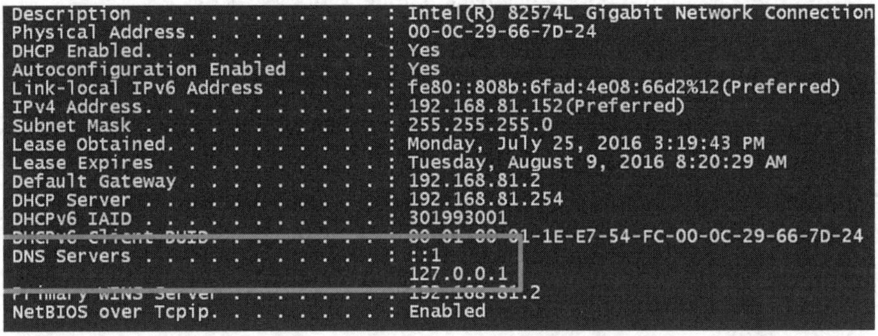

```
Description . . . . . . . . . . . : Intel(R) 82574L Gigabit Network Connection
Physical Address. . . . . . . . . : 00-0C-29-66-7D-24
DHCP Enabled. . . . . . . . . . . : Yes
Autoconfiguration Enabled . . . . : Yes
Link-local IPv6 Address . . . . . : fe80::808b:6fad:4e08:66d2%12(Preferred)
IPv4 Address. . . . . . . . . . . : 192.168.81.152(Preferred)
Subnet Mask . . . . . . . . . . . : 255.255.255.0
Lease Obtained. . . . . . . . . . : Monday, July 25, 2016 3:19:43 PM
Lease Expires . . . . . . . . . . : Tuesday, August 9, 2016 8:20:29 AM
Default Gateway . . . . . . . . . : 192.168.81.2
DHCP Server . . . . . . . . . . . : 192.168.81.254
DHCPv6 IAID . . . . . . . . . . . : 301993001
DHCPv6 Client DUID. . . . . . . . : 00-01-00-01-1E-E7-54-FC-00-0C-29-66-7D-24
DNS Servers . . . . . . . . . . . : ::1
                                    127.0.0.1
Primary WINS Server . . . . . . . : 192.168.81.2
NetBIOS over Tcpip. . . . . . . . : Enabled
```

7. Verify DNS functionality by typing **`nslookup`** followed by **`www.google.com`**. You should see a list of IP addresses that service google.com. To allow all incoming network traffic from the Linux host, type
   `netsh advfirewall firewall add rule name="Allow all traffic from Linux" dir=in action=allow protocol=any remoteip=192.168.1.210`
8. Press ENTER. Type **`exit`** and press ENTER to close the PowerShell window.

Exercise 3-3: Configure the DNS Server in Windows Server 2012 R2

1. Make sure you are logged into your Srv2012-1 virtual machine with the Administrator account.
2. Click the Start menu and type **dns**. When the DNS tool is displayed, press ENTER.
3. In the left navigator of the DNS manager window, expand your server name and right-click Forward Lookup Zones. Choose New Zone.
4. Click Next on the Welcome to the New Zone Wizard.

5. Accept the default of a Primary zone, and then click Next.
6. For the Zone name, type **fakezone.com** and then click Next.
7. Accept the defaults for the rest of the wizard and click Finish.
8. Expand Forward Lookup Zones and click fakezone.com. On the right, notice the default SOA and NS DNS records.
9. A reverse lookup zone should be created for the subnet. On the left, right-click Reverse Lookup Zones and choose New Zone. Click Next.
10. Continue through the wizard. Create a Primary IPv4 Reverse Lookup Zone. For the Network ID, type **192.168.1**. Accept the defaults for the rest of the wizard and click Finish.
11. Right-click fakezone.com and choose New Host (A or AAAA record).
12. In the New Host window, specify **www** for the name, and for the IP enter **192.168.1.200**. Enable the option Create Associated Pointer (PTR) Record. Click Add Host and then click OK. If the New Host window pops up, click its close box.
13. Select fakezone.com on the left, and notice the new A record for www.fakezone.com.
14. Start PowerShell. Type **`nslookup`** followed by **`www.fakezone.com`**, pressing ENTER after each command you type. You should see the Address (192.168.1.200) returned for the host.
15. Type **`set type=ptr`** and press ENTER after each typed command. Watch for the case and spacing; it's very unforgiving!
16. Type **`192.168.1.200`**. It should return the name of www.fakezone.com—this comes from our reverse lookup zone.
17. Type **`exit`** and press ENTER.
18. Type **`get-dnsserver`**. PowerShell will then return info about the DNS server, including the zones.

Exercise 3-4: Install the DHCP Server in Windows Server 2012 R2

1. Make sure you are logged into your Srv2012-1 virtual machine with the Administrator account.
2. Start PowerShell from the taskbar and type
   `install-windowsfeature dhcp -includemanagementtools`
3. Click the Start button and type **DHCP**. When the DHCP tool is displayed, click it.
4. In the left navigator in the DNS Manager window, expand SRV2012-1.
5. Select IPv4, and then right-click IPv4 and choose New Scope. Click Next.
6. For the name, type **LabScope1** and click Next.

7. For the starting IP address, enter **192.168.1.50**, and for the ending IP address, enter **192.168.1.80**. Click Next four times.
8. For the router (default gateway), enter **192.168.1.200** and click Add. Click Next.
9. For the parent domain, enter **domain1.local** and click Next three times, and then click Finish.
10. On the Srv2012-2 virtual machine, go to a command prompt and type **`ipconfig /release`,** then **`ipconfig /renew`**
11. On Srv2012-1, in the DHCP tool, expand IPv4 and then expand Scope [192.168.1.0] LabScope1. Click Address Leases. You will see that an IP address has been leased to Srv2012-2.

Exercise 3-5: Install an Active Directory Server in Windows Server 2012 R2

1. Make sure you are logged into your Srv2012-1 virtual machine with the Administrator account.
2. Start PowerShell from the taskbar and type
   `install-windowsfeature ad-domain-services -includemanagementtools`
3. Start the Server Manager GUI tool (second taskbar icon from the left).
4. Click the flag notification icon in the upper right; you will see a message stating that you must "Promote this server to a domain controller." Click the link.
5. Choose Add A New Forest, and within the Deployment Configuration window and for the root domain name, type **fakedomain.local**. Then click Next.
6. Enter **Pa$$w0rd** for the DSRM password and click Next.
7. Accept the defaults for the remainder of the wizard and then click Install. After a few minutes, your server will restart.
8. Log back in using the Fakedomain\Administrator account with a password of Pa$$w0rd.
9. If prompted to change the password, type **Pa$$w0rdwindows**.
10. Click the Start button and type **Active**. When Active Directory Users and Computers is displayed, click it. The fakedomain.local AD domain now exists.
11. Click the Start button and type **DNS**. When the tool is displayed, click it.
12. In the DNS Manager window, expand the server name on the left, and then expand Forward Lookup Zones. Notice the fakedomain.local zone.

13. Expand fakedomain.local, and then click _tcp. Notice the four service location records for the domain controller.
14. Start PowerShell from the taskbar and type **`get-aduser -filter *`** to verify that AD is accessible via PowerShell. You will see a list of AD user accounts.

NOTE The lab instructions use a hybrid of command line and GUI tools. The idea is to get used to using both.

Exercise 3-6: Install the Red Hat Enterprise Linux 7 Operating System

1. Start VMware Workstation and ensure the RHEL7-1 virtual machine is selected.
2. In the navigation panel on the left, click Edit Virtual Machine Settings.
3. Notice the Network Adapter on the left. Click Network Adapter, and on the right select Custom: Specific Virtual Network and choose VMnet5 from the drop-down list.
4. On the left, click CD/DVD, and on the right, click Use ISO Image File. Click Browse and select the Red Hat Enterprise Linux 7 trial ISO file downloaded as per the instructions in Appendix A of this book. Click OK.
5. In the navigation panel on the left, click Power On This Virtual Machine. The virtual machine begins booting from the Linux installation media.
6. From the Red Hat Enterprise Linux 7.1 text installation screen, press I and then ENTER to install the product.

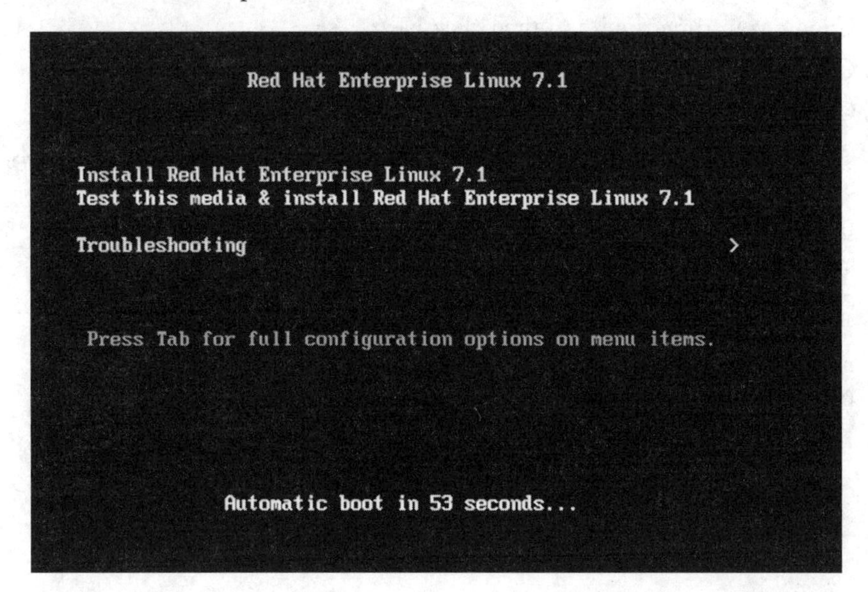

7. On the language selection screen, leave English selected and click Continue.
8. On the Installation Summary screen, click Installation Destination. The three virtual hard disks will be listed. Click the 20 GB disk listing and then click Done in the upper left.
9. Click Software Selection and choose Server With A GUI. Then click Done in the upper left.
10. Click Begin Installation.
11. As files are copied, you can specify the root user. Click Root Password and type **`Pa$$w0rdLinux`** into the Root Password and Confirm fields. Click Done.
12. Once installation is complete, click the Reboot button in the bottom right.
13. After the server reboots, click License Information. Then click I Accept The License Agreement and click Done.
14. Click Finish Configuration at the bottom right.
15. On the Subscription Management Registration page, choose No, I Prefer To Register At A Later Time. Click the Forward button.
16. On the Language screen, ensure that English (United States) is selected and click Next.
17. On the Input Sources screen, click Next.
18. On the Login screen, click Create A Local Account and enter the following:
    Full Name: **User One**
    Username: **uone**
    Password: **Pa$$w0rdLinux**
19. Click Next.
20. Choose your time zone, and then click Next.
21. Click Start Using Red Hat Enterprise Linux Server.
22. Close the GNOME help screen.
23. Click the Applications menu in the upper left, and then choose System Tools, Settings.
24. In the Hardware group, click Network. Ensure that Wired is selected on the left, and then click the configure icon (cog icon) at the bottom right.
25. Click IPv4 on the left. On the right, change Automatic (DHCP) to Manual. Enter the following information:
    Address: **192.168.1.210**
    Netmask: **255.255.255.0**
    Gateway: **192.168.1.200**
    In the DNS server section, type **192.168.1.200**.
26. Click Apply.

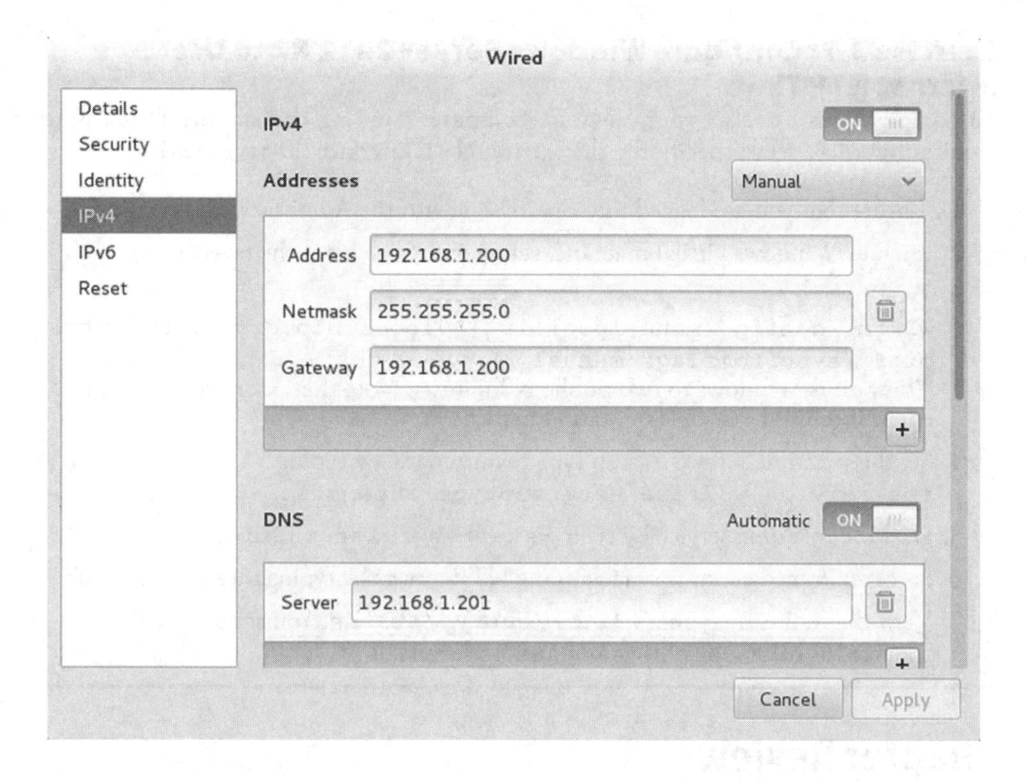

27. To the right of the Wired network connection, click the slider so that it changes from OFF to ON. Click the close button to close the Settings dialog box.
28. From the Applications menu choose Utilities, Terminal. Type **`ifconfig`** and press ENTER. Notice that the network interface (which may have a name such as eno16777736) is using the 192.168.1.210 IP address.
29. Name the server: From the Linux terminal prompt, type
    `hostnamectl --static set-hostname rhel7-1`
    Then verify that the hostname has been changed by typing **`hostname`**.
30. Create a snapshot of the installation in case you need to revert to this configuration in the future: From the VMware VM menu, choose Snapshot, Take Snapshot. Type **Fresh Installation** for the name, and then click Take Snapshot. You may have to wait a few minutes as the snapshot is created.

NOTE Throughout this book, you will learn about not only Windows Server operating systems, but also Red Hat Enterprise Linux OSs, in both physical and virtual environments. This includes hands-on exercises and troubleshooting tips.

Exercise 3-7: Configure Windows Server 2012 R2 to Use Internet NTP Time

To complete this exercise, your VMware computer running the lab virtual machines requires Internet access, specifically the externalNAT interface for Srv2012-1.

1. Ensure that you are logged into Srv2012-1 with the Administrator account.
2. In your Windows virtual machine, start PowerShell from the taskbar.
3. Type
   `w32tm /config /manualpeerlist:"0.pool.ntp.org 1.pool.ntp.org" /syncfromflags:manual`
   This points Windows to two public NTP hosts. Note the space between the two entries within the double quotation marks.
4. Set the w32time service startup type to automatic by typing
   `set-service w32time -startuptype automatic`.
5. Start the w32time service by typing **`start-service w32time`**.
6. Force an immediate time sync with the NTP servers by typing **`w32tm /resync`**.
7. View the results by typing **`w32tm /query /status`**. You should see the "Source" as being one of the pool.ntp.org servers.

Chapter Review

This chapter focused on how to install, configure, manage, and maintain server operating systems, whether they run on physical hardware or within virtual machines.

Server Roles

The type of workload handled by a server must be planned before server installation, and in some cases, these roles can be co-located on the same server.

DHCP

DHCP servers allow centrally configured IPv4 and IPv6 settings to be deployed to DHCP clients using TCP ports 67 and 68. DHCP scopes contain IP address ranges as well as additional settings such as lease duration, default gateways, DNS servers, reservations, exclusions, and more. Specific DHCP settings can be delivered to certain types of DHCP clients using vendor class identifiers. IPv4 clients that cannot reach DHCP will be auto-configured with an APIPA address with a prefix of 169.254.

Name Resolution

DNS servers are queried by clients on UDP port 53 primarily for name resolution, where an FQDN is supplied and a corresponding IP address is returned. Given an IP address, a DNS server can also perform a reverse lookup to return a name. DNS is a hierarchy of domains, where different DNS servers control different parts of the DNS namespace. The most common type of DNS resource record managed by administrators is an A record (IPv4) that is used for resolving names to IP addresses; the equivalent for IPv6 is an AAAA record.

WINS is used for resolving computer names to IP addresses, but unlike DNS it is not a hierarchy, but rather a flat list of NetBIOS computer names.

NTP

NTP is used to synchronize time for network devices from a time source. Connectivity for this protocol occurs over UDP port 123. Stratum 0 NTP devices are a trusted time source. Stratum 1 devices are NTP servers that get their time from a Stratum 0 device. Stratum 2 devices are NTP servers that get their time from Stratum 1 servers, and so on.

Directory Services

A directory service is a network database containing network-related objects such as users, computers, and groups. Often this is replicated among multiple servers to provide high availability and service localization.

Microsoft Active Directory uses domain controllers to house and replicate the directory service database. Clients discover domain controllers via DNS service location records.

Other Server Roles

Web servers use HTTP to transmit HTML web pages to web browser clients. Clients request the pages over TCP port 80 or 443 (HTTPS). HTTPS requires a server-side SSL/TLS certificate to secure the connection. Web site developers can build server-side/client-side code for site functionality. Enterprise Web SSO uses an underlying directory service, often in the form of identity federation.

Application servers can consist of multiple components such as a front-end web server and a back-end database that serve a specific business purpose.

File and print servers enable connectivity to these resources over the network and must have properly configured ACLs to allow access. CUPS (Common UNIX [and Linux] Printing System) is the standard UNIX/Linux printer sharing solution.

SMTP mail servers transfer mail between SMTP mail hosts; POP and IMAP are message retrieval protocols used by mail client software. IMAP allows synchronization between different devices, unlike POP.

Routing and remote access servers have at least two network interfaces and can be configured for IP routing, NAT, or VPNs.

Virtualization Servers

Hypervisors are software that run virtual machines and manage access to physical hardware. Type 1 hypervisors have direct access to physical hardware; Type 2 hypervisors rely on an underlying operating system to manage hardware access.

Hardware for the hypervisor must be planned relative to the virtual machines and their workloads that it will host. More RAM would be needed to run multiple virtual machines than just one, and some IT workloads such as large database servers will require more resources such as RAM.

Guests are virtual machines running on a hypervisor host, and each is configured with its own set of virtual hardware to accommodate its IT workloads properly. Settings such as dynamic memory can more efficiently use host memory among multiple virtual machines.

Server Installation

Hardware and software compatibility lists must be consulted before installing servers to ensure the smooth installation and running of IT services. Server OSs can be installed from bootable media or over the network, including PXE boot. PXE booting occurs over the network without local media, and services such as Microsoft RIS/WDS provide this functionality.

Server OS images can be used as well, and a server installation from media or an image can be completely automated using answer files or enterprise deployment solutions. A virtual machine deployed on-premises or in the cloud can use virtual machine images (or templates), which allow easy server deployment in mere minutes.

Server Administration Methods

Server administration methods include the following:

- Locally at the console
- Remotely using GUI tools such as Microsoft RSAT or RDP
- Remotely using Telnet or SSH
- Remotely using PowerShell or WinRM

KVM is used to connect to numerous servers where a single keyboard, video display, and mouse is used. KVM enables technicians to switch to different servers for management, whether servers have physical connections to KVM or over IP.

Out-of-band administration provides hardware-level remote access to a host without relying on the OS software running. Common solutions include Dell's iDRAC and HP's iLO; the server hardware must support this type of remote administration and it must be configured with IP settings.

Server Documentation

Server documentation includes the following:

- OEM service manuals
- Hardware and software inventory
- Log files
- Network/dataflow diagrams
- Service level agreements
- Baseline documentation
- Recovery documentation

The server asset life cycle, from procurement to disposal, must be documented, including configuration changes during the useful life of the server.

Server Maintenance

Proactive maintenance includes the application of firmware and software updates, ensuring that server room and data center environmental controls are in place, plugging servers into UPS systems, and making sure that a recovery procedure exists in the event of server failure.

Patch management can be centralized and automated using a tool such as WSUS or SSCM for Windows environments. Reports can be run to ensure that updates have been successfully applied.

Reactive maintenance involves viewing log entries, responding to alerts including error codes, server LCD messages, and so on.

Questions

1. Through which methods can on-premises servers communicate with cloud-based virtual machine servers? Choose two.

A. Site-to-site VPN connection

B. IPv6 leased connection

C. Dedicated leased connection

D. PKI

2. Which server role provides centralized IP configuration settings for clients?

A. DNS

B. IIS

C. RDP

D. DHCP

3. You need to configure DHCP to deliver a specific IP address to a specific network printer. What should you configure?

A. DHCP scope

B. DHCP reservation

C. Default gateway

D. PXE

4. Your network consists of Windows 10 computers and Android smartphones. You need to ensure that the Android devices are given IP addresses that place them on their own isolated VLAN. What should you do?

   A. Configure a DHCP vendor class identifier.

   B. Plug the Android devices into switch ports grouped into a VLAN.

   C. Configure a DHCP reservation.

   D. Configure a DHCP scope.

5. Your users report that they cannot access Internet resources today, although yesterday this worked fine. At a user station, you notice the IP address begins with 169.254. Why can't user stations reach the Internet?

   A. A DHCP server cannot be reached.

   B. An incorrect subnet mask has been specified.

   C. An incorrect default gateway has been specified.

   D. An incorrect DNS server has been specified.

6. Which Windows command shows DHCP lease information?

   A. `ipconfig /release`

   B. `arp -a`

   C. `nslookup`

   D. `ipconfig /all`

7. What type of DNS record is used to resolve FQDNs to IP addresses?

   A. MX

   B. PTR

   C. A

   D. AAAA

8. Which port does a DNS server listen on for client queries?

   A. UDP 53

   B. TCP 53

   C. UDP 3389

   D. TCP 3389

9. You install a Windows DNS server named DNS1. Clients on the network are configured to use DNS1 for name resolution. Users report they are able to connect to Internet resources by name. You need to ensure that DNS resolves only internal names. What should you do?
   A. Remove the DNS server default forwarders.
   B. Remove the DNS server default stub zones.
   C. Add DNS server root hints.
   D. Remove the DNS server root hints.

10. You need to configure firewall ACLs to allow DNS server zone transfer traffic. Which port should your ACL allow?
   A. UDP 53
   B. TCP 53
   C. UDP 80
   D. TCP 80

11. WINS and DNS are used for name resolution. How do WINS and DNS differ?
   A. WINS uses a hierarchical naming structure; DNS uses a flat naming structure.
   B. WINS uses a flat naming structure; DNS uses a hierarchical naming structure.
   C. WINS uses AAAA records for IPv6; DNS uses A records for IPv6.
   D. WINS uses UDP port 53 for client queries; DNS uses TCP port 53 for client queries.

12. Your network servers point to NTP time servers connected to reference clocks. Which type of NTP time servers do you have on your network?
   A. Stratum 0
   B. Stratum 1
   C. Stratum 2
   D. Stratum 3

13. You are configuring firewall ACLs. You need to ensure that NTP traffic is allowed through. Which port must you specify in your ACL rule?
    A. UDP 161
    B. TCP 161
    C. UDP 123
    D. TCP 123

14. Which server role stores network configuration objects in a centralized and replicated database?
    A. Directory service
    B. CUPS
    C. DNS
    D. DHCP

15. Your intranet has a web server containing sensitive data. You want to encrypt communications between web browser clients and the web server. What should you do?
    A. Issue a PKI certificate for each client web browser. Install the certificates on the web server.
    B. Issue a PKI certificate for each client web browser. Install the certificates on each client.
    C. Issue a PKI certificate for the web server. Install the certificate on the web server.
    D. Issue a PKI certificate for the web server. Install the certificate on each client station.

16. Which file and print sharing protocol is used by Windows devices?
    A. Samba
    B. NFS
    C. SMB
    D. CUPS

17. Your firewall has an ACL that allows inbound traffic destined for TCP port 25 to your company's DMZ. What type of traffic is this?
    - **A.** POP
    - **B.** SNMP
    - **C.** IMAP
    - **D.** SMTP

18. What term is used to refer to a host with at least two network interfaces?
    - **A.** NIC teaming
    - **B.** Multihomed
    - **C.** MultiNICed
    - **D.** NIC homing

19. Which term is used to refer to a running virtual machine on a hypervisor?
    - **A.** Host
    - **B.** Node
    - **C.** Device
    - **D.** Guest

20. Which type of hypervisor has direct access to physical hardware?
    - **A.** Type 1
    - **B.** Type 2
    - **C.** Type A
    - **D.** Type B

21. You need to ensure that your cloud backup solution has guaranteed uptime. What must you have to ensure this?
    - **A.** Network diagram
    - **B.** Dataflow diagram
    - **C.** Service level agreement
    - **D.** Change control policy

22. You have a Linux image that will be deployed to numerous virtual machines. The image should be pulled down over the network without providing boot media. Which option should you use?

    A. PXE

    B. DHCP

    C. DISM

    D. USB

23. You want data center technicians to be able to scan equipment physically to facilitate hardware inventory gathering. What should you use?

    A. Bluetooth

    B. RFID

    C. Wi-Fi

    D. 4G

24. Which PowerShell cmdlet opens an interactive session with a remote host?

    A. `Invoke-Command`

    B. All PowerShell cmdlets using the `-computername` parameter

    C. `Enter-PSSession`

    D. `Winrs`

25. Which of the following are considered out-of-band server management solutions? Choose two.

    A. SSH

    B. iDRAC

    C. iLO

    D. RDP

Questions and Answers

1. Through which methods can on-premises servers communicate with cloud-based virtual machine servers? Choose two.

   A. Site-to-site VPN connection

   B. IPv6 leased connection

   C. Dedicated leased connection

   D. PKI

   A, C. Site-to-site VPNs traverse the Internet and can link local and cloud networks together. Dedicated leased connections do not traverse the Internet and could also be used to link on-premises and cloud networks. B and D are incorrect. IPv6 supersedes IPv4 and has a larger address space as well as security and quality of service improvement, but there is no such thing as an IPv6 leased connection. PKI is a hierarchy of security certificates; it can be used to secure traffic but not to link two networks together.

2. Which server role provides centralized IP configuration settings for clients?

   A. DNS

   B. IIS

   C. RDP

   D. DHCP

   D. DHCP provides centralized IP settings that DHCP clients can use. A, B, and C are incorrect. DNS is a centralized name lookup service. IIS is Microsoft's web server product. RDP is Microsoft's Remote Desktop Protocol.

3. You need to configure DHCP to deliver a specific IP address to a specific network printer. What should you configure?

   A. DHCP scope

   B. DHCP reservation

   C. Default gateway

   D. PXE

   B. DHCP reservations tie an IP address to a MAC address of a device on the network. A, C, and D are incorrect. DHCP scopes contain address ranges and settings such as DNS server and default gateways. A default gateway sets the IP address(es) of the router(s) interface on the local network and enables traffic to be sent outside of the LAN. PXE is a network booting option often used for machine imaging purposes.

4. Your network consists of Windows 10 computers and Android smartphones. You need to ensure that the Android devices are given IP addresses that place them on their own isolated VLAN. What should you do?

A. Configure a DHCP vendor class identifier.

B. Plug the Android devices into switch ports grouped into a VLAN.

C. Configure a DHCP reservation.

D. Configure a DHCP scope.

A. Vendor class identifiers can determine which type of device is connecting to DHCP and can assign IP settings for that type of device. B, C, and D are incorrect. Android devices do not have Ethernet ports for network cables. DHCP reservations tie an IP address to a device MAC address. DHCP scopes contain IP address ranges and related settings, but the scope applies to all devices by default.

5. Your users report that they cannot access Internet resources today, although yesterday this worked fine. At a user station, you notice the IP address begins with 169.254. Why can't user stations reach the Internet?

A. A DHCP server cannot be reached.

B. An incorrect subnet mask has been specified.

C. An incorrect default gateway has been specified.

D. An incorrect DNS server has been specified.

A. APIPA addresses are the result of a device not being able to contact a DHCP server. B, C, and D are incorrect. An incorrect subnet mask, default gateway, or DNS server won't matter if the station is using a 169.254 address prefix.

6. Which Windows command shows DHCP lease information?

A. `ipconfig /release`

B. `arp -a`

C. `nslookup`

D. `ipconfig /all`

D. The `ipconfig /all` command shows IP information including that related to DHCP. A, B, and C are incorrect. The `ipconfig /release` command releases DHCP-acquired IP configurations. The `arp -a` command shows IP address to MAC address resolution information. nslookup is a DNS diagnostic tool.

7. What type of DNS record is used to resolve FQDNs to IP addresses?
   - **A.** MX
   - **B.** PTR
   - **C.** A
   - **D.** AAAA

C. A records, also called host records, resolve FQDNs to IPv4 addresses. A, B, and D are incorrect. MX records are mail exchange records used to locate SMTP mail servers. PTRs are pointer records used in reverse lookup zones to return a name, given and IP address. AAAAs are IPv6 host records.

8. Which port does a DNS server listen on for client queries?
   - **A.** UDP 53
   - **B.** TCP 53
   - **C.** UDP 3389
   - **D.** TCP 3389

A. Client DNS queries target the DNS server on UDP port 53. B, C, and D are incorrect. TCP 53 is used for zone transfers between DNS servers. UDP 3389 is not normally used. TCP 3389 is the default RDP port on Windows hosts.

9. You install a Windows DNS server named DNS1. Clients on the network are configured to use DNS1 for name resolution. Users report they are able to connect to Internet resources by name. You need to ensure that DNS resolves only internal names. What should you do?
   - **A.** Remove the DNS server default forwarders.
   - **B.** Remove the DNS server default stub zones.
   - **C.** Add DNS server root hints.
   - **D.** Remove the DNS server root hints.

D. DNS server root hints allow for Internet name resolution. A, B, and C are incorrect. There are no forwarders or stub zones by default, and adding DNS server root hints will not resolve the issue.

10. You need to configure firewall ACLs to allow DNS server zone transfer traffic. Which port should your ACL allow?

A. UDP 53

B. TCP 53

C. UDP 80

D. TCP 80

B. TCP port 53 is used for zone transfer traffic between DNS servers. A, C, and D are incorrect. UDP 53 is used for DNS client queries, UDP 80 is not normally used, and TCP 80 is the default HTTP web server port.

11. WINS and DNS are used for name resolution. How do WINS and DNS differ?

A. WINS uses a hierarchical naming structure; DNS uses a flat naming structure.

B. WINS uses a flat naming structure; DNS uses a hierarchical naming structure.

C. WINS uses AAAA records for IPv6; DNS uses A records for IPv6.

D. WINS uses UDP port 53 for client queries; DNS uses TCP port 53 for client queries.

B. WINS simply resolves NetBIOS computer names to IP addresses; there is no hierarchy as there is in DNS. A, C, and D are incorrect. WINS is not hierarchical; DNS is. DNS A records are for IPv4; AAAA records are for IPv6. UDP 53 is used only for DNS client queries; TCP 53 is used for DNS server zone transfers.

12. Your network servers point to NTP time servers connected to reference clocks. Which type of NTP time servers do you have on your network?

A. Stratum 0

B. Stratum 1

C. Stratum 2

D. Stratum 3

C. Stratum 2 NTP servers point to Stratum 1, which in term uses a reference clock (Stratum 0). A, B, and D are incorrect. Stratum 0 is for reference clocks, Stratum 1 are time servers connected to reference clocks, and Stratum 3 servers point to Stratum 2 time providers.

13. You are configuring firewall ACLs. You need to ensure that NTP traffic is allowed through. Which port must you specify in your ACL rule?

A. UDP 161

B. TCP 161

C. UDP 123

D. TCP 123

C. NTP uses UDP port 123. A, B, and D are incorrect. UDP 161 is for SNMP, TCP 161 and 123 are not normally used.

14. Which server role stores network configuration objects in a centralized and replicated database?

A. Directory service

B. CUPS

C. DNS

D. DHCP

A. A directory service is a centralized and replicated database that stores network objects such as users, groups, and computers. B, C, and D are incorrect. CUPS is the UNIX- and Linux-based print server standard. DNS is used for name resolution. DHCP provides centralized IP settings for DHCP client devices.

15. Your intranet has a web server containing sensitive data. You want to encrypt communications between web browser clients and the web server. What should you do?

A. Issue a PKI certificate for each client web browser. Install the certificates on the web server.

B. Issue a PKI certificate for each client web browser. Install the certificates on each client.

C. Issue a PKI certificate for the web server. Install the certificate on the web server.

D. Issue a PKI certificate for the web server. Install the certificate on each client station.

C. Only the web server requires a PKI certificate. A, B, and D are incorrect. Clients do not need a PKI certificate for secured web server traffic.

16. Which file and print sharing protocol is used by Windows devices?

A. Samba

B. NFS

C. SMB

D. CUPS

C. Windows file and print sharing uses the SMB protocol. A, B, and D are incorrect. Samba enables Linux clients to contact Windows SMB shared resources. NFS is the UNIX and Linux file sharing standard. CUPS is the UNIX and Linux print server standard.

17. Your firewall has an ACL that allows inbound traffic destined for TCP port 25 to your company's DMZ. What type of traffic is this?

A. POP

B. SNMP

C. IMAP

D. SMTP

D. SMTP mail traffic has a destination port of TCP 25. A, B, and C are incorrect. POP uses TCP port 110, SNMP is UDP 161, and IMAP is TCP 143.

18. What term is used to refer to a host with at least two network interfaces?

A. NIC teaming

B. Multihomed

C. MultiNICed

D. NIC homing

B. A host with at least two NICs is said to be multihomed. A, C, and D are incorrect. NIC teaming groups multiple NICs together for bandwidth aggregation or load balancing. MultiNICed and NIC homing are made-up words.

19. Which term is used to refer to a running virtual machine on a hypervisor?

A. Host

B. Node

C. Device

D. Guest

D. A virtual machine is also called a guest. A, B, and C are incorrect. The hypervisor is referred to as the host. A node is a network device that can transmit and receive packets. A device is a node that can transmit and receive data on a network.

20. Which type of hypervisor has direct access to physical hardware?

A. Type 1

B. Type 2

C. Type A

D. Type B

A. Type 1 hypervisors have direct access to hardware without going through an operating system. B, C, and D are incorrect. Type 2 hypervisors go through an existing operating system for hardware access. Types A and B are not used to refer to hypervisors.

21. You need to ensure that your cloud backup solution has guaranteed uptime. What must you have to ensure this?

A. Network diagram

B. Dataflow diagram

C. Service level agreement

D. Change control policy

C. Service level agreements specify details such as guaranteed uptime. A, B, and D are incorrect. Network and dataflow diagrams are useful documentation for troubleshooting, change management, and inventory purposes. A change control policy dictates steps that must be taken to make configuration changes.

22. You have a Linux image that will be deployed to numerous virtual machines. The image should be pulled down over the network without providing boot media. Which option should you use?

A. PXE

B. DHCP

C. DISM

D. USB

A. PXE boots over the network and pulls down a small operating system to the local machine, often for imaging purposes. B, C, and D are incorrect. DHCP is used with PXE, but it does not provide boot and imaging options. DISM is a Windows command line tool that can be used to service Windows image files. Using a USB would mean technicians would have local boot media.

23. You want data center technicians to be able to scan equipment physically to facilitate hardware inventory gathering. What should you use?

A. Bluetooth

B. RFID

C. Wi-Fi

D. 4G

B. RFID enables devices to be scanned with RFID tags for inventory and tracking purposes. A, C, and D are incorrect. Bluetooth, Wi-Fi, and 4G are wireless technologies, but they are not designed specifically for inventory gathering.

24. Which PowerShell cmdlet opens an interactive session with a remote host?

A. `Invoke-Command`

B. All PowerShell cmdlets using the `-computername` parameter

C. `Enter-PSSession`

D. `Winrs`

C. Interactive PowerShell sessions can be started with `Enter-PSSession`. A, B, and D are incorrect. `Invoke-Command` and the `-computername` parameter for some cmdlets allow remote code execution, but not interactively. Winrs is a Windows command line remote management tool.

25. Which of the following are considered out-of-band server management solutions? Choose two.

A. SSH

B. iDRAC

C. iLO

D. RDP

B, C. Dell's iDRAC and HP's iLO are hardware-based, out-of-band remote management solutions. A and D are incorrect. SSH is used to manage any device securely and remotely with an SSH listener. RDP is used to manage Windows computers remotely.

CHAPTER 4

Storage

In this chapter, you will

- Learn about various storage technologies
- Understand why SSDs are superior to HDDs
- Plan storage capacity
- Learn about cloud storage options
- Understand network storage
- Learn how to install storage devices
- Recognize ways to maintain file systems
- Discover a variety of RAID configuration options

Today's server storage implementations can be configured from a wide array of options based on several considerations, including whether the stored data is directly available to the server or whether it is accessible to the server over a network.

A variety of storage technologies are in use today. Larger server rooms and data centers tend to use a collection of rack-mounted storage arrays available over a storage area network (SAN). For cloud-computing consumers, additional storage can be provisioned in seconds with the click of a mouse. Disks can be grouped together to increase disk read and write performance, to increase fault tolerance when disks fail, or both.

You need to understand storage options at both hardware and software levels, because when the data storage is seen by the server operating system, it needs to be configured—initialized, partitioned, and formatted. In this chapter, you will learn how to plan, choose, and configure storage to meet business needs.

Storage Technologies

A wide array of factors will influence your storage decisions, including decisions regarding where the storage will exist. Are you using cloud storage? Are the storage disks located inside the server itself, or are they accessible over an enterprise network?

Similar to server form factors, storage device dimensions and form factors have to be considered so that storage devices can be physically accommodated within servers or storage arrays. Today, 3.5-inch large form factor (LFF) hard drives are common. (This measurement refers to the diameter of the disk platters. Small form factor (SFF) disks are 2.5 inches. Note that you don't need to be concerned with form factors when it comes to external USB drives.)

Regardless of the type of storage in use, two of your main concerns will be the storage capacity and how quickly you can read and write to storage. At the server level, today's storage (per disk) falls somewhere in the 1 to 8 terabyte (TB) range, but this is constantly evolving. Of course, grouping disks together provides vastly greater storage capacity.

Magnetic Hard Disks

Old-school hard disks use magnetism to store data on metal platters. Hard disk drives (HDDs) are vacuum-sealed and contain multiple platters, each having read and write heads on an actuator arm to read and write data as the platter spins. You can see the actuator arm extended over the hard disk platter in Figure 4-1. Numerous factors influence disk speeds, as listed in Table 4-1.

The norm for desktop disks is 7200 RPMs; laptop disk speeds are around 5400 RPMs. Fast server hard drives spin at 15,000 RPMs, and you'll pay more for these drives than for slower 10,000 RPM drives. Keep in mind that an increase in RPMs means a decrease in rotational latency, which translates to faster data access times.

Solid-State Drives

Solid-state drives (SSDs) have no moving parts, which means less physical wear and tear, less power required (no motors to drive), less heat, and less noise (less ventilation needs, as they run cooler because of reduced power draw). The biggest problem with SSDs, at least at the time of this writing, is that larger capacity SSDs are more expensive than the equivalent capacity magnetic hard disks.

Externally, SSDs aren't much different from regular hard drives. Magnetic hard drives and SSDs are both plugged in using the Serial Advanced Technology Attachment (SATA) interface. Configuring and using the disk in the server operating system is the same regardless of drive type.

Figure 4-1 The internal components of a magnetic hard disk

Disk Characteristic	Description
Revolutions per minute (RPMs)	The faster a disk spins, the quicker we can read or write to it. A 10,000 RPM disk performs better than a 5400 RPM disk.
Seek time	The position of the read/write head over the disk platter determines the amount of time it takes to locate data on the disk.
Rotational latency	Before data is transferred, the disk platter must spin to the correct position to read or write. This is normally measured in fractions of a second; a smaller value is better in this case.
Bus width	The amount of bits that can be transferred at the same time. This is not as important for disk storage as it once was; fast disk transmission technologies often use serial rather than parallel transmission schemes.
Input/output operations per second (IOPS)	How often a disk can perform disk I/O operations depends on the specific workload, but generally more is better.
Transfer rate	The per-second rate at which data is moved into and out of disks indicates speed of data transfer; for example, a 6 Gbps transfer rate is superior to a 2 Gbps rate.

Table 4-1 Storage Speed Factors

Modern enterprise server environments often use a hybrid of SSDs and slower magnetic hard disks that are configured in different storage tiers. Different vendor solutions use varying methods of defining what gets stored on the faster SSDs; generally, frequently accessed data will reside on SSDs and less frequently accessed data is stored on the slower magnetic hard disks.

Public cloud providers also charge a premium when SSD storage is used. For example, when provisioning virtual machines in the cloud, we can opt for better performance by choosing a higher disk IOPS value. In the cloud, it's important to deprovision unneeded resources (such as storage) to avoid charges.

Flash drives are SSDs with no mechanical parts—everything is electronic. But isn't that the same as a USB drive? Not always. Some large external USB drives are simply enclosures that contain an internal magnetic hard disk. CompactFlash memory is used for smaller devices such as cameras, audio recorders, and the like. Both flash storage types are shown in Figure 4-2.

Hybrid Drives

You can probably guess what a hybrid drive is—a combination of hard disk and solid-state technology in the same package. Often called solid-state hybrid drives (SSHDs), they consist of spinning platters as well as the faster flash memory. These drives cache frequently accessed data on the faster flash memory to improve performance.

Figure 4-2 A USB flash drive and a 32GB SDHC (high capacity) flash memory card

Cost-wise, SSHDs fall between traditional hard drives and SSDs. Consider the following price comparisons (in US dollars):

- 1TB hard drive: $70
- 1TB SSHD: $95
- 1TB SSD: $320

You can see why SSDs are often used only for frequently accessed files or any type of disk-intensive activities.

Storage Tiers

All storage and data are not equal: SSDs offer better performance than hard disks, and valuable data should be quickly accessible. Storage administrators can configure storage-tier policies that determine which type of data will be stored on which specific storage media. In the industry, this is generally referred to as *hierarchical storage management* (HSM).

As an example, EMC, the same company that owns VMware, offers the fully automated storage tiering (FAST) feature. Microsoft Windows Server 2012 R2 also offers storage tier capabilities; you'll need both SSD and HDD to set this up. After creating a storage pool from the physical disks and upon creating a virtual disk in the pool, you'll get the option to create storage tiers on the virtual disk.

Because many servers today access data storage over a network, it makes sense to place tiered storage capabilities in front of SAN storage. Different vendor solutions have different naming conventions for storage tiers. Here are some examples:

Windows Server

- Tier 1 (SSD)
- Tier 2 (HDD)

EMC

- Extreme performance tier (fastest)
- Performance tier (middle of the road)
- Capacity tier (slowest)

Tier 1 storage (SSD) is used for frequently accessed and important data; Tier 2 storage (HDD) is used for less frequently accessed data. But how do storage solutions determine whether one piece of data is more important than another? As mentioned, storage administrators can configure storage tier policies that categorize data accordingly.

Disk Interfaces

Over the years, some disk interface standards have stood the test of time and have evolved, while others have been replaced by newer technologies. Take, for instance, the old IDE disk interface standard that was common in the 1980s and 1990s, which is no longer commonly used. Instead, SATA (Figure 4-3) and Fibre Channel are the norm in server environments.

Table 4-2 lists common disk interface characteristics.

Optical Drives

Optical drives have begun to fade away. When is the last time you burned a CD or DVD, or even a Blu-ray Disc? Probably a long time ago. With the availability of cheap and fast external USB devices, consumers have moved away from optical media in favor of USBs because USBs are easy to work with, accommodate many writes—and they just work! Writing multiple times to an open CD, on the other hand, can be tricky, and you need the right software to do it.

Figure 4-3 SATA disk data cable connectors

Disk Interface	Details
Serial-attached SCSI (SAS)	• Serial bit transmission • Hot-pluggable (can be swapped out while a machine is running) • Newer iteration of the older SCSI standard • More expensive than SATA • Smaller storage capacity than SATA • Designed for constant use • Used often for servers
Serial ATA (SATA)	• Serial bit transmission • Not designed for constant use • Used often in personal workstations
Small Computer System Interface (SCSI)	• Parallel bit transmission • Many standards have evolved over the years, including SAS; traditionally SCSI used parallel transmission, SAS uses serial-based transmission • Used often for servers
Universal serial bus (USB)	• Serial bit transmission • Convenient external connectivity • Used often in personal workstations
Fibre Channel (FC)	• Used in storage area networks • Host bus adapters are required in servers to access SAN storage • Used often for servers

Table 4-2 Disk Interfaces

Write Once Read Many (WORM) drives preceded optical drives. They allowed data to be written once to the device, with many reads. WORM drives worked well in archiving situations. Newer operating systems, including Windows, support optical media burning without requiring that you install additional software. For servers, this isn't as important—servers should never be used as a desktop! But there are times when servers need a local optical drive to boot from for recovery purposes or to install an operating system. As long as the server has a USB interface, you'll be able to plug in an external optical drive if needed. With the advent of server virtualization, Preboot Execution Environment (PXE) network boot, and operating system imaging, installing from optical media has become less common.

Cloud Storage

Public cloud storage has become popular for consumers and enterprises, and no wonder! All that's needed is an Internet connection and a cloud provider subscription.

You can provision (and deprovision) storage instantaneously and pay only for the space you use. There could be legal or regulatory restrictions that prevent the use of public cloud storage, and certainly cloud storage is not appropriate for *every* scenario—it's just another option.

Your on-premises storage (servers, storage enclosures) can be configured to replicate or back up to the cloud as well, so hybrid solutions are also possible. The great thing about cloud storage is that somebody else deals with the disk devices, their configuration, and their availability on the network. As cloud consumers, we can connect from pretty much any device (such as a smartphone, as shown in Figure 4-4) on any network and still get to our files.

Direct-Attached Storage

Direct-attached storage (DAS) is the traditional server storage model in which storage disks are housed inside the server chassis and are locally available only to that server. So if the server is not accessing storage over some kind of a network, it's DAS.

Network-Attached Storage

File-sharing protocols such as Microsoft Server Message Block (SMB) and the UNIX Network File System (NFS) enable user connectivity to shared file systems over a network. The fact that these higher layer protocols (SMB and NFS) are used is a factor that distinguishes network-attached storage (NAS) from storage area networks (SANs). Another factor is that servers connect to NAS storage over a network consisting of standard network equipment and using standard network protocols such as Internet Protocol (IP). SANs are specialized high-speed networks designed to transmit disk I/O traffic using protocols designed for this use.

NAS can come in the form of a hardware appliance, such as the Dell device shown in Figure 4-5—essentially a disk enclosure with wired and wireless network connectivity

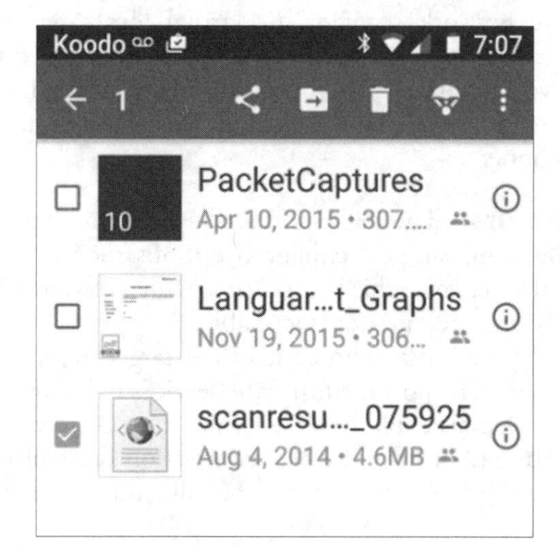

Figure 4-4 Accessing cloud storage from an Android smartphone

Figure 4-5 PowerVault NX3200 NAS device, Courtesy of Dell Inc.

that has web management built into its firmware. In other cases, your NAS storage might be served up from a server configured solely for this purpose.

iSCSI

The acronym iSCSI stands for Internet Small Computer System Interface (SCSI). SCSI is a decades-old standard used primarily for disk storage. To this day, it continues to evolve and is common in server environments. iSCSI makes storage accessible to hosts over a standard TCP/IP network on a small scale within a company.

The "i" in iSCSI refers to the fact that standard network equipment, such as standard Ethernet switches and cabling, can be used along with IP. What happens is SCSI disk I/O commands generated by a host (the iSCSI initiator) are placed inside of IP packets. IP packets have the delivery details, such as the identity of the server or appliance serving up the disk space (the iSCSI target). Standard network hardware and software makes iSCSI possible; compared to a SAN, iSCSI is cheaper, slower, and less reliable.

A separate network segment, or virtual local area network (VLAN) configured within or between network switches, should be dedicated for iSCSI use; there's enough overhead involved already by stuffing disk commands into IP packets that need to be addressed and transmitted. What makes this solution attractive is its price tag, and it gets the job done.

iSCSI Initiators The iSCSI initiator can be implemented as software or hardware. Hardware initiators support enhanced options such as a server booting the operating system over the network; this isn't possible with software initiators because the OS has to be running before the initiator is available.

In order for the initiator to contact the target, it first needs some kind of network address and port. The port identifies the services running on the host, and in this case it's TCP port 3260. This could be a hostname such as storage1.acme.local or an IP address such as 172.16.54.56. After the host connection is established, we then specify the logical unit number (LUN) using an iSCSI qualified name (IQN) such as iqn.2012-06.com.sample:target0.

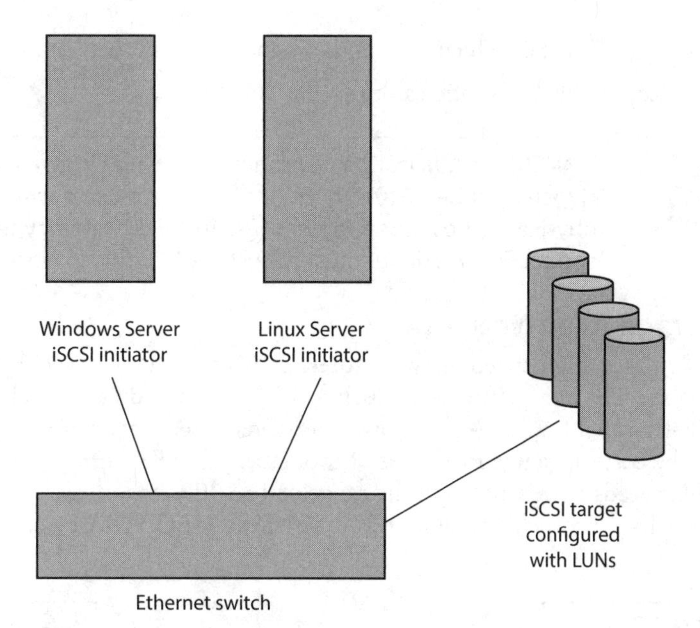

Figure 4-6 iSCSI initiators connect to iSCSI targets using TCP/IP

iSCSI Targets The iSCSI target hosts the disk space on an IP network, and that space gets consumed by servers as depicted in Figure 4-6. Storage administrators carve out different chunks of disk space for servers to consume. These chunks of disk space are called logical unit numbers, because traditional storage protocols such as SCSI used a unique numeric value to refer to disk storage.

NOTE iSCSI LUNs can also be consumed by some client operating systems and devices. For example, a Windows 10 machine can consume an iSCSI LUN; to Windows 10, it's just more available disk space.

FCoE

Fibre Channel (FC) is a high-speed transmission method often used to connect servers to network storage. Despite "fibre" being in the name, it does not require fiber-optic cabling; standard twisted pair copper cables will work just fine. Because the FC standards are designed for speed and reliability, they are more often used in data centers or by service providers.

Fibre Channel over Ethernet (FCoE) stuffs disk commands into Ethernet frames as opposed to using higher level IP packets, which introduce more overhead. But for this to work, we need the correct hardware, as seen in Figure 4-7:

- Converged network adapters (CNAs) in each server, which combine Ethernet and FC functionality in a single card

- FCoE switches, which serve as the connection point between servers and storage arrays
- Copper or fiber-optic cables

EXAM TIP Virtualization environments such as VMware and Microsoft Hyper-V enable virtual machines to communicate with a SAN through a physical FC host bus adapter (HBA) installed in the hypervisor host. The correct FC HBA driver must be installed for this to work.

Storage Area Networks

A SAN is a high-speed network used exclusively for connecting to network storage using specific storage protocols such as FC, as opposed to general-use protocols such as TCP/IP. You'll find SANs used in larger enterprises, data centers, and service providers, and the cost can range from tens of thousands of dollars into the millions!

FC speeds currently fall in the range of 1 to 32 Gbps; there is less overhead than with higher level protocols such as IP. Servers need a FC HBA to connect to SAN storage.

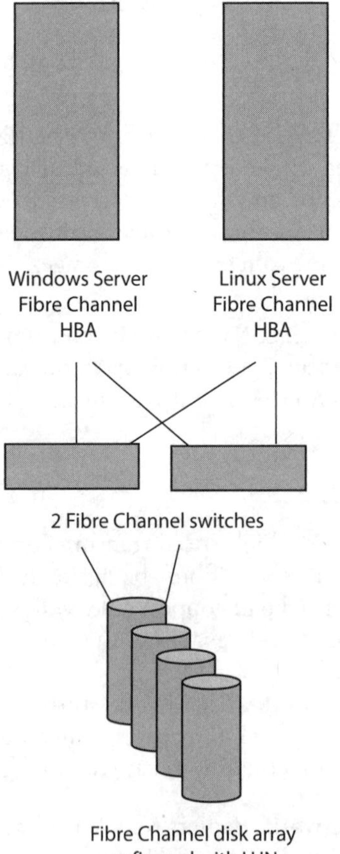

Figure 4-7 A Fibre Channel SAN using redundant switches

The HBA has a unique identifier called a *World Wide Name (WWN)*. The HBA can have multiple ports, each of which can connect to different FC switches for redundancy. Storage arrays are connected to FC switches. Collectively, this topology is referred to as a *fabric*. Other devices take on this nomenclature, too, as in *fabric switches*.

Storage administrators configure LUNs and LUN masks to determine which servers can use which configured storage. A LUN uniquely identifies disk space on the storage array. A LUN mask is normally configured at the HBA level. For example, we might want to prevent Windows Server from seeing specific LUNs used by Linux servers.

NOTE Larger SANs will use zoning instead of LUN masking. Zoning is configured at the FC switch level and it does not apply to FCoE or iSCSI. It groups nodes into zones, much like organizing devices on their own IP subnet. This enables us to control LUN visibility to all nodes in the same zone. To achieve this with FCoE or iSCSI, we would use separate VLANs.

Storage Capacity and Future Growth

When it comes to servers, a myriad of questions need answers. What is the server's purpose? How many users will be connecting at once? How critical is it that the server stay up and running? Planning servers before jumping into the actual configuration is paramount. One part of this is trying to anticipate server storage needs. And this is where cloud computing (specifically, Infrastructure as a Service, or IaaS) can be very useful.

When you work with storage on-premises, you have to order storage, wait for it to be shipped, plug it in, configure it, and then it can be used. If, over time, you didn't need all of the storage, well, you paid for it all either way. In some cases, cloud storage makes a lot of sense. By definition, cloud services must support the following:

- A pool of resource shared by multiple tenants
- IT services available on demand from anywhere using any device
- Rapid elasticity (I need more disk space right now!)
- User (not service provider) provisioning and deprovisioning
- Metered services (pay only for the storage you've allocated)

Base 2 vs. Base 10

Imagine one of your users asking you to explain a kilobyte. Would you say, "It is a term to express 1000 bytes," or would you say, "It expresses 1024 bytes"? Those 24 little bytes can really add up when you're calculating server storage needs, especially in a data center or service provider environment!

We humans normally express numbers using base 10. Why? There are a few theories:

- We have 10 digits on our two hands.
- The pope said so in the Middle Ages.
- Our financial systems do it this way.

It really doesn't matter why. It just is. Computers, however, don't do base 10—they do base 2, or binary, where everything is collections of 0's and 1's. So with base 10, we could say $10^3 = 1000$ ($10 \times 10 = 100$, $100 \times 10 = 1000$). With base 2, we would say $2^{10} = 1024$ ($2 \times 2 = 4$, $4 \times 2 = 8$, and so on). Therefore, a 1 terabyte (TB) drive is 1,099,511,627,776 bytes (that's 1 trillion and change), not just 1 trillion. The difference here is 99 billion bytes!

Where Did All the Disk Space Go?

Remember the old saying, "If you build it, they will come"? Well, for disk space our statement of wisdom will be, "If you make it available, it will be consumed." As storage capacity increases and becomes affordable, we seem to have a need to gobble it all up for storing movies, music collections, company data, operating system images, and so on. Here is a partial list of disk space consumers:

- Operating system files
- Operating system patches and service packs
- Operating system images
- Driver and application updates
- Log files
- Temporary files
- Data files
- Data backups and archives

You can imagine that a customer-transaction database for a large online retailer would consume an increasing amount of disk space, especially over time. Any application server resulting in data is a potential item to consider. File servers housing thousands of user home directories are prime candidates for running out of space. Some companies have policy-driven software that automatically archives data not accessed frequently to slower, cheaper storage media (a different storage tier), or even to the cloud.

Using Less Disk Space

What can we do to use less storage space? Disk quotas can limit how much disk space is used either in a folder (regardless of who places content there) or even by user (such as on a file server). Some quota tools support *soft* quotas, where the quota is not enforced, but a log entry is made noting that the quota has been reached. *Hard* quotas are enforced. Windows Server user quotas can be set using the GUI, as shown in Figure 4-8.

As a server technician, when you create server disk volumes, you have the option of *thin provisioning*, which is also referred to as *overbooking* or *overcommittal of disk space*. Here's how thin provisioning works:

1. A server admin adds 500GB of new storage to a server.
2. The admin creates disk volume 1, which is thinly provisioned during creation and is set to a size of 500GB.

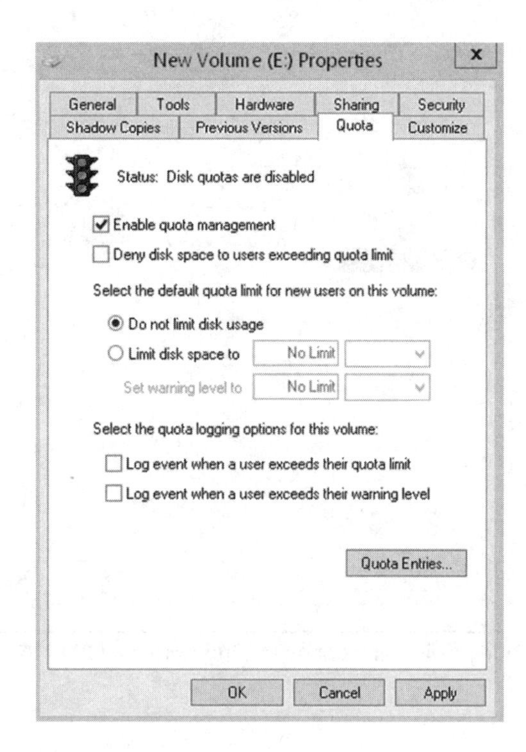

Figure 4-8 Setting user disk quotas on a Windows server

3. The admin creates disk volume 2, which is thinly provisioned during creation and is set to a size of 500GB.

Wait a minute! That's 1TB of disk space we may use down the road, but there is only 500GB of physical storage! The beauty here lies in the fact that both disk volumes will use disk space as they grow over time, but in the end we are limited to 500GB. With thin provisioning, we don't have to know ahead of time exactly how much space each volume will end up needing. Figure 4-9 shows thin provisioning being configured within the Windows Server 2012 R2 operating system.

Compression

Disk compression tools save disk space by reducing redundant occurrences of data. Windows and Linux servers let you work with compression in the GUI or at the command line. For example, on a Windows server, we can compress all files on drive D: with the following command:

```
compact /c /i /d:\
```

From a terminal prompt on a Linux host, we could use

```
gzip -r zipped_budgets.gz /budgets_2014 /budgets_2015
```

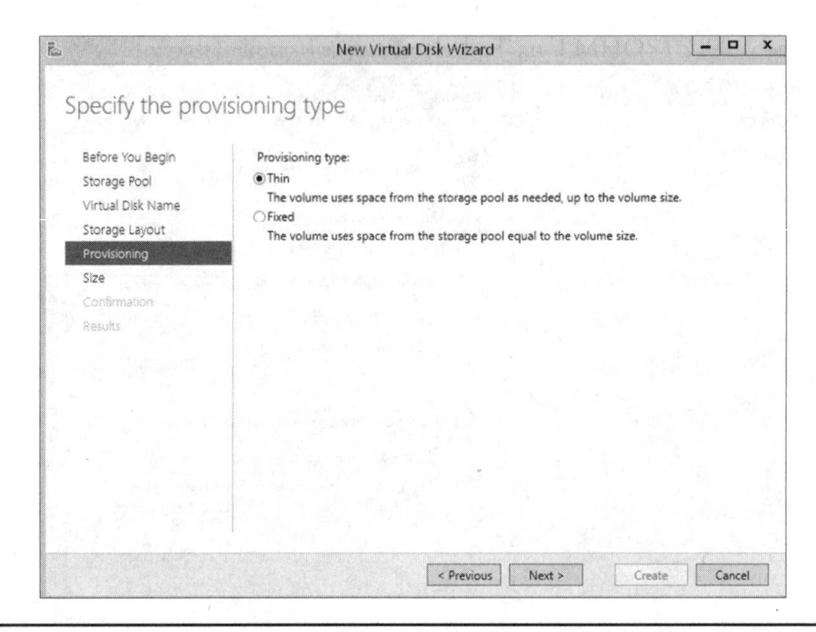

Figure 4-9 Thin provisioning option in Windows Server 2012 R2

Data Deduplication

Data deduplication can remove redundant data blocks to conserve space. Windows Server 2012 R2 includes data deduplication for NTFS volumes, but it's not installed by default. There are also tools available to measure where your current disk space is being used to aid in planning future storage capacity. One example is Microsoft's File Server Resource Manager (FSRM), shown in Figure 4-10, which is included with the Windows Server OS.

Windows Image Files

The standard file type for storing Windows images is the .WIM format. You can save disk space by storing multiple images of the same operating system within a single .WIM file. Suppose you have five Windows 10 images used within the company, and each image is approximately 10GB, for a total of 50GB. If you were to store those five images in a single .WIM, the total consumed disk space might be only 25GB. The reason is *single-instance storage*; multiple copies of files are stored only once, thus saving space.

You can use the Deployment Image Servicing and Management (DISM.exe) tool to work with Windows image files. DISM is built into newer operating systems such as Windows 10 and Windows Server 2012 R2.

The following example creates an image of drive C: and appends it to Z:\win10_images.wim with a name of win10_sales:

```
Dism /Append-Image /ImageFile:Z:\win10_images.wim /CaptureDir:
C:\ /Name:win10_sales
```

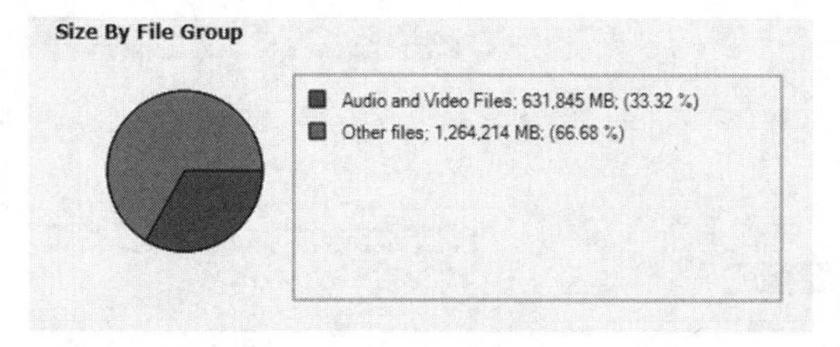

Size by File Group		
File Group	Total size on Disk	Files
Audio and Video Files	631,845 MB	15050
Image Files	22,636 MB	41653
Executable Files	20,447 MB	1812
Compressed Files	5,831 MB	784
Office Files	2,328 MB	4023
Temporary Files	1,209 MB	285
System Files	464 MB	1406
Web Page Files	53.5 MB	3444
Text Files	15.3 MB	1143
E-mail Files	0.77 MB	8
Backup Files	0.26 MB	26
All other files	1,211,229 MB	31602

Figure 4-10 FSRM storage report

The following example applies the win10_sales image stored in the win10_images.wim file to the C: drive:

```
Dism /Apply-Image /ImageFile:Z:\win10_images.wim /name:win10_sales
/ApplyDir:C:\
```

Of course, DISM isn't the only game in town; other tools such as imagex.exe, Microsoft Deployment Toolkit (MDT), and Microsoft System Center Configuration Manager (SCCM) do a fine job when working with Windows images.

RAID Configuration

Groups of disks not yet configured to work together are called JBOD—Just a Bunch of Disks. The Redundant Array of Independent Disks (RAID) takes a much more structured approach and is widely used in enterprise computing ecosystems—and it has been for years.

RAID lets us group multiple physical disks together as a logical manageable unit for two reasons: improved disk I/O performance and fault tolerance. To the operating system, it might see what it thinks is one disk when in reality the RAID array might consist of five disks working together.

Hardware RAID support is normally integrated on server motherboards, but if it isn't, you can get expansion cards (a RAID controller) to make this possible. Software RAID (see Figure 4-11) is built into server operating systems, but, of course, if something goes

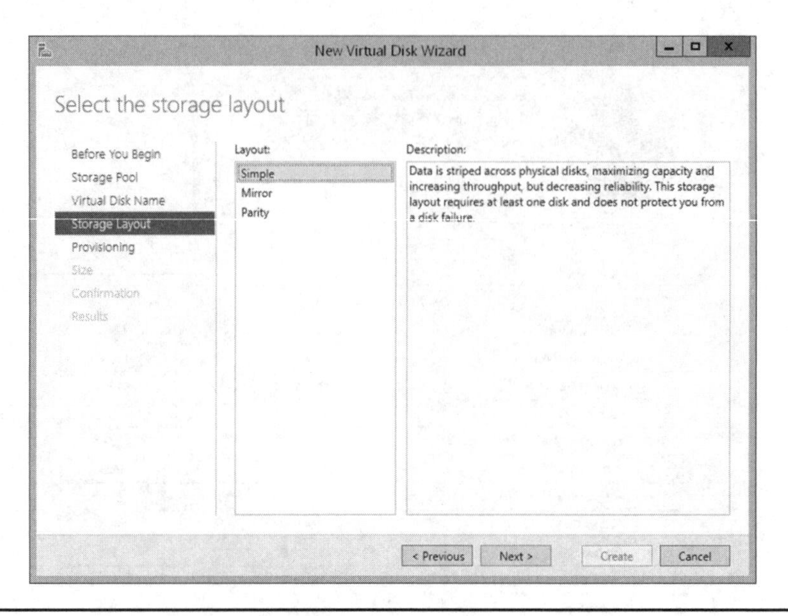

Figure 4-11 Configuring software RAID using Windows Server 2012 R2

wrong with the OS, something might go wrong with the RAID disk array. Not only that, but remember that firmware designed for one purpose always outperforms software designed for many uses, so use hardware RAID whenever possible!

Hardware RAID array controllers often have some of their own battery-backed cache. This works well when disk writes to the array aren't committed immediately and an issue such as a power outage occurs. Upon restart, cached data is actually committed to disk. In the spirit of redundancy (remove single points of failure!), you can also use redundant RAID controllers. Interestingly, RAID level 1 (disk mirroring), when using two disks connected to two different controllers, is called *duplexing*. Figure 4-12 show how hardware RAID storage shows up in Windows Server 2012 R2.

RAID Levels

Many RAID levels consist of various disk configurations. The following sections summarize the characteristics of common RAID levels.

RAID 0

- Uses disk striping
- Requires at least two disks
- Data to be written to disk is broken into blocks (stripes) that are evenly written across the disk array
- Improves disk I/O performance
- Offers no fault tolerance

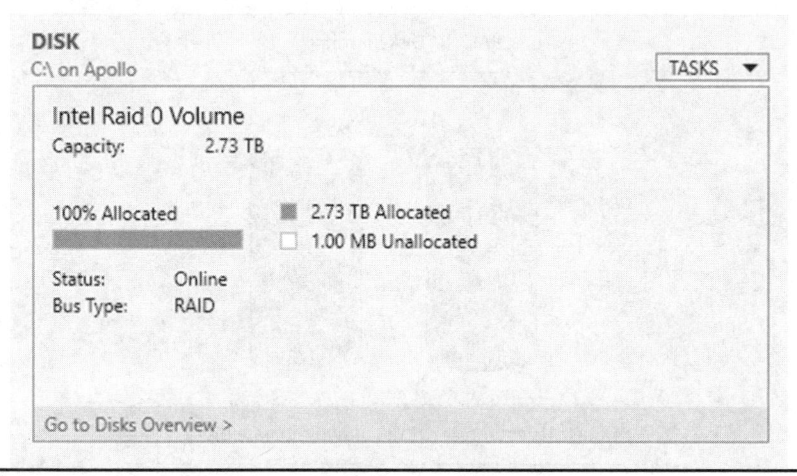

Figure 4-12 An Intel RAID 0 volume in Windows Server 2012 R2

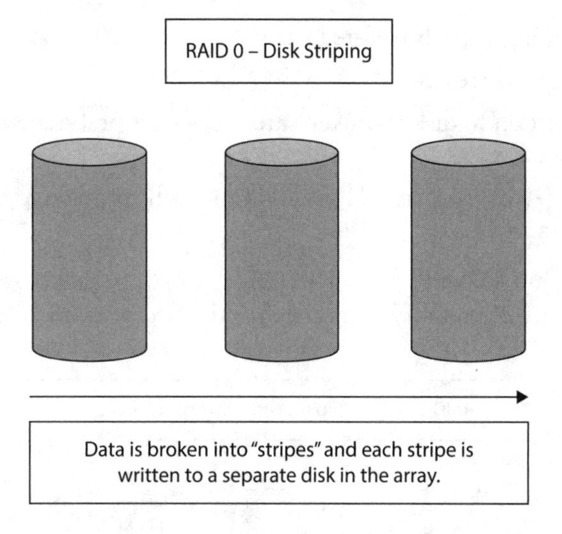

RAID 1

- Uses disk mirroring
- Requires at least two disks
- Data written to a disk partition on one disk is also written to a disk partition on a different disk
- Can use only 50 percent of your disk space
- Tolerates a disk failure
- Does *not* replace backups

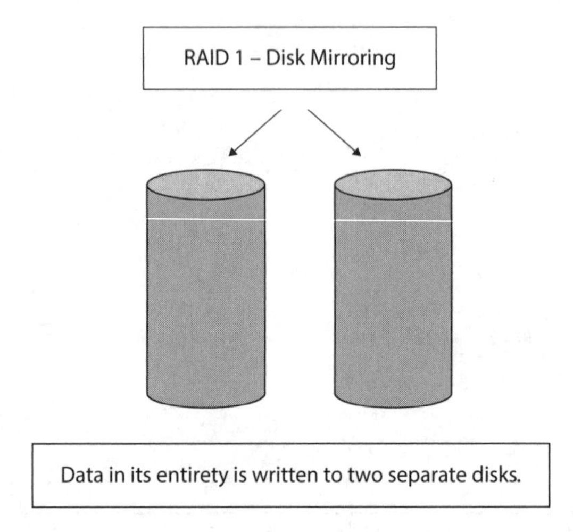

RAID 5

- Uses disk striping with distributed parity
- Requires at least three disks
- Data to be written to disk is broken into blocks (stripes) that are evenly written across the disk array
- Stores parity (error recovery) information for each stripe on a separate disk from its related data stripe
- Tolerates a single disk failure
- Can reconstruct in memory and on demand any data from failed disk

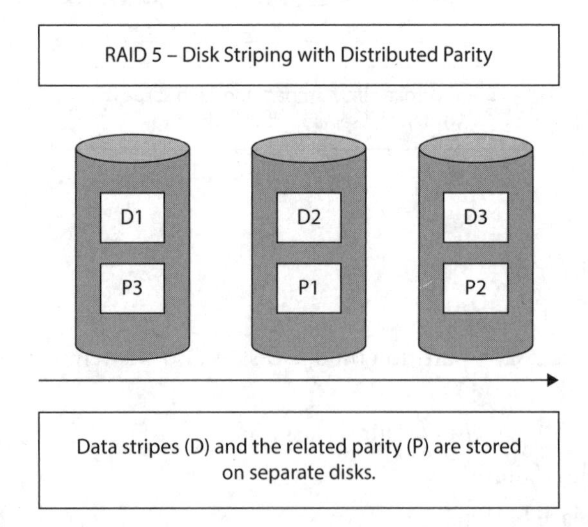

RAID 6

- Uses double parity RAID
- Requires at least four disks
- Data to be written to disk is broken into blocks (stripes) that are evenly written across the disk array
- Stores two parity (error recovery) stripes on each disk
- Never stores parity and its related data on the same disk
- Tolerates two disk failures
- Can reconstruct in memory and on demand any data from failed disks

RAID 10

- Uses RAID level 1, and then 0
- Uses disk mirroring followed by striping
- Provides fault tolerance *and* performance
- Requires at least four disks
- Stripes data across mirrored pairs
- Tolerates multiple disk failures as long as they are not in the same mirrored pair
- Is useful for busy (many reads/writes) databases

EXAM TIP You will be tested in some way on your RAID knowledge. Make sure you understand how to visualize the RAID levels in terms of where data versus parity are stored, how many disks are required, and when a specific RAID level solves a problem.

Storage Device Installation

Installing storage devices begins with knowing what you have, and then progresses to knowing what you need. A rack-mounted server with an integrated SAS RAID controller may or may not accept SATA disks; it depends on the specific RAID controller. In the same way, a disk subsystem might accept only 4 disks, or it might accept 128. But after the connectivity is taken care of, disk space must be configured appropriately and file systems created.

MBR and GPT

When servers can see disk space, whether storage is DAS, NAS, or over a SAN, the next step is to make the space usable. This means initializing disks, partitioning them, and formatting those partitions with a particular file system. Disk initialization is required for server operating systems to be able to use the space, and you can choose either master boot record (MBR) or GUID Partition Table (GPT) for this. MBR and GPT are a function of the server's firmware (BIOS/UEFI) and the operating system, not the disk itself.

MBR is the old 1980s 32-bit standard for disk initialization that supports a maximum of four primary disk partitions, each being no larger than 2TB in size. Another MBR option is to create three primary partitions and one extended partition in which you can then create multiple logical drives, but this is rare these days.

GPT is a newer, 64-bit standard for initializing disk space that supports many very large partitions (the values vary depending on the operating system and file system used). Windows Server 2012 R2 will allow up to 128 partitions, each being up to 256TB in size, although theoretically the partition size could be up to 9.44 zettabytes (ZB). GTP also stores partitioning information in multiple places on the disk, which makes it much more resilient to corruption compared to MBR. Booting from a GPT-initialized disk requires UEFI (as opposed to BIOS) and, in the case of Windows Server OSs, also requires a 64-bit operating system.

Windows systems can use the diskpart.exe command line tool or the GUI Disk Management (shown next) and Server Manager tools to work with disks. Server Manager doesn't even give you the option of initializing a disk using MBR. Those using Linux systems can use the old `fdisk` command to work with MBR; the `gdisk` command is used for GPT.

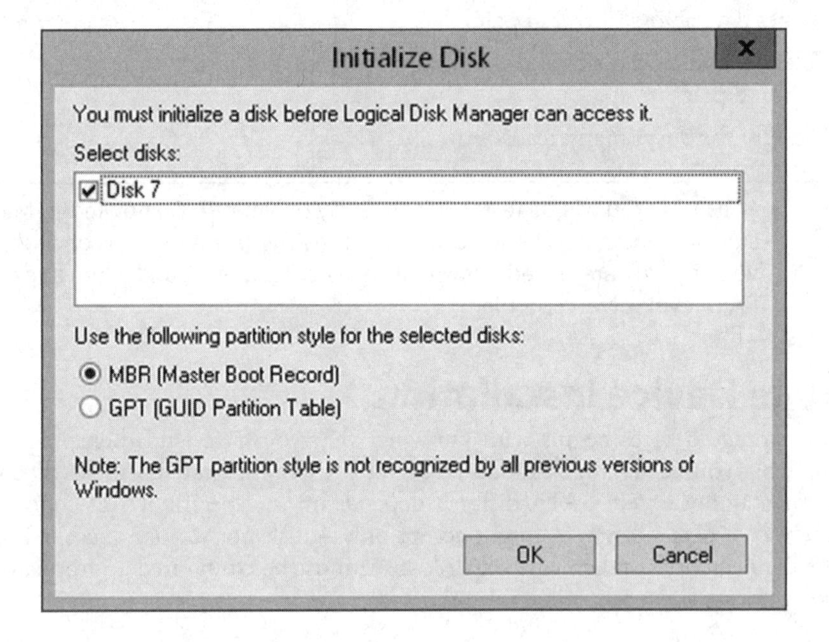

File Systems

File systems are determined when you format a disk partition. Each server OS supports various file systems—some old, some new—that can meet your requirements. For example, if you want user disk quota and file encryption support on a Windows server, you should be using NTFS.

Windows Server OSs generally support the following file systems:

- File Allocation Table (FAT)
- FAT32
- Extended FAT (exFAT)
- New Technology File System (NTFS)
- Resilient File System (ReFS)

NTFS (shown next), which supersedes FAT and FAT32, is a journaled file system that supports compression, encryption, file system security, larger file and partition sizes, and user disk quotas, to name just a few features. FAT32 and exFAT are used most commonly with removable storage such as flash drives, although you can format flash drives as NTFS.

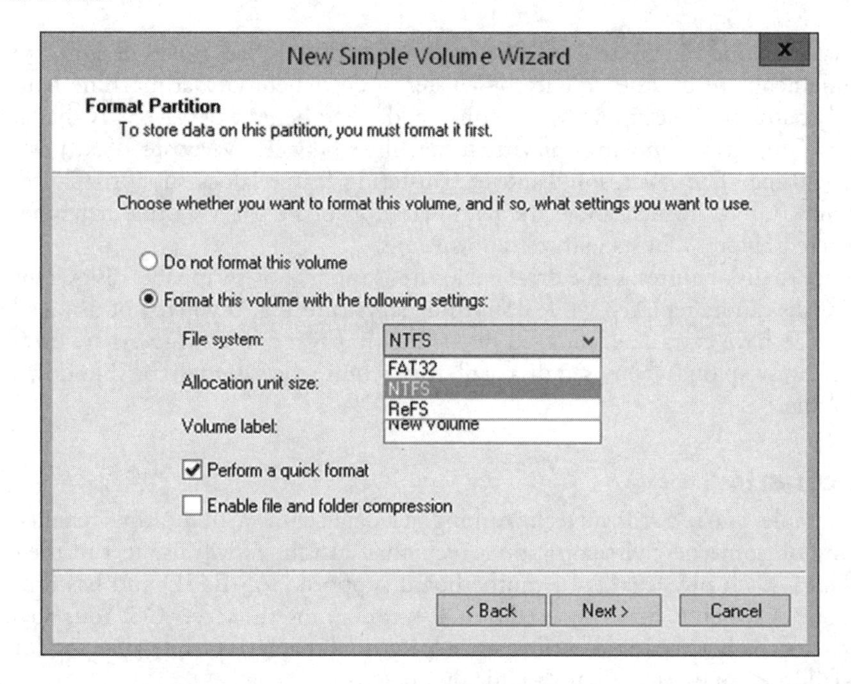

ReFS is a newer file system made available in the Windows Server 2012 R2 OS that is designed to be more resilient to file system corruption. It boasts new features including the ability to scan for and correct file system corruption while the disk volume is mounted and in use. But it has drawbacks: for example, ReFS doesn't support data deduplication or user disk quotas.

UNIX and Linux server OSs generally support the following file systems:

- UNIX File System (UFS)
- Zettabyte File System (ZFS)

- Extended File System (EXT2, 3, 4)
- ReiserFS

EXT4 and ReiserFS are common in today's Linux environments, although development support for ReiserFS appears to be waning. Both of these file systems are *journaled*, which means all file system write transactions are logged before being committed to disk. This makes the file system less susceptible to corruption, which can occur with a power loss, for example.

EXAM TIP Don't confuse network file-sharing protocols with local file system types. For instance, Network File System (NFS) is a UNIX and Linux file-sharing protocol, just like Server Message Block (SMB) is a Windows file-sharing protocol. We don't format local disk volumes as NFS or SMB.

The Virtual Machine File System (VMFS) is specific to VMware. It was designed to support simultaneous read/write activity by cluster nodes where virtual machine hard disk files and snapshots (checkpoints) are concerned. One benefit of VMFS is that it enables the live migration (moving) of virtual machines between VMware ESXi hosts with zero downtime. The Microsoft Failover Clustering feature does support Cluster Shared Volumes (CSVs), which allow the live migration of Hyper-V virtual machines between clustered Hyper-V hosts with zero downtime.

For resilience to disk failures, some drive enclosures support hot-swappable disks. This means failed disks can be replaced while everything stays running. If you're not using all the disks, you can have extra ones plugged in—these are *hot spares*. *Cold spares* are extra disks that you can swap out when used disks fail; they require the system to be shut down when you do this.

Sample Scenario 1

In this first example, you're a storage tech working in a data center with multiple tenants. You're working on some new virtualization servers that customers will use to run their virtual machines. Each physical server motherboard supports SAS RAID and has four SATA ports, one of which is currently used by a disk containing the server OS. Your boss is after you to get the best possible performance for virtual machines while allowing for the possible failure of one disk. What should you do?

Given this scenario, the best solution is to acquire three fast, high capacity SATA disks and configure them using hardware RAID in a stripe set with distributed parity (RAID 5). RAID 5 needs at least three disks; RAID 6 needs four, which is not an option here. With RAID 5, you're spreading the disk I/O workload across three disks while also writing parity information in case one disk fails.

Sample Scenario 2

Your company is using a Fibre Channel SAN with multiple FC switches connected to SSD and hard disk storage arrays. A new blade server has arrived. The blade will run

Windows Server 2012 R2 Hyper-V by booting from the SAN and will host two virtual machines running customer management software. You must ensure that both virtual machines have redundant connectivity to a log file storage volume and an application database storage volume on the SAN. Log files should be stored as archives on slower disks, while database access must be as fast as possible. How should you go about this?

The first clue here is redundant SAN connectivity—this means you need a dual-port FC HBA for multiple paths to different FC switches. You will also need the correct HBA driver so that the two virtual machines can talk to the SAN directly.

Storage administrators will have to configure three LUNs in this case: one to host the Windows Server 2012 R2 OS (boot from SAN), a second LUN for log files, and a third LUN for the database. Storage tiers need to be configured so that the database and related files are available on fast SSDs, while logs are stored on hard disks.

Hands-on Exercises

Exercise 4-1: Configure a Windows Server 2012 R2 iSCSI Target

1. Make sure your Srv2012-1 virtual machine is running in VMware Workstation and that you are logged on using the Administrator account with a password of Pa$$w0rd.

Install the iSCSI target software from PowerShell

2. Click the Windows Start menu and enter **powershell**. When it shows up in the search results, press ENTER.
3. Enter `install-windowsfeature fs-iscsitarget-server`. After a few moments, the software is installed. You can ignore the warning about automatic updating.
4. Enter `get-windowsfeature *isci*`. The asterisks are wildcards that will show features containing the text iSCSI. Notice there is an X in the box, which implies that the software has indeed been installed.

Configure iSCSI storage on the target

5. Start Server Manager (second icon from the left in the taskbar).
6. In the navigator on the left, click File And Storage Services, and then click Disks. You will create a dedicated storage volume for iSCSI virtual disks.
7. Right-click the first listed Offline disk and choose Bring Online. Click Yes.
8. Right-click the same disk again and choose New Volume. Click Next multiple times to accept the wizard defaults. When prompted that the selected disk will be brought online and initialized as a GPT disk, click OK.
9. In the Specify The Size Of The Volume Windows, for the volume size, enter **30GB**. Click Next.

10. Select drive letter I (for iSCSI) and click Next.
11. Enter a volume label of **iSCSI Virtual Disks** and click Next.
12. On the summary screen click Create, and then click Close.

Create iSCSI virtual disks for consumption over the network

13. Within Server Manager, in the navigator on the left, click iSCSI.
14. Click the Tasks button on the right and choose New iSCSI Virtual Disk.
15. Click the Browse button and navigate to drive I: to store the iSCSI virtual disks. Click Select Folder. Click Next.
16. Enter **iscsi_lun1** for the name and click Next.
17. Enter **10GB** for the size and click Next.
18. Ensure that New iSCSI Target is selected and click Next. This is where you specify which network hosts are allowed to access this iSCSI storage.
19. For the name, enter **LocalServers** and click Next.
20. Click Add. From the Type drop-down list, select IP Address.
21. In the Value field to the right, enter **192.168.1.210**. This is the IP address of your Red Hat Linux server, which will consume this storage. Click OK.
22. Click Next twice, click Create, and then click Close. Your iSCSI vdhx file is created.

Exercise 4-2: Use the Red Hat Enterprise Linux 7 iSCSI Initiator to Connect to an iSCSI Target

1. On the Windows iSCSI target server, open Server Manager and navigate to iSCSI. Select the iSCSI virtual disk, and then look under iSCSI Targets and take note of the target IQN, shown in the following illustration; you'll need this in a few steps.

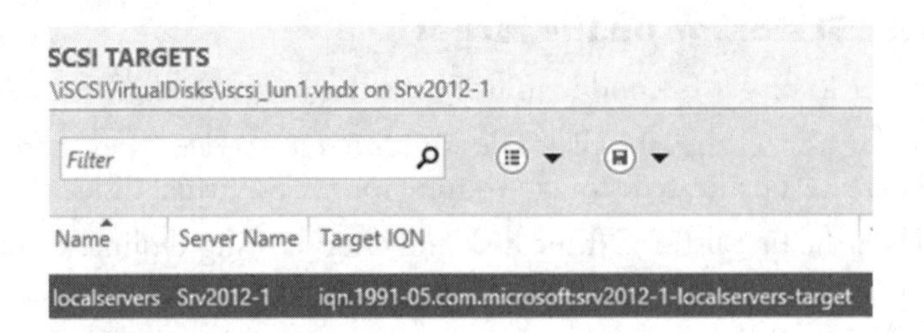

2. Make sure your RHEL7-1 virtual machine is running in VMware Workstation and that you are logged in as user root with a password of Pa$$w0rdLinux.

3. Open a terminal window. From the Applications menu in the upper left, start a new terminal session. Enter
   `iscsiadm --mode discovery --type sendtargets --portal 192.168.1.200`
4. Enter
   `iscsiadm --mode node --targetname the_IQN_noted_in_Step_1 --portal 192.168.1.200 --login`
5. Enter
   `lsblk --scsi | grep iscsi`
6. Notice (from step 5) the connected iSCSI disk and the name of it (for this example, we will assume the name is sdd).
7. Enter **`fdisk /dev/sdd`** and press ENTER.
8. Press N (for new partition) and then press ENTER, and keep pressing ENTER to accept the defaults to use the entire disk for this primary partition.
9. Press W (for write) to save the changes to disk.
10. To format the new partition, enter **`mkfs /dev/sdd1`**.
11. Create a mount point folder by entering **`mkdir /project-x`**.
12. Mount the new partition into the folder by entering **`mount /dev/sdd1 /project-x`**.
13. Verify the mount succeeded by entering **`mount | grep project`**.
14. Switch to the Windows Server iSCSI target, and in the Server Manager iSCSI view, click Tasks, Refresh. Notice the Virtual Disk Status column now shows Connected. Also notice the Initiator ID shows the Linux host IP address. The Linux host is now consuming the disk space over the network.

Exercise 4-3: Configure Software RAID Using Windows Server 2012 R2

This exercise demonstrates how two disk volumes can be thinly provisioned to use all available space in the storage pool.

1. Make sure your Srv2012-1 virtual machine is running in VMware Workstation and that you are logged on using the Administrator account with a password of Pa$$w0rd.
2. Start the Server Manager GUI tool (second icon from the left in the taskbar).
3. In the left-hand navigator, click File And Storage Services, and then click Storage Pools. You will see Primordial listed. Click Primordial and look at the Physical Disks (bottom right). We will create a new storage pool from these disks.
4. In the upper right, click Tasks, New Storage Pool and then click Next.

5. Enter the name of the storage pool, SwRaid, and click Next.
6. Click the checkbox for each of the three listed 60GB SAS disks. Click Next, then Create, and then Close. The new SwRaid storage pool is listed instead of Primordial.
7. Right-click the SwRaid storage pool and choose New Virtual Disk. Note that "virtual disk" in this context has nothing to do with virtualization. Click Next twice.
8. Enter the name of the new virtual disk, Vdisk1, and click Next.
9. On the Select The Storage Layout screen, ensure that Simple is selected to configure disk striping across the three disks. Then click Next.
10. For the Provisioning Type, choose Thin and click Next.
11. Enter 145GB as the size and click Next. Then click Create and Close.
12. The New Volume wizard will automatically be displayed. Click Next five times to accept the defaults. On the Confirm Selections screen, take note of the drive letter for the new disk volume. Click Create and then Close.
13. In the left hand navigator, click Volumes. On the right, notice the new drive letter (for example, E:).
14. Start Windows Explorer and notice the new drive letter for your new striped volume.
15. Back in Server Manager, make sure you are back under File And Storage Services on the left and that you've clicked Storage Pools. Repeat steps 7–14 in this exercise, except enter **Vdisk2** for the name of the virtual disk.

Exercise 4-4: Configure Software RAID Using Red Hat Enterprise Linux 7

1. Make sure your RHEL7-1 virtual machine is running in VMware Workstation and that you are logged in as user root with a password of Pa$$w0rdLinux. If you choose to log in to Linux with a regular (nonroot) user account, you'll have to precede the command instructions in this lab with `sudo` followed by a space. This will run the commands with elevated privileges.
2. Open a terminal command prompt (choose Applications | Utilities | Terminal).
3. Enter **`lsblk --scsi`** to list SCSI disk block devices. You should see sda, sdb, and sdc. These are three separate disks. We will create a disk mirror between sdb and sdc.
4. Enter **`fdisk /dev/sdb`** and press ENTER. Press N (new partition), and then press ENTER four times to create a primary partition that consumes the entire disk.
5. Press T to change the partition type, and then enter **`fd`** to set the type to Linux raid autodetect.

6. Press W to write the changes to disk.
7. Repeat steps 4–6 in this exercise, except enter **`fdisk`** with **`/dev/sdc`** instead of /dev/sdb.
8. Enter **`fdisk -l /dev/sdb /dev/sdc`** to verify that the Linux RAID autodetect partition flag has been set on both disk partitions. Notice the partitions are /dev/sdb1 and /dev/sdc1.
9. Create a software RAID 1 (mirroring) configuration:
   `mdm --create /dev/md1 -level=1 --raid-devices=2 /dev/sdb1 /dev/sdc1`
10. Press Y (for yes, to continue creating the array).
11. Verify your work: **`mdadm --detail /dev/md1`**
12. Make a useable file system on the mirrored array: **`mkfs -t ext4 /dev/md1`**
13. Make a mount directory: **`mkdir /cust_trans`**
14. Mount the file system to a directory so it is ready to use:
    `mount /dev/md1 /cust_trans`

Exercise 4-5: Monitor Disk Space Using File Server Resource Manager

1. Make sure your Srv2012-1 virtual machine is running in VMware Workstation and that you are logged on using the Administrator account with a password of Pa$$w0rd.
2. From the taskbar, start PowerShell; this is the second icon to the right of the Start button.
3. Enter
   `install-windowsfeature fs-resource-manager -includemanagementtools`
4. Click the Start button, type **file**, and wait a moment. When File Server Resource Manager is displayed, click it.
5. In the left-hand navigator, right-click Storage Reports Management and choose Generate Reports Now. Notice you can also schedule reports.
6. In the Select Reports To Generate list, scroll down and choose Large Files.
7. Click the Edit Parameters button, and in the Minimum File Size field type **25**. Then click OK.
8. Click the Scope tab. Then click the Add button and scroll down and choose Local Disk (C:). Click OK.
9. Choose Wait For Reports To Be Generated And Then Display Them and click OK.

10. This will open a Windows Explorer window with your HTML report. Double-click the Large Files HTML report and review the data.

Exercise 4-6: Set a Disk Quota Using File Server Resource Manager

1. Make sure your Srv2012-1 virtual machine is running in VMware Workstation and that you are logged on using the Administrator account with a password of Pa$$w0rd.
2. Using Windows Explorer, create a folder called Projects on the root of any drive letter other than C:.
3. Click the Start button, type **file**, and wait a moment. When File Server Resource Manager is displayed, click it.
4. In the left-hand navigator, expand Quota Management by clicking the triangle icon.
5. Left-click Quotas in the left navigator, and then right-click Quotas and choose Create Quota.
6. For the Quota Path, enter any local drive letter other than C:, followed by **Projects**, for example, **E:\Projects**.
7. Under How Do You Want To Configure Quota Properties?, choose Define Custom Quota Properties. Click the Custom Properties button.
8. Set the limit to 200MB and ensure that it is configured as a Hard quota.
9. Click OK, then Create, and then choose Save The Custom Quota Without Creating A Template and click OK.
10. Copy C:\Windows\Fonts to the Projects folder. Once the limit of 200MB is exceeded, you will get a message stating that there isn't enough free space. Click Cancel.

Exercise 4-7: Retrieve Disk Information Using PowerShell

1. Make sure your Srv2012-1 virtual machine is running in VMware Workstation and that you are logged on using the Administrator account with a password of Pa$$w0rd.
2. From the taskbar, start PowerShell.
3. Enter `get-physicaldisk > c:\diskinfo.txt` and press ENTER. This writes a list of physical disks and related information into a text file called diskinfo.txt.
4. Enter `get-volume >> c:\diskinfo.txt` and press ENTER. This appends disk volume info to the existing diskinfo.txt file.
5. Enter `notepad c:\diskinfo.txt` and press ENTER to view the results. Close Notepad.

Chapter Review

Server storage is a crucial part of server planning, including potential future disk space requirements. This is especially true for data center administrators, because consumers expect storage to be available when they decide to provision more space.

Storage Device Characteristics

Characteristics such as RPMs, seek time, rotational latency, bus width, and IOPS all contribute to the overall transfer rate of data into and out of hard disks.

Hard disks consist of read and write heads on mechanical arms that move over the spinning platters. Solid-state drives (including flash drives) have no moving parts; everything is electronic. SSDs generally perform faster but are more expensive than hard disks.

Disk Interfaces

Disk interfaces include

- SAS (common in servers)
- SATA
- SCSI
- USB
- Fibre Channel (used in SANs)

Local and Network Storage

DAS storage is available locally to a server without using a network. NAS uses file-sharing protocols such as SMB and NFS to make network storage available. SANs use specific disk block I/O protocols for high-speed access to network storage. SAN-specific equipment includes FC HBAs in each server, FC switches, and storage arrays. LUNs represent disk space available over the network. Techniques such as LUN masking and zoning are used to restrict server access to specific LUNs.

iSCSI enables storage consumption by hosts over a standard TCP/IP network. iSCSI initiators connect to iSCSI targets either on the same or a different subnet. iSCSI traffic should be kept separate from other TCP/IP traffic by configuring a dedicated iSCSI VLAN.

FCoE incurs less overhead than iSCSI because it packages disk I/O commands directly into Ethernet frames instead of higher level IP packets. CNAs and FCoE switches are required, but fiber-optic cabling is not; copper-based cables will also work.

Storage Capacity Planning

Planning for future storage capacity can be measured using base 2 or base 10. Base 2 is more specific (binary) and more closely reflects actual required disk space. Compression, data deduplication, disk quotas, and thin provisioning are options for optimizing disk space use.

RAID

RAID treats multiple physical disks as a group. The operating system sees only one logical disk. RAID is used to squeeze more disk I/O performance (multiple disks reading and writing instead of just one) and to provide fault tolerance (disks that will fail).

- **RAID 0** Disk striping
- **RAID 1** Disk mirroring
- **RAID 5** Disk striping with distributed parity
- **RAID 6** Disk striping with dual distributed parity
- **RAID 10** Combines RAID 1 with RAID 0

Disk Initialization and File Systems

MBR and GPT do not refer to a type of hard disk; disks are initialized in an operating system as either MBR or GPT. MBR allows a maximum of four partitions each with a maximum potential size of 2TB. GPT limits are imposed by specific operating systems; Windows Servers allow up to 128 GPT partitions, each being 256TB in size. Booting from GPT requires UEFI.

After disk initialization and partitioning, file systems are created. Windows servers typically use NTFS, where Linux servers vary: Ext3, Ext4, and ReiserFS are common. VMFS is a file system specific to VMware hosts that enables concurrent reading and writing to a disk volume by multiple cluster nodes, similar to Microsoft CSV.

Questions

1. A new 4TB drive is added to a server. You notice that the server operating system can use only 2TB. What is the most likely cause of the problem?

   A. The drive was initialized as GPT.

   B. The drive was initialized as MBR.

   C. The operating system has not been updated.

   D. Compression is enabled.

2. What hard disk dimension is considered the standard?

   A. 1.75-inch

   B. 3-inch

   C. 5.5-inch

   D. 3.5-inch

3. Which disk speed factor does *not* apply to SSDs?
   A. IOPS
   B. Capacity
   C. Rotational latency
   D. Transfer rate

4. Which disk interface standard is the most common in servers?
   A. SAS
   B. IDE
   C. SATA
   D. EIDE

5. Your server environment requires the ability to replace a failed disk while systems remain running. What type of disk system must you use?
   A. Hot-swappable
   B. UEFI
   C. Drive-swappable
   D. RAID

6. Identify the Windows supported file systems. Choose two.
   A. eFAT
   B. ReFS
   C. XFS
   D. NTFS

7. How does a SAN differ from NAS?
   A. There is no difference.
   B. SANs use IP and NAS does not.
   C. SANs are local server storage and NAS is not.
   D. SANs use specific block I/O protocols and NAS uses standard file-sharing protocols.

8. One of your locations is using iSCSI for server network storage. You want to ensure that regular TCP/IP traffic does not impede iSCSI performance. What should you do?
   - **A.** Use a separate VLAN for iSCSI.
   - **B.** Configure LUN masking.
   - **C.** Configure LUN zoning.
   - **D.** Enable iSCSI CHAP authentication.

9. Which statement regarding software iSCSI initiators is true?
   - **A.** Targets are accessible only through FC switches.
   - **B.** They do not support OS booting from SAN.
   - **C.** IPv6 must be configured.
   - **D.** iSCSI targets must reside on the same subnet with iSCSI initiators.

10. Your boss has asked you to determine what equipment must be ordered to set up a new FCoE environment. Which FCoE item is required?
    - **A.** NAS device
    - **B.** CNA
    - **C.** UEFI
    - **D.** RAID controller

11. You are a Linux server administrator. To plan future disk space requirements, you would like to track user disk space consumption. What should you configure?
    - **A.** Hard quotas
    - **B.** GPT
    - **C.** NTFS
    - **D.** Soft quotas

12. As you configure three new server disk volumes, you are unsure as to how large each volume should be. What should you configure?
    - **A.** Thin provisioning
    - **B.** Thick provisioning
    - **C.** RAID 0
    - **D.** RAID 1

13. Which RAID level offers the best performance?

A. RAID 0

B. RAID 1

C. RAID 2

D. RAID 3

14. Which type of storage would be considered Tier 2 storage?

A. SCSI

B. IDE

C. SSD

D. HDD

15. Which type of storage combines disk platters with flash memory?

A. SSHD

B. SSD

C. HHDD

D. HDD

16. In an attempt to save disk space, Sean wants to store multiple Windows Server 2012 images in a single .WIM file. Which command should Sean use?

A. `Dism /Append-Image /File:Z:\win10_images.wim /CaptureDir:C:\ /Name:win10_sales`

B. `Dism /Add-Image /ImageFile:Z:\win10_images.wim /CaptureDir:C:\ /Name:win10_sales`

C. `Dism /Append-Image /ImageFile:Z:\win10_images.wim /CreateFrom:C:\ /Name:win10_sales`

D. `Dism /Append-Image /ImageFile:Z:\win10_images.wim /CaptureDir:C:\ /Name:win10_sales`

17. You are planning the use of a new 8TB HDD. Six disk partitions are required for varying file storage uses. How should you initialize the disk?

A. GPT

B. MBR

C. RDP

D. TCP

18. Which features do NTFS file systems offer beyond FAT32 file systems? Choose two.
    - **A.** Encryption
    - **B.** Auditing
    - **C.** Imaging
    - **D.** PXE

19. What benefit does VMFS offer over NTFS?
    - **A.** Encryption
    - **B.** Simultaneous journaling from multiple nodes
    - **C.** Auditing
    - **D.** Simultaneous read/write from multiple nodes

20. Your server requires storage that will be supplied over the network. What must the storage administrator configure for your server?
    - **A.** NTFS
    - **B.** VMFS
    - **C.** DAS
    - **D.** LUN

Questions and Answers

1. A new 4TB drive is added to a server. You notice that the server operating system can use only 2TB. What is the most likely cause of the problem?
    - **A.** The drive was initialized as GPT.
    - **B.** The drive was initialized as MBR.
    - **C.** The operating system has not been updated.
    - **D.** Compression is enabled.

    B. MBR-initialized disks have a maximum partition size of 2TB. A, C, and D are incorrect. GPT partitions are not limited to 2TB. Operating system updates do not determine partition size. Compression of the file system would not cause only 2 of 4TB to be available.

2. What hard disk dimension is considered the standard?

A. 1.75-inch

B. 3-inch

C. 5.5-inch

D. 3.5-inch

D. Most hard disk platters have either a 2.5- or 3.5-inch diameter. A, B, and C are incorrect. 1.75-, 3-, and 5.5-inch are not standard hard disk dimensions.

3. Which disk speed factor does *not* apply to SSDs?

A. IOPS

B. Capacity

C. Rotational latency

D. Transfer rate

C. Rotational latency is related to the amount of time it takes for hard disk platters to spin to the correct position; SSDs do not have spinning platters. A, B, and D are incorrect. IOPS is the number of disk I/O functions that can be performed within 1 second. Capacity is the size of the drive. The transfer rate is a measurement of how quickly data can move into and out of a storage device.

4. Which disk interface standard is the most common in servers?

A. SAS

B. IDE

C. SATA

D. EIDE

A. SAS disks are designed to work 24/7 at high speeds and thus are well suited for servers. B, C, and D are incorrect. IDE and its successor EIDE are deprecated disk interface standards. SATA is commonly used in desktops and servers, but SAS is more common on the server side.

5. Your server environment requires the ability to replace a failed disk while systems remain running. What type of disk system must you use?

A. Hot-swappable

B. UEFI

C. Drive-swappable

D. RAID

A. Hot-swappable components can be replaced while a system is running. B, C, and D are incorrect. UEFI is a firmware standard that succeeds BIOS. Drive-swappable is a fictitious term. RAID organizes multiple physical disks to work together for fault tolerance and/or performance reasons.

6. Identify the Windows supported file systems. Choose two.
   - **A.** eFAT
   - **B.** ReFS
   - **C.** XFS
   - **D.** NTFS

   B, D. The ReFS file system was introduced with Windows Server 2012 R2 and reduces the amount of file system corruption problems. NTFS is the most common Windows Server file system type; it is a journaled file system that supports additional features such as encryption, file security, compression, and disk quotas. A and C are incorrect. eFAT is a fictitious term. XFS is a file system used by SGI IRIX operating system and some flavors of Linux.

7. How does a SAN differ from NAS?
   - **A.** There is no difference.
   - **B.** SANs use IP and NAS does not.
   - **C.** SANs are local server storage and NAS is not.
   - **D.** SANs use specific block I/O protocols and NAS uses standard file-sharing protocols.

   D. SANs do not use IP or file-sharing protocols; instead, they use block I/O protocols such as Fibre Channel. A, B, and C are incorrect. SANs and NAS are not the same. NAS uses standard file-sharing protocols such as SMB and NFS. SAN solutions do not use IP and they are not considered local storage; instead, they are considered network storage.

8. One of your locations is using iSCSI for server network storage. You want to ensure that regular TCP/IP traffic does not impede iSCSI performance. What should you do?
   - **A.** Use a separate VLAN for iSCSI.
   - **B.** Configure LUN masking.
   - **C.** Configure LUN zoning.
   - **D.** Enable iSCSI CHAP authentication.

   A. VLANs can be used to isolate one type of network traffic from another for performance reasons. Placing iSCSI traffic on its own VLAN accomplishes this. B, C, and D are incorrect. LUN masking and zoning are used to control host access to network storage. iSCSI CHAP is indeed used for authenticating initiators to targets, but it is not related to improving network performance.

9. Which statement regarding software iSCSI initiators is true?

   A. Targets are accessible only through FC switches.

   B. They do not support OS booting from SAN.

   C. IPv6 must be configured.

   D. iSCSI targets must reside on the same subnet with iSCSI initiators.

   B. Software iSCSI initiators can be used only when the operating system is already running; therefore, SAN booting using this solution is not possible. A, C, and D are incorrect. iSCSI does not require FC switches; standard Ethernet equipment works just fine. IPv6 is not required for iSCSI; IPv4 works well. Initiators and targets do not have to reside on the same subnet.

10. Your boss has asked you to determine what equipment must be ordered to set up a new FCoE environment. Which FCoE item is required?

    A. NAS device

    B. CNA

    C. UEFI

    D. RAID controller

    B. CNAs combine FCoE and NIC functionality; each host needing access to network storage requires a CNA. A, C, and D are incorrect. NAS devices provide access to network storage using file-sharing protocols such as NFS and SMB; this is not required with FCoE. UEFI is a firmware standard that succeeds BIOS. RAID controllers can group multiple physical disks together for fault tolerance and/or performance reasons, but this is not FCoE-specific equipment.

11. You are a Linux server administrator. To plan future disk space requirements, you would like to track user disk space consumption. What should you configure?

    A. Hard quotas

    B. GPT

    C. NTFS

    D. Soft quotas

    D. Soft quotas can log the fact that disk space thresholds have been exceeded. A, B, and C are incorrect. Hard quotas actually prevent additional files from being stored on a server once the quota is reached, so they aren't as useful as soft quotas for tracking purposes. GPT is a newer disk partitioning scheme that supersedes MBR and allows for a larger number and capacity for partitions. NTFS is a common Windows file system standard that supports features such as file encryption, compression, auditing, and disk quotas.

12. As you configure three new server disk volumes, you are unsure as to how large each volume should be. What should you configure?

A. Thin provisioning

B. Thick provisioning

C. RAID 0

D. RAID 1

A. Thin provisioning enables administrators to set a disk volume to grow to a maximum size if required, but the space is not allocated in its entirety, thereby allowing other thinly provisioned disk volumes to consume that same space as needed. B, C, and D are incorrect. Thick provisioning allocates disk volume space immediately and therefore cannot share that space simultaneously with other disk volumes. RAID 0, disk striping, is used to improve disk I/O performance. RAID 1, disk mirroring, is used for redundancy in case one disk fails.

13. Which RAID level offers the best performance?

A. RAID 0

B. RAID 1

C. RAID 2

D. RAID 3

A. RAID 0, disk striping, groups multiple physical disks together for disk I/O. When writing data to the RAID 0 array, the data is broken into blocks (stripes), each of which is concurrently written to a physical disk in the array, thus resulting in improved performance. B, C, and D are incorrect. RAID 1, disk mirroring, is used for fault tolerance. A disk write to one disk is duplicated on another disk. When one disk fails, the other has an up-to-date copy of the data. RAID 2 stripes bits of data but still writes error recovery information. RAID 3 stripes bytes of data but still uses a dedicated parity disk for error recovery.

14. Which type of storage would be considered Tier 2 storage?

A. SCSI

B. IDE

C. SSD

D. HDD

D. Hard disk drives are considered to be Tier 2 storage. A, B, and C are incorrect. SCSI and IDE are disk interfaces that are not organized into storage tiers. SSD would be considered Tier 1 storage.

15. Which type of storage combines disk platters with flash memory?
   - **A.** SSHD
   - **B.** SSD
   - **C.** HHDD
   - **D.** HDD

A. Solid-state hybrid drives combine flash memory with disk platters. B, C, and D are incorrect. SSDs are flash memory only. HHDD is a fictitious acronym. HDDs are disk platters only.

16. In an attempt to save disk space, Sean wants to store multiple Windows Server 2012 images in a single .WIM file. Which command should Sean use?
   - **A.** `Dism /Append-Image /File:Z:\win10_images.wim /CaptureDir:C:\ /Name:win10_sales`
   - **B.** `Dism /Add-Image /ImageFile:Z:\win10_images.wim /CaptureDir:C:\ /Name:win10_sales`
   - **C.** `Dism /Append-Image /ImageFile:Z:\win10_images.wim /CreateFrom:C:\ /Name:win10_sales`
   - **D.** `Dism /Append-Image /ImageFile:Z:\win10_images.wim /CaptureDir:C:\ /Name:win10_sales`

D. The `/Append-Image` switch adds images to a single .WIM file. A, B, and C are incorrect. There is no `/File`, `/Add-Image`, or `/CreateFrom` switch for the `dism` command.

17. You are planning the use of a new 8TB HDD. Six disk partitions are required for varying file storage uses. How should you initialize the disk?
   - **A.** GPT
   - **B.** MBR
   - **C.** RDP
   - **D.** TCP

A. GPT allows more than four disk partitions. B, C, and D are incorrect. MBR allows up to a maximum of four partitions. RDP is the Remote Desktop Protocol that is used to connect to a Windows computer over a network; it is not related to storage, nor is TCP. TCP is the Transmission Control Protocol; it is a reliable connect-oriented transport protocol within the TCP/IP suite.

18. Which features do NTFS file systems offer beyond FAT32 file systems? Choose two.

A. Encryption

B. Auditing

C. Imaging

D. PXE

A, B. NTFS file systems support encryption and auditing, which are not supported with FAT32 file systems. C and D are incorrect. Imaging and PXE are not file system features. Imaging is a convenient way of deploying operating systems without performing a manual installation. PXE allows booting over the network instead of from local media and is normally used for imaging operations.

19. What benefit does VMFS offer over NTFS?

A. Encryption

B. Simultaneous journaling from multiple nodes

C. Auditing

D. Simultaneous read/write from multiple nodes

D. VMware's VMFS is designed to allow multiple cluster nodes to read and write to the same file system at the same time. A, B, and C are incorrect. Encryption and auditing are available with NTFS file systems. Simultaneous journaling is not a valid feature.

20. Your server requires storage that will be supplied over the network. What must the storage administrator configure for your server?

A. NTFS

B. VMFS

C. DAS

D. LUN

D. A logical unit number is a unit of disk space with a unique ID that is prepared by a storage administrator for use by a specific server. A, B, and C are incorrect. NTFS and VMFS are file systems that are not required for network storage. DAS refers to direct-attached, or local server, storage.

CHAPTER 5

Network Concepts

In this chapter, you will

- Learn about the OSI model
- Identify proper cable installation and management techniques
- Recognize the role of network interface cards, switches, and routers
- Learn how to configure IPv4 and IPv6 including subnetting
- Understand TCP and UDP port numbers
- Identify network infrastructure services including DHCP, DNS, and WINS

Every server technician is exposed to networking at the hardware and software levels at some point in time. You may not be the network infrastructure expert in your organization, but your servers will interface with the network infrastructure in various ways. The TCP/IP protocol suite has long been used on corporate networks as well as the Internet. As such, Server+ candidates are required to have a solid understanding of both IPv4 and IPv6.

The OSI Model

Telephony and network communications involve both hardware and software components. The Open Systems Interconnection (OSI) model is a widely accepted seven-layer approach to mapping and explaining these components. The IT industry will often refer to "Layer 3 switches," "Layer 7 firewalls," "Layer 2 addresses," and so on.

The OSI layers are not tangible or visible in any way; they are a concept, albeit an important one. Not all layers need to be involved in the transmission and receipt of data between two devices.

Here are the seven layers:

- **Layer 7** Application layer
- **Layer 6** Presentation layer
- **Layer 5** Session layer
- **Layer 4** Transport layer
- **Layer 3** Network layer
- **Layer 2** Data link layer
- **Layer 1** Physical layer

Layer	Characteristics
7—Application	• Software that may or may not involve user interaction • Operating systems can use this layer without user knowledge or consent
6—Presentation	• How data is presented • Differing character sets • Encryption and decryption
5—Session	• Session establishment, maintenance, and tear-down • Does not imply authentication • Session IDs
4—Transport	• Responsible for end-to-end data transmission • Can require acknowledgment of sent data • Port addresses (port numbers)
3—Network	• Routing of network packets • IP addresses • Routers, Layer 3 switches
2—Data link	• Methods of accessing transmission media • MAC addresses • Bridges, Layer 2 switches, network interface cards
1—Physical	• Electrical specifications • Cables, connectors • Wireless specifications • Hubs, repeaters

Table 5-1 OSI Model Layers

One way to remember the seven layers, starting from the top, is by using a mnemonic: "All People Seem To Need Data Processing." Table 5-1 explains the purpose of each layer.

Let's apply the OSI model to the action of viewing a secured web site (HTTPS) using a web browser:

1. The user enters a URL into the address line of a web browser. The application layer (7) is involved at this point.
2. Because an HTTPS connection is being used, the presentation layer (6) is involved due to encryption.
3. HTTPS traffic uses TCP as a transport mechanism. TCP establishes a session with the receiving host before transmitting data, so the session layer (5) is used here.
4. TCP is a transport layer (4) protocol. Layer 4 addresses are port addresses; HTTPS web servers normally listen for client connections on TCP port 443.

5. If the client and server are on different networks, a router gets involved. Routers are Layer 3 (the network layer) devices. IP addresses would still be involved even on the same network, and IP addresses are Layer 3 addresses.
6. On the LAN, MAC addresses (hardware addresses) are used. This applies to the data link layer (2), as does the specific mechanism for gaining access to the transmission medium.
7. Finally, the physical layer (1) is involved whether a wired or wireless connection is used for connectivity.
8. The same type of activity takes place on the other end of the connection, but instead it moves up the layers of the OSI model.

Cable Installation and Management

Wireless networking in the form of cellular 3G, 4G, and Wi-Fi communications has exploded in popularity for user devices. But for servers and infrastructure equipment in the enterprise, data center, and server room, wired networking is required and ubiquitous. Many organizations use a hybrid of both wired and wireless communications, and these apply to the physical layer (1) of the OSI model.

Cable Placement

Large server rooms and data centers use racks to mount equipment—but what about all the power and data cables? Power cables for equipment are normally located in the back of the rack, as are network cables for servers, storage arrays, KVM switches, and the like. Cable management arms can be used to organize cables for rack-mounted devices. As the rack-mounted device is slid out on a rail, the arm containing the cables expands, so we don't have to worry about cables being pulled tight.

In the case of rack-mounted network switches and similar equipment, network cables are plugged into ports on the front of the equipment. Either way, we need an organized way to channel these bundles of cables both horizontally and vertically using cable management trays or channels built into the rack.

Plastic cable ties and hook-and-loop fasteners can be used to keep bundles of network cables together. These bundles are fed into cable channels, which can be built into racks or added to existing racks. The cable channels can also extend from racks to other locations in the server room or data center as required.

NOTE Cable channel placement, especially near ceilings, must be carefully planned. We don't want thick bundles of cables and cable trays hampering the effectiveness of fire suppression systems or airflow mechanisms.

Cable Labeling

Most people like spaghetti, but not in server rooms. Dealing with bundles of unlabeled knots of network cables is not so great; check out Figure 5-1 to see what I mean. Have

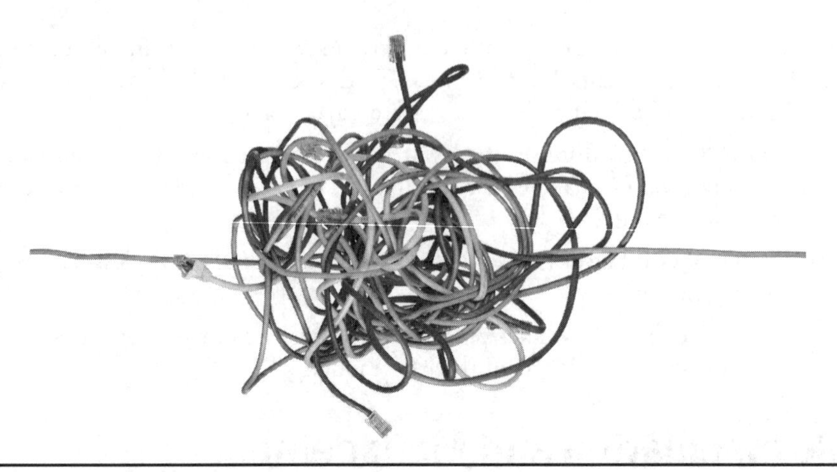

Figure 5-1 A mess of network cables

you ever had to trace network cables in a server room or wiring closet? It can go one of two ways:

- A good experience due to labeling and proper cable management
- A frustrating experience due to a snake pit of tangled cables

Network wall jacks, as well as the other end of the cable on the patch panel in the server room or wiring closet, need to be correctly labeled. From the patch panel, we use shorter network cables that get plugged into network equipment such as Ethernet switch ports. These patch cables also must be correctly labeled.

You must establish and follow a labeling standard. Using things such as IP addresses or computer names for labeling isn't a great idea, because they are both easily changed. You might use a wall-jack labeling scheme, or a location-based scheme (Floor 9, Room 2, Jack 1 might become f9r2j1). Or you might simply use incrementing numbers (jack1, jack2, jack3, and so on). Printing these values on small stickers or cable labels makes your life much easier when you're tracing cables and troubleshooting. Color-coded cables can also help. For example, cables plugged into infrastructure equipment such as switches and routers might all be colored orange.

Cable Types

There are many different types of network cables, but regardless of your choice, cables must be properly organized and labeled. When routing cables around corners, make sure you don't exceed the cable bend radius, which determines the degree to which you can bend a cable without damaging the wires inside it. For example, for CAT5 and CAT6 network cables, the bend radius is four times the diameter of the cable—this works out to be about 1 inch. Fiber-optic cables, on the other hand, have a bend radius of about 2 inches.

Several questions need to be addressed to determine cable selection criteria, including the following:

- What type of connectors does our equipment support?
- Over what distance must the transmission travel?
- Could electromagnetic interference (EMI) resistance be a problem?
- Can eavesdropping be a problem for cable transmissions?

Copper Cables

Copper cables contain copper wires that transmit electrical signals. Shielded twisted pair (STP) and unshielded twisted pair (UTP) cables contain eight copper wires grouped into four pairs. Each pair of wires is twisted at a specific rate to reduce crosstalk interference from adjacent wires. The higher the transmission rate (higher frequencies), the greater the number of twists per inch. A UTP cable is shown in Figure 5-2.

NOTE Network cables alone do not determine how quickly data is transmitted. Other factors, including network card and switch port configuration, as well as distance covered, greatly influence network speeds.

Figure 5-2
UTP cable with RJ-45 connector

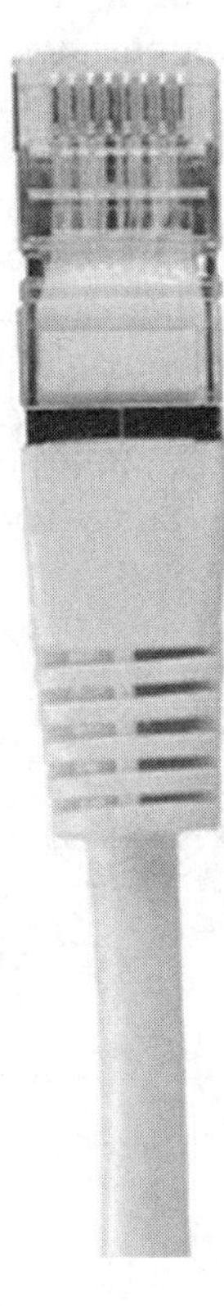

STP cables have a shielding layer that sends interfering electronic signals to a ground wire that protects signals being transmitted within the cable. UTP does not have a shielding layer so it is more susceptible to EMI produced from objects such as machinery in a manufacturing plant.

Copper Cable Connectors RJ-11 connectors are used for standard four-wire telephone cables. RJ-45 connectors are used for UTP and STP cables. These connectors are plastic with tiny metal plates that connect to the copper wires in the cable, thus allowing for electrical conductivity when plugged into an RJ-11 or RJ-45 socket. RJ-45 connectors are shown in Figure 5-3.

Modern office phone systems use the Voice over Internet Protocol (VoIP), where each phone is a node on the network with a unique IP address. Older office phone systems used private branch exchange (PBX) devices (or virtual machine appliances).

A PBX is used essentially as an internal office phone system, for which you can configure extension numbers (the office would need only a single telephone number), hold music, voicemail settings, call forwarding, and a full complement of telephony options. Back in the day, RJ-11 connectors linked office phones to the PBX.

Common Copper Cable Uses When the eight copper wires in a network cable are in the same position at both ends (the pin 1 wire on one end corresponds to pin 1 on the other end of the cable), we have a *straight-through cable*. This is the most common type of copper-based network cable; we use it to plug stations into network wall jacks, to connect patch panel connections to switch ports, and to interconnect network infrastructure equipment such as switches.

Crossover cables reverse the receive and transmit wires on each end of the cable. We can use this to plug stations directly into each other without a switch, or, if required, we can use these to link equipment together such as switches. Most modern network switches don't require crossover cables; they can automatically detect whether a straight-through cable is being used and properly match the other end of the link. Crossover cables are often red, or they have red connector covers.

Rollover cables are used for administrators to connect locally to network equipment such as the console port on a router. These are easy to identify; the cable is flat and is normally light blue in color.

Figure 5-3
RJ-45 connectors

CAT5, CAT5e, CAT6 Copper cable categories are distinguished from one another by the transmission speeds they can accommodate at higher frequencies. This is accomplished by increasing the number of twists per inch for each wire pair. So the CAT5 network cable standard has more twists per inch than a CAT3 cable, which means CAT5 can transmit data at a much higher rate than CAT3. Remember that network cards and network equipment also factor into transmission speeds.

Copper network cables generally have a maximum transmission distance of 100 meters (328 feet), after which the signal degrades significantly. (You can multiply meters by 3 to get an approximation of the distance in feet.) Repeaters can be placed at every 100 meters to extend the distance of the network. A network switch or router can be used as a repeater. Table 5-2 shows the differences between copper cable types. Unless otherwise stated, it is understood that 100 meters is the maximum distance.

EXAM TIP Newer copper cable standards will work with older network equipment. This is useful when you're upgrading cabling before upgrading equipment. The only issue is whether or not the existing equipment can transmit or receive at the rated speeds for the cable standard.

Fiber-optic Cables

Fiber-optic cables transmit light instead of electrical signals, so they are not susceptible at all to EMI. We need special network cards and equipment to transmit and receive data over fiber-optic.

Cable Standard	Maximum Transmission Rate	Frequency
CAT5 • Also called 100BASE-T or Fast Ethernet	10 or 100 Mbps	100 MHz
CAT5e • Gigabit Ethernet • Also called 1000BASE-T	1000 Mbps (1Gbps)	100 MHz
CAT6 • More resistant to interference • Also called 1000BASE-TX or 10GBASE-T (55m only)	1 Gbps (100m) or 10 Gbps (55m)	250 MHz
CAT6a • More expensive than CAT6	10 Gbps	500 MHz
CAT7 • Individual wire pair shielding • Useful in high EMI environments • Also called 10GBASE-T • Cables are larger and heavier	10 Gbps at 100m	600 MHz

Table 5-2 Copper Cable Categories

Contrary to popular belief, the term "fiber-optic" does not always means faster transmission rates, although many vendors market it this way, such as FibreOP for the home. Fiber-optic cables enable signals to travel longer distances than their electrical counterparts, however, since light can travel much farther than electrical signals, which can also degrade over long distances. For example, where twisted pair copper network cables generally max out at 100 meters, fiber-optic can travel hundreds of kilometers. Figure 5-4 shows a fiber-optic cable.

Each individual glass or plastic core fiber can carry different light wavelengths, which means it can carry multiple signals over different channels. This is often used on service provider backbones and requires optical multiplexer and demultiplexing equipment.

Fiber-optic offers benefits such as the following:

- Multiple channels carried in a single fiber rather than requiring many copper network cables
- Not susceptible to EMI
- Lightweight, so it works well in places such as aircraft
- No possibility of sparks, so it's good in explosive environments
- Difficult to eavesdrop (wiretap)

Fiber-optic cabling is rarely used for desktop computing environments because of its cost, but it is used for server networks and internetwork connections.

There are two general types of fiber-optic cabling: single-mode and multi-mode. *Single-mode* fiber has a smaller diameter (less than 10 micrometers) than multi-mode fiber (about 50 micrometers in diameter) and it supports greater distances, but this means that single-mode is more expensive than multi-mode. *Multi-mode* is useful for distances less than 2 kilometers (1.2 miles).

Bear in mind that a single fiber-optic cable could consist of more than one single-mode fiber core.

Figure 5-4
Fiber-optic cable with straight-tip connectors

Connector Type	Details
Straight-tip (ST)	• Spring-loaded male/female connectors • Round, elongated connector • Commonly used with multi-mode fiber
Subscriber connector, standard connector (SC)	• Snap-in connector • Somewhat square-shaped
Local connector (LC)	• Snap-in connector • Smaller than SC • Commonly used with single-mode fiber
Small form-factor pluggable (SFP)	• Modular transceiver for network connectors • Most often used with fiber-optic networks • Can be used with copper-cable networks

Table 5-3 Common Fiber-optic Cable Connectors

NOTE Imagine the great distance covered using submarine fiber-optic cables linking Halifax, Nova Scotia, to Dublin, Ireland—we're talking 12,000 kilometers, or 7400 miles! Check out www.submarinecablemap.com/ to see undersea fiber links around the planet.

Fiber-optic Connectors Just as copper cables have their specific connectors, so, too, do fiber-optic cables. Table 5-3 lists common fiber-optic connectors.

Network Hardware

It takes varying pieces of network equipment working together to result in a functioning network infrastructure. This section gets into network cards, network switches, and routers.

Network Interface Cards

Network cables have connectors that are supposed to plug into something, and one of those items is a network interface card (NIC). Most modern computers have wired NICs embedded on the motherboard; servers, including blade servers, often have multiple onboard NICs. Some blade server models allow a daughter circuit board (a NIC) to be plugged into the blade server motherboard.

You must carefully choose NICs to support your needs, which may include the following:

- Supports your network topology (Ethernet, token ring)
- Includes the correct connector sockets (RJ-45, fiber ST)
- Supports the correct speeds (1 Gbps, 10 Gbps Ethernet)

MAC Address

All network cards have a unique 48-bit hexadecimal hardware address, also called a physical address or *Media Access Control* (MAC) address. Whether we work with Bluetooth or Wi-Fi wireless NICs or a wired Ethernet or token ring NIC, they all have a MAC address, which looks something like this: 90-48-9A-11-BD-6F.

On a Windows system, you can see the MAC address for your network interface(s) by typing **`ipconfig /all`**. On Linux, type **`ifconfig`**.

The MAC address is a hardware-unique identifier used only on the local area network (LAN). So, for instance, when you connect to an Internet web server, your machine must know the web server's IP address, but it's not concerned with the web server's MAC address. You might wonder what role the MAC address then plays; in our example, your machine must know the MAC address of the router, or *default gateway*, to get traffic out of the LAN.

MAC addresses can also be used to control connections. One great example of this is MAC address filtering at the switch port level or with a wireless router; if your MAC address is not on the "allowed" list, you can't connect. However, MAC addresses can be spoofed, or forged, so don't rely solely on MAC address filters for security. MAC addresses are also called *Layer 2 addresses*.

Common NIC Features

Modern desktop and server motherboards often have integrated network cards. You can configure a series of options depending on how you plan on using the cards.

Wake-on-LAN One common NIC feature is Wake-on-LAN (WoL). WoL must also be supported by the BIOS or unified extensible firmware interface (UEFI). It allows a powered-down system to still feed enough power to the NIC so that it can be woken up remotely with a specially crafted packet. Although this can work well for desktops that you want to push updates to in the middle of the night, servers are generally left on all the time.

PXE The Preboot Execution Environment (PXE) NIC feature works with the BIOS or UEFI boot sequence to allow network boot. This means that instead of starting an operating system from a local disk, a small operating system image gets pulled across the network from a PXE boot server to local RAM. PXE boot works best with Dynamic Host Configuration Protocol (DHCP) to assign IP settings dynamically to PXE boot clients, and this is common as a server network imaging solution.

Duplexing Depending on your NIC and its operating system driver, you might also have the option of configuring half-, full-, or automatic-duplex settings. Full-duplex allows receiving and transmitting at the same time, while half-duplex allows either transmitting or receiving at one time, but not both. This is also a function of the switch port the NIC is plugged into. As its name implies, the automatic setting senses the speed when talking to the switch port.

If you connect a device configured for full-duplex with a device configured with half-duplex, you'll end up with degraded network performance—if they can communicate at all. This is why the auto-configuration option is recommended for this setting.

NIC Teaming *NIC teaming* is used to group multiple NICs together, similar to grouping multiple disks together in a RAID array. A NIC team can be used to aggregate the bandwidth of multiple NICs together for better performance, or it can be used for communications redundancy in case one NIC fails. You might encounter vendor terms such as "NIC bonding" or "NIC balancing"; it all falls under the same umbrella.

NIC teaming can be a function of a server operating system (such as Windows Server 2012 R2) and/or the network switch. NIC teaming configuration on the Windows platform is shown in Figure 5-5. If you were to configure NIC teaming for bandwidth aggregation in an operating system, network traffic leaving the server could take advantage of this feature, but not inbound traffic (how would the sending station or switch know about the NIC teaming?). You may have to involve your switch administrator to configure switch port aggregation for the switch ports your server NICs are plugged into.

Network Switches

For wired networks, most modern network equipment uses twisted pair cabling to plug devices into wall jacks, which in turn use short patch cables to plug into switch ports back in a wiring closet or server room.

Figure 5-5 Adding NICs to a NIC team using Windows Server 2012 R2

For very small networks, a 4-port switch might do the trick. In larger networks, multiple 24-port switches might be linked together to accommodate large numbers of devices. With most modern switches, a standard twisted pair straight-through cable can be used to link switches together, although you may come across some that require a cross-over cable (receive and transmit wires are reversed on either end of the cable). Higher end switches will use fiber-optic cabling to link together, or trunk, switches.

VLANs

By default, all physical switch ports are configured within the same virtual local area network (VLAN). A VLAN is a way of grouping devices together so that they can talk as if they were on the same physical LAN. A router is needed for devices on different VLANs to communicate. Layer 3 switches have built-in routing capabilities, so it's convenient to configure inter-VLAN routing using a single device.

A VLAN might simply group physical switch ports together. For example, switch ports 1–12 might be called VLAN1 and switch ports 13–24 might be called VLAN2. Even though all ports are physically on the same switch, without a router, a device on VLAN1 will not be able to communicate with a device on VLAN2.

Another way to create a VLAN is by having the switch examine the IP address of the device plugged into the port. For example, regardless of physical port, devices plugged into the switch with a network prefix of 172.16.0.0 would be considered to be on the same VLAN, so they can talk to each other without requiring a router.

Switch administrators can also control VLAN membership by MAC address, by protocol used on the client device, and by higher level applications in use. So a device with a MAC address of 90-48-9A-11-BD-6F could be configured to be in VLAN1. Devices using FTP could be grouped together into their own VLAN.

Network people normally configure VLANs to improve network efficiency. Having a number of devices that talk frequently on their own small network instead of everybody on a large network makes sense. Creating a VLAN creates a new broadcast domain. Broadcasts are network transmissions addressed to all devices on the network; they don't cross VLANs, so multiple VLANs can reduce traffic overall.

Another primary reason for multiple VLANs is security; accounting devices might be placed on a separate VLAN from the rest of the network, for example.

Layer 2 and Layer 3 Switches

Most switches are Layer 2 devices because they work with MAC addresses. Higher end switches will have IP routing capabilities and are Layer 3 switches.

A switch has its own memory where it tracks which device MAC addresses are plugged into its ports. This is done so that, instead of broadcasting transmissions to every port (like a hub does) to find a specific MAC address, it simply consults its MAC address table in memory. This reduces network chatter and essentially creates a collision domain for each switch port. Why does this matter? Unlike a hub, switches allow multiple concurrent network conversations.

The cheapest, least functional switches are not manageable. This means you supply power to the switch, plug devices into the switch ports, and that's it—you can't configure

Figure 5-6 A UTP cable plugged into an Ethernet switch port

it any further, and you certainly can't connect to it over the network for management purposes. Figure 5-6 shows a UTP cable with RJ-45 connector plugged into a switch port. Most enterprises use managed switches that are assigned a valid IP configuration so that various remote management tools such as web browsers and SSH can be used by administrators to connect remotely over the network.

The following list includes common items you might configure on a switch:

- Port duplex mode and speed
- VLANs
- Disabled (unused) switch ports
- TCP/IP settings (for managed switches)
- Port aggregation (for NIC teaming)
- Port multicast support

Routers

Routers have at least two interfaces that interconnect networks. A large company might use dozens of routers to interconnect its internal networks. The Internet consists of thousands of interconnected routers (many more than this if you count personal wireless routers that many homes tend to use).

A router has memory that stores routing tables. Routers use routing protocols such as Routing Information Protocol (RIP) and Open Shortest Path First (OSPF) to exchange routing information with one another.

To look up the best way to send packets to a remote network, routers consult their routing tables, which include information about other IP networks and characteristics (routing metrics) such as the route cost, how many hops (routers) the packet would have to go through before arriving at its destination, and so on.

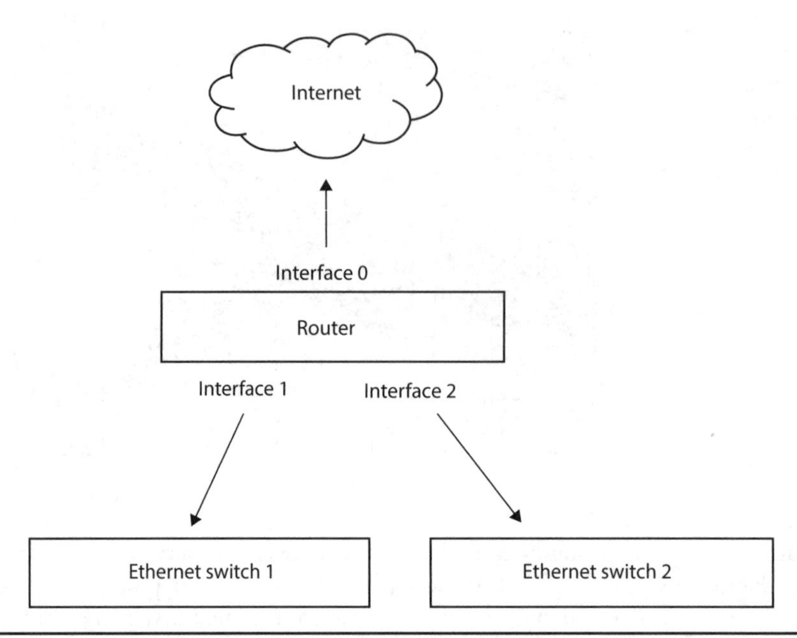

Figure 5-7 A simple network infrastructure

Because it deals with IP addresses and transferring network traffic to remote networks, a router is said to be a Layer 3 device. Remember that Layer 3 of the OSI model is the network layer.

Figure 5-7 shows a router with three interfaces. Interface 0 is public-facing with a connection to the Internet. Interfaces 1 and 2 each connect to a separate internal network switch where other network devices such as printers, desktops, and servers would be plugged in. Each router interface must be configured with the correct TCP/IP settings—lucky for you, this is covered in the next section!

Configuring IPv4

We all know how old-school telephones work. With a local number, the first three numbers identify the local exchange, or central office, and the last four numbers identify a specific telephone. IP addresses work similarly, where a single IP address consists of both a network and node (host) portion.

For communication on today's enterprise networks (and the Internet), devices must have a unique IP address—unique, at least on their LAN, or subnet. Have you ever wondered why, for example, you can use an IP address of 192.168.1.100 on your home network, and your friend on their home network can use the same IP address? How does that work if you can both get on the Internet? The answer is Port Address Translation (PAT).

PAT

Port Address Translation allows many internal IP addresses to connect through a PAT router to the Internet using a single public IP address (the one assigned to the public interface of the PAT router). The PAT router uses a unique source port number from the internal sending machine to track external connections and their responses. This works well to get a bunch of internal devices on the Internet with a single public IP address.

Check this out from home or work on different devices (including smartphones and tablets) by visiting www.whatismyip.com/. You'll see that all your internal devices appear to be coming from the same Internet IP address. Figure 5-8 illustrates how many internal IP addresses can get to the Internet using a single public IP address by tracking port numbers.

NAT

Network Address Translation (NAT) maps external IP addresses on the NAT router to corresponding internal IP addresses for devices on the internal network. This is useful when you want to allow *inbound* connections to hosts on a private network through a NAT router. So there is a 1:1 correlation between external and internal IP addresses.

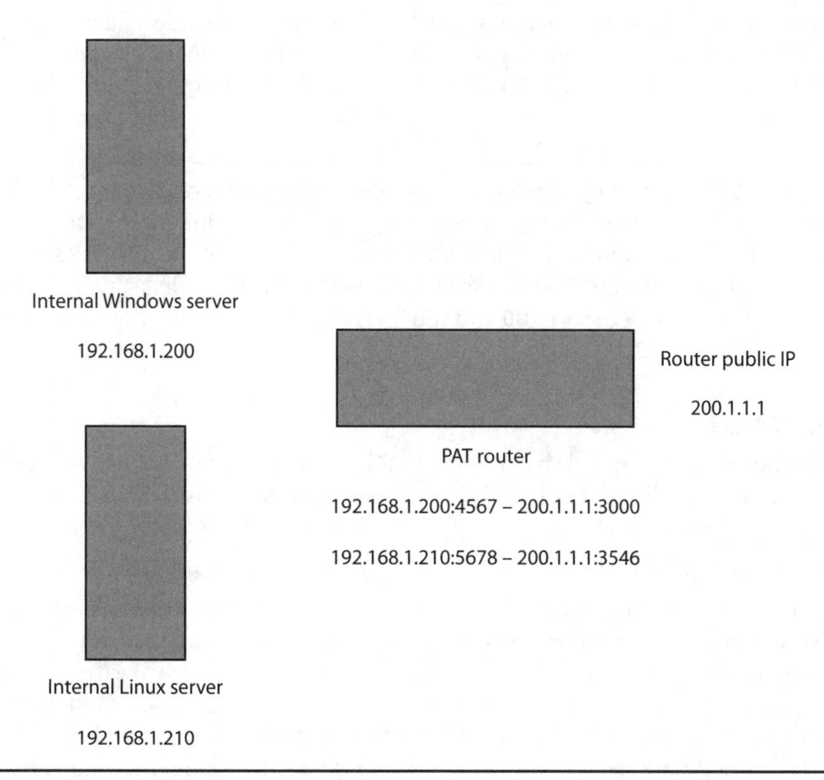

Figure 5-8 PAT router port table

IP

The Internet Protocol (IP) is a big deal. We hear about it all the time at work and in the media when the latest Internet hack spreads like wildfire. It is the specific TCP/IP protocol that enables traffic to shoot around the Internet, and it applies to Layer 3 of the OSI model.

Devices that want to communicate on a TCP/IP network must have a valid IP address (among other things), but IP is also responsible for routing packets to different networks all over the planet. Routers look at IP addresses to determine the best way to get traffic to a remote network efficiently. This applies to both IPv4 and the newer IPv6.

IPv4 Addressing

The swinging 1960s led to the development of a communications protocol in the early 1970s by the US government, which we still use today over the Internet. IPv4 was not designed to be used the way it is being used today; there have been countless changes and security fixes. You don't want to know what happened to IP versions 1, 2, and 3.

An IPv4 address is 32 bits long, but most of us are used to seeing it expressed in decimal with a period separating each 8-bit group, such as 192.168.1.1., the binary equivalent of which is 11000000 10101000 00000001 0000001. Each grouping of 8 bits is called a *byte* or *octet*.

Since we're working with binary 0's and 1's, the smallest possible value for an octet is 0 (00000000 in binary) and the largest is 255 (11111111 in binary), so you'll never see an IPv4 address like 267.3.52.378—it's not possible. IP addresses are also referred to as Layer 3 addresses.

NOTE Many organizations use specific internal IP ranges for certain types of devices. For instance, servers might always be configured in the 200 to 210 host range, and network printers might be in the 220 to 230 host range. So if your IPv4 network prefix is 192.168.1, the first server IP address would be 192.168.1.200 and the first network printer IP address would be 192.168.1.220.

Subnet Mask

Earlier in the section we stated that a single IP address consists of both network and node (host) portions. The subnet mask defines this. For example, consider the following:

IP address: 192.168.1.1
Subnet mask: 255.255.255.0

The first octet of the subnet mask (255) means all of the binary bits are set to 1's. This means this entire octet identifies a part of our network; the same is true for the next two octets. The result in this example is that the first three octets identify the network the device is a member of (192.168.1.0/24). A trailing 0 is normally used to identify a network address. The slash 24 (which is called CIDR notation) means there are 24 binary bits in the subnet mask, so /24 and 255.255.255.0 have the same meaning. That leaves us with one octet (the fourth octet) to address devices, or hosts, on the 192.168.1.0 network. The device address in this example is simply 1.

NOTE Many wireless routers have their internal WLAN IP address set to 192.168.1.1. In this case, either start using addresses from 192.168.1.2 onward or reconfigure the IP address of the wireless router.

Reserved Internal IP Address Ranges

The address 127.0.0.1 is a reserved local loopback address used for testing, but there are entire ranges of IP address designed for internal use on enterprise networks. Internet routers don't forward this type of traffic, but your organization's internal routers can. The address ranges follow:

- 10.0.0.0–10.255.255.255
- 172.16.0.0–172.31.255.255
- 192.168.0.0–192.168.255.255

Public unique IP addresses are allocated by your Internet service provider (ISP), and depending on your needs, you might have only one or dozens of them. If, for instance, you wanted to host your own public web site on your own network, you would need a unique public IP address (and DNS name, too).

An example of a public IPv4 address is 199.126.129.77. IP addresses can be configured manually, as shown in Figure 5-9. With IPv4, there is a shortage of addresses.

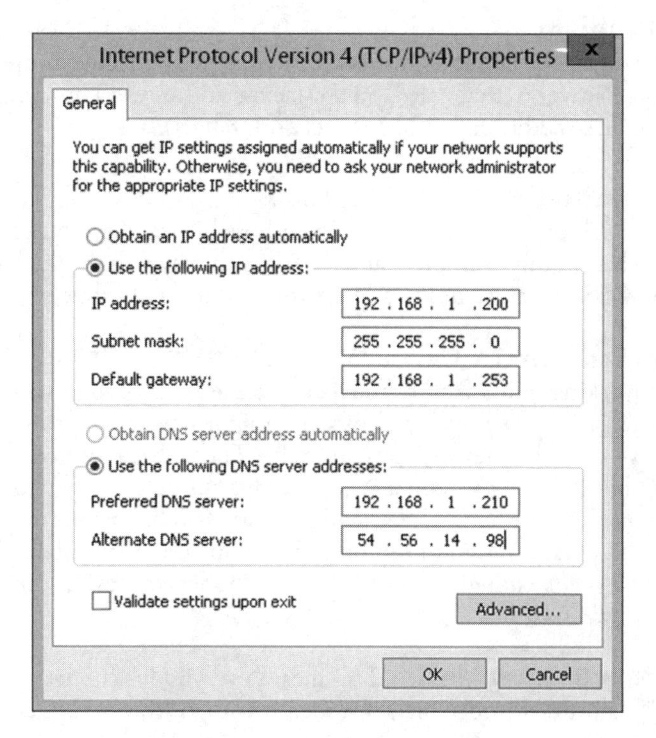

Figure 5-9 Manual configuring of IPv4 settings in Windows

Mathematically, 2^{32} equals 4 billion and change. In other words, there are around 4 billion unique IPv4 addresses possible. This is where PAT, NAT, and IPv6 come in.

When to Use Subnetting

There are times when you'll have a single IP network address but more than one network to allocate IP addresses to. Other than acquiring additional network addresses, your only option is to subnet.

Subnetting takes an existing network address and further subdivides it into subnetworks, or subnets, to enable communication between devices on the various subnets. But where do you configure this? On the router? On each device? The answer to all is "yes." Subnetting is implemented in the IP addressing and subnet mask configured on all affected devices. We need an example.

I've run into plenty of IT people who state they don't need to bother learning anything about subnetting, especially with the advent of PAT and NAT. I disagree, certainly for the purposes of the Server+ SK0-004 exam! It's like a carpenter stating that he or she doesn't have to understand trigonometry. So let's get started with the trig!

The Sample Scenario

You are a network specialist. Your organization's ISP provides the company with a single network address of 200.200.1.0/24. From the /24, you know you have a 24-bit subnet mask, stated otherwise as 255.255.255.0. So you have one octet, the last one (8 bits) to work with.

The Problem

You have one IP network address, but your public-facing router is connected to three separate networks that need public-facing addresses. The company cannot afford to acquire three additional public IP network ranges.

The Solution

You will subnet. This is done by using host bits so that you can address your subnets. Remember, in this example you have 8 bits to play with in the last octet. But how many bits of the 8 must you use to address three additional subnets?

How Many Bits? Use the formula $2^{\text{number of borrowed host bits}} - 2$. The first 2 is used since you're working in binary (0's and 1's); there are only two possible values. The *number of borrowed host bits* is how many bits you might need to use so that you can address your subnets—so it's a guessing game initially. The – 2 is required because a subnet address cannot be all 0's or 1's in binary, so you must subtract these two invalid possibilities.

If you calculate $2^3 - 2$, you end up with 6. This means you could have six unique subnet addresses, yet you need only three. But if you calculate $2^2 - 2$, you end up with only two—not enough; you need three subnet addresses. So it's settled. You will be borrowing 3 host bits.

The New Subnet Mask This means everybody's subnet mask will change from /24 to /27. Expressed in decimal, this means you go from a subnet mask of 255.255.255.0

to 255.255.255.224. It's 224 because in binary, the last octet is 11100000. Converted to decimal, this is 224. Now you have only 5 bits to address devices on each subnet!

Subnet Addresses Next you have to come up with valid subnet IDs. One way to do this is to map the last octet (in our specific case) manually to a binary conversion table. Here's the table. I would recommend committing it to memory, because it *will* help with this kind of stuff. Start with 128 and keep cutting it in half until you get to 1. Then plot your binary 8 bits into the table.

128	64	32	16	8	4	2	1
1	1	1	0	0	0	0	0

Now look at the right-most binary "1." It falls under 32, so 32 is your first subnet address, and it is the mathematical value you will use to determine other subnet addresses. So, 32, 64, 96, and so on (keep adding 32).

- Your first subnet address is 200.200.1.32/27.
- Your second subnet address is 200.200.1.64/27.
- Your third subnet address is 200.200.1.96/27.

What happened to IP addresses 1–31? They're gone; you lose IP addresses when you subnet because you have less host bits to work with. Next you need to calculate valid IP address ranges within each subnet.

Subnet IP Ranges Your first subnet address value is 32 and the next is 64. Since 32 identifies the subnet itself, you can't use 32 (200.1.1.32) as a host address. Instead, you start at 33. You can't use 64 because it identifies the second subnet, so 63 is valid, right? Wrong: 63 is the broadcast address for subnet 32, so it's off limits. How on Earth are you expected to know that? The number 63 in binary is 0011 1111, and 001 is 32, and when you set the rest of the bits (001 defines subnet 32, so all of the bits after 001) to 1's it means broadcast—it's just a rule you have to remember.

So 63 is no, but 62 is valid. So here is your valid IP address range for subnets 32, 64, and 96:

- Subnet 32: 200.1.1.33–200.1.1.62
- Subnet 64: 200.1.1.65–200.1.1.94
- Subnet 96: 200.1.1.97–200.1.1.126

Remember that some of those IPs need to be assigned to the appropriate router interface connected to each network—and everybody gets configured with the 255.255.255.224 subnet mask. Subnetting can be useful for addressing on VLANs. One way a switch administrator creates a VLAN is to group physical switch ports into their own network (a VLAN). Yet another method is to group devices into a VLAN (regardless of physical switch port) based on their IP address. You might want VLANs to isolate network traffic for performance or security reasons.

Configuring IPv6

IPv6, unlike IPv4, was designed with the knowledge of how the world's computing devices are interconnected. IPv6 is different from IPv4 in many ways, including the fact that broadcasts are not used; instead, there is a heavy reliance on multicasting. On the security side, IP Security (IPSec) support is required for IPv6 implementations. IPSec can encrypt and sign network transmissions and can also be used with IPv4.

Software broadcasts don't exist with IPv6, like they do with IPv4. Unicast transmissions (from one sender to one target), multicast transmissions (from one sender to a group of devices registered with a multicast listening address), and anycast transmissions (from one sender to the nearest member of a multicast group) are used instead.

IPv6 Addressing

Here's the biggest change: where the IPv4 address space consists of 32 bits, IPv6 uses 128 bits, so it is four times larger! Let's do the math:

- IPv4: $2^{32} = 4,294,967,296$
- IPv6: $2^{128} = 340,282,366,920,938,463,463,374,607,431,768,211,456$

IPv4 has about 4 billion different IP addresses and IPv6 has 340 undecillion! Instead of expressing the address in decimal form (such as is the case with IPv4), IPv6 addresses are expressed in hexadecimal. Hex is base 16; we use numbers 0–9 and letters A–F where A = 10, B = 11, C = 12, D = 13, E = 14, and F = 15.

Each of the eight parts of an IPv6 address is 16 bits long (a hextet), and of course $8 \times 16 = 128$. Instead of separating each hextet with a period, a full colon is used. Consider the following IPv6 address:

fe80::883b:ced4:63f3:f297%8

Notice the two full colons together. This can be used once in an IPv6 address—it represents a series of 0's, which is really the absence of a value. Also take note of the %8 at the end. This is a network interface identifier. The IPv6 local loopback address for testing is simply ::1.

The preceding IPv6 address is a *link-local address* because of the fe80 prefix. Through multicast neighbor solicitation messages, IPv6 nodes can discover network settings from routers and also assign themselves a local IP address that always starts with fe80. This isn't quite the same as an IPv4 Automatic Private IP Address (APIPA) configuration; IPv6 nodes *always* have a link-local address, even if they acquire another IPv6 address through DHCP or are configured with a static IPv6 address.

The following list describes common IPv6 network prefixes:

- **FE80** Self-assigned link-local address
- **FF** Multicast traffic

- **2001** Global unicast address
- **FC00** Unique unicast, similar to private IP ranges

IPv6 Settings

IPv6 uses DHCP, default gateways, and DNS servers in the same way that IPv4 hosts do; just enter the IPv6 addresses for these components into the appropriate places. Instead of a subnet mask, IPv6 terminology favors "network prefix," and it is expressed in Classless Inter-Domain Routing (CIDR) format, such as /64, shown in Figure 5-10.

Modern operating systems and devices support IPv6. For example, Windows Server 2012 R2 has IPv6 enabled by default. Some operating systems may not have IPv6 enabled by default but can have it up and running in seconds if you configure it. You might consider disabling IPv6 in your network interface settings if you are sure it's not needed in your environment. Reducing the server attack surface includes disabling unused components.

Believe it or not, June 6, 2012, was World IPv6 Launch day. The purpose was for many ISPs and major web sites to enable IPv6 support and leave it running, which they did. Break out the bubbly!

Internet Protocol Version 6 (TCP/IPv6) Properties

General

You can get IPv6 settings assigned automatically if your network supports this capability.
Otherwise, you need to ask your network administrator for the appropriate IPv6 settings.

○ Obtain an IPv6 address automatically
◉ Use the following IPv6 address:

IPv6 address: 1:2:3:4::abcd
Subnet prefix length: 64
Default gateway: 1:2:3:4::aabb

○ Obtain DNS server address automatically
◉ Use the following DNS server addresses:

Preferred DNS server: 1:2:3:4::aacc
Alternate DNS server: 2:3:4:5::aacc

☐ Validate settings upon exit

Advanced...

OK Cancel

Figure 5-10 Manually configuring IPv6 settings in Windows

Transition Technology	Description
6to4	• Allows IPv6 traffic over the IPv4 Internet • Routers on both ends must support IPv6 • Routers have an IPv6 address configured on their internal interface
Intra-Site Automatic Tunnel Addressing Protocol (ISATAP)	• Allows IPv6 traffic on an internal IPv4 network • The IPv4 address is embedded within the IPv6 address
Teredo	• Allows IPv6 traffic over the IPv4 Internet through NAT • The Teredo server must reside on the IPv4 Internet • Public Teredo servers and relays are available

Table 5-4 IPv6 Transition Technologies

IPv6 Transition Technologies

The Internet in 2016 uses primarily IPv4. As IPv6 becomes more and more common, we'll need a way to get IPv6 traffic sent through the IPv4 Internet. Table 5-4 describes IPv6 transition technologies.

Network Infrastructure Services

Network infrastructure is similar to a physical city infrastructure, which include roads, bridges, and highways that enable the movement of people and goods. In a network environment, some fundamental services are required for large-scale IP addressing, name-to–IP address resolution, and internetwork connectivity.

Default Gateway

The term "default gateway" is an unfortunate choice of words; "gateways" have many meanings, but the term has become standard over the years ("default router" would have made much more sense).

The *default gateway* is a router on your LAN through which you send traffic leaving the LAN. Without it, you are limited to communication with hosts on your local network. Each device that must communicate with devices on other networks must be configured with at least one default gateway IP address.

EXAM TIP One thing to be careful of is ensuring that you configure the IP address for the router interface connected to *your* network. Routers have at least two interfaces to interconnect networks. A second thing to watch out for is using the correct subnet mask. You must be able to talk to your router (default gateway) on your LAN.

DNS Servers

It's probably fair to say that nobody remembers the IP addresses for all of the Internet services (including web sites) that they use. Instead, we humans have an easier time remembering names. It's no problem remembering www.mheducation.com, but try memorizing 52.72.96.223, and doing similarly for hundreds of different sites where the IP address can change periodically.

Domain Name Service (DNS) is a lookup service that can run on a server or some kind of network appliance such as a router. As users, we normally have a name, but we need the corresponding IP address (your computer needs an IP address, not a name), and this is called a *forward lookup*. Occasionally, you might already know the IP address, but you're looking for the corresponding name, and this is called a *reverse lookup*.

Devices on a TCP/IP network must be configured with at least one DNS server IP address (and I would strongly recommend at least two). If the DNS server is down or the client can't connect to it for some reason, it's fair to say that everything grinds to a halt—and we can remember server and web site names easily but not their IP addresses.

Using the Windows `ipconfig /all` command will reveal which DNS servers our network interfaces are configured to use, as shown in the next illustration. On a Linux host, we can open the /etc/resolv.conf and add DNS server IP addresses to the file. Use the `nslookup` command in both Windows and Linux to test connectivity to DNS servers.

```
Command Prompt
   DHCPv6 IAID . . . . . . . . . . . : 486559830
   DHCPv6 Client DUID. . . . . . . . : 00-01-00-01-1D-A1-C5-44-F8-A9-63-6F-15-67

   DNS Servers . . . . . . . . . . . : fec0:0:0:ffff::1%1
                                       fec0:0:0:ffff::2%1
                                       fec0:0:0:ffff::3%1
   NetBIOS over Tcpip. . . . . . . . : Enabled

Wireless LAN adapter Wi-Fi:

   Connection-specific DNS Suffix  . : silversides.local
   Description . . . . . . . . . . . : Qualcomm Atheros AR956x Wireless Network
Adapter
   Physical Address. . . . . . . . . : 90-48-9A-11-BD-6F
   DHCP Enabled. . . . . . . . . . . : Yes
   Autoconfiguration Enabled . . . . : Yes
   IPv4 Address. . . . . . . . . . . : 192.168.1.157(Preferred)
   Subnet Mask . . . . . . . . . . . : 255.255.255.0
   Lease Obtained. . . . . . . . . . : Thursday, June 9, 2016 12:30:00 PM
   Lease Expires . . . . . . . . . . : Saturday, June 11, 2016 7:14:38 AM
   Default Gateway . . . . . . . . . : 192.168.1.1
   DHCP Server . . . . . . . . . . . : 192.168.1.1
   DNS Servers . . . . . . . . . . . : 8.8.8.8
                                       192.168.1.1
   Primary WINS Server . . . . . . . : 192.168.1.1
   NetBIOS over Tcpip. . . . . . . . : Enabled

Tunnel adapter isatap.silversides.local:

   Media State . . . . . . . . . . . : Media disconnected
   Connection-specific DNS Suffix  . : silversides.local
   Description . . . . . . . . . . . : Microsoft ISATAP Adapter
   Physical Address. . . . . . . . . : 00-00-00-00-00-00-00-E0
   DHCP Enabled. . . . . . . . . . . : No
   Autoconfiguration Enabled . . . . : Yes

Tunnel adapter isatap.{80A7D3E4-4324-46B7-89B6-A1B66C7C41C8}:

   Media State . . . . . . . . . . . : Media disconnected
   Connection-specific DNS Suffix  . :
   Description . . . . . . . . . . . : Microsoft ISATAP Adapter #3
   Physical Address. . . . . . . . . : 00-00-00-00-00-00-00-E0
   DHCP Enabled. . . . . . . . . . . : No
```

DNS Hierarchy

DNS is a hierarchical naming structure. Top-level domains include suffixes such as .com, .edu, .net, and others. Second-level domains are those such as mheducation, google, and so on. When you add the host name (normally www for Internet web sites), you get a *fully qualified domain name (FQDN)* such as www.mheducation.com.

The domain suffix can be configured when you configure TCP/IP settings on a device. So if you are configuring IP on a server named server1, you might configure a domain suffix of widgets.com, which results in a FQDN of server1.widgets.com.

Prior to DNS servers becoming common, each TCP/IP device used a local text file called *hosts* to resolve names to IP addresses. You can imagine how difficult that would be to manage on a large scale.

WINS Servers

The Windows Internet Naming Service (WINS) isn't used often anymore. It is an old Microsoft standard for resolving NetBIOS computer names (such as computer1) to an IP address. It's a flat structure; there's no hierarchy as we have in DNS.

Prior to WINS servers becoming common, each Microsoft system used a local text file called *lmhosts* to resolve NetBIOS computer names to IP addresses.

DHCP

Now that you know about configuring TCP/IP settings manually on each device, let's dive into how this gets done on a larger scale. DHCP, much like DNS, is a standard network service that runs on a server or some network device such as a router (including Wi-Fi routers). To cut to the chase, DHCP is nothing more than TCP/IP settings configured centrally and delivered to clients over the network. But wait! How can that work if a client doesn't have an IP address in the first place? Read on.

Devices that attempt to acquire TCP/IP settings using DHCP execute a four-packet exchange as follows:

1. DHCP discovery
    - Client sends a network broadcast seeking a DHCP server.
    - If this fails, the client assigns itself an automatic private IP address (APIPA) that has a prefix of 169.254. This enables communication only on the LAN with other devices in the 169.254 range.
2. DHCP offer
    - Each DHCP server (if more than one) responds via broadcast with an IP address lease offer.
    - The DHCP client works with the first offer it receives.
3. DHCP request
    - The client broadcasts its acceptance of the offer, which is received by the DHCP server.

4. DHCP acknowledgment
   - The DHCP server sends an ACK packet to the client along with any additional configured TCP/IP settings.

DHCP clients will attempt to renew their leases before they expire. The time interval differs between different versions of operating systems, but generally it's at 50 percent of the lease. Use the `ipconfig /all` Windows command to view DHCP server and lease information, as shown in the next illustration. If you're a Linux person, you can use the `cat` command to view the contents of the DHCP lease file, which normally resides under /var/lib/dhcp.

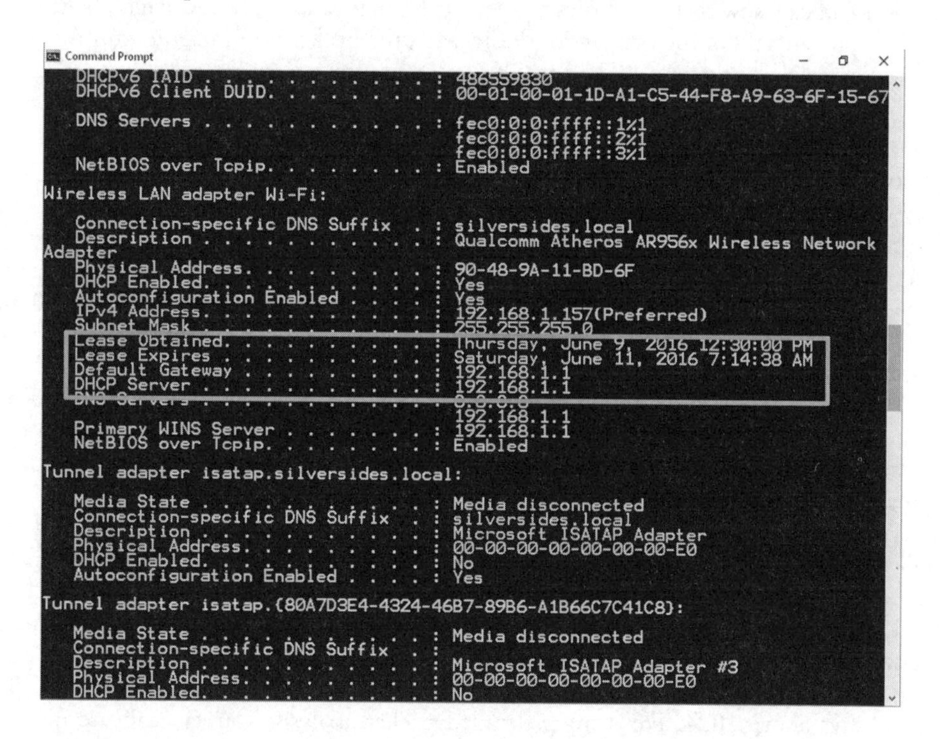

TCP and UDP

TCP is one type of transport available in the TCP/IP suite; User Datagram Protocol (UDP) is the other. Software developers determine whether TCP or UDP will be used. In some rare cases, it might even be a configuration option within a network service or application.

TCP

You'll come across plenty of literature that states that TCP is a "connection-oriented reliable protocol." Great. What exactly does that mean?

It means that a session is established between two communicating devices before transmitting data for the purposes of negotiating session parameters. This is done with the TCP three-way handshake. Let's detail this packet exchange:

1. **SYN** Initial sequence number (ISN) is sent by the initiator and is used to track data sent and received.
2. **SYN ACK** Sent back from the target, this is an acknowledgment of receipt of the initiator's ISN and also includes the target's ISN.
3. **ACK** Sent by the initiator, this acknowledges receipt of the target's ISN.
4. Data can now be transmitted between the parties and is acknowledged by the opposite end of the connection; otherwise, the packet is retransmitted if the sender doesn't get an ACK from the recipient after a time interval.

Port Numbers

Network services running on a TCP/IP device need some kind of unique identifier. Let's say your server has a single IP address of 200.200.1.1 and you're running a web site and an SMTP mail server. How can you uniquely identify the web server versus the mail server on the same IP address? Easy! Via the *port address*. It's similar conceptually to a separate channel of communication. Web servers normally listen on TCP port 80 and SMTP mail servers normally listen on TCP port 25, although administers can set the listening ports for most services.

Port addresses are also referred to as Layer 4 addresses, whether TCP or UDP. Despite this, protocols such as HTTP, DNS, and SMTP, to name just a few, are Layer 7 protocols. Remember that higher layers in the OSI model rely on some or all lower layers, depending on the specific protocol.

Port numbers are software addresses that uniquely identify network services, and they fall within the range of 0 to 65,536, where the first 1024 are reserved for well-known services, such as those listed in Table 5-5.

Use the `netstat` command in Windows operating systems to see which port you are connected to for a given network service, as well as the local client port used. Client ports and channels are used for network services to transmit data back to clients, and the values are always above 1024. For a more detailed packet analysis, you can capture network traffic using tools such as Wireshark, as shown in Figure 5-11.

UDP

UDP is much simpler than TCP. Because it is neither connection-oriented nor reliable, there is much less overhead at the cost of reliability. You can see this in Figure 5-12. UDP is often used for data transmissions where timing is crucial such as with VoIP, streaming applications, and multi-user gaming, to name just a few uses.

UDP does not use a three-way handshake; there are no sequence numbers and there are no acknowledgments for each packet transmitted. It basically sends out packets and then immediately forgets about it. Like TCP, UDP-based network services are also uniquely identified with a port number. Table 5-6 shows some common UDP-based services.

Protocol	Description	TCP Port Number
Domain Name Service (DNS)	• Hierarchical name lookup service • DNS server-server replication uses TCP port 53	53
File Transfer Protocol (FTP)	• A standard way of transferring files over the Internet • Allows the uploading and downloading of files regardless of operating system	20, 21
File Transfer Protocol Secure (FTPS)	• Adds cryptographic support to FTP by way of Secure Sockets Layer (SSL) or the newer Transport Layer Security (TLS)	21
Hyper Text Transfer Protocol (HTTP)	• Web server protocol • Web browsers connect over HTTP • Web pages written in HTML	80
Hyper Text Transfer Protocol Secure (HTTPS)	• HTTP protocol over a secure connection using SSL or TLS • Widely used on the Internet	443
Internet Message Access Protocol (IMAP)	• Client mail retrieval protocol • Allows mail sync from multiple devices	143
Lightweight Directory Access Protocol (LDAP)	• Provides access to a networked database such as Microsoft Active Directory	389
Post Office Protocol version 3 (POP3)	• Client mail retrieval protocol	110
Remote Desktop Protocol (RDP)	• Used to administer Windows computers remotely	3389
Secure Copy (SCP)	• Transfers files over SSH • Options must be specified at the command line • Not interactive like SFTP	22
Secure File Transfer Protocol (SFTP)	• Transfers files over SSH with file system management capabilities	22
Simple Mail Transfer Protocol (SMTP)	• Transfers mail between mail servers	25
Secure Shell (SSH)	• Enables remote device administration over an encrypted connection	22
Telnet	• Insecure remote device command line administration • Usernames and passwords sent in clear text	23

Table 5-5 Common TCP-based Network Services

```
⊟ Transmission Control Protocol, Src Port: 59668 (59668), Dst Port: https (443), Seq: 0, Len: 0
    Source port: 59668 (59668)
    Destination port: https (443)
    [Stream index: 17]
    Sequence number: 0    (relative sequence number)
    Header length: 32 bytes
  ⊟ Flags: 0x02 (SYN)
      0... .... = Congestion Window Reduced (CWR): Not set
      .0.. .... = ECN-Echo: Not set
      ..0. .... = Urgent: Not set
      ...0 .... = Acknowledgement: Not set
      .... 0... = Push: Not set
      .... .0.. = Reset: Not set
    ⊞ .... ..1. = Syn: Set
      .... ...0 = Fin: Not set
    Window size: 8192
  ⊞ Checksum: 0xdf7a [validation disabled]
  ⊞ Options: (12 bytes)
```

Figure 5-11 A Wireshark HTTPS packet capture showing the fields within a TCP header

```
⊟ User Datagram Protocol, Src Port: 55828 (55828), Dst Port: domain (53)
    Source port: 55828 (55828)
    Destination port: domain (53)
    Length: 45
  ⊞ Checksum: 0x2b4e [validation disabled]
⊟ Domain Name System (query)
    [Response In: 242]
    Transaction ID: 0xebe4
  ⊞ Flags: 0x0100 (Standard query)
    Questions: 1
    Answer RRs: 0
    Authority RRs: 0
    Additional RRs: 0
  ⊞ Queries
```

Figure 5-12 A Wireshark DNS packet capture showing UDP header fields

Protocol	**Description**	**UDP Port Number**
Network Time Protocol (NTP)	• Synchronizes device clocks on a network	123
Domain Name Service (DNS)	• Hierarchical name lookup service • DNS client queries contact the DNS server on UDP port 53	53
Dynamic Host Configuration Protocol (DHCP)	• Delivers centrally configured TCP/IP settings to clients over the network	67, 68
Simple Network Management Protocol (SNMP)	• Monitors and manages network device or service	161

Table 5-6 Common UDP-based Network Services

Hands-on Exercises

Exercise 5-1: Manually Configure IPv6 on Windows Server 2012 R2

1. Make sure your Srv2012-1 virtual machine is running in VMware Workstation and that you are logged on using the Domain Administrator account (Fakedomain\Administrator) with a password of Pa$$w0rd, or if you changed the password, use it.
2. From the Windows start menu, enter **Network**. When the option is displayed, click Network And Sharing Center.
3. On the left, click Change Adapter Settings.
4. Right-click the Internal network adapter and choose Properties.
5. In the Properties window, shown next, click Internet Protocol Version 6 (TCP/IPv6), and then click Properties.
6. Choose Use The Following IPv6 Address.
7. In the IPv6 Address field, enter **1:2:3:4::abcd**.
8. In the Subnet Prefix Length field, enter **64**.
9. For the Preferred DNS Server, enter **::1**. Click OK, and then Close.

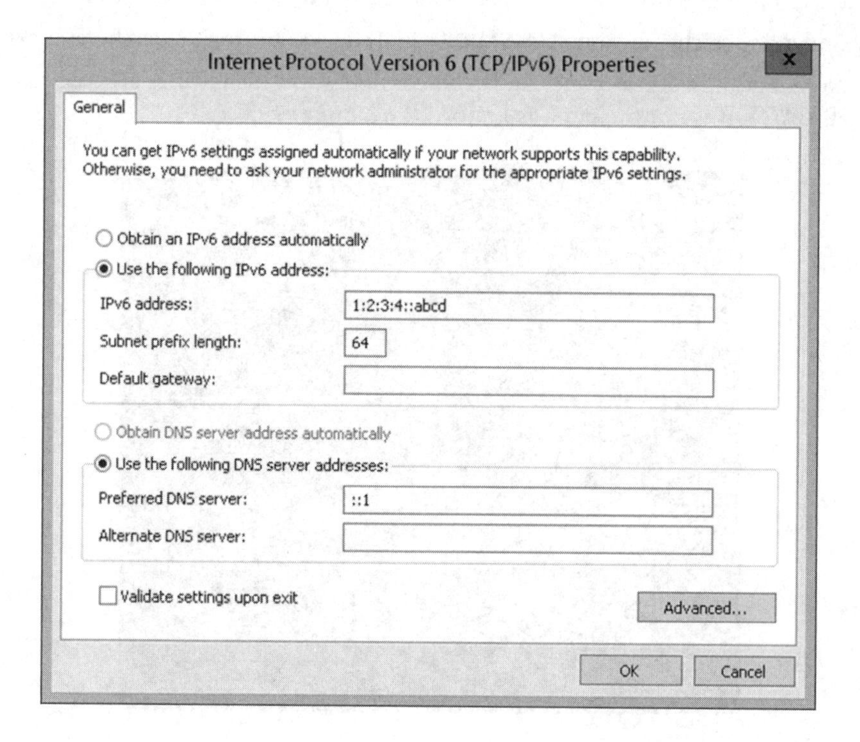

10. From the Windows start menu, enter **cmd**. When it is displayed, click Command Prompt.
11. Type **`ipconfig`** and press ENTER. Notice that the Internal network adapter has both an IPv6 address and a link-local IPv6 address.
12. Type **`ping 1:2:3:4::abcd`** and press ENTER. You should see four replies.

Exercise 5-2: Manually Configure IPv6 on Red Hat Enterprise Linux 7

1. Make sure your RHEL7-1 virtual machine is running in VMware Workstation and that you are logged in as user root with a password of Pa$$w0rdLinux. If you are not logged in with the root user account, you will need to precede Linux commands with `sudo` for elevated privileges. Also ensure that the Srv2012-1 virtual machine is running.
2. Choose Applications | Utilities and open a terminal window.
3. Enter **`gedit /etc/sysconfig/network-scripts/ifcfg-eno16777736`** (the suffix interface name on your system may differ; enter **`ls /etc/sysconfig/network-scripts`** to find out) and press ENTER.
4. Ensure that IPV6INIT is set to yes. Change IPV6_AUTOCONF to no.
5. Add a line to the bottom: **`IPV6ADDR=1:2:3:4::bcde/64`**, as shown next.

   Note that most Linux commands and configuration file settings are case-sensitive. IPv6ADDR is not the same as IPV6ADDR; be careful!

```
TYPE=Ethernet
BOOTPROTO=none
DEFROUTE=yes
IPV4_FAILURE_FATAL=no
IPV6INIT=yes
IPV6_AUTOCONF=no
IPV6_DEFROUTE=yes
IPV6_FAILURE_FATAL=no
NAME=eno16777736
UUID=36fe88e0-37ed-418f-8a98-a5c3c91adbae
DEVICE=eno16777736
ONBOOT=no
IPADDR=192.168.1.210
PREFIX=24
GATEWAY=192.168.1.200
DNS1=192.168.1.201
IPV6_PEERDNS=yes
IPV6_PEERROUTES=yes
IPV6ADDR=1:2:3:4::bcde/64
~
```

6. Close and save the configuration file.
7. Type **service network restart** and press ENTER to put the settings into effect.
8. Type `ifup eno16777736` and press ENTER (your interface name may be different; you can type `ifconfig` to see its name). This will bring up the network interface.
9. Type `ifconfig`. You will notice the inet6 listed address of 1:2:3:4::bcde.
10. Switch to the Srv2012-1 virtual machine and open a command prompt. Type `ping -6 1:2:3:4::bcde`. This is the IPv6 address of the Linux server. You should see four replies.

Exercise 5-3: Install and Configure NAT on Windows Server 2012 R2

1. Make sure your Srv2012-1 virtual machine is running in VMware Workstation and that you are logged on using the Administrator account with a password of Pa$$w0rd.
2. On the Linux virtual machine, in a terminal window, type `ping 192.168.1.200`. This is the Internal IP address of Srv2012-1, and you should get a reply. Press CTRL-C to stop the pinging.
3. Type `ping 200.1.1.1`. This is the External NAT IP address of Srv2012-1, and you should *not* get a reply at this point. Press CTRL-C to stop the pinging.
4. From the Start menu on Srv2012-1, enter **network**. When the Network And Sharing Center option is displayed, click it.
5. On the left, click Change Adapter Settings. Right-click ExternalNAT, choose Properties, choose TCP/IPv4, and click Properties.
6. Choose Use The Following IP Address and enter **200.1.1.1**. Ensure the Subnet Mask is set to **255.255.255.0** and the Preferred DNS Server is set to **127.0.0.1**. Click OK and then Close.
7. Start PowerShell (second icon to the left after the Start menu button).
8. Enter `install-windowsfeature routing -includemanagementtools`
9. After the role is installed, from the Windows Start menu, type **Rout**. When the Routing And Remote Access option appears, click it.
10. Right-click Srv2012-1 in the left panel and choose Configure And Enable Routing And Remote Access. Click Next.
11. Choose Network Address Translation (NAT) and click Next.

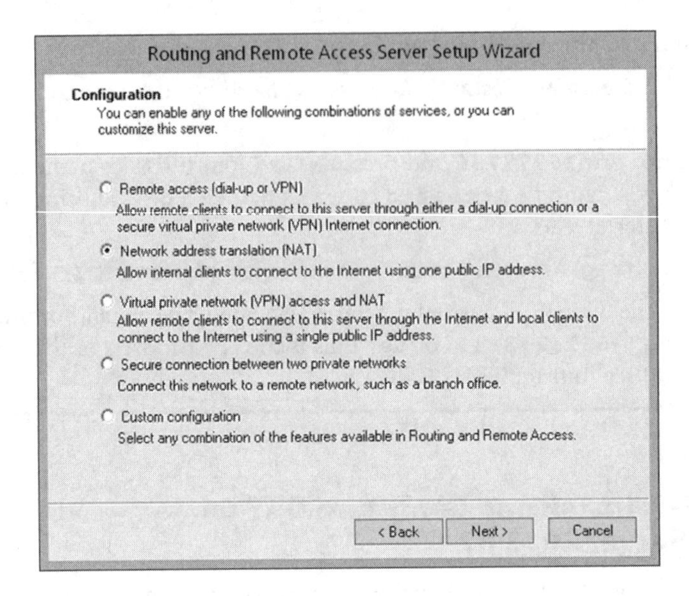

12. Click ExternalNAT for the public interface. Click Next.
13. Choose I Will Set Up Name And Address Services Later. Click Next and then Finish.
14. To allow ICMP ping packets to Srv2012-1, from PowerShell, enter the following:

```
New-NetFirewallRule -DisplayName "Ping Allowed"
-Direction Inbound -Action Allow -Protocol icmpv4
-Enabled true
```

15. On the Linux virtual machine, in a terminal window, type **`ping 200.1.1.1`**. You should now see a reply, since NAT allows routing of IP packets; all outbound traffic from internal hosts will assume the address of 200.1.1.1.

NOTE Network devices can use NAT only if the internal IP address of the NAT router is set as their default gateway.

Exercise 5-4: Use Wireshark to Capture and Analyze HTTP Traffic

This exercise can be completed from any Windows computer that has access to the Internet, where the computer allows downloading and installing software from the Internet.

1. Using your web browser, go to www.wireshark.org. Download and install the appropriate Windows Installer and then accept all installation defaults. Leave the web browser open.
2. From the Start menu, launch Wireshark.
3. If prompted when you start Wireshark, click the network interface whose Packets column displays a changing number (this means network activity). If you are not prompted, choose Capture | Interfaces, and then choose the interface that has packet activity. Then, to the right of the network interface, click the Start button.
4. Switch over to your web browser and connect to www.mheducation.com.
5. Switch back to Wireshark, and choose Capture | Stop. Notice all of the captured network packets.
6. In the address bar (it should currently say Apply A Display Filter), type **http** and press ENTER. Now only HTTP network traffic is shown; viewing web sites uses HTTP.
7. Choose Edit | Find Packet. On the newly displayed search line, click Display Filter and change it to String. In the field to the right, type **mheducation**. Click the Find button on the far right. The first HTTP packet containing mheducation is selected.
8. In the middle of the screen, you will see packet headers. Expand Transmission Control Protocol. Notice the source and destination port values. If the packet is a transmission to the web site, the destination port will be 80 and the source port will be a higher value; otherwise, the port numbers will be reversed. These are Layer 4 addresses.
9. In the packet header section, expand Internet Protocol Version 4. You may need to scroll down a bit to see the source and destination IP addresses. These are Layer 3 addresses.
10. In the packet header section, expand the Ethernet II header. Notice the source and destination MAC addresses. These are Layer 2 addresses.
11. Close Wireshark without saving the capture.

NOTE Do you see how the OSI model layers are reflected in sequence (Layers 2, 3, 4, and so on) when viewing packet headers? This is not a coincidence.

Chapter Review

It seems server experts must also be network experts—this is true! Your servers can interact with a large variety of services and network components on a large scale, and you must understand how all the moving parts work together.

The OSI Model

The seven-layer OSI model is used to explain communication hardware and software, and the layers, beginning with Layer 7, are application, presentation, session, transport, network, data link, and physical.

- Higher level software applies to Layer 7, the application layer
- How data is presented applies to Layer 6, the presentation layer
- The establishment, maintenance, and termination of sessions apply to Layer 5, the session layer
- Port numbers apply to Layer 4, the transport layer
- IP addresses apply to Layer 3, the network layer
- MAC addresses apply to Layer 2, the data link layer
- Cables, connectors, and electrical specifications apply to Layer 1, the physical layer

Cables and Connectors

Groups of cables should be bundled together and routed in cable channels in racks throughout server rooms and data centers. Cable management arms prevent cables from being pulled tight when rack-mounted equipment is pulled out on rails from the rack. Labeled or color-coded cables keep things organized and facilitate troubleshooting.

RJ-11 connectors are used for telephone cables, and RJ-45 connectors are used for twisted pair copper network cables, which transmit electronic signals. CAT5 cabling supports transmissions at 10 or 100 Mbps. CAT5e has more cable pair twists per inch and supports up to 1000 Mbps. CAT6 supports 1 Gbps over 100 meters or 10 Gbps over 55 meters.

Fiber-optic cables transmit light waves and can travel greater distances without amplification. Single-mode fiber is used for longer distances than multi-mode fiber. Common connectors include ST, SC, LC, and SFP.

Network Interface Cards

Network interface cards can be integrated on server motherboards or are available as expansion cards. NICs have a unique 48-bit hardware address called a MAC address and support enhanced features such as Wake-on-LAN, PXE boot, and NIC teaming. NIC teaming groups multiple network cards together for the purpose of redundancy or greater bandwidth.

IPv4 and IPv6

IPv4 uses 32-bit IP address, where each 8 bits is expressed in decimal format and separated by a period. TCP/IP configuration settings can be configured manually on each device or centrally using DHCP. The subnet mask determines which portion of the IP address designates the network and which portion designates the host on that network.

Subnetting occurs when host bits are borrowed to address subnetworks beyond the original network. This is done when additional network addresses cannot be acquired. When subnetting, all affected devices use the same new subnet mask.

Port Address Translation enables multiple internal IP nodes to access a public network, such as the Internet, using a single public IP address. The network address exposes internal hosts by mapping public IP addresses on the NAT router to internal private IP addresses.

IPv6 improves upon IPv4 with a larger 128-bit address space, security using IPSec, and more efficient network traffic management. IPv6 addresses are exposed in hexadecimal, where every 16 bits is separated by a full colon.

The default gateway is used when a device is transmitting data to a remote network outside of the LAN, and it must be on the same subnet as the device; it is the IP address of a router. DNS servers provide a lookup service, most often for names-to–IP addresses. Devices should point to at least one DNS server IP address for name resolution.

IP, TCP, and UDP

In the TCP/IP suite, IP is responsible for routing. TCP provides connection-oriented reliable transmissions, whereas UDP does not and is therefore quicker. Network services listen on a port address for client connections; the port must be unique on a given IP address. The first 1024 ports are reserved for well-known services such as an HTTP web server listening on TCP port 80.

Questions

1. Which of the following is a valid concern regarding ceiling cable channels?

A. Distance

B. EMI

C. Fire suppression

D. Security

2. What is the primary difference between the categories of copper-based network cables?

A. Twists per inch

B. Shielding

C. Type of NICs

D. Distance

3. Which type of connector is commonly used with CAT6 cables?
   - A. RJ-11
   - B. SFP
   - C. TX
   - D. RJ-45

4. Aaron is a network technician linking two older Ethernet switches together with a straight-through network cable. He later realizes the interswitch connection is not working. What should Aaron do?
   - A. Replace the straight-through cable with a rollover cable.
   - B. Replace the straight-through cable with a crossover cable.
   - C. Replace the straight-through cable with a null modem cable.
   - D. Replace the straight-through cable with a switch cable.

5. You are planning the cabling for your company's data center. A network speed of 10 Gbps is preferred. The maximum distance between servers and network switches is approximately 30 meters. Keeping costs to a minimum, what type of network cabling should be used?
   - A. CAT5
   - B. CAT6
   - C. CAT6a
   - D. CAT7

6. Which type of fiber-optic cable should be used for the network backbone on a university campus?
   - A. Single-mode
   - B. Unimode
   - C. Dual-mode
   - D. Multi-mode

7. Which spring-loaded fiber-optic cable connector is commonly used with multi-mode fiber cables?
   - **A.** SC
   - **B.** LC
   - **C.** ST
   - **D.** LT

8. Which of the following statements best describe a MAC address? Choose two.
   - **A.** They are used to route network packets.
   - **B.** Packets being sent to hosts on remote networks are addressed to that host's MAC address.
   - **C.** MAC addresses are 48 bits long.
   - **D.** Each server NIC has a unique MAC address.

9. A data center uses disk images to deploy new physical servers quickly. Rather than have technicians apply the operating system images locally from disk media, network imaging is desired. Which technology must be configured?
   - **A.** Wake-on-LAN
   - **B.** NIC teaming
   - **C.** Full duplex
   - **D.** PXE

10. Server1 has an IP address of 200.1.1.40/27. From Server1, you are attempting to make an SSH connection to Server2, whose IP address is 200.1.1.70/27, but you cannot connect. What might the problem be?
   - **A.** /27 is invalid.
   - **B.** 200.1.1.0 is a reserved IP range.
   - **C.** A default gateway is not properly configured on both servers.
   - **D.** UDP port 22 is blocked on Server2.

11. Which of the following is a valid IPv6 link-local address?
   - **A.** fe80::883b:ced4:63f3:f297
   - **B.** fd75::883b:ced4:63f3
   - **C.** fe80::883b:ced4:63f3:fh97
   - **D.** fd75::883b:ced4:63g3

12. Widgets, Inc., has offices in London and Paris. The IT team has been directed to deploy IPv6 for test VLANs in both cities in anticipation of the eventual requirement of using IPv6. What should be configured to ensure that servers in each city test VLAN can communicate over the Internet?
    A. 6to4
    B. ISATAP
    C. Teredo
    D. NAT

13. A help desk technician is addressing network connectivity issues being experienced by a user, Charlie. Charlie's station is unable to connect to a customer financial history database server on the same subnet named sect1-423.widgets.local, even though other stations do not have this problem; the error messages states "Unknown Host." The technician successfully pings the default gateway to verify a valid IP configuration from Charlie's station. What should the technician do next?
    A. Nothing. The server is down.
    B. Verify that Charlie's station has a default gateway configured.
    C. Verify that Charlie has authenticated to the server first.
    D. Verify that Charlie's station is properly configured with at least one DNS server.

14. Your smartphone receives an alert stating that ServerHFX-234 is not responding. You connect to the server using hardware remote control and issue the `ipconfig` command. You then notice the server IP address is 169.254.46.63. Why is the server having communication problems?
    A. The machine was unable to reach a DHCP server.
    B. The machine must be configured with a private IPv4 address.
    C. The machine is not configured with a DNS server IP address.
    D. The machine is not configured with a valid subnet mask.

15. A colleague, Courtney, discusses the newly installed Layer 3 switches in the wiring closet. What benefit does a Layer 3 switch offer beyond a Layer 2 switch?
    A. Bridging
    B. Switching
    C. Routing
    D. VLANs

16. Which of the following are valid methods of configuring VLANs? Choose two.

A. Username

B. IP address

C. Switch port

D. PKI certificate

17. What type of address applies to Layer 2 switches?

A. IP

B. Port

C. LUN

D. MAC

18. What type of address applies to Layer 3 switches?

A. IP

B. Port

C. LUN

D. MAC

19. Which software communication method is not used with IPv6?

A. Broadcast

B. Unicast

C. Multicast

D. Anycast

20. A new web server is installed with an Intranet web site. User authentication to the site is not required. Your boss asks you to configure the firewall appliance to enable people to browse to the new site. Which port should you open on the firewall appliance?

A. 25

B. 110

C. 80

D. 443

Questions and Answers

1. Which of the following is a valid concern regarding ceiling cable channels?
   - **A.** Distance
   - **B.** EMI
   - **C.** Fire suppression
   - **D.** Security

   C. Ceiling cable channels must be oriented carefully to avoid reducing the effectiveness of fire suppression systems. A, B, and D are incorrect. Although distance is a concern, because cables have a maximum effective distance, this is much less relevant than fire suppression. EMI can be a concern if ceilings have fluorescent lighting and cables are unshielded, neither of which is mentioned. Ceiling cable channels have no bearing on security.

2. What is the primary difference between the categories of copper-based network cables?
   - **A.** Twists per inch
   - **B.** Shielding
   - **C.** Type of NICs
   - **D.** Distance

   A. More twists per inch for copper wire pairs means less interference from adjacent wires. This allows for transmissions at higher frequencies, which results in greater bandwidth. B, C, and D are incorrect. Although some categories of cables differ in their shielding, this is not as prevalent a difference as twists per inch. The type of NIC and distance are not distinguishing differences between different copper cable categories.

3. Which type of connector is commonly used with CAT6 cables?
   - **A.** RJ-11
   - **B.** SFP
   - **C.** TX
   - **D.** RJ-45

   D. RJ-45 connectors are common with CAT6 cables. A, B, and C are incorrect. RJ-11 connectors are used with telephone cables. SFP is a hot-pluggable network transceiver used most often to interconnect fiber cables. TX is not a valid network cable connector type.

4. Aaron is a network technician linking two older Ethernet switches together with a straight-through network cable. He later realizes the interswitch connection is not working. What should Aaron do?

   A. Replace the straight-through cable with a rollover cable.

   B. Replace the straight-through cable with a crossover cable.

   C. Replace the straight-through cable with a null modem cable.

   D. Replace the straight-through cable with a switch cable.

   B. Crossover cables reverse the transmit and receive wires at either end, which is sometimes required for older network switches. A, C, and D are incorrect. Rollover cables are used to connect administrative stations to the console port on network equipment such as routers. Null modem cables are used to link modem devices directly together. There is no such thing as a switch cable.

5. You are planning the cabling for your company's data center. A network speed of 10 Gbps is preferred. The maximum distance between servers and network switches is approximately 30 meters. Keeping costs to a minimum, what type of network cabling should be used?

   A. CAT5

   B. CAT6

   C. CAT6a

   D. CAT7

   B. CAT6 cabling supports 10 Gbps over distances up to 55 meters. A, C, and D are incorrect. CAT5 supports up to 1 Gbps. CAT6a and CAT7 would work but are more costly than CAT6.

6. Which type of fiber-optic cable should be used for the network backbone on a university campus?

   A. Single-mode

   B. Unimode

   C. Dual-mode

   D. Multi-mode

   D. Multi-mode fiber should be used over shorter distances, such as on a university campus. A, B, and C are incorrect. Single-mode fiber is often used over longer distances and is more expensive than multi-mode. Unimode and dual-mode fiber are not common terms.

7. Which spring-loaded fiber-optic cable connector is commonly used with multi-mode fiber cables?
   - **A.** SC
   - **B.** LC
   - **C.** ST
   - **D.** LT

   C. ST connectors are commonly used with multi-mode fiber-optic cables. A, B, and D are incorrect. SC connectors are square shaped and not spring-loaded. LC connectors, like SC, are square snap-in connectors that are commonly used with single-mode fiber-optic cables. LT is not a valid type of connector.

8. Which of the following statements best describe a MAC address? Choose two.
   - **A.** They are used to route network packets.
   - **B.** Packets being sent to hosts on remote networks are addressed to that host's MAC address.
   - **C.** MAC addresses are 48 bits long.
   - **D.** Each server NIC has a unique MAC address.

   C, D. MAC addresses are 48 bits long and expressed in hexadecimal format. Each server NIC will have its own unique MAC address. A and B are incorrect. IP addresses are used to route packets, not MAC addresses. Transmitting nodes do not know the MAC address of a target node on a remote network.

9. A data center uses disk images to deploy new physical servers quickly. Rather than have technicians apply the operating system images locally from disk media, network imaging is desired. Which technology must be configured?
   - **A.** Wake-on-LAN
   - **B.** NIC teaming
   - **C.** Full duplex
   - **D.** PXE

   D. PXE booting makes it possible to boot from a NIC to retrieve a small operating system from a boot server that runs locally in server RAM. This is commonly used for imaging. A, B, and C are incorrect. Wake-on-LAN is used to wake up powered-down systems and should be used for desktops and not servers. NIC teaming is used to group together server NICs to increase bandwidth or redundancy. Full-duplex communication enables traffic to be sent and received simultaneously over the network cable.

10. Server1 has an IP address of 200.1.1.40/27. From Server1, you are attempting to make an SSH connection to Server2, whose IP address is 200.1.1.70/27, but you cannot connect. What might the problem be?

A. /27 is invalid.

B. 200.1.1.0 is a reserved IP range.

C. A default gateway is not properly configured on both servers.

D. UDP port 22 is blocked on Server2.

C. A default gateway is not properly configured on both servers. A, B, and D are incorrect. The /27 is a valid subnet mask, 200.1.1.0 is not a reserved IP range, and SSH uses TCP (not UDP) port 22.

11. Which of the following is a valid IPv6 link-local address?

A. fe80::883b:ced4:63f3:f297

B. fd75::883b:ced4:63f3

C. fe80::883b:ced4:63f3:fh97

D. fd75::883b:ced4:63g3

A. fe80::883b:ced4:63f3:f297 is a valid IPv6 link-local address. Link-local addresses are self-assigned by IPv6 nodes and enable LAN communications. This type of address is always present on IPv6 nodes. B, C, and D are incorrect. fd75::883b:ced4:63f3 is not a link-local address; the prefix must be fe80. In addition, fe80::883b:ced4:63f3:fh97 and fd75::883b:ced4:63g3 are invalid; hexadecimal allows only numbers 0–9 and letters A–F.

12. Widgets, Inc., has offices in London and Paris. The IT team has been directed to deploy IPv6 for test VLANs in both cities in anticipation of the eventual requirement of using IPv6. What should be configured to ensure that servers in each city test VLAN can communicate over the Internet?

A. 6to4

B. ISATAP

C. Teredo

D. NAT

A. 6to4 enables IPv6 networks to communicate over the IPv4 Internet; routers in both locations must support IPv6 on their internal interfaces. B, C, and D are incorrect. ISATAP is used on an IPv4 intranet, not the Internet. The Teredo standard allows IPv6 communication over the IPv4 Internet for IPv6 nodes behind NAT routers.

13. A help desk technician is addressing network connectivity issues being experienced by a user, Charlie. Charlie's station is unable to connect to a customer financial history database server on the same subnet named sect1-423.widgets.local, even though other stations do not have this problem; the error messages states "Unknown Host." The technician successfully pings the default gateway to verify a valid IP configuration from Charlie's station. What should the technician do next?

    A. Nothing. The server is down.

    B. Verify that Charlie's station has a default gateway configured.

    C. Verify that Charlie has authenticated to the server first.

    D. Verify that Charlie's station is properly configured with at least one DNS server.

    D. DNS allows connections to hosts by name instead of IP addresses. A, B, and C are incorrect. We know the server is not down because other stations can connect. The default gateway is not used for communication on the local subnet. Authentication is not the problem, because we know the error is that the server name is not even a known host.

14. Your smartphone receives an alert stating that ServerHFX-234 is not responding. You connect to the server using hardware remote control and issue the `ipconfig` command. You then notice the server IP address is 169.254.46.63. Why is the server having communication problems?

    A. The machine was unable to reach a DHCP server.

    B. The machine must be configured with a private IPv4 address.

    C. The machine is not configured with a DNS server IP address.

    D. The machine is not configured with a valid subnet mask.

    A. Systems will assign themselves an APIPA address beginning with 169.254 when a DHCP server cannot be contacted. B, C, and D are incorrect. The symptom does not indicate in any way that the server needs a private IPv4 address, DNS server, or subnet mask configuration.

15. A colleague, Courtney, discusses the newly installed Layer 3 switches in the wiring closet. What benefit does a Layer 3 switch offer beyond a Layer 2 switch?

    A. Bridging

    B. Switching

    C. Routing

    D. VLANs

C. Layer 3 switches can use IP routing to transmit packets to destination networks instead of relying solely on MAC addresses and switch ports. A, B, and D are incorrect. Bridging is a Layer 2 mechanism for network segmentation that is based on MAC addresses. Although switching can apply to Layers 2 and 3, it is not solely related to Layer 3. Virtual local area networks (VLANs) are available also with Layer 2 switches, such as port-based VLANs, which group devices together based on the switch ports they are plugged into.

16. Which of the following are valid methods of configuring VLANs? Choose two.

A. Username

B. IP address

C. Switch port

D. PKI certificate

B, C. Switch administrators can configure VLAN membership by IP address and by switch port. A and D are incorrect. Usernames and PKI certificates are not used to configure VLAN membership.

17. What type of address applies to Layer 2 switches?

A. IP

B. Port

C. LUN

D. MAC

D. MAC addresses are Layer 2 addresses. The MAC address is the hardware address of a network interface. A, B, and C are incorrect. IP addresses are Layer 3 addresses, ports are Layer 4 addresses, and a LUN is a unique value assigned to network storage.

18. What type of address applies to Layer 3 switches?

A. IP

B. Port

C. LUN

D. MAC

A. IP addresses are Layer 3 addresses. B, C, and D are incorrect. Port addresses apply to Layer 4, LUNs are unique values assigned to network storage, and MAC addresses are Layer 2 hardware addresses.

19. Which software communication method is not used with IPv6?

A. Broadcast

B. Unicast

C. Multicast

D. Anycast

A. IPv6 does not use software broadcasts. B, C, and D are incorrect. IPv6 unicasts are one-to-one transmissions, multicasts are one-to-many, and anycasts are sent to the nearest member of a multicast group.

20. A new web server is installed with an Intranet web site. User authentication to the site is not required. Your boss asks you to configure the firewall appliance to enable people to browse to the new site. Which port should you open on the firewall appliance?

A. 25

B. 110

C. 80

D. 443

C. HTTP web servers normally listen for client connections on TCP port 80. A, B, and D are incorrect. SMTP uses port 25, POP3 uses 110, and HTTPS uses 443.

CHAPTER 6

Security

In this chapter, you will

- Examine different types of security controls
- Determine how to secure resource access
- Identify best practices for hardening networks and servers
- Learn how encryption protects server data

This chapter provides a great reference for technicians responsible for setting up security controls that protect not only servers, but the network environment in which those servers live. A few scary security examples are scattered throughout the chapter to put you in the security frame of mind.

Physical Security

Technological security solutions are great; they solve business problems efficiently and are absolutely required for businesses to remain competitive and safe. But sometimes old-school methods can be overlooked. Security measures such as firewalls and antimalware won't help if your server disks are not behind locked doors in a protected facility.

Premises Access

The first line of physical defense is perimeter security comes from the following:

- Fencing
- Lighting
- Locked gates
- Security guards
- Guard dogs
- Limited access to areas of a facility
- Motion-sensing security systems

It doesn't make sense for every organization and government agency to implement all of these measures, but some of them can be implemented to improve security.

Access to a physical structure is always an issue. And it is a very big deal when it comes to data centers, because hundreds or thousands of customers' data is stored in a data center and is ideally replicated to other data centers for fault tolerance. This is why some providers are reluctant to supply even the addresses of their data centers.

Security guards are important for building security, even if their services are shared by multiple tenants. A visiting guest who is expected to enter a secured facility should be placed on an access list ahead of time so guards can refer to the list when the guest arrives and provides identification. Many business complexes require that you present some kind of ID card, or in some cases a photo ID, before you can enter the facility, especially after hours.

Mantraps are used at building entrances where high security is a must. A second inner door opens only after the first outer door has closed (and locked). This prevents tailgating—when an unauthorized person slips into a door behind you.

Of course, security cameras would capture somebody slipping in behind you. Every facility has a policy regarding surveillance footage retention, if it is retained at all. The mere presence of a security camera can serve as a deterrent to bad behavior, as can signage stating that the area is being watched. The wording on signage can be important for legal reasons: you don't want parties claiming they didn't know they were being watched and that their privacy rights have been violated.

Once people have physical access to the facility, internal physical controls can further keep sensitive information safe. A clean desk policy means not leaving sensitive documents in areas where anybody can see them, and locking sensitive documents or even backup tapes in a locked cabinet is better than leaving them out in the open.

Card-based Access

Radio-frequency identification (RFID) chips are embedded in many types of cards, including building access cards and toll cards for roads and bridges. RFID was designed to be used for inventory and asset tracking, but its use has expanded in a variety of ways.

You might be wondering how an RFID card differs from a smartcard. Smartcards, such as debit and credit cards, are designed to be used for payment systems, and they have more security built in. RFID chips have a longer wireless range than smartcards, which introduces more security vulnerabilities. Payment cards normally encrypt wireless transmissions to the receiving terminal, and these days that's done often using near-field communication (NFC). RFID cards, on the other hand, are not encrypted. With either card type, the primary benefit is convenience. You may have to enter a PIN to use a card, but it's still very easy to use. The downside is that somebody may be able to scan private data stored on a card.

The type of data stored on a card varies from one vendor's card to another, but generally you can expect the following:

- Card type
- Account numbers
- Account expiry
- Account holder name
- Card and account expiration dates
- PIN, or a hash of a PIN

Figure 6-1 Embedded chip on a payment card

Forging a smartcard is extremely difficult to do, since we're talking about a microprocessor chip embedded into a card (Figure 6-1)—and an average thief will not be able to reproduce this.

The Human Element

People are the biggest security threat of all. Companies should implement strict hiring and background check policies to ensure that employees can be trusted with sensitive information. Still, no system is perfect; consider, for example, intelligence agent Jeffrey Delisle of the Royal Canadian Navy, who supplied sensitive information to a Russian spy agency beginning in 2007.

The other aspect of the human security element is user awareness and training. The best technical safeguards are not effective if users don't understand threats such as social engineering and e-mail phishing; it pays to be paranoid and cynical! Providing documentation to employees about security awareness is usually not effective. Instead, lunch-and-learn sessions presented by dynamic speakers will make these important issues much more memorable.

Authentication

Authentication is the process of proving one's identity. Technicians generally assume that authentication applies only to individuals, but it can also be used to prove the identity of

- Users
- Devices
- Services
- Applications

Everybody is familiar with supplying a username and password to authenticate to a system. At the device level, a smartphone with a virtual private network (VPN) app might need a unique device Public Key Infrastructure (PKI) security certificate that is trusted by the VPN server before the user even gets a chance to provide their credentials to the VPN. Or a client desktop might require a unique PKI certificate before being given access to a restricted web site. Normally, secured web sites require a PKI certificate only server-side, but for very sensitive sites, clients might need a certificate, too.

A security certificate can be applied to the software, so that when it runs it can authenticate to another component for proper functionality. For example, a web service might use a PKI certificate to authenticate to a back-end database.

Successful authentication is required before access is granted to computing resources such as web sites, databases, files, and so on. There are various categories of authentication, as discussed in the following sections.

Identity Federation

Today's business computer environments are increasingly complex: there are business-to-business connectivity requirements as well as on-premises–to–public cloud connections. There needs to be a way to centralize authentication that supports Single Sign-On (SSO).

Identify federation strives to provide a single centralized identity store. "Single" doesn't mean it can't be replicated to multiple servers. Think of a company that plans to use public cloud services and has Microsoft Active Directory user accounts configured on-premises. Why re-create users and passwords in the cloud?

Web applications can be configured to trust security tokens issued from a trusted identity store. Security tokens contain *claims*, or assertions about a user or device. For example, a user claim might consist of an e-mail address and a date of birth. Different applications will consume different claims; it depends on the app.

With identify federation, apps don't have to handle authentication themselves; instead, they consume trusted security tokens containing claims. Replicating credentials from on-premises to the cloud enables web SSO, so users don't have to keep entering their credentials when they access different resources.

EXAM TIP Web SSO between on-premises networks and public cloud providers is achieved by replicating an on-premises directory service to a cloud-based directory service.

Microsoft Active Directory Federation Services (ADFS) does this nicely, as do other solutions such as the open-source Shibboleth product. Figure 6-2 shows how claims can be configured: the Employee-ID attribute in the left column is changed in the claim to EmpID. This would occur if a consuming web app needed to see a claim with EmpID and not Employee-ID; this will vary from application to application.

Something You Know

This type of security is stored in your head and hopefully nobody else's. A password, PIN, mother's maiden name, color of your first car, middle child's nickname—stuff about you that shouldn't be easy to figure out or find on social media or through web searches.

Most authentication today still relies on a username and password combination. Even though this consists of two items, they both fall under a single category (something you know), so we call this *single-factor authentication*.

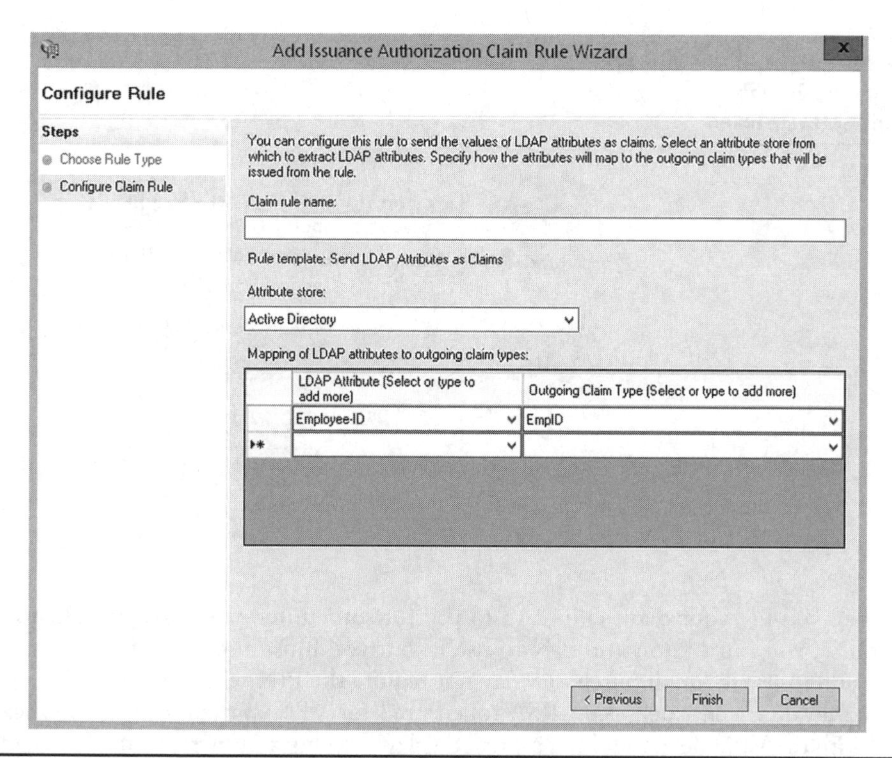

Figure 6-2 Mapping an LDAP attribute to an outgoing claim

EXAM TIP Watch out for questions that reference multifactor authentication, and make sure the methods are from different authentication categories.

The problem with the traditional password is that it's not really all that secure—and users hate it. If you're using passwords, you have to change them periodically based on your organization's security policy. This is a tedious task; users are normally required to change their passwords to something they've never used before, and the new password must meet complexity requirements, such as some uppercase and lowercase letters, numbers, symbols. No wonder users get exasperated!

Problems with passwords result in user frustration, less time spent at work being productive, increased help desk costs, and—as if that's not enough—they are not very secure. Nevertheless, a username/password combination is still the number one authentication system in use today—go figure!

Something You Have

Some authentication mechanisms require that you have physical possession of something—a smartcard, for example, or a hardware token (also called security tokens or key fobs). These days, some apps can act as software tokens. Administrators make token files available to users to import into their software token application, as shown in Figure 6-3.

Figure 6-3 Configuring the RSA SecurID software token

When you use your debit chip card to pay for something, you're using a smartcard. Of course, you must know the PIN to use it, but you must also have the card in your possession to use it. Small purchases may not require the PIN with some cards.

A hardware token, such as an RSA token used for VPN authentication, is synchronized with the VPN device and has a small display showing a numeric value that changes periodically—every 90 seconds, for instance. This numeric value must be entered within an acceptable timeframe, in addition to some other type of authentication, such as username and password, before access to the VPN is granted.

Another example of something you have is a PKI security certificate. Your smartphone might use this to establish trust (at the device level) between the phone and a VPN appliance. The same holds true with servers that must trust each other before transmitting sensitive information.

Something You Are

Each and every one of us is biologically unique in some way. Nothing is perfect, though; a fingerprint scan could be defeated by forcing somebody to press their finger on a scanner—or, in a gruesome scenario, by an attacker taking a finger with them to place on a scanner.

This category of authentication, called *biometric authentication,* uses unique identifying characteristics, including the following:

- Fingerprint
- Voice recognition
- Facial recognition
- Speech or gesture recognition
- Behavioral recognition

- Retinal scan
- Iris scan
- Handwriting recognition

For years, certain laptop models have included built-in fingerprint scanners; of course, you can use an external fingerprint scanner connected via USB. Fingerprint scans generally require a unique eight-point match for successful authentication. This means the fingerprint scan must already exist somewhere on the system.

Many vendors offer products that enable biometric authentication integration with existing systems. For example, we could store fingerprints with Microsoft Active Directory user accounts by extending the schema (blueprint) to enable this to be stored as an attribute of a user.

Biometric authentication might also be configured to enable access to more sensitive data than would be available with only username and password authentication.

Under Lock and Key

You might use a proximity or swipe card to gain access to a building and to certain floors or areas. Keypads are another option for opening doors, as well as arming and disarming security systems; you have to know the code. Keypads are great for server rooms—we don't want unfettered access to racks of equipment that includes storage media. Server room doors should never be left open, even for ventilation reasons; HVAC should be taking care of that!

A data center can contain thousands of physical servers (and tens or hundreds of thousands of virtual machines). Many rack systems for data centers have doors on the front and back that can be locked; this controls physical access to the fronts and backs of rack-mounted equipment.

It might be important to use a lock-down security cable to protect expensive data projection units, but these are replaceable and don't contain sensitive company data as laptops would. Yet how often do we see laptops being locked down compared to projection units?

Mobile devices introduce enormous risks, yet they are ubiquitous at home just as they are at work. As with USB thumb drives, mobile devices and storage media are easily lost, stolen, forgotten at a client site, and so on.

Logical Access Control

Managing individual user access to resources is difficult to manage on a large network; therefore, it is rarely done. Auditing individual users makes sense to reduce information overload, however.

Groups

The standard procedure for resource access in most of today's networks is as follows:

1. Create a group following company standards.
    - Naming conventions

2. Grant resource permissions to the group.
   - Web site
   - Database
   - Files/folders
   - Categories of data
3. Add members to the group.
   - Users
   - Devices
   - Other groups (group nesting)

NOTE Adding group members in Microsoft Active Directory requires that the user added to the group log off and log back on again. The access token that contains groups memberships is updated only upon initial user logon.

Anyone in a group who, for example, has been granted read and write permission to a file will inherit those permissions, because the user is a member of the group. One problem with groups is that you might need hundreds of groups to manage resources access, and that's a lot of additional items to manage. Then there's the issue of group membership being static (members are manually added and removed).

Some tools enable dynamic group membership, for example, based on some kind of characteristic, such as whether an employee is full-time or part-time—but you're still managing a group. Be careful of distribution list groups, which is the case with Microsoft Active Directory (see Figure 6-4), because this type of group (versus a security group) cannot be assigned permissions; it is designed for use by e-mail systems.

Dynamic Access Control

Other solutions such as Microsoft Windows Server 2012 R2 Dynamic Access Control (DAC) offer alternatives (see Figure 6-5). DAC is nothing new, other than the fact that it is now built into the OS. DAC looks at user and device Active Directory (AD) attributes to determine what level of access, if any, is granted to files and folders (*resources*). This can be done without groups, but somebody must have filled in the user and device attributes in AD. For example, DAC may enable only read access to a folder for full-time employees in Orlando, yet full-time employees at headquarters may be given read and write permissions.

Roles

Roles are similar to groups, but one difference is that a role might apply to a single individual, such as a CEO. As we do with groups, we assign resource permissions to roles and we then assign a role occupant. The occupant then gets the role permissions.

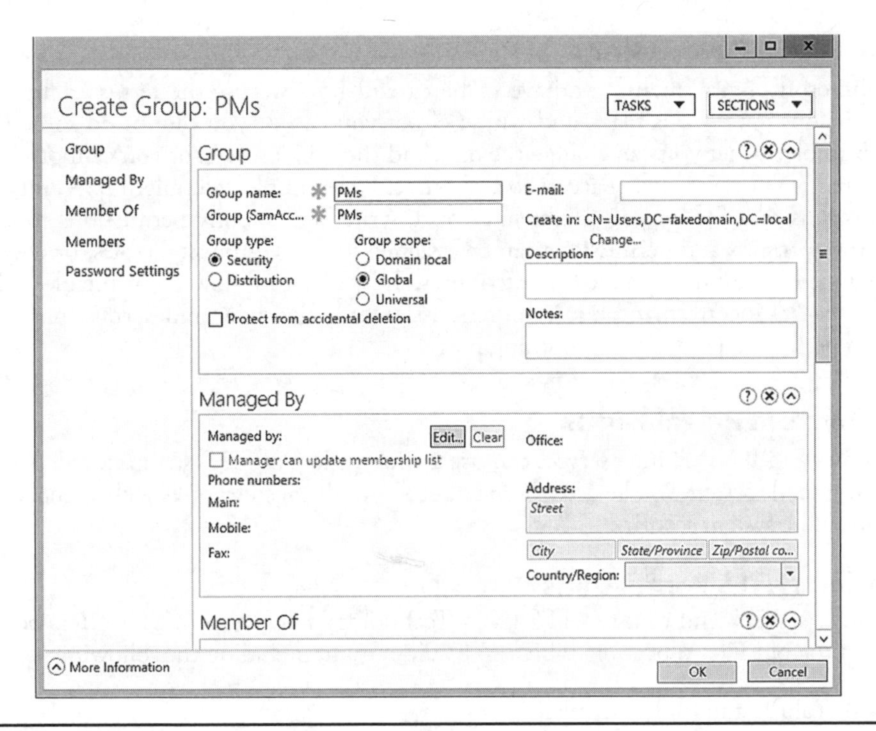

Figure 6-4 Creating a group using the Active Directory Administrative Center

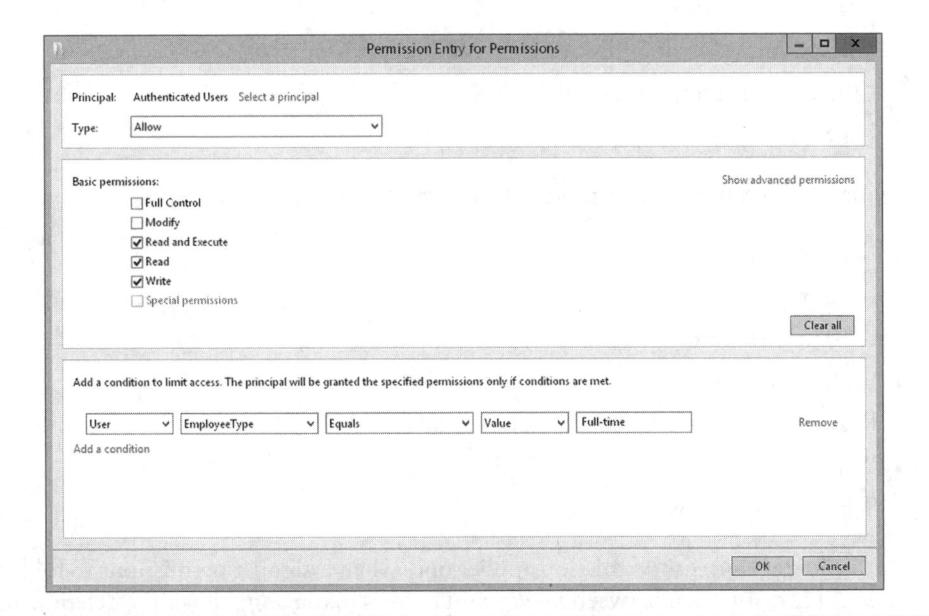

Figure 6-5 Configuring conditional file system permissions in Windows Server 2012 R2

Rights and Permissions

In Microsoft environments, we have to be careful how we use the terms "rights" and "permissions." A *right* is black-and-white: either you can or you cannot do something. For example, either you can change the date and time on a server, or you cannot.

Permissions are a degree of access to a resource. For example, you might have only read permissions to a file, or you might have read, write, and modify permissions to a file. Either way, rights and permissions can be assigned to users, groups, or roles, or they can be assigned conditionally based on attributes. Take care to follow the principle of least privilege—it's inconvenient, but it matters: assign only the rights and permissions necessary to perform a job task, and nothing more.

File System Permissions

Windows and UNIX/Linux servers can use a wide variety of file system types depending on how the file system will be used. Some offer more advanced features such as encryption and local file system security.

Windows NTFS Permissions

Windows servers tend to use NTFS (New Technology File System). This offers benefits beyond the old File Allocation Table (FAT) file system, including the following:

- Local file and folder permissions
- File and folder encryption using Encrypting File System (EFS)
- File system auditing
- File system journaling (disk recovery and repair is quicker)
- Data deduplication to save disk space
- Disk space quotas

Standard NTFS permissions (Figure 6-6) include

- Full control
- Modify
- Read and execute
- List folder contents
- Read
- Write
- Special permissions

The list folder contents permission applies only when assigning permissions to folders, not files. A big distinction between *modify* and *write* is that *modify* allows file deletion and *write* does not. Special permissions provide a further degree of granularity; for instance, you may want to allow the creation of folders but not new files (both are possible if a user is allowed to write).

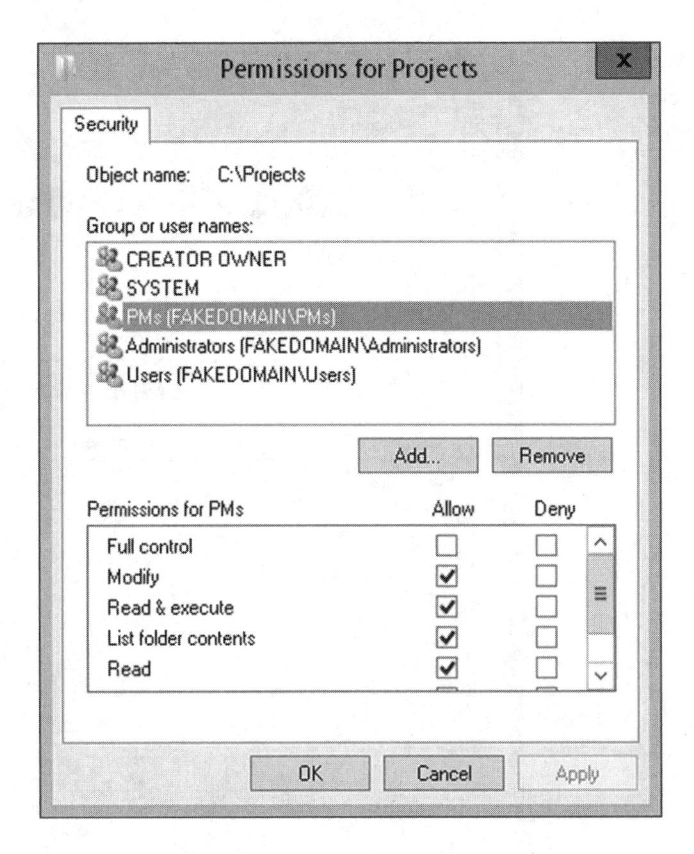

Figure 6-6 NTFS standard permissions

NTFS permissions can be assigned to a drive, a folder, or a file. When assigned to a drive or folder, the permissions are inherited by subordinate file system objects. You can either allow or deny permissions.

Permissions inheritance can be altered by clicking the Disable Inheritance button—you get to this screen by right-clicking a file or folder and choosing Properties, click the Security tab, then click the Advanced button. You can also alter permissions inheritance by adding a new access control list (ACL) entry for a user, group, or computer with a different set of permissions that will then apply from that point in the file system downward.

Windows Shared Folder Permissions

Individual files cannot be shared over the network, but folders can. To control network access to shared folders, we configure share permissions (Figure 6-7). As with applying permissions to any resource, groups are normally used.

There are three shared folder permissions:

- Full Control
- Change
- Read

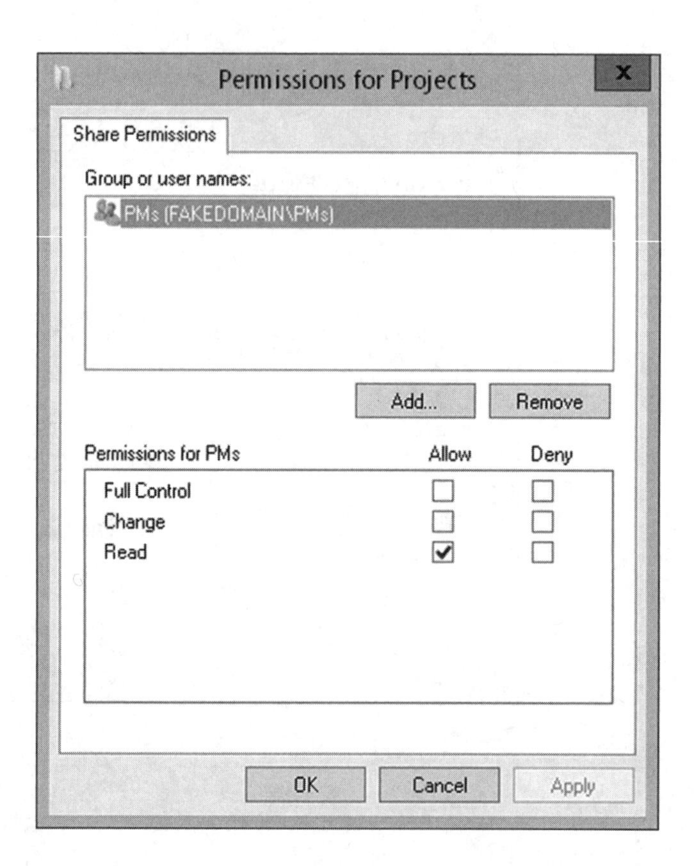

Figure 6-7 Shared folder permissions

NOTE When combining both NTFS and share permissions, the most restrictive permissions will apply. A common strategy is to be a bit more liberal with share permissions and then lock things down granularly with NTFS permissions.

Linux File System Permissions

Many types of file systems are available for UNIX and Linux operating systems, including ReiserFS, Ext4, and XFS, to name a few.

Some file systems support extended permissions, but here we will look at the standard permissions that will work on any type of UNIX/Linux file system:

- Read (r), 4
- Write (w), 2
- Execute (x), 1

You're probably wondering what the listed numbers mean. The *r*, *w*, and *x* should be self-explanatory. Read has an internal value of 4, write is 2, and execute is 1.

Three sets of these three permissions (r, w, and x) apply to the following:

- Owner of the file or directory
- A group associated with the file or directory
- Everyone else

That's why you'll sometimes see commands such as `chmod 760 project_b.txt` (see Figure 6-8). The `chmod` means "change mode"; it's how we set file system permissions at a shell prompt (there are Linux GUI shells that will allow this to be done without typing).

Back to the example: `chmod 760 /projects`. The `7` applies to the file or directory owner; it is the sum of 4 + 2 + 1 (r + w + x), so it means the owner has read, write, and execute permissions. The `6` value is the sum of 4 + 2 (r + w), so the group associated with the file or directory has read and write permissions. The `0` means that neither read, write, nor execute has been assigned to everybody else.

The `chmod` command also has a `-R` command line switch that recursively applies permissions to a directory and everything in and under it. Note that delete and modify are both included in the write permission. If you are logged into Linux as the root superuser account, these file system permissions are not applied, because they are for non-root users.

NOTE Don't forget that Linux commands are case-sensitive! So **`Chmod`** and **`chmod`** are not the same thing!

Peripheral Devices

Access control should also be considered for peripheral devices such as printers, data projectors, and USB devices.

Projectors

Because a data projector doesn't store sensitive company information and its contents won't endanger human lives, there's not too much more you can do to lock it down

```
root@rhel7-1:/projects
[root@rhel7-1 projects]# chmod 760 project_b.txt
[root@rhel7-1 projects]# ls -l
total 4
-rwxrw----. 1 root root 10 Jul 26 08:36 project_b.txt
[root@rhel7-1 projects]#
```

Figure 6-8 Setting file system permissions in Linux

beyond preventing it from being physically stolen. Modern projectors support Wi-Fi, so they can be discovered on the network—but, again, there's not a huge threat here.

Printers

Printers are another story. Some printers store queued jobs for a period of time, which could conceivably be retrieved by a determined malicious user. Whether or not the network printer is managed by a centralized print server, access to manage the printer must be secure. Change the default administrative username and password and make sure HTTPS administrative access is enabled (as opposed to HTTP).

One benefit of using a print server to manage printers is centralized management and security control. If you use a Windows print server or a Linux CUPS print server, you can determine what printing privileges are granted to different groups of users.

EXAM TIP Even though users can print directly to printers without a print server, remember that print servers provide centralized security and management.

USB

This is a catch-all category; pretty much any type of peripheral can be plugged into a computer via USB, and this is really important from a security standpoint. Malware infections are scary and can infect your server depending on what you plug into USB ports—not just into servers themselves, but also into any device that in some way can contact your servers.

Scary USB devices include

- Smartphones
- Tablets
- Storage media
- Halloween skeletons (these do exist—search it up)

Ransomware sends a chill of fear down the backs of all server geeks. This type of malware is in epidemic mode as of the writing of this book. It executes on an infected computer and encrypts any files that the infected computer can write to, including server drives. The only way to get a decryption key is to pay a ransom in Bitcoins, assuming you'd get the key anyway. If you're lucky, you'll be able to rebuild affected systems quickly from images and backup—but it's not always that easy.

One way to mitigate USB threats is to disable USB ports for storage media, while allowing peripherals such as printers, keyboards, and mice. There are ways to enforce this centrally, such as using Group Policy in an Active Directory environment, as shown in Figure 6-9. Of course, antimalware solutions can help with some infections, but not all of them. The best security measure? User awareness and education! Ransomware is usually spread by phishing e-mails or by people clicking on web page links or opening file attachments they weren't expecting via e-mail.

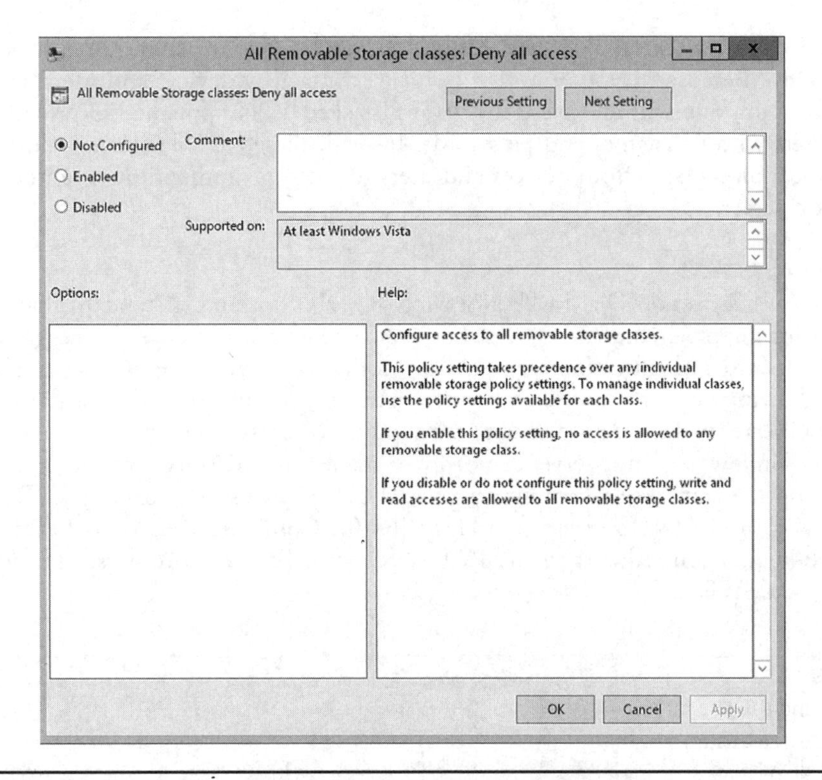

Figure 6-9 Configuring Group Policy to block access to removable storage

Network Security

Networks are cool: millions of interconnected devices share data around the planet in a matter of seconds. But this also means the bad guys (and gals) have an infrastructure in place to ply their despicable trade. On a corporate network, one important consideration is strictly controlling access to your networks in the first place.

NAC

Network Access Control (NAC) is often referred to as "port-based security." These ports are logical, not physical—you can think of a port as some kind of entry point into a network.

When IT techies chat about NAC, you'll also hear them mention "802.1x." IEEE 802.1x is a worldwide standard for port-based security, or controlling access into your network. Think of the various network edge devices that enable connections to the network:

- Network switches
- Wireless routers
- VPN appliances

These edge devices should never perform authentication for connecting devices and users. Why? Because they are the first point of contact by devices and users, and they could be compromised, and we don't want a hacked VPN appliance to provide malicious users with usernames and passwords. Instead, these edge devices should forward authentication requests from devices and users to a central authentication authority—a RADIUS server.

RADIUS Servers

Remote Authentication Dial-In User Service (RADIUS) is an old standard that persists today, with improvements made over the years. The idea is that edge devices (RADIUS clients) forward authentication requests from connecting devices and users (supplicants) before allowing network access. Only after successful centralized authentication via the RADIUS server will the device or users be allowed to access the network.

Your Windows or Linux server can easily be made into a RADIUS server by installing the appropriate software and configuring a RADIUS shared secret between the RADIUS clients and the RADIUS server (see Figure 6-10). Configure RADIUS clients to forward authentication requests to the RADIUS server. For Wi-Fi routers, use the WPA Enterprise or WPA2 Enterprise option.

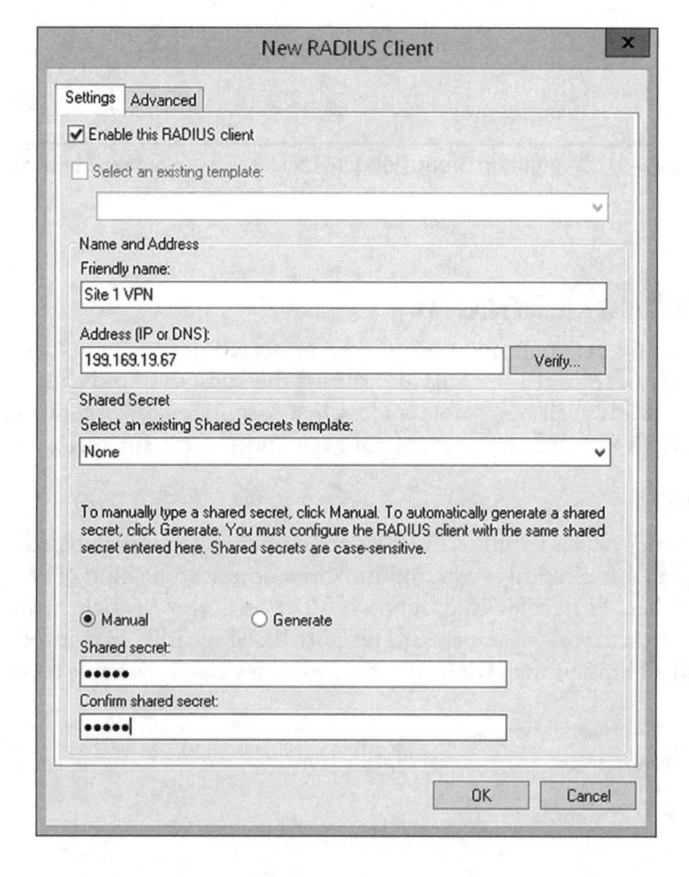

Figure 6-10 Configuring a VPN appliance as a trusted RADIUS client

TACACS

Terminal Access Controller Access-Control System (TACACS) and its newer variant TACACS+ are designed to handle frequent authorization requests within a session; RADIUS is designed primarily for authentication at the beginning of a session. TACACS+ enhances security by encryption transmissions, and it is based on the TCP transport mechanism as opposed to UDP, which is used by RADIUS. TACACS+ is normally used to administer network devices, while RADIUS is used primarily for centralized authentication.

VLANs

A virtual local area network is similar conceptually to adding a new network segment to your existing network infrastructure. Technically, creating a new VLAN creates a new broadcast domain (just like a new physical network would). Network broadcasts are addressed to all devices on a network, although routers do not forward these broadcasts to other networks.

Let's say, for example, that you have a 24-port OSI Layer 3 Ethernet switch. By default, all 24 ports are grouped into the same VLAN. This means that if you plug in 24 network devices and configure them on the same IP subnet, they can all communicate with one another.

There are times, however, when you may want to split your 24-port switch into smaller networks. Why would you do this? Because smaller networks perform better than larger ones, and you might want isolation between networks—maybe a VLAN for deploying images to new computers (which slows down the network), and a separate VLAN for accounting computers.

From a security perspective, separate VLANs present a simple security barrier. A router is needed to allow communication between VLANs, and a Layer 3 switch can do this, too; a Layer 2 switch does not have routing capabilities. VLANs are covered it more detail in Chapter 5.

NOTE Make sure you plug each physical server network interface card (NIC) into the correct switch port, especially if using port-based VLAN membership; otherwise, devices may not be able to communicate with the server.

VLAN Attacks

Even though traffic from one VLAN should not be able to reach a different VLAN without a router, as with everything in IT, there are vulnerabilities that actually let this happen—including, but not limited to, the following:

- **MAC flooding attacks** Fills MAC table limited memory on switches, which causes otherwise isolated traffic to be visible on other VLANs
- **VLAN hopping** Attacker spoofs the identity of another switch, and the attacker station then becomes a member of multiple VLANs

It's one thing to identify weaknesses, but what can we do about it? Switch administrators can enforce strong port security, allowing connections from specific or a limited number of MAC addresses—and, of course, the latest firmware updates should always be applied to network equipment.

Firewalls

Firewalls control inbound and outbound traffic, whether for an entire network or for a single network device. Some firewalls look only at IP addresses, port numbers, and protocol types, while others (OSI Layer 7 firewalls) perform deep packet inspection. The best approach is to block everything, and then create firewall rules to allow only traffic that is necessary.

Firewalls can be hardware- or software-based. Hardware-based appliances are generally more stable and can handle more traffic than their software counterparts. Just remember that hardware appliances also get firmware updates, so be sure to subscribe to vendor update notifications.

Host-based Firewalls

A host-based firewall runs as software on a specific host. Windows computers use the Windows firewall (configured through the GUI or the command line), while UNIX and Linux systems can use command line tools such as iptables. These are both considered OSI Layer 4 firewalls because they can allow or deny traffic based on the following:

- Source IP address
- Destination IP address
- Source port
- Destination port
- Protocol type

Some Windows services such as Active Directory require multiple ports for communication, in which case it is possible to work with groups of firewall rules, some of which are already included in Windows.

Windows Firewall The Windows Firewall can be configured in the GUI (Figure 6-11) or through the command line. Consider the following PowerShell example (not case-sensitive), which allows Active Directory–related communications by using a supplied firewall rule group:

```
Enable-NetFirewallRule -DisplayGroup "Active Directory Domain Services"
```

We could also add a custom firewall rule using PowerShell. In this example, assume we've installed an SSH listener on our Windows host and want to allow inbound SSH traffic:

```
New-NetFirewallRule -Protocol TCP -LocalPort 22 -Direction Inbound -Action
Allow -DisplayName SSHAdmin
```

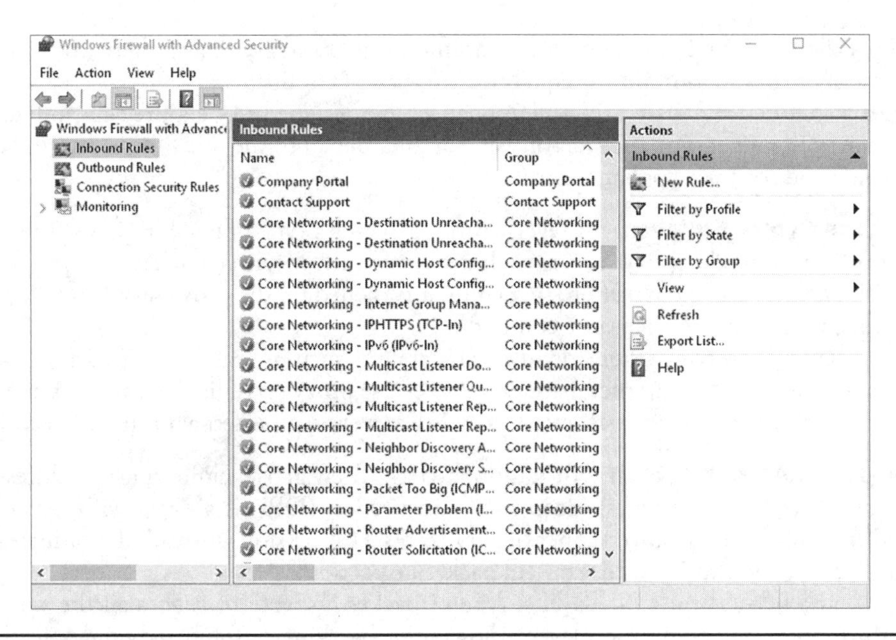

Figure 6-11 Creating a firewall rule using the Windows Firewall GUI

Linux Firewall You can use a variety of methods to configure a Linux firewall. Traditionally, the `iptables` command is used. Some Linux variants, such as Red Hat Enterprise Linux Server 7.1, have evolved to different tools such as FirewallD.

To allow incoming SSH administrative traffic, an `iptables` command would look like this:

```
iptables -A INPUT -p tcp -m tcp --dport 22 -j ACCEPT
service iptables save
```

`-A` means to add to the `INPUT` chain, `-p` means protocol, `-m` means match, `--dport` is the destination port, and `-j` means jump to `ACCEPT` (the target of this rule).

We could then list firewall rules with the following command:

```
iptables -L
```

Network-based Firewalls

Routers or specialized appliances function as network-based firewalls. These devices have at least two network interfaces. They are placed on the network where network traffic that must be examined will flow into and out of the network, such as between the Internet and an internal network. These are often called "perimeter firewalls."

Routers can be configured with network access control lists (ACLs) to control inbound and outbound traffic. For example, to configure a network ACL on a Cisco router, we would type the following:

```
interface ethernet0
ip access-group 102 in
access-list 102 permit tcp any any eq www
```

This allows (`permit`) incoming (`in`) traffic from anywhere to anywhere (`any any`) as long as the destination port is equal (`eq`) to www (TCP 80).

Dedicated network-based firewall appliances are designed to be a firewall (unlike an operating system running firewall software) and hardened to the hilt. They come in both hardware and software appliance forms.

Reverse Proxy Servers A reverse proxy server is a type of network-based firewall. Forward, or "normal," proxy servers fetch items from the Internet, such as web pages, on behalf of an internal client. Often, that content is cached on the proxy server to speed up subsequent requests for that same content.

Reverse proxy servers listen for incoming traffic, such as traffic destined for a web server. Although to the Internet it appears the reverse proxy server is the real web server, it isn't; it simply forwards requests quietly to a web server on an internal protected network.

Deep Packet Inspection In addition to basic firewall packet filtering (IP addresses, port numbers, protocol types), deep packet inspection (DPI) is a given with network-based firewalls. This advanced functionality tracks TCP sessions instead of treating each packet separately: this is called "stateful packet inspection."

DPI goes beyond the OSI Layer 4 type of packet inspection; it goes all the way up to OSI Layer 7, the application layer. Allowing or blocking traffic based on details such as payload content provides much more functionality than allowing or blocking traffic based solely on packet headers.

Many public cloud companies offer various types of firewalls in the cloud, a part of Security as a Service (SECaaS). For example, the Microsoft Azure cloud uses Network Security Groups (NSGs) to control inbound and outbound traffic at the subnet, virtual machine, and virtual NIC (VNIC) levels, as shown in Figure 6-12.

Distributed Denial-of-Service Attacks Not all distributed denial-of-service (DDoS) attacks are sophisticated; conceptually speaking, DDoS attacks are like jamming a communication channel with static so nothing meaningful gets through. The "distributed" part of DDoS means an attacker could have hundreds or thousands of infected computers (zombies and zombie nets) at their disposal to execute the attack.

Packet flooding can bring down a victim server or an entire network if enough machines send enough bogus traffic in a short period of time. Servers and network infrastructure equipment can handle only so much traffic at a time; too much garbage traffic means legitimate traffic doesn't get processed, and therein lies the issue. Of course, it takes nothing to spoof the source IP address of the zombie computers that ran the attack, so tracking down the culprit machines is made more difficult.

One common mitigation technique is to "black hole" the traffic—to discard traffic destined for the victim. Of course, this means legitimate traffic is also lost, so the attacker is still achieving their malicious objective. Depending on the specific DDoS attack, router ACLs could block some traffic as well, but doing this could require hundreds of ACL rules. Suffice it to say the standard firewalls are *not* designed to mitigate DDoS attacks.

DDoS perpetrators often demand payment from victims before they will turn off the packet tap. You might remember the BetCRIS DDoS attacks in the 2003. (BetCRIS is an online sports betting site.) Attackers would launch a DDoS against BetCRIS before

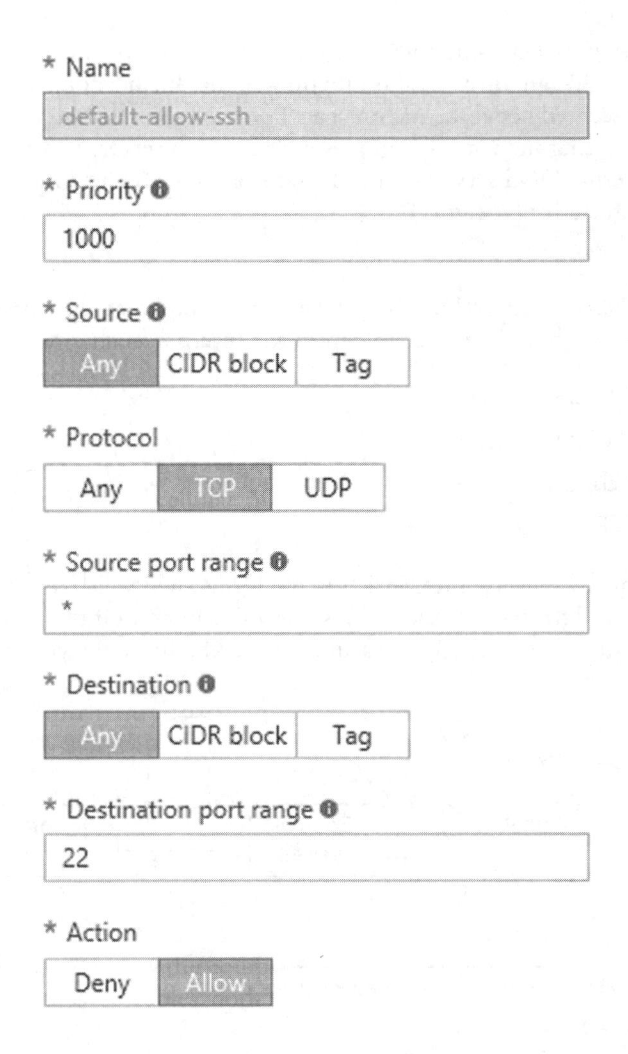

Figure 6-12 A Microsoft Azure Network Security Group rule

major live sporting events. The attackers demanded US $40,000 to cease the attacks for up to 12 months. For every day offline, BetCRIS lost up to US $100,000. Although a software developer was able to block that particular attack, further attacks by DDoS extortionists are expected, and this type of attack is becoming more problematic for other online businesses.

Security Zones

Planning a network layout involves dealing with sensitive systems residing on protected internal networks and services that should be visible to the Internet on external public-facing networks. An *intranet* is an internal network that can offer connection services like those found on the Internet.

Isolation is key—firewalls control traffic from the Internet into the public-facing network, which in turn has a second firewall that further controls traffic into and out of an internal secured network. You must always make sure that internal data is not replicated to a public-facing network—examples include DNS servers in a public network replicating with internal DNS servers—and the same goes for replicating directory services (such as Microsoft Active Directory).

DMZ

A *demilitarized zone* (DMZ) is an external public-facing network in which we place services that should be reachable from the Internet, such as the following:

- VPN appliances
- SMTP mail servers
- Web servers
- FTP servers

Normally, a reverse proxy exists in the DMZ, which listens for client requests for these services, and the services themselves exist on a different internal network that is protected by a firewall. Figure 6-13 shows an example of a firewall layout in a DMZ network.

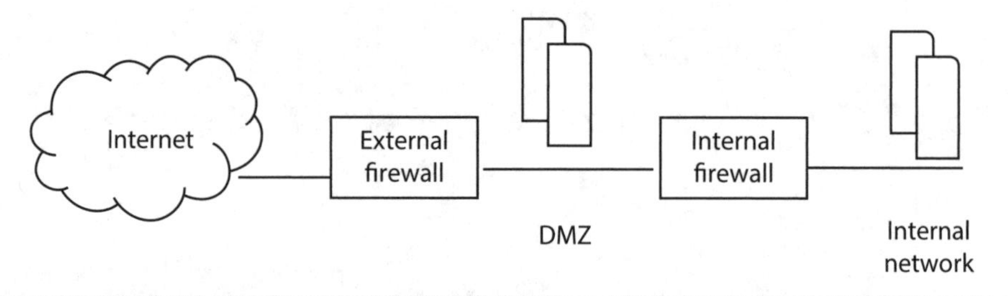

Figure 6-13 Firewalls in a DMZ network layout

EXAM TIP You could see an exam question about placement of firewalls or rules on a network architecture diagram. Remember that public services should exist in the DMZ either literally, or they should be accessible from the DMZ through a reverse proxy.

PKI

A *Public Key Infrastructure* (PKI) is a hierarchy of digital security certificates issued to users, devices, or services for the purposes of security. PKI certificates can be used to encrypt and digitally sign sensitive e-mail messages, to encrypt files, to authenticate a smartphone to a VPN, to secure a web site over HTTPS, and for other purposes.

The certificate authority (CA) is at the top of the hierarchy, and it can have subordinate CAs, such as in a large organization where each region may want its own CA. Finally, the actual PKI certificates are issued by either the CA or a subordinate CA, as pictured in Figure 6-14.

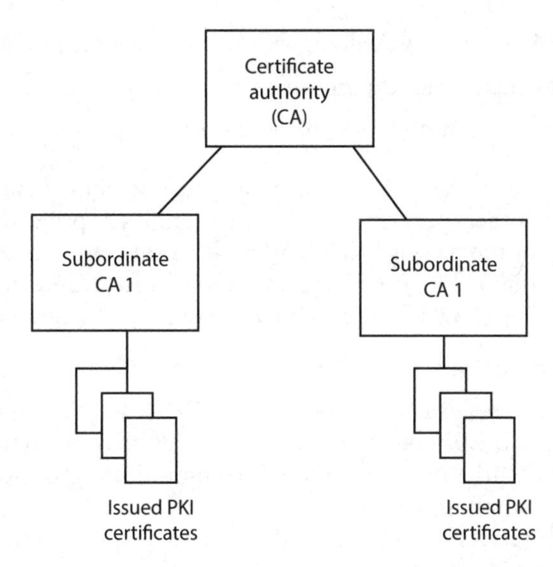

Figure 6-14
PKI hierarchy

You can install your own CA within your organization, which can then issue self-signed PKI certificates as you see fit. Certificates can be manually requested and issued or automatically issued, which is possible using Microsoft Group Policy.

The root, or top-level, CA should be kept offline, because if it is compromised, so, too, are all certificates issued within that hierarchy.

Instead of an internal CA, you can also pay a fee and acquire PKI certificates issued to third-party trusted CAs on the Internet, such as Google, DigiCert, and Symantec (formerly Verisign), to name a few.

PKI Certificate Contents

The certificate itself, also called an X.509 certificate, can be used as a file (ideally password-protected), or it can be burned into a magnetic strip or smartcard. But what exactly is stored in a PKI certificate?

When a certificate is issued by a CA or an intermediary CA, a template is used that contains details on what should be stored in the certificate. Common items in the certificate (along with examples) include the following:

- Serial number
- Subject name
  - User e-mail address, FQDN of web site
- A unique mathematically related public- and private-key pair
  - The private key must be kept secret
- Certificate use
  - E-mail or file encryption, code signing for developers

- Digital signature of CA along with signature algorithm used
- Date of issuance and expiration date
  - Certificate can no longer be used once it expires

The certificate can be exported with particular attributes, such as when a certificate is exchanged with other users for e-mail encryption. Encrypting an e-mail message requires the public key of the message recipient(s). So in this case, the recipient exports only the public key portion of the certificate and provides it to the sender. The mathematically related private key is used by the recipient to decrypt the message.

SSL and TLS

Secure Sockets Layer was developed in the 1990s by Netscape, and the version most widely used is SSL 3.0. Like its successor, Transport Layer Security (TLS), SSL provides encryption and authentication between communicating devices over a network. TLS version 1.3 is in draft as of this writing.

HTTP web servers use TCP port 80 for unencrypted connections and port 443 for HTTPS encrypted connections (the port numbers may vary, but these are normally used). The same is true for other higher level protocols such as SMTP, POP3, and so on. Whether you use SSL or TLS, a PKI certificate is required.

When the option is available, TLS should be used if it is supported by the applications, because SSL versions 2 and 3 are known to have serious security vulnerabilities. Modify the registry on a Windows server to disable SSL 3.0 and enable TLS 1.2. Using OpenSSL with Linux also supports TLS; this is configured per application (web site, web browser, and so on).

IPSec

Even though it's built into IPv6, Internet Protocol Security (IPSec) also works with IPv4. Contrary to popular belief, IPSec is not used solely for VPNs.

Unlike SSL and TLS, IPSec is not configured for each application. Consider that fact that if you want to secure an HTTP web server and an SMTP mail server you need to acquire a PKI certificate and configure both apps to use the certificates. With IPSec, you can secure network traffic without acquiring PKI certificates for each individual app or server.

IPSec applies policy settings to computers, and this dictates how IPSec will be used. For example, on a Windows Server 2012 R2 computer, IPSec is configured as part of the Windows Firewall under Connection Security Rules. It can be configured to be used where both parties communicating over a network use IPSec to secure network traffic, regardless of the protocol being used.

This is an interesting concept, because all the network traffic within your organization could be encrypted and authenticated using IPSec without your having to configure security for each app or network service. Even ping traffic could be encrypted. Some enterprise networks don't encrypt internal network traffic, but many threats can cause havoc within a network. If you have the option, you should encrypt all internal traffic.

Configuring IPSec requires some kind of key for authentication. Figure 6-15 shows key options when configuring Windows Firewall, including using the Kerberos protocol, certificates, and preshared keys.

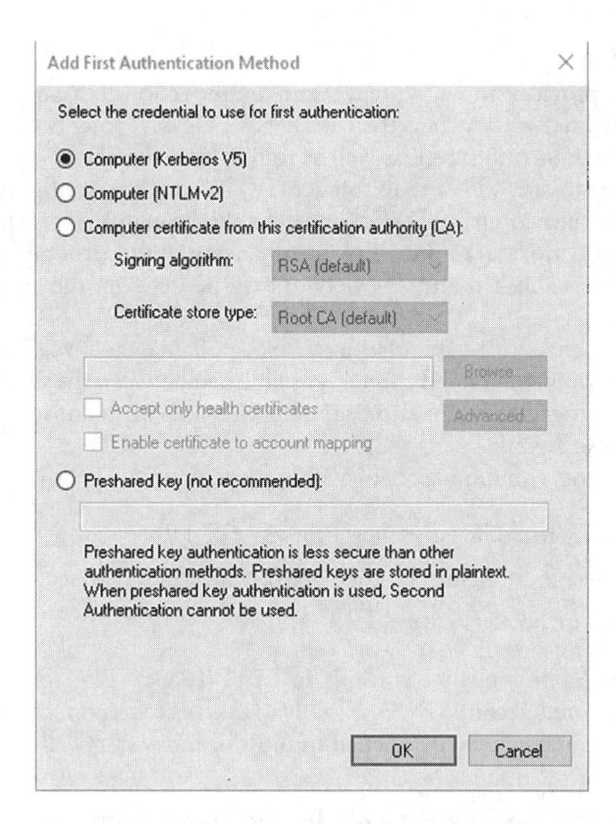

Figure 6-15 IPSec authentication options

EXAM TIP For computers joined to an Active Directory domain, the Kerberos protocol is the best choice for authentication. A preshared key is the weakest option, because it is a symmetric key, which means that the same key is used for encryption and decryption. The difficulty with symmetric keys is how to distribute them securely—knowledge of the symmetric key is all that is required for decryption.

IPSec Tunnel Mode

IPSec tunnel mode is normally used between two endpoint VPN devices, such as a site-to-site VPN over the Internet. It works by encrypting the entire original IP packet (not just the payload) and adding a new IP header so that the transmission can get to the other end of the tunnel.

Tunnel mode can also be used between a client and server or VPN appliance. In technical jargon, the original IP packet is said to be "encapsulated" in a new IPSec packet.

IPSec Transport Mode

IPSec transport mode doesn't encrypt the entire original IP packet (headers and payload), but just the payload itself. Communication between devices is protected regardless of the protocol being used.

VPNs

A VPN provides an encrypted, secured connection to a target private network over an untrusted network such as the Internet. VPNs have long been used by people who work from home or who travel, as well as to link sites together over the Internet.

Client-to-site VPNs require client VPN software configured to connect to a VPN appliance in a company DMZ (or reachable through a reverse proxy in the DMZ). Once a user authenticates to the VPN, ideally using multifactor authentication, the encrypted tunnel is established and any network traffic between the client and VPN appliance is secured.

Site-to-site VPNs require a VPN appliance at two different network sites. A point-to-point encrypted tunnel is established between the two VPN appliances that link networks together. It can also be used between an on-premises network and a pubic cloud provider's network.

The most common types of VPN protocols are

- Point-to-Point Tunneling Protocol (PPTP)
- Layer 2 Tunneling Protocol with IPSec (L2TP/IPSec)
- Secure Sockets Layer (SSL) tunnel

If the VPN appliance is using an L2TP/IPSec VPN, the VPN client software must be configured accordingly. SSL VPNs have become popular because they use standard HTTPS ports, which are opened in most of today's firewalls.

Intrusion Detection and Prevention Systems

Intrusion detection (ID) and intrusion prevention (IP) play a big role in securing hosts and networks by looking for anomalous, or suspicious, activity that doesn't match normal network usage patterns.

Host Intrusion Detection System

A host intrusion detection system (HIDS) detects suspicious activity related to a specific host, such as an HTTP web server running multiple web apps. By monitoring network traffic into and out of the host, operating system, and application logs, the ID engine can determine whether something is out of the ordinary.

A HIDS must be configured to look for abnormalities; sophisticated solutions can monitor host activity over time and generate a baseline of normal activity. One benefit of a HIDS is that it can read traffic that is encrypted over the network; once the host decrypts that traffic, it can be examined. ID systems can send alert notifications to technicians, who can then take further action.

Network Intrusion Detection System

A network intrusion detection system (NIDS) is a standalone appliance that watches network activity, looking for anomalies. For this to work, the NIDS must be able to see all of the traffic.

In a network-switched environment, switch administrators will have to configure the switch to copy all packets to the port to which the NIDS is connected.

Here's an example: Using the open source Snort IDS, rules are created that determine what gets monitored. The Snort command line or configuration file specifies output log file locations for alert messages. To assign a unique Snort ID (sid) and to generate an alert for ICMP traffic from any host to any host, our Snort rule is configured as follows:

```
alert icmp any any -> any any (msg:"ICMP Traffic Detected";sid:3000003;)
```

Intrusion Prevention Systems

Intrusion prevention systems (IPSs) extend the functionality of IDSs by taking steps to prevent further damage when malicious activity is detected. Like IDSs, IPSs must be tuned for the specific host (HIPS) or network (NIPS) environment they will be monitoring.

An IPS can, for example, detect malware and remove or prevent the infection from spreading. Another example is excessive packets received from a remote network in a short amount of time; an IPS could block further traffic from that network address.

Hardening

Hardening a server reduces its attack surface. In a data center, server hardening is done through a centralized configuration and not on each and every individual server. Server operating system images can be hardened so that newly installed servers are reasonably safe right from the start.

Keeping systems secure is an ongoing process. Periodic vulnerability scans should be conducted to detect weakness in hardware, operating systems, and applications. Some vulnerability scanners can automatically correct, or remediate weaknesses; others will only report the discovered vulnerabilities. Often, patching and following secure configuration guidelines reduces vulnerabilities.

Operating System Hardening

There's no reason why a HIDS or HIPS shouldn't be implemented on each and every server. It makes sense for each server to have a dedicated component that watches for malicious activity, including malware, and either notifies administrators or takes some kind of corrective action.

The good news is that most modern server operating systems do not have much installed by default, so right away you're off to a good start. The following list contains common items addressed when hardening servers:

- Apply firmware updates to BIOS/UEFI RAID controllers.
- Set a CMOS boot password to prevent changing the boot order.
- Enable CPU No-eXecute (NX bit) at the BIOS level.
    - Prevent certain memory pages from running executable code.
    - Stop buffer overflow attacks.
- Lock the server chassis or rack case.

- Disable Wake-on-LAN.
    - We don't want servers brought down for maintenance to be remotely awakened.
- Apply operating system updates.
- Apply application software updates.
- Follow OS and application configuration best practices.
- Enable multifactor authentication.
- Install a HIDS/HIPS component.
- Keep your antimalware solution up to date.
- Configure a host-based firewall.
    - Block unused ports.
- Disable unused services and daemons.
- Disable unused accounts.
- Rename or disable default accounts.
- Enable auditing or logging related to the IT workload.
    - Copies of log entries should be forwarded to a different host.
    - Log forwarding is possible using Windows Event Log Forwarding and Linux syslog forwarding.
- Follow the principle of least privilege when assigning rights and permissions.
- Enable network encryption for all traffic if possible.
    - Traffic on internal networks should also be encrypted (consider using IPSec).
- Encrypt data at rest on all storage media.

None of these items should be a surprise, especially since most organizational security policies will insist on these configurations.

Hardware Hardening

In addition to applying the latest firmware updates for server hardware, applying firmware updates for network infrastructure and network devices is crucial. Hardware to consider includes the following:

- Routers
- Switches
- SAN switches
- SAN backup devices
- Disk arrays
- Network printers
- VPN appliances

- Firewall appliances
- Wireless access points
- Wireless routers

When it comes to devices such as network switches, there is an entire set of configuration items to consider when hardening. For instance, unused switch ports should be disabled; switch ports should not allow numerous MAC addresses, which could indicate a VLAN MAC flooding attack; remote Telnet administration should be disabled in favor of SSH; and so on.

Application Hardening

Many hardening techniques that apply to hardening server operating systems also apply to application hardening. You need to have a strong knowledge of the application before locking it down so that you can keep it functional.

Patching is always crucial—whether for operating systems, drivers, or specific application patches. For example, plenty of Microsoft Office memory corruption vulnerabilities have been addressed by patches. To be fair, the open source LibreOffice has had its share of vulnerabilities, often in the form of buffer overflows.

Hardening an application also includes modifying its default configuration. For instance, you might choose to disable collaborative sharing features in an app to prevent sensitive data leakage, or you might configure macro security in a spreadsheet to allow only trusted digitally signed macros to execute.

Using PowerShell scripts for automating Windows Server administrative tasks is becoming more and more popular. One way to allow only digitally signed scripts to run is by configuring the script execution policy to run only digitally signed scripts from a trusted signer, as shown in Figure 6-16.

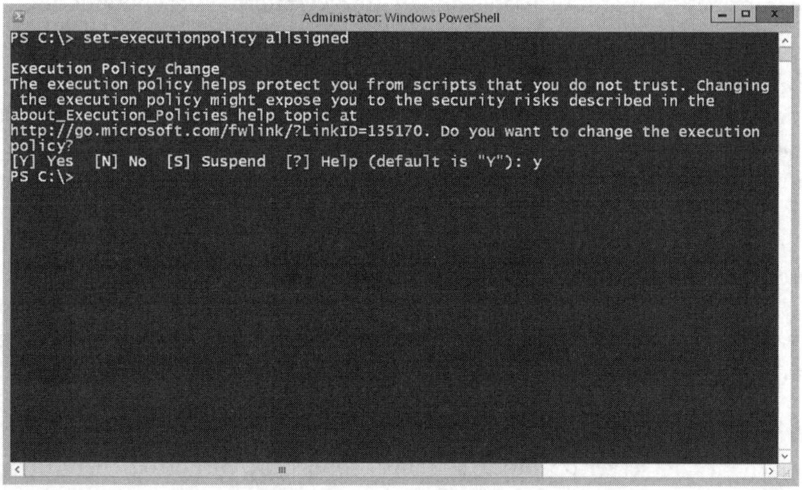

```
Administrator: Windows PowerShell
PS C:\> set-executionpolicy allsigned

Execution Policy Change
The execution policy helps protect you from scripts that you do not trust. Changing
 the execution policy might expose you to the security risks described in the
about_Execution_Policies help topic at
http://go.microsoft.com/fwlink/?LinkID=135170. Do you want to change the execution
policy?
[Y] Yes  [N] No  [S] Suspend  [?] Help (default is "Y"): y
PS C:\>
```

Figure 6-16 Hardening the PowerShell script execution policy

Data Security

Data, however it is being used, should always be encrypted when possible using strong encryption ciphers. Encrypted data presents another layer of defense that malicious users have to overcome. Data can exist in various states:

- **Data in use** Currently being processed
- **Data in motion** Transmitted over a network
- **Data at rest** Stored on media

Encryption requires at least one key. A symmetric key is used to encrypt and decrypt. With *asymmetric encryption*, a pair of keys is used, one for encryption and one for decryption. PKI certificates contain related public and private key pairs, so, for example, if data is encrypted with the public key, only the related private key can decrypt the data.

Data and Mobile Devices

Mobile device use in a business environment presents an enormous threat. Centralized management of mobile device options is absolutely paramount, including logical partitioning, or containerization. Business apps, settings, and data must be kept separate from user personal apps, settings, and data if users will be using personal mobile devices.

A centralized data leakage prevention tool must be used to ensure, for example, that sensitive file attachments cannot be stored on removable thumb drives or shared on social media sites.

Geofencing is another great way to control where mobile device apps can be used. In retail, for example, potential customers in a mall might have access to coupons online only when they are in the mall. On the security side, a mobile device app that can access sensitive information might be usable only within certain physical boundaries.

Encrypting Data at Rest

Encryption of data at rest prevents unauthorized access to stored sensitive data. We talked about encrypting data as it gets transmitted over the network; here the focus is on protecting data when it's stored on media.

The Payment Card Industry Data Security Standard (PCI-DSS) requires (since 2006) merchants handling customer payment card information to encrypt not only data transmission on a network, but also data at rest; otherwise, they face steep fines. The Health Insurance and Portability and Accountability Act (HIPAA) in the United States requires that private health information data be protected. There are many such data protection requirements for different types of data throughout the world.

Windows BitLocker

Windows client and server operating systems support the BitLocker encryption feature (the client must be running the Enterprise Edition of the OS). BitLocker encrypts entire disk volumes and removable USB thumb drives. Group Policy settings can be configured to require BitLocker encryption on certain types of drives and to prevent data writes to unencrypted drives.

The Trusted Platform Module (TPM) is a firmware standard built into most laptop, desktop, and server motherboards. TPM can store cryptographic keys used for encrypting and decrypting BitLocker disk volumes, and it can also detect unauthorized system startup modifications such as changes to the boot sequence. If a motherboard fails, the decryption key would be unavailable even if the disk drive were moved to another computer, so it's important to store decryption and recovery keys in a safe location.

If a malicious user were to steal BitLocker-encrypted hard disks or thumb drives, the data would be inaccessible without the decryption key. You can see BitLocker configuration options in Figure 6-17.

Other, third-party, disk volume encryption tools can be used on Windows servers, including Symantec Endpoint Encryption and Sophos Safeguard Enterprise, to name a few.

Windows Encrypting File System

Individual files and folders can be encrypted to provide data confidentiality. Microsoft has long included the Encrypting File System (EFS) within its Windows operating system. EFS ties encrypted files and folders to specific users (unlike disk volume encryption). Encryption and decryption are possible using the GUI as well as the cipher.exe command line tool.

The first time a Windows user encrypts a file using EFS, a PKI security certificate is automatically generated if the user doesn't already have one on the machine.

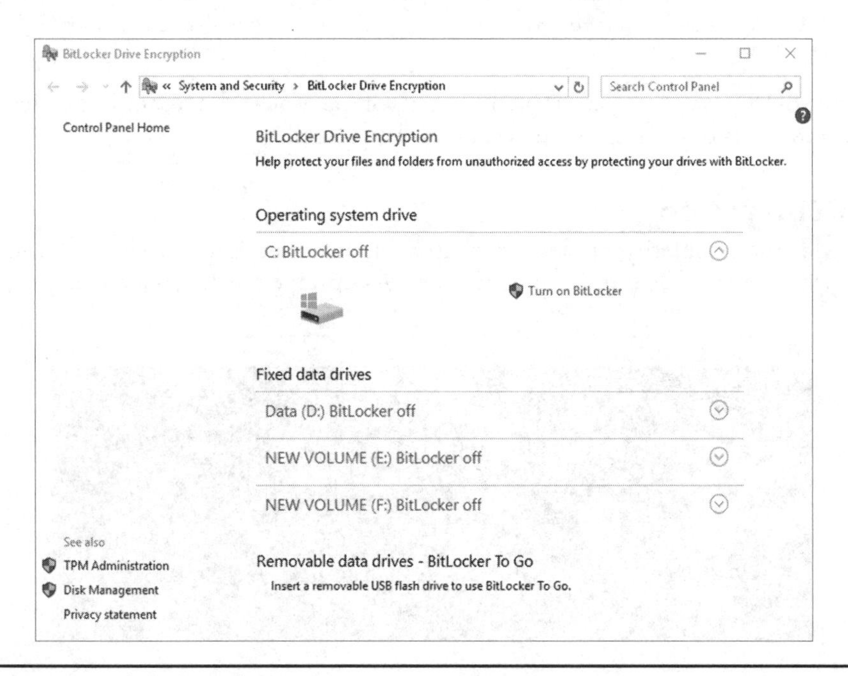

Figure 6-17 Windows BitLocker settings

The certificate contains a unique public and private key pair for the user that is employed for EFS encryption and decryption.

Technically, EFS uses a bulk encryption key, a file encryption key (FEK), to encrypt blocks of data. The user's public key (from their PKI certificate) is used to encrypt the FEK, which is stored with the file. Each encrypted file has a different FEK. To decrypt files, the user's private key (from their PKI certificate) reveals the FEK, which in turn decrypts the blocks of data.

The user PKI certificate must be backed up to a safe location. EFS data recovery agents can be configured to grant administrators the ability to decrypt user EFS-encrypted files. In a Microsoft Active Directory environment, the domain Administrator account can decrypt files on any station joined to the domain.

Files can be encrypted using the following command, where `/e` means encrypt:

```
cipher.exe /e D:\Projects\Project_A.txt
```

OpenSSL

Red Hat Enterprise Linux 7.1 includes the openssl package, which, among other things, can encrypt files. Other Linux distributions might first require a package to be installed before file encryption is possible.

To encrypt a file, use this command:

```
openssl enc -aes-256-cbc -in project_b.txt -out project_b_encrypted.txt
```

To decrypt a file, use this command:

```
openssl enc -d -aes-256-cbc -in project_b_encrypted.txt -out project_b_
decrypted.txt
```

Figure 6-18 shows the unencrypted contents of the project_b.txt sample file (test data) and the contents of the encrypted version of the same file.

Tape Encryption

Even with the popularity of cloud backup solutions, tape is still widely used for data backup purposes. It's common practice for backup tapes to be rotated (reused) on a

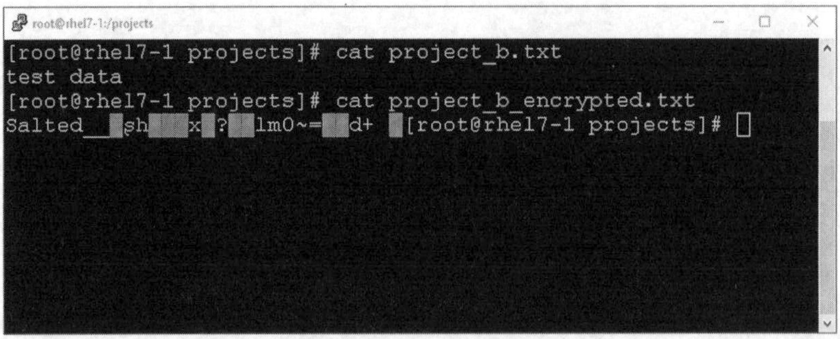

```
root@rhel7-1:/projects
[root@rhel7-1 projects]# cat project_b.txt
test data
[root@rhel7-1 projects]# cat project_b_encrypted.txt
Salted__ sh x ? lm0~= d+ [root@rhel7-1 projects]#
```

Figure 6-18 Viewing unencrypted and encrypted text file content in Linux

periodic basis, but when they contain a fresh data backup, they're often stored offsite for added security.

Tape media normally contains sensitive information and should be encrypted in case the tapes fall into the wrong hands. Data classification makes it easy to determine what needs to be encrypted and what does not.

Today's enterprise servers tend to use storage area network (SAN) storage. Having an enterprise-class SAN means having SAN-based backup solutions, which are far more efficient than having a backup solution for each server and its local disks. In addition to having backups stored offsite, onsite tapes can be stored in a safe.

Several considerations are related to SAN-based tape backup security:

- **Which user account performs backups** Root or Administrator?
- **Scripts are normally used before and after backup** Are malicious scripts present?
- **When encryption occurs** Does it occur during or after backup?
- **The human element** Have thorough background checks been performed on backup administrators?
- **Reliability** Is the offsite tape storage provider trustworthy?

Compliance with data protection laws often drives the data backup policy within an organization, including encryption requirements. Remember that encryption requires keys; proper key management is crucial in order to decrypt data when needed.

Secure Media Disposal

Deleting files (soft wiping) from storage media doesn't remove it permanently. Even the casual Windows user knows to check the Recycle Bin for files that have been mistakenly deleted. Even repartitioning a drive and copying files to it doesn't necessarily mean you can't restore some of the old data from the media. (Imagine being the head of IT for a medical practice that repartitioned hard disks from old PCs before giving the PCs to schools and charities. It has happened!)

Disk Scrubbing

Disks don't get dirty and therefore don't need to be scrubbed for cleanliness. "Scrubbing" in this context means making it as difficult as possible to retrieve data previously stored on the media. This is done by writing useless random data to the disk in multiple passes (called a hard wipe).

Government laws and regulations in some parts of the world require that specific disk scrubbing solutions be used to ensure there are no data remnants. Figure 6-19 shows a screen from Disk Scrubber from Summit Computer Networks. Zeroing out all sectors on a disk is a common method of wiping a disk to minimize the possibility of data recovery. This technique writes a zero byte to all storage locations on a disk.

Physical Destruction

Organizational security policy, driven by laws or regulations, could require the physical destruction of storage media. An often crucial and overlooked aspect of destroying

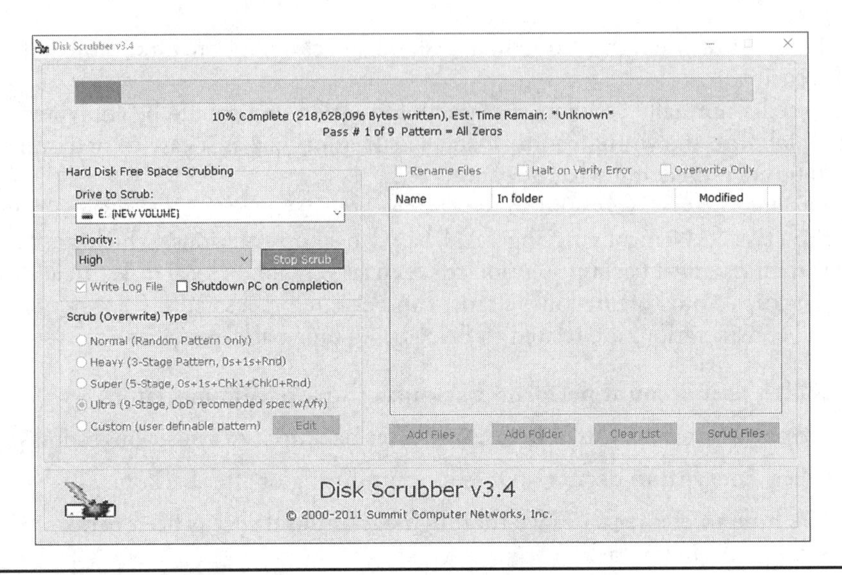

Figure 6-19 Disk scrubbing

storage media is *sorting* to ensure that sensitive storage devices are the ones that get destroyed. There have been cases of bad sorting, which have, for example, resulted in sensitive Canadian military personnel information being exposed—not a great salute for people who put their lives on the line for their country.

One way to make sure data is very difficult to recover is to drill physical holes into hard disk platters. Physical shredding using an industrial shredder or burning storage media can also be effective.

Remote Wipe

Mobile device management (MDM) solutions enable the centralized management of mobile devices. MDM tasks include

- Software deployment
- Update deployment
- Device configuration policies
- Device partitioning

Administrators can remotely wipe lost or stolen smartphones to protect sensitive data and apps, as shown in Figure 6-20. Also bear in mind it takes only one compromised mobile device that can access the network to bring down or compromise servers, so remote wiping is a big deal. The wipe can reset the entire device to factory settings (a full wipe), or it can wipe only corporate apps and data (a selective wipe).

Selective wipes make sense in bring your own device (BYOD) scenarios, where employees use their personal mobile devices to perform work tasks. Many organizations pay a small monthly stipend to employees to offset the cost of the devices.

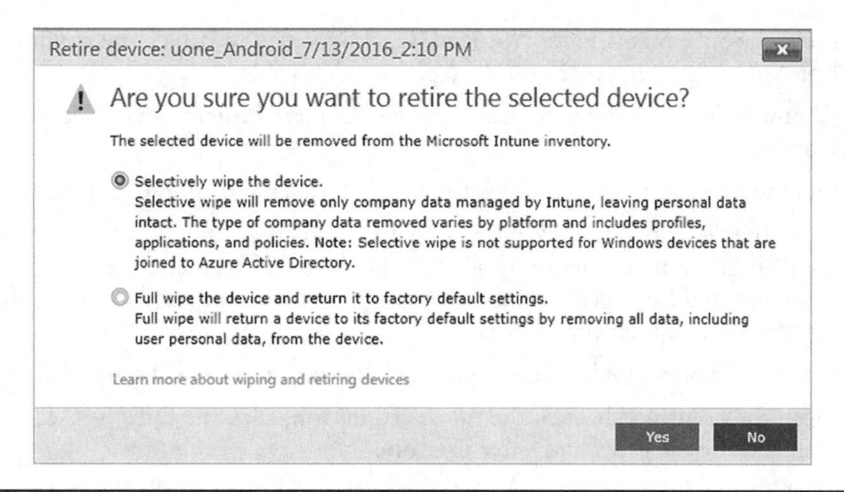

Figure 6-20 Microsoft Intune device wiping options

Hands-on Exercises

Exercise 6-1: Set NTFS File System Permissions

1. Ensure that you are logged into Srv2012-1 with the Domain Administrator account (Fakedomain\Administrator) with a password of Pa$$w0rd.
2. Click the Start button, enter **Active**, and click Active Directory Users And Computers when it is displayed.
3. In the left navigator, right-click fakedomain.local and choose New, Organizational Unit.
4. Enter **ProjectManagers** for the name and click OK.
5. Expand fakedomain.local in the left navigator, right-click ProjectManagers, and choose New, User.
6. Enter **User** for the first name, **One** for the last name, and **uone** for the user logon name. Click Next.
7. For the password, enter **Pa$$w0rd**. Uncheck the option for changing the password at next logon and then click Next and then Finish.
8. Right-click ProjectManagers and choose New, Group; name it **PMs**. Accept all other defaults.
9. Add **User One** as a member of the PMs group. Double-click the PMs group within the ProjectManagers organizational unit. Then click the Members tab, click Add, and enter **user one**. Then click OK twice.
10. Start Windows Explorer (fourth icon from the left on the taskbar at the bottom of the screen; it looks like a yellow folder). Create a folder called Projects on C:\ by right-clicking Local Disk (C:) in the left navigator and choosing New, Folder.

11. From the Start menu, enter **Notepad**. Click Notepad to launch the application. Enter some random text in the Notepad windows.
12. Choose File | Save, and enter the name **C:\Projects\Project_A.txt**. Close Notepad.
13. In Windows Explorer, right-click the Projects folder and choose Properties.
14. Open the Security tab, click Edit, click Add, and enter **PMs**. Click OK. Notice the PMs group is automatically allowed the Read & Execute, List Folder Contents, and Read permissions. Click the check mark under the Allow column for Modify, and then click OK twice.
15. Open the Projects folder. Then right-click Project_A.txt and choose Properties.
16. Open the Security tab, click the Advanced button, click the Effective Access tab. then click Select a user and enter **user one**.
17. Click OK and then click View Effective Access. Scroll down the list and notice the individual permissions allowed (green check mark). Click OK.

Exercise 6-2: Set Shared Folder Permissions

1. Ensure that you are logged into Srv2012-1 with the Domain Administrator account (Fakedomain\Administrator) with a password of Pa$$word.
2. Start PowerShell (third icon from the left on the taskbar at the bottom of the screen).
3. Enter
   ```
   new-smbshare -name Project -path c:\projects -readaccess
   "fakedomain\PMs"
   ```
   Then press ENTER. This grants only read access to members of the PMs group.
4. Verify step 3 in Windows Explorer by right-clicking C:\Projects, choosing Properties, clicking the Sharing tab, clicking Advanced Sharing, and then clicking Permissions. You will see the PMs group with Read access. Click Cancel twice.
5. Open the Security tab, click the Advanced button, and then click the Effective Access tab. Then click the Select A User link, enter **user one**, and click OK. Then click View Effective Access. Notice now that essentially only read and listing permissions are available. When you combine NTFS and share permissions, the most restrictive permissions prevail.

Exercise 6-3: Set File System Permissions in Linux

1. Ensure that you are logged into RHEL7-1 with the root account with a password of Pa$$w0rdLinux. If you do not have permissions to run the following command, precede each command on the same line with sudo followed by a space. Press the ENTER key after you issue each command.

2. Choose Applications | Utilities, and start a terminal session.
3. Enter **`cd /`**. Enter **`mkdir projects`**. Then enter **`ls -ld projects`**. Notice that the default group permissions for the root group are set to r-x.
4. Enter **`groupadd sales`**.
5. Enter **`useradd utwo -G sales`**. User Two is now a member of the sales group.
6. Enter **`chgrp sales /projects`**. Then enter **`ls -ld projects`**. Notice that the default group is now sales.
7. Enter **`chmod g+w /projects`**. This adds the write permission for the group assigned to projects. Enter **`ls -ld /projects`**. Notice that the group permissions are now rwx.

Exercise 6-4: Use EFS to Encrypt Files in Windows

1. Ensure that you are logged into Srv2012-1 with the domain Administrator account. Press the ENTER key after you issue each command.
2. From the Start menu, open a command prompt by entering **cmd**. Then click the prompt when it is displayed.
3. Enter **`md c:\budgets`**.
4. Start Notepad and type random text into the new file. Save the file as **c:\budgets\budget1.txt** and close Notepad.
5. From the command prompt, enter
   `cipher.exe /e c:\budgets`
6. Enter **`cipher.exe c:\budgets`** and notice the "E" to the left of the budget.txt file name; this shows that the file is now encrypted using EFS.

Exercise 6-5: Use OpenSSL to Encrypt Files in Linux

1. Ensure you are logged into **RHEL7-1** with the root account with a password of Pa$$w0rdLinux. If you do not have permissions to run the following command, precede each command on the same line with `sudo` followed by a space. Press the ENTER key after you issue each command.
2. Choose Applications | Utilities, and start a terminal session.
3. Enter **`mkdir /projects2`**.
4. Enter **`vi /projects2/project_b.txt`**.
5. Press the I key. Enter some random text. Press ESC, and enter **`:wq`** to write and quit out of the new file.
6. Enter **`openssl enc -aes-256-cbc -in project_b.txt -out project_b_encrypted.txt`** to encrypt the new file. Enter **Pa$$W0rd** when prompted.

7. Delete the original file by entering **rm /projects2/project_b.txt**. If prompted, press Y to remove the file.
8. Enter **cat /projects2/project_b_encrypted.txt** and notice that the file content is encrypted.
9. Enter **openssl enc -d -aes-256-cbc -in project_b_encrypted.txt -out project_b_decrypted.txt**
10. Enter **cat /projects2/project_b_decrypted.txt** to view the file contents.

Exercise 6-6: Use iptables to Set Firewall Rules in Linux

1. Ensure that both the Srv2012-1 and RHEL7-1 virtual machines are running. For Windows, make sure you are logged on as Fakedomain\Administrator with a password of Pa$$w0rd. For Linux, make sure you are logged in as root with a password of Pa$$w0rdLinux. If you do not have permissions to run the following command, precede each command on the same line with sudo followed by a space. Press the ENTER key after you issue each command.
2. From a command prompt on Srv202-1, enter **ping 192.168.1.210**. You should get a response; this is the IP address of the Linux server.
3. Ensure that you are logged into RHEL7-1 with the root account.
4. Choose Applications | Utilities, and start a terminal session.
5. Enter **iptables -A INPUT -p icmp -j DROP** to block all incoming ICMP traffic.
6. From a command prompt on Srv202-1, enter **ping 192.168.1.210** once again. This time you should *not* get a response.
7. From a terminal prompt on RHEL7-1, enter **iptables -F** to flush (remove) rules.
8. From a command prompt on Srv2012-1, ping the Linux server again. You should get a response.

Exercise 6-7: Enable Encrypted Communication on a Windows IIS Web Server

1. Ensure that you are logged into Srv2012-1 with the domain Administrator account.
2. Start Server Manager (second icon from the left on the taskbar).
3. Click Add Roles And Features.

4. Accept defaults and keep clicking Next until you reach the Select Server Roles screen.
5. Add a check mark to the Web Server (IIS) option if prompted to install tools accept. Continue through the wizard accepting defaults.
6. After IIS is installed, start Internet Explorer on Srv2012-1. If prompted to accept recommended settings, do so.
7. In the address bar, enter **http://srv2012-1.fakedomain.local.** The IIS default web page should be displayed. Close Internet Explorer.
8. From Server Manager, click Add Roles And Features.
9. Accept defaults and keep clicking Next until you reach the Select Server Roles screen.
10. Add a check mark to Active Directory Certificate Services. This role allows the creation of a PKI hierarchy. If prompted to add additional roles and features, click Add Features. Continue through the rest of the wizard, accepting defaults until you reach the end of the wizard. Then click Install, and then Close.
11. In Server Manager, click the flag notification icon in the upper right. Click the Configure Active Directory Certificate Services On This Server link to complete the Certification Authority configuration. Proceed through the wizard and select the Certification Authority check box on the Select Role Services To Configure screen. Create an Enterprise CA, and accept the defaults for the remainder of the settings.
12. From the Start menu, enter **mmc.exe**, and when the Management Console displays, click it.
13. Choose File | Add / Remove Snap-in, select Certificates on the left, click Add, choose Computer Account, and then click Next, then Finish, and then OK.
14. In the left navigator expand Certificates. Right-click Personal and choose All Tasks, Request New Certificate.
15. Click Next twice. Add a check mark to Domain Controller and click Enroll. This creates a PKI certificate for your server that can be used to secure the IIS web site. Click Finish to close the Certificate Enrollment window.
16. From the Start menu, enter **IIS**. When Internet Information Services (IIS) Manager is displayed, click it.
17. On the left, expand your server name, and then expand Sites.
18. Right-click Default Web Site and choose Edit Bindings.
19. Click Add, and from the Type drop-down list, choose https.
20. From the SSL Certificate drop-down list, choose Srv2012-1.fakedomain.local and click OK.
21. Select the http binding from the list and choose Remove. Close the dialog box.

22. Start Internet Explorer and enter **http://srv2012-1.fakedomain.local** in the address bar. Then press ENTER. You will see a webpage not found error, since we removed the http binding. If it displays the web page, you may need to clear your IE browser history by pressing ALT-T, and then choosing Delete Browsing History.
23. In the address bar, enter **https://srv2012-1.fakedomain.local** (notice the https). Click OK on the Security Alert message. The web page appears over an HTTPS connection.

Chapter Review

This chapter covered various aspects of locking down computer environments, from physical security, to server hardening, to data encryption.

Physical Security

Restricted access to facilities is possible using fencing, lighting, security guards, guard dogs, gates, mantraps, door locking mechanisms, and security solutions such as motion detection systems. Large data centers replicate data to other data centers to ensure high availability of IT services and data. Individual servers as well as server room racks have locking mechanisms to prevent equipment tampering.

Modern access and payment cards, such as RFID chip cards and smartcards, have embedded circuits that can transmit data wirelessly.

Authentication

User, device, and service authentication falls into three categories:

- Something you know
- Something you have
- Something you are

Multifactor authentication uses at least two of these categories. Authentication can be centralized using identity federation.

Logical Access Control

Users can be placed into groups or roles, which are granted permissions to resources. Some server operating systems support conditional access based on user, device, and resource attributes.

Windows administrators assign NTFS and share permissions to control network access to files. The most restrictive permission applies when combining share and NTFS permissions. Linux server administrators can use the `chmod` command to work with file system permissions.

Network Security

Network Access Control (802.1x) limits which users and devices can connect to a network through edge devices such as network switches, wireless routers, and VPN connections. Edge devices (RADIUS clients) should be configured to forward authentication requests to a central RADIUS authentication server.

VLANs organize network nodes into virtual networks, even within a single physical switch. This can be done by MAC or IP address, by grouping physical switch ports together, and so on. VLANs allow administrators to isolate network traffic for performance and security reasons.

Firewalls

Firewalls regulate traffic into and out of networks and individual hosts. Packet-filtering firewalls examine packet headers, looking at characteristics such as source and destination IP address, port address, and protocol type. Deep packet inspection firewalls examine payload content beyond packet headers.

Reverse proxy servers are listeners on a publicly visible network that forward traffic to a specific network service on an internal protected network.

Network services, firewalls, and proxy servers must be placed in the correct network security zone. Demilitarized zones (DMZs) enable the safe placement of publicly visible servers while protecting systems on internal networks. Firewalls control traffic between the Internet and the DMZ, and between the DMZ and internal networks.

PKI

Public Key Infrastructure is a hierarchy of security certificates issued to users, devices, or services. The certificates contain keys that provide security in the form of authentication and encryption. Certificate authorities issue certificates.

PKI certificates contain numerous items such as the subject name, a serial number, and a unique public and private key pair. The private key is sensitive and must not be shared with other parties. Certificates have an expiration date, after which they can no longer be used.

SSL and the newer TLS provide authentication and encryption for network services such as web sites. Keys from PKI certificates make this possible; in most configurations, only the server needs a PKI certificate, not each connecting client.

IPSec

IPSec is used to authenticate and encrypt network transmissions using either transport or tunnel mode. Tunnel mode is used for point-to-point connections such as with VPNs. Transport mode can be used for all devices on a LAN to encrypt network traffic that normally might not support encryption.

IPv6 requires IPSec; it is optional for IPv4. On Windows servers, IPSec is configured through the Windows Firewall using Connection Security Rules.

VPNs

Virtual private networks enable encrypted connections to a private network over an untrusted network. Common VPN types include PPTP, L2TP/IPSec, and SSL. Different types of VPNs require different ports to be open in firewalls—SSL VPNs are firewall friendly since they use TCP port 443, which is also used by HTTPS.

VPN clients require that software be configured to connect to the VPN. All traffic between the client and VPN appliance is encrypted. The VPN appliance decrypts received traffic and sends it to the internal network.

Intrusion Detection and Prevention

Intrusion detection systems (IDSs) send administrative alerts when suspicious activity is detected. Network traffic, log files, and local operating system process execution are tracked for anomalies. Intrusion prevention systems (IPSs) take this a step further by taking action to stop the activity from continuing.

IDS and IPS solutions can run on a specific host or on the network to view all network traffic, if placed properly. Rules must be configured to ensure that IDS and IPS solutions are effective in a specific network environment.

Hardening

Hardening applies to networks, servers, and applications, and it includes activities such as disabling unused ports and services, applying patches, encrypting data in transit and at rest, and so on.

Logging must be enabled on all devices, and log copies should be forwarded to other hosts in case a device is compromised and logs are cleared.

Firmware updates should also be a part of hardening, along with setting CMOS passwords on servers and ensuring that antimalware solutions are kept up to date. Storage area network devices, VPN appliances, routers, switches, and wireless routers should also be hardened.

Data Security

Encryption is used to ensure that only authorized users can access sensitive data. When the same key is used for encryption and decryption, it is called *symmetric encryption*; when different (yet mathematically related) keys are used, it is called *asymmetric encryption*. PKI certificates contain related public and private key pairs.

Data encryption can be applied to data in use, data in transit, and data at rest. Ideally, encryption should be used everywhere (networks, servers, backup tapes, desktops), but encryption must be enforced on removable media and mobile devices.

Secure Media Disposal

Techniques such as disk scrubbing (software) can overwrite storage media to prevent data retrieval. Physical techniques such as physical media destruction ensure that sensitive data cannot be retrieved.

Lost or stolen mobile devices can either be fully wiped or selectively wiped. Selective wiping removes only company apps, settings, and data.

Questions

1. Which physical security control prevents tailgating?
   - A. RFID card
   - B. Mantrap
   - C. Security guard
   - D. Fencing

2. Which modern short-distance wireless standard is used for payment cards and terminals?
   - A. NFC
   - B. Bluetooth
   - C. Wi-Fi
   - D. 4G

3. Which term is used to describe the act of tricking people into divulging sensitive information?
   - A. Threat engineering
   - B. Mailing
   - C. Scanning
   - D. Social engineering

4. Your VPN requires multifactor authentication. Which of the following solutions should you use?
   - A. Smartcard, PIN
   - B. Username, password, PIN
   - C. Username, PIN
   - D. Password, PIN

5. Your network consists of multiple web applications. To connect to each application, a user e-mail address and date of birth are required. What should you do?
   A. Direct users to enter their e-mail address and date of birth when connecting to each web app.
   B. Configure user claims with identify federation, and configure the web apps to trust the identity provider.
   C. Configure device claims with identify federation, and configure the web apps to trust the devices.
   D. Issue PKI certificates to users, and configure the web apps to trust user PKI certificates.

6. Which VPN authentication tool uses a changing numeric code synchronized with the VPN appliance?
   A. Key fob
   B. USB thumb drive
   C. Smartcard
   D. PKI certificate

7. Which of the following statements regarding Active Directory groups is false?
   A. Permissions management is simplified.
   B. Groups can be nested.
   C. Group membership changes take effect while affected users are logged in.
   D. Groups can contain computers.

8. Stacey needs access to budget files stored on a file server in a folder called Budgets. She is a member of the Managers group. The Managers group has been allowed read, read & execute, list folder contents, and write permissions. Stacey complains that she receives an "Access denied" message when she tries to delete budget files. What should you do?
   A. Decrypt the budget files.
   B. Grant the Managers group write permissions on each individual file.
   C. Grant the Manager group modify permission to the budgets folder.
   D. Add Stacey as an EFS data recovery agent.

9. Trinity is a member of the Executives group, which has been granted the read permission to a shared folder called Expenses. Trinity is also a member of the Site A group, which has been granted the NTFS read and write permissions to the Expenses folder. What permissions will Trinity have to a file in the Expenses folder?

   A. Read

   B. Read and write

   C. Write

   D. No permissions

10. Which Linux command is used to set file system permissions?

   A. `set-acl`

   B. `chmod`

   C. `chperm`

   D. `set-perm`

11. What type of malware encrypts data files and demands payment before providing a decryption key?

   A. Malware

   B. Trojan

   C. Virus

   D. Ransomware

12. Which security standard controls port-level access to a network?

   A. 802.1x

   B. 802.3

   C. 802.5

   D. 802.11

13. A smartphone is attempting to authenticate to a RADIUS server through a Wi-Fi router. The Wi-Fi router is configured with WPA2 Enterprise. What term is used to describe the smartphone?

   A. RADIUS client

   B. RADIUS supplicant

   C. RADIUS authenticator

   D. RADIUS consumer

14. Your network uses four Ethernet switches linked together to interconnect 80 computers. Ten of the computers are used by the accounting department and are configured with IPSec. Accounting department computers do not need to communicate with other computers. How can you keep accounting computer traffic more secure?
    - A. Encrypt network communications using HTTPS.
    - B. Configure a new VLAN for the accounting department computers.
    - C. Encrypt network communications using BitLocker.
    - D. Configure accounting department computer to use only IPv6.

15. Which type of VLAN attack overloads switch MAC table memory?
    - A. VLAN hopping
    - B. Big MAC attack
    - C. MAC flooding attack
    - D. VLAN spanning tree

16. Your firewall can filter traffic based on MAC addresses. Which term correctly identifies your firewall?
    - A. Layer 2
    - B. Layer 3
    - C. Layer 4
    - D. Layer 7

17. Your firewall can filter traffic based on UDP and TCP port numbers. Which term correctly identifies your firewall?
    - A. Layer 2
    - B. Layer 3
    - C. Layer 4
    - D. Layer 7

18. Your firewall can filter traffic based on the contents of packet payloads. Which term correctly identifies your firewall?
    - A. Layer 2
    - B. Layer 3
    - C. Layer 4
    - D. Layer 7

Questions and Answers

1. Which physical security control prevents tailgating?
   - A. RFID card
   - B. Mantrap
   - C. Security guard
   - D. Fencing

   B. Mantraps close and lock an outer door before allowing you to open an inner door. This prevents people from tailgating, or slipping in behind you. A, C, and D are incorrect. RFID cards, such as toll bridge pass cards, use radio frequencies to transmit data wirelessly. Security guards might notice somebody slipping into a secured facility behind you, but that is not their primary purpose as it is for a mantrap. Fencing does not prevent tailgating.

2. Which modern short-distance wireless standard is used for payment cards and terminals?
   - A. NFC
   - B. Bluetooth
   - C. Wi-Fi
   - D. 4G

   A. Near-field communication (NFC) is a short-distance wireless standard used often by payment cards and terminals. B, C, and D are incorrect. Bluetooth is a short-range wireless standard used by headsets, speakers, and so on, but it is not used for payment card systems. Wi-Fi is not short-range and is not used by payment systems; neither is 4G, a cellular data network standard.

3. Which term is used to describe the act of tricking people into divulging sensitive information?
   - A. Threat engineering
   - B. Mailing
   - C. Scanning
   - D. Social engineering

   D. Social engineering involves tricking people into divulging sensitive information. A, B, and C are incorrect. Threat engineering is a made-up term. Mailing is used to send messages. Scanning is performed to gather information about a network.

4. Your VPN requires multifactor authentication. Which of the following solutions should you use?

A. Smartcard, PIN

B. Username, password, PIN

C. Username, PIN

D. Password, PIN

A. The smartcard is something you have, and the PIN is something you know—this is multifactor authentication. B, C, and D are incorrect. Usernames, passwords, and PINs constitute a single authentication category—something you know.

5. Your network consists of multiple web applications. To connect to each application, a user e-mail address and date of birth are required. What should you do?

A. Direct users to enter their e-mail address and date of birth when connecting to each web app.

B. Configure user claims with identify federation, and configure the web apps to trust the identity provider.

C. Configure device claims with identify federation, and configure the web apps to trust the devices.

D. Issue PKI certificates to users, and configure the web apps to trust user PKI certificates.

B. Claims contain attributes such as e-mail addresses and dates of birth. Identity federation servers provide these digitally signed claims to apps that are configured to trust the identity provider. A, C, and D are incorrect. Users should not have to enter details for each and every app. The required claim attributes are tied to users, not devices. PKI certificates themselves do not provide claims-based authentication.

6. Which VPN authentication tool uses a changing numeric code synchronized with the VPN appliance?

A. Key fob

B. USB thumb drive

C. Smartcard

D. PKI certificate

A. Key fobs, also called hardware or software tokens, depending on what is being used, have a changing numeric code that must be entered in addition to other credentials for authentication to succeed. B, C, and D are incorrect. USB thumb drives do not provide anything related to authentication; they are used for storage. Smartcards and PKI certificates can be used for authentication, but they do not have a changing numeric code.

7. Which of the following statements regarding Active Directory groups is false?
   - **A.** Permissions management is simplified.
   - **B.** Groups can be nested.
   - **C.** Group membership changes take effect while affected users are logged in.
   - **D.** Groups can contain computers.

C. Users must log off and back in for their group membership changes to be in effect. A, B, and D are incorrect. The remaining options are all true; therefore, they do not address the purpose of the question.

8. Stacey needs access to budget files stored on a file server in a folder called Budgets. She is a member of the Managers group. The Managers group has been allowed read, read & execute, list folder contents, and write permissions. Stacey complains that she receives an "Access denied" message when she tries to delete budget files. What should you do?
   - **A.** Decrypt the budget files.
   - **B.** Grant the Managers group write permissions on each individual file.
   - **C.** Grant the Manager group modify permission to the budgets folder.
   - **D.** Add Stacey as an EFS data recovery agent.

C. To delete files, users need the NTFS modify permission. A, B, and D are incorrect. The question does not state that files are encrypted, so decryption and recovery agents do not apply. It is clear that the granted permissions (including write) do not allow deletions.

9. Trinity is a member of the Executives group, which has been granted the read permission to a shared folder called Expenses. Trinity is also a member of the Site A group, which has been granted the NTFS read and write permissions to the Expenses folder. What permissions will Trinity have to a file in the Expenses folder?
   - **A.** Read
   - **B.** Read and write
   - **C.** Write
   - **D.** No permissions

A. When combining share and NTFS permissions, the most restrictive permission applies. B, C, and D are incorrect. Because the most restrictive (the read share permission) applies, the other answers cannot be correct.

10. Which Linux command is used to set file system permissions?

A. `set-acl`

B. `chmod`

C. `chperm`

D. `set-perm`

B. `chmod` (change mode) is used to set Linux file system permissions. A, C, and D are incorrect. These commands do not exist in Linux.

11. What type of malware encrypts data files and demands payment before providing a decryption key?

A. Malware

B. Trojan

C. Virus

D. Ransomware

D. Ransomware encrypts files that infected computers have write access to and demand payment before supposedly supplying a decryption key. A, B, and C are incorrect. Malware is a catch-all term; ransomware is more specific. Trojans are a form of malware that appear to be benign but are malicious. A virus is a form of malware that attaches to files.

12. Which security standard controls port-level access to a network?

A. 802.1x

B. 802.3

C. 802.5

D. 802.11

A. 802.1x is an IEEE standard that defines port-level security mechanisms for devices connecting to a network. B, C, and D are incorrect. 802.3 is the Ethernet standard, 802.5 is the token ring standard, and 802.11 defines the Wi-Fi standard.

13. A smartphone is attempting to authenticate to a RADIUS server through a Wi-Fi router. The Wi-Fi router is configured with WPA2 Enterprise. What term is used to describe the smartphone?

    A. RADIUS client

    B. RADIUS supplicant

    C. RADIUS authenticator

    D. RADIUS consumer

    B. In a RADIUS authentication environment, client devices are referred to as supplicants. A, C, and D are incorrect. RADIUS clients are edge devices such as Wi-Fi routers and network switches. RADIUS authenticator and consumer are not valid terms in this context.

14. Your network uses four Ethernet switches linked together to interconnect 80 computers. Ten of the computers are used by the accounting department and are configured with IPSec. Accounting department computers do not need to communicate with other computers. How can you keep accounting computer traffic more secure?

    A. Encrypt network communications using HTTPS.

    B. Configure a new VLAN for the accounting department computers.

    C. Encrypt network communications using BitLocker.

    D. Configure accounting department computer to use only IPv6.

    B. VLANs provide security by isolation network communications. A, C, and D are incorrect. There is no need to encrypt using HTTPS if IPSec is already in use. BitLocker encrypts disk volumes, not network communications. IPv6 by itself would not provide security.

15. Which type of VLAN attack overloads switch MAC table memory?

    A. VLAN hopping

    B. Big MAC attack

    C. MAC flooding attack

    D. VLAN spanning tree

    C. MAC flooding attacks overwhelm the limited switch memory to retain MAC addresses plugged into switch ports, which makes traffic flood to all ports, much like a hub. This means traffic not normally visible becomes visible to all switch ports. A, B, and D are incorrect. VLAN hopping occurs when a malicious user spoofs packet data so that their station can become a member of multiple VLANs. Big MAC attack is a phrase coined by a well-known fast-food chain in the 1970s. VLAN spanning tree is not a type of VLAN attack.

16. Your firewall can filter traffic based on MAC addresses. Which term correctly identifies your firewall?

A. Layer 2

B. Layer 3

C. Layer 4

D. Layer 7

A. MAC addresses are OSI Layer 2 (data link) addresses. B, C, and D are incorrect. MAC addresses do not apply to OSI Layers 3, 4, or 7.

17. Your firewall can filter traffic based on UDP and TCP port numbers. Which term correctly identifies your firewall?

A. Layer 2

B. Layer 3

C. Layer 4

D. Layer 7

C. Port numbers apply to OSI Layer 4, the transport layer. A, B, and D are incorrect. Port numbers do not apply to OSI Layers 2, 3, or 7.

18. Your firewall can filter traffic based on the contents of packet payloads. Which term correctly identifies your firewall?

A. Layer 2

B. Layer 3

C. Layer 4

D. Layer 7

D. Packet payload inspection applies to OSI Layer 7, the application layer. A, B, and C are incorrect. OSI Layers 2, 3, and 4 cannot read packet payload data.

CHAPTER 7

Troubleshooting and Performance Optimization

In this chapter, you will

- Learn how to apply a troubleshooting methodology to real-world problems
- Troubleshoot hardware, software, storage, and network problems
- Apply troubleshooting skills to resolve security issues
- Optimize server and network performance

Working in IT means solving problems—after all, IT solutions exist to solve business problems. This chapter focuses on how to troubleshoot a wide variety of issues to get people productive as quickly as possible.

Troubleshooting Methodology

Solving IT issues is a combination of knowledge, experience, and the application of a sound troubleshooting methodology. When things that once worked no longer work, always ask yourself, "What has changed?" Finding the answer could involve reviewing server log files, asking other technicians, and a host of other activities.

Following is the general troubleshooting methodology:

1. Identify the problem.
2. Establish a theory of probable cause.
3. Test the theory.
4. Establish a plan of action.
5. Implement a solution or escalate.
6. Verify functionality.
7. Perform root cause analysis.
8. Document the solution.

Let's cover these steps in more detail.

Identify the Problem

We have to be able to identify exactly what the problem is before we can solve it. This can be difficult it if involves specific functionality in a custom app, so in some cases the end user can help by further explaining the issue.

Problems are usually reported through a help desk ticketing system, which should be customized to fit your environment. For example, if your company uses Custom App 1 and Custom App 2, these should be selectable from a drop-down list when users are creating a help desk ticket.

Troubleshooting over the phone requires the person reporting the issue to be clear in stating the problem. Technicians often ask users questions (check your IP address, make sure you've clicked on this and that), and this can make problem identification (and problem resolution) tricky if user responses are unclear. If possible, technicians should remotely control the network device.

The best people to ask questions of are the stakeholders affected by the problem, whether they are end users, other technicians, or management. Ask when the problem began appearing, or if there were any recent changes—not only to the server itself, but to anything in its environment. For example, a change in a switch's VLAN configuration could affect user access to a server.

EXAM TIP Watch for troubleshooting questions that indirectly imply that a change was made that results in a problem. Although the change itself may not be the problem, how it was implemented may be.

Identify the Problem Scope

Problem scope is often overlooked. Who or what is affected by the issue? For example, if the problem is related to Internet connectivity, does it affect

- Only a single server?
- All devices on a specific network?
- All devices on all networks?

CompTIA Server+ technicians need to know where to focus their troubleshooting time.

Reproduce the Problem

To solidify your knowledge of the actual problem, it helps if you can re-create the issue. For example, perhaps you must go through a very specific series of steps on a server to request a PKI certificate that results in an error, but the problem occurs only when you choose a specific certificate template.

Reproducing problems might involve changing system configuration settings—so it's important to back up all settings and data prior to making any changes. In some cases, you might even create a server image (if you don't already have one) in case the server OS becomes inoperable.

Check the Log Files

There are many types of log files, listed here. For example, Figure 7-1 shows the DNS server log on a Windows server.

- Windows event viewer logs
- UNIX/Linux logs
  - Normally stored under /var/log
  - Certain apps can store logs under /var/opt
- IDS/IPS logs
- Firewall logs
- VPN appliance logs
- Audit logs
  - File system
  - Privilege use
  - Account management
  - Account logon
- Client operating system logs
- OS component logs
  - Group Policy
  - CUPS
  - DNS (Figure 7-1)
  - DHCP

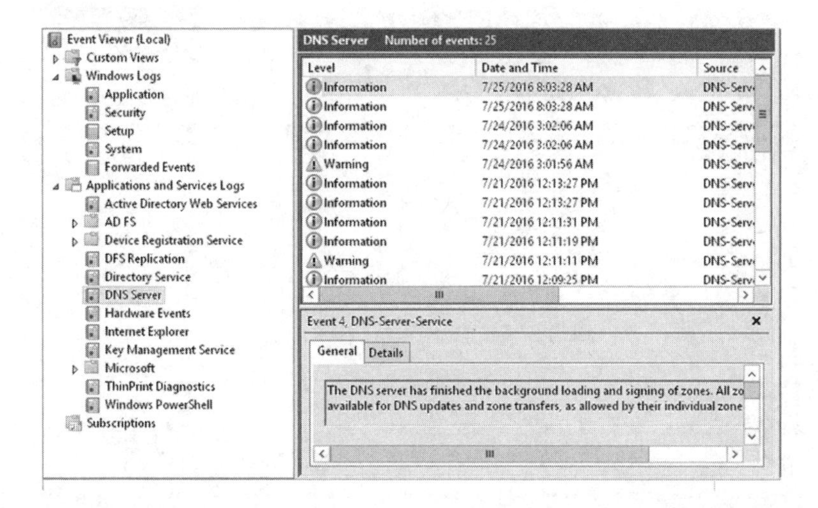

Figure 7-1 Windows Server DNS log

Log files should not only be stored on the device, but in a larger enterprise (especially a data center), log forwarding or a central log viewing tool is critical. Figure 7-2 shows log files stored locally on a Linux host.

UNIX and Linux support log forwarding through the traditional syslog dameon or its successor, syslog-ng. Filters are created to determine which type of messages are forwarded to other hosts. Windows machines can be configured with event subscription to forward certain type of log message to other hosts. Log forwarding is especially important for edge devices like VPN appliances or public web sites in a DMZ.

Viewing or graphing log files over time can demonstrate when a problem appears. The Windows Reliability Monitor history shown in Figure 7-3, for example, can help.

Figure 7-2 Viewing log files in the Linux /var/log directory

```
[root@rhel7-1 projects]# ls /var/log
anaconda                 messages-20160801
audit                    pluto
boot.log                 pm-powersave.log
btmp                     ppp
btmp-20160801            qemu-ga
chrony                   rhsm
cron                     sa
cron-20160724.gz         samba
cron-20160801            secure
cups                     secure-20160724.gz
dmesg                    secure-20160801
dmesg.old                speech-dispatcher
firewalld                spooler
gdm                      tallylog
glusterfs                tuned
lastlog                  wtmp
libvirt                  Xorg.0.log
maillog                  Xorg.0.log.old
maillog-20160724.gz      Xorg.9.log
maillog-20160801         Xorg.9.log.old
messages                 yum.log
messages-20160724.gz
[root@rhel7-1 projects]#
```

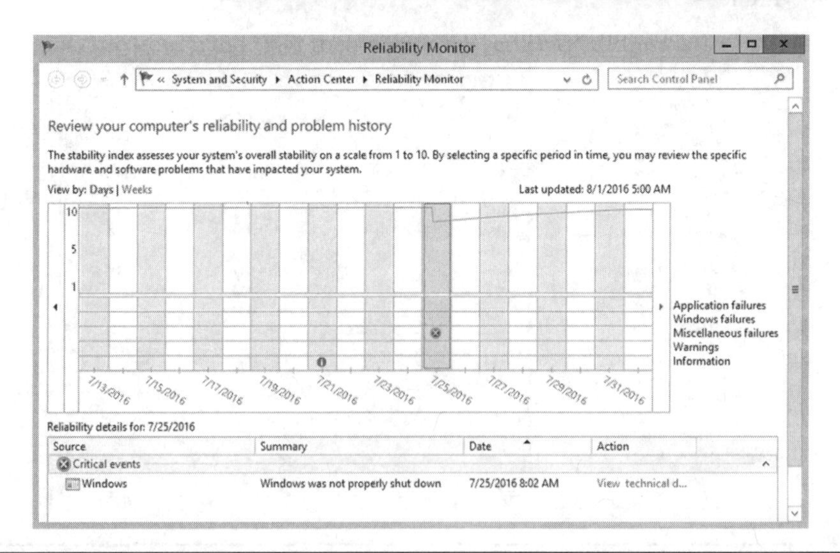

Figure 7-3 Windows Reliability Monitor history

Read the Documentation

Solving problems quickly requires being very organized. If, for instance, you are responsible for maintaining SUSE Linux Enterprise Server 11 computers, you should have OS documentation readily available, perhaps through an organized list of bookmarks in your web browser.

Hardware documentation for RAID controllers, network printers, hardware firewall appliances, and the like should be easily accessible. In some cases, if you work with the same equipment often, you should pore over this documentation so that you're prepared—be proactive!

Implementation documentation is especially important, because it is unique for each organization. You might know everything there is to know about Microsoft Server 2012 R2, but if you don't know how it is configured, especially in a large network, you may as well know nothing at all!

Server documentation will define which roles the server houses and how they are configured. From this information, you can also determine the server's network configuration, firewall settings, patch history, and other important factors.

Network documentation shows server placement and the role the server plays relative to other servers and network devices. Troubleshooting server issues without specific implementation documentation makes the process long, tedious, and less effective, and it costs much more because it requires more time to fix. It's worth paying the up-front costs to have proper documentation.

NOTE Experienced IT consultants will not begin troubleshooting in an unfamiliar computing environment without first taking time to first absorb implementation documentation.

Establish a Theory of Probable Cause

As server technicians, we don't want to troubleshoot issues by first testing complex solutions; we check the obvious stuff first. Is the network cable plugged in? Does the NIC link indicator light show an active connection? Is the user in a group that should have permissions to access a file?

This can become tricky when you rely on other parties to provide accurate information about the problem. Where possible, verify that what you are told on the phone or through a help desk ticket is, in fact, correct. For example, a user complaining about being unable to print to Network Printer B might be having problems because she's unknowingly printing to Network Printer Z. Check the obvious!

With regard to the scope issue, once you begin to formulate a theory of probable cause, you might find that this symptom occurs on other servers or devices, too.

Test the Theory

Your organization should have a sandbox testing environment used for a variety of reasons, including troubleshooting. This is often a virtual network with multiple virtual machines that mimic the production environment where possible (sometimes easier said than done). Make sure system configuration settings and data are backed up before you change settings and test theories.

As an example, reconfiguring a host-based firewall on a server to resolve a network service communication issue might break other network services, or it might violate corporate security policy. Back up existing settings first, and follow proper change management procedures. Once your theory is determined to be a viable resolution to the problem, formulate the appropriate steps to be taken in the production environment.

Establish a Plan of Action

Solving a server- or network-related problem first requires problem identification, followed by the establishment of a theory of probable cause. When you test the theory and it proves to be effective in removal of the issue, you need to develop a plan of action.

The plan includes detailed steps that will be taken against affected systems, notification of stakeholders, and, for complex problems, an implementation timeline. Simple problem resolution is much less formal and may be entirely in the control of a single technician who can solve the problem in seconds, such as simply adding a user to a group so that the user can access a file.

Implement a Solution or Escalate

After you have established a plan of action, it must be implemented. Depending on the scope or complexity, a team of technicians may have to be assembled and notified of their roles.

Imagine a network problem created by switch VLANs that have been incorrectly implemented in a large data center. If the problem exists on hundreds or thousands of switches, many technicians might be required to solve the problem quickly, or, where possible, an automation script might be used.

In some cases, you may need to escalate to another party with the expertise and authority to resolve the problem. For instance, when troubleshooting Internet connectivity in a branch office, if you determine that network connectivity within your branch office is working, you may escalate the issue to technicians in headquarters, where Internet traffic is centrally routed.

Remember to change one thing at a time. Changing multiple settings at once makes it difficult to determine exactly which action solved the problem. If a change doesn't fix the issue, reverse it before moving to other tests.

Verify Functionality

Don't be tempted to declare victory too quickly! Thorough testing is required to ensure that the problem is indeed solved.

If the problem existed within custom software, you may need to involve a user who works with the custom software daily to test functionality before you can state that the problem has been resolved. Then put preventative measures in place to ensure that the same issue doesn't occur again. If the problem resulted from a user tinkering on their Windows workstation, perhaps locking down settings using Group Policy is an appropriate resolution.

From a consulting perspective, the problem isn't solved until the customer is satisfied. IT service frameworks such as Information Technology Infrastructure Library (ITIL) are based on this foundation.

Perform Root Cause Analysis

When the true cause of an IT problem is known, solutions come much more quickly. At the same time, preventative measures are effective because they are focused.

Conceptually, this is similar to putting out a fire and preventing other fires from occurring by identifying sources of a fire—such as leaving the stove on after cooking. In the case of IT, perhaps it involves preventing the use of non-company–issued USB devices to stop malware infections. In other words, you must treat the root cause and not just the symptoms.

Understand that you may be looking for multiple related root causes, not just one. To prevent similar problems in the future, remember that the key question is, "Why?"

The following list offers a sense of how to deal with root cause analysis:

- Why did machines get infected with malware?
  - *Cause:* User personal USB devices were not blocked.
  - *Solution:* Block personal USB device use.
- Why were newly hired users unable to access required files?
  - *Cause:* They were not added to the required groups.
  - *Solution:* Create new users from a template that includes required groups.
- Why was file server response time brought to a crawl?
  - *Cause:* A disk failed in a RAID 5 array so data was rebuilt on demand (Figure 7-4).
  - *Solution:* Ensure that hot spare disks are always available in the RAID array so that data can be rebuilt on disk and served quickly to users.

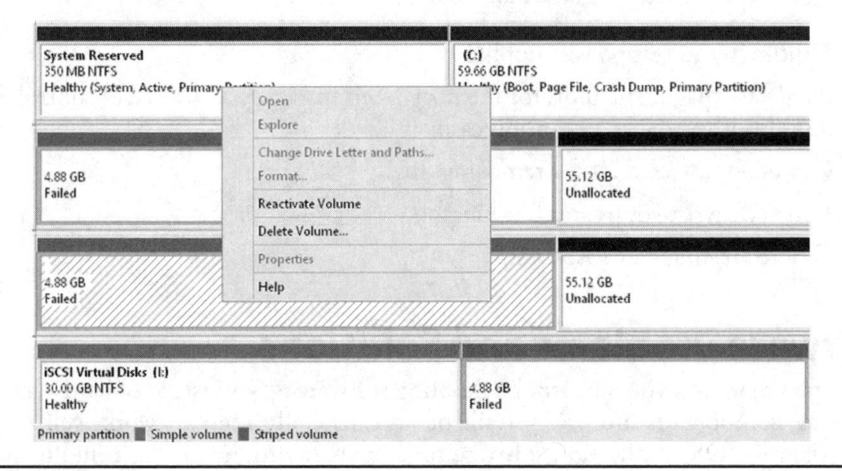

Figure 7-4 Windows Server 2012 R2 failed software RAID 5 array

Document the Solution

Throughout the troubleshooting process, your structured approach will eventually reveal a root cause and related remedies to prevent future occurrences. You need to document the result as well as the steps taken along the way.

Many organizations use help desk ticketing software that integrates searchable knowledge functionality. When tickets are closed because solutions were found, this information is stored with metadata in a database that can be quickly searched in the future to avoid having to go through the entire troubleshooting process again if the same problem occurs.

As a result, in some cases, IT configurations change, business processes are improved, and security controls are further hardened.

Hardware Problems and Solutions

These days, when hardware is properly maintained, it is pretty resilient to problems. Proper maintenance includes applying firmware updates when they are available. There's also the issue of overheating, which greatly reduces the life expectancy of equipment and can cause erratic behavior.

NOTE Most servers and related equipment have hardware sensors that detect environmental conditions such as temperature. You may need to install software for this data to be available.

Table 7-1 lists common hardware problems and solutions. Sometimes the problem is server add-on hardware such as expansion cards (including those for blade enclosure backplanes), or onboard components integrated with the motherboard. In other cases, some hardware components may simply be incompatible with others; refer to documentation for more information.

You may want to keep the following hardware and software tools handy when troubleshooting server and network hardware issues:

- Multimeter to test power supplies
- Hardware diagnostic tools for memory (seen in Figure 7-5), RAID controllers, disks, motherboards, expansion cards
- Can of compressed air for removing dust
- Antistatic wrist straps and ESD mats
- Tool for testing bad RAM chips

Software Problems and Solutions

More often than not, you'll be troubleshooting software issues instead of hardware issues. Hardware components are pretty resilient and generally tend to work well together. Other than the OS, application software runs in an environment that could be hosting

Hardware Problem	Possible Cause	Possible Solution
BIOS failure	• Overheating • Unsupported features • Newer options might require UEFI, not BIOS (eg., secure boot)	• Keep server rooms and data centers cool • Ensure optimized airflow to introduce cool air and remove warm air • Update (flash) the BIOS
POST failure	• TPM firmware detects a boot configuration change • Failed hardware components such as a bad RAM chip or non-ECC RAM	• Enter TPM recovery code and configure boot options • Replace failed components
Memory failure	• Often shows up as a POST failure • Random OS freezes or reboots	• Run memory diagnostics • Replace failed components
Processor failure	• Overheating • Throttling slows down the CPU as temperature increases, resulting in poor performance	• Ensure HVAC is running correctly to keep server rooms and data centers cool
Boot sequence	• Operating system not found due to changing of disk order and partitions • Trying to boot from USB may fail if unsupported or not enabled in the BIOS	• Configure bootable disk order in BIOS • Configure bootable disk partitions in OS • Flash BIOS so that USB boot is supported
Storage failure	• Drive failure that can result in disk I/O failures • RAID array drive failures can result in slow file I/O performance	• Run disk diagnostics to verify disk failure • Replace failed components • Have hot spare disks in place
Power failure	• Power supply • Power surge	• Use redundant power sources • Use a UPS • Ensure that UPS batteries are functional • Use surge protectors
Environment failure	• HVAC malfunction causes overheating • Accumulated dust hampers airflow and adds a layer of insulation to chips • Not enough humidity increases ESD	• Ensure that HVAC is keeping server rooms and data centers cool • Clear dust from components and cool air intake fans • Ensure that HVAC keeps a consistent relative humidity

Table 7-1 Common Hardware Issues and Solutions

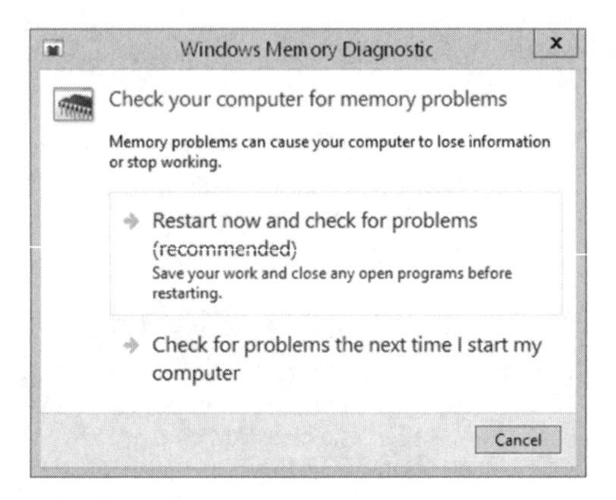

Figure 7-5 Windows Server 2012 R2 built-in memory tester

literally millions of other software components; no wonder we spend a lot of troubleshooting time here!

Don't forget to check the obvious. For example, a mobile phone user may unknowingly mute a phone microphone during a conversation and assume there is a transmission or phone problem. This is called discontinuous transmission (DTX), and simple issues like this are easily avoided with user training. Many organizations expect users to learn how to use new hardware and software solutions magically without providing training, but this is not a place to cut corners!

Table 7-2 lists commons software problems, causes, and solutions.

Software Problem	Possible Cause	Possible Solution
Logon failure	• Incorrect credentials • Corrupt user profile • Cannot locate authentication server	• Reset user password • Save old user profile, remove corrupt user profile and registry references • Ensure that client station points to correct DNS server
User unable to access resource	• Insufficient permissions • Encryption is enabled • Windows User Account Control (UAC) configuration is too restrictive • UNIX/Linux sudo is not configured to allow user access to certain commands	• Check user effective access • Check group membership • Ensure that user has decryption key
Memory leak	• Poorly written software • Malware • Runaway processes that keep consuming resources	• Reboot server to reclaim memory • Run antimalware scan • Patch software • Find functionally equivalent software that does not result in memory leaks

Table 7-2 Common Software Issues and Solutions (*Continued*)

Software Problem	Possible Cause	Possible Solution
Blue Screen of Death (BSoD)	• Unstable device driver • Bad RAM chips	• Update, replace, or roll back driver • Run memory diagnostics • Replace failed RAM chip • Restart the Windows server, press `F8`, attempt to boot using the last known good configuration (LKGC)
Disk drive unmountable	• File system corruption • Not supported by local OS	• Run a disk scan to correct file system errors • Format drive with file system supported by the local OS
Logs cannot be written to	• Log disk volume is full	• Free up disk space • Store logs in alternate location with more free disk space • Archive old log messages
Slow OS performance	• OS disk is full • Disks are fragmented • System resources lacking • CPUs are busy • Virtual memory swap file or partition is on slow disk, is using too much space, or is corrupt	• Free up space on the OS drive • Extend the OS drive capacity • Defragment drive • Reduce the amount of processes running concurrently • Place virtual memory swap configuration of fast disks with plenty of free disk space
Software patches are not being applied	• Previous software dependencies are not present • Patches don't match platform architecture (x86 vs. x64)	• Apply previous dependencies first • Acquire patches for appropriate platform architecture
Service failure	• Dependency services failed to start • Service account has insufficient permissions • Service account password has expired	• Ensure that dependent services are started first • Grant the service account required permissions • Set service account password
OS cannot be shut down	• Hangs can be caused by runaway background processes • Updates are still being applied	• Use Task Manager in Windows or Linux `kill` command to terminate offending process • Wait until updates have finished being applied
Users cannot print	• Windows print spooler service is unresponsive • Printer is offline • Incorrect or corrupt printer driver	• Restart Windows print spooler service • Ensure that printer has paper, ink, correct network configuration, and bring online • Uninstall, then reinstall up-to-date printer driver • Remove and reconfigure printer in OS

Table 7-2 Common Software Issues and Solutions

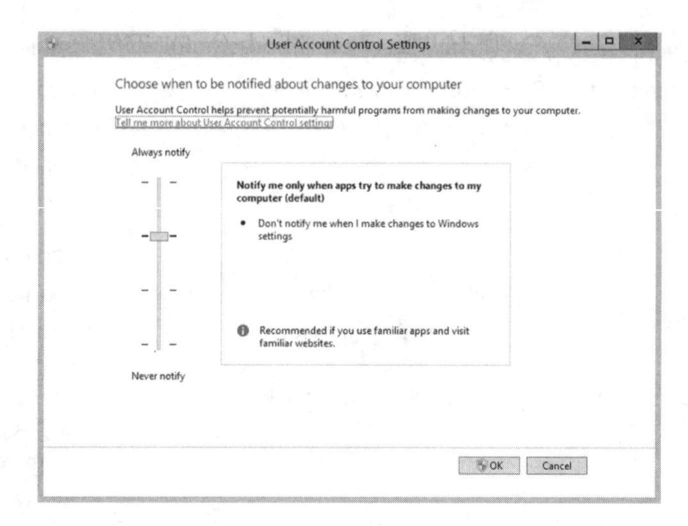

Figure 7-6 User Account Control settings on Windows Server 2012 R2

As a prepared CompTIA Server+ technician, you will have software utilities available at all times to resolve software issues quickly. Some restrictions, such as installing or running applications, can be related to UAC configuration, as shown in Figure 7-6.

Remember to check related logs for clues. For instance, if a DNS server doesn't seem to be responding to DNS queries from clients, yet it's up and running on the network, check the DNS server and client logs.

You can monitor resource use in Windows using a variety of tools:

- Task Manager
- Resource Monitor
- Performance Monitor
- Data Collector Sets

The Windows Resource Monitor (Figure 7-7) gives you further insight as to which processes are consuming the most disk I/O time; the other tools do not provide this detail.

Data Collector Sets (DCSs) are similar to Performance Monitor in that you can add metrics that you want to monitor. DCSs differ from Performance Monitor in that you can control when to start and stop collecting this data, and you can configure alert notifications when certain thresholds have been exceeded. For example, if CPU utilization goes beyond 80 percent for a period of time, administrators can be notified in a variety of ways (Figure 7-8).

UNIX and Linux environments provide various tools to troubleshoot software issues:

- `top` Lists top processes consuming resources
- `ps` Lists running processes

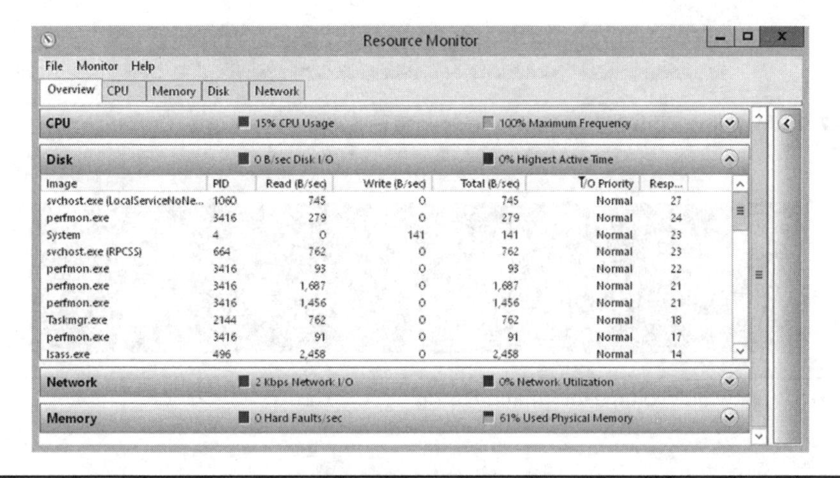

Figure 7-7 Viewing disk I/O statistics in Resource Monitor

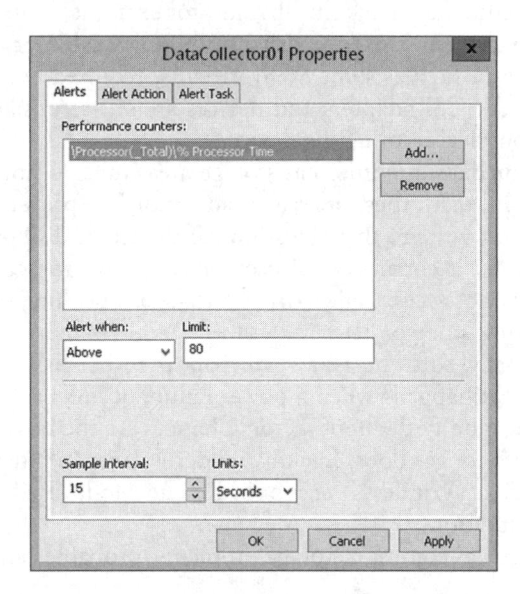

Figure 7-8 An alert Data Collector Set based on CPU usage

- **`kill`** Terminates processes
- **`df`** Shows disk free space

Windows environments have built-in tools for mapping drives, such as the GUI, `net use` command (Figure 7-9), or the `new-psdrive` PowerShell cmdlet. You can also use the GUI to view disk, file, and folder properties by right-clicking and choosing Properties.

Using PowerShell, the `get-volume` cmdlet shows file system health status as well as size statistics (Figure 7-10).

```
C:\>net use O: \\192.168.1.200\j$ /persistent:yes
The command completed successfully.
```

Figure 7-9 Mapping a drive letter in Windows with `net use`

```
PS C:\> get-volume

DriveLetter FileSystemLabel FileSystem DriveType HealthStatus OperationalStatus SizeRemaining       Size
----------- --------------- ---------- --------- ------------ ----------------- -------------       ----
F           NEW VOLUME      FAT        Fixed     Healthy      OK                      2.93 GB    2.93 GB
D           Data            NTFS       Fixed     Healthy      OK                      6.53 GB   14.17 GB
            Recovery        NTFS       Fixed     Healthy      OK                    566.33 MB     600 MB
C                           NTFS       Fixed     Healthy      OK                     81.53 GB  212.83 GB
E           NEW VOLUME      FAT32      Fixed     Healthy      OK                      1.95 GB    1.95 GB
```

Figure 7-10 View disk volume information using `get-volume`

Storage Problems and Solutions

Always remember to check the obvious; for example, loose or faulty power or data cables for disk devices can cause the drive to be unavailable or available intermittently. Some disk I/O buses, such as some SCSI variants, required both ends of the bus to be terminated. Newer SCSI adapters and devices are self-terminated, whereas older equipment requires a physical terminating device.

Storage media sometimes has storage areas that do not reliably store data; disk-scanning tools will mark these areas as "bad sectors" to prevent the server OS from attempting future disk write to these locations. If the entire disk partition (or volume, if it spans multiple disks) is corrupt, or if users do not have the correct permissions, they might receive a "cannot access logical drive" message. The same is true for servers attempting to access network storage.

Occasionally, software issues will appear to be disk-subsystem issues. Consider, for example, what happens when a power failure occurs in the midst of applying server OS patches that modify the boot sector. Chances are the boot sector will be corrupt and the server will no longer boot. Luckily, modern server OS installation media often provides a repair option (Windows) or a boot Rescue Mode (Red Hat Enterprise Linux) to deal with such situations.

Table 7-3 lists common storage problems, probable causes, and possible solutions.

Windows Tools

You can manage and troubleshoot disks on Windows servers in a number of ways. In some cases, you might even wipe and repartition a problematic disk—just make sure you've made a backup of the disk contents beforehand.

Command line tools include the following:

- Diskpart.exe
- Defrag.exe
- PowerShell cmdlets

Storage Problem	Possible Cause	Possible Solution
Slow file access	• Failed RAID 5 array is rebuilding data-on-demand in memory; can tolerate one disk failure in the array • Failure of RAID controller disk write cache or battery • Disk array contains mismatched drive speeds	• Ensure that hot spare disks are always available • Consider using RAID 6, which can tolerate two simultaneous drive failures • Without write caching, RAID arrays cannot queue disk requests that cannot be services right away; replace faulty components • Disk arrays with both slow and fast disks will use the slower speed
Data unavailable	• Failed server • Failed HBA	• Ensure high availability with failover clustering, data backups, and data replication to other sites • Ensure redundant SAN paths in case of HBA or switch failure
Failed backup	• Failed network connection • Media failure	• Ensure that there are redundant network connections for LAN and cloud-based backup • Ensure that extra backup media is always available, and store media appropriately • Perform period restore drills to ensure that restores will not fail • Have at least two backups of critical data in case a restore from one fails
Unavailable drives	• OS failure • Physical disk failure • RAID controller failure • Blade enclosure backplane failure • Network connection failure	• View LED indicators and drive error lights to catch problems before they grow • Ensure redundant network paths to critical applications and data • Failed RAID controllers or disk devices can sometimes be resolved by replacing failed components and attempting to rebuild the array • Replace failed hardware components
Unable to mount storage device	• Corrupt file system • Corrupt mass storage driver • Insufficient user permissions • Incorrect partition type	• For Windows, run a disk scan to ensure the file system is not corrupt • For Linux and Windows, ensure that user permissions are configured correctly to enable users to mount local and network storage • Some OSs cannot properly read disk partitions created with other OS versions; use the correct partition type that is understandable by the server OS

Table 7-3 Common Storage Issues and Solutions

Newer Windows OSs (such as Windows 10 and Windows Server 2012 R2) no longer include the old fdisk command line utility; it has been replaced with diskpart.exe. At the GUI level, you can use tools such as these:

- Disk Management
- Server Manager
- Disk Defragmenter
- Disk Cleanup
- Error Checking

For example, the following set of `diskpart` commands wipe (clean) the third disk in a machine and then convert the disk to a GUID Partition Table (GPT), which enables larger capacity partitions as well as a larger number of partitions than a master boot record (MBR). (See Chapter 4.) A 50GB primary partition is created, formatted as NTFS, and assigned drive letter E:.

```
diskpart
select disk 2
clean
convert gpt
create partition primary size=500000
format quick fs=ntfs label="Website Content"
assign letter="E"
```

Using Microsoft PowerShell, you could initialize, partition, and format a disk, as shown in the following example:

```
Initialize-Disk -Number 2
New-Partition -DiskNumber 2 -AssignDriveLetter -Size 500gb
Format-Volume -FileSystem NTFS
```

PowerShell also includes cmdlets for troubleshooting file system issues:

```
Repair-Volume -DriveLetter E -OfflineScanAndFix
```

Linux Tools

Like Windows, some UNIX and Linux variants provide a bootable rescue mode to troubleshoot disk boot problems, often from OS installation media. From rescue mode, or in some cases, within the OS itself, you can use tools to manage and troubleshoot at the command line, including the following:

- **`df`** Shows disk free space
- **`fsck`** Checks file systems for corruption
- **`xfs_repair`** Checks for and repairs an XFS file system
- **`iostat`** Shows disk I/O statistics for storage devices

- **lsof** Lists open files and provides further details
- **mdadm** Linux software RAID array management

For example, to repair an unmounted XFS file system on /dev/sdc1, as shown in Figure 7-11, you would use this command:

```
xfs_repair /dev/sdc
```

Sometimes a lack of free disk space can cause many, often performance-related, problems. The Linux disk free (`df`) command (Figure 7-12) has a `-h` (human readable) switch to show file systems and their disk space usage statistics in terms of megabytes, gigabytes, and so on, instead of in units of 1KB blocks:

```
df -h
```

```
[root@rhel7-1 /]# xfs_repair /dev/sdc1
Phase 1 - find and verify superblock...
Phase 2 - using internal log
        - zero log...
        - scan filesystem freespace and inode maps...
        - found root inode chunk
Phase 3 - for each AG...
        - scan and clear agi unlinked lists...
        - process known inodes and perform inode discovery...
        - agno = 0
        - agno = 1
        - agno = 2
        - agno = 3
        - process newly discovered inodes...
Phase 4 - check for duplicate blocks...
        - setting up duplicate extent list...
        - check for inodes claiming duplicate blocks...
        - agno = 0
        - agno = 1
        - agno = 2
        - agno = 3
Phase 5 - rebuild AG headers and trees...
        - reset superblock...
Phase 6 - check inode connectivity...
        - resetting contents of realtime bitmap and summary inodes
        - traversing filesystem ...
        - traversal finished ...
        - moving disconnected inodes to lost+found ...
Phase 7 - verify and correct link counts...
done
```

Figure 7-11 Repairing an XFS file system using `xfs_repair` in Linux

Figure 7-12 Viewing disk free space in Linux using the `df` command

```
[root@rhel7-1 /]# df -h
Filesystem               Size  Used Avail Use% Mounted on
/dev/mapper/rhel-root     18G  3.0G   15G  18% /
devtmpfs                 908M     0  908M   0% /dev
tmpfs                    917M  140K  917M   1% /dev/shm
tmpfs                    917M   33M  884M   4% /run
tmpfs                    917M     0  917M   0% /sys/fs/cgroup
/dev/sda1                497M  124M  373M  25% /boot
[root@rhel7-1 /]# 
```

```
[root@rhel7-1 /]# iostat
Linux 3.10.0-229.el7.x86_64 (rhel7-1)   07/31/2016      _x86_64_
)

avg-cpu:  %user   %nice %system %iowait  %steal   %idle
           0.09    0.00    0.14    0.03    0.00   99.74

Device:            tps    kB_read/s    kB_wrtn/s    kB_read    kB_wrtn
fd0               0.00         0.00         0.00         12          0
sda               0.14         2.04         1.52    2141112    1601364
sdb               0.00         0.00         0.00       2260          0
sdc               0.00         0.00         0.00       2260          0
dm-0              0.02         0.00         0.08       4136      86888
dm-1              0.15         1.93         1.44    2024515    1512362
```

Figure 7-13 Viewing disk I/O statistics using the `iostat` Linux command

To determine which Linux disk device has the most I/O activity, use the `iostat` command, as shown in Figure 7-13.

Network Problems and Solutions

Network problems can be hardware related, software related, or both. For example, physical network cables can sometimes have problems. A *time-domain reflectometer* (TDR) is used to measure the continuity of electronic signals through circuit boards and the wires within a network cable to identify faults.

EXAM TIP Don't confuse TDRs with tone and probe generators. TDRs are used to identify where cable faults exist, while tone and probe generators are used to identify specific cables in large cable bunches, by sending a tone through wires in a wall jack and identifying that signal at the other end of the cable in a wiring closet.

Optical time-domain reflectometers (OTDRs) result in traces that are used to show where fiber-optic cables are terminated and can show locations of cable breaks. OTDRs are expensive devices that require expertise to use and to interpret results.

Many network problems stem from incorrect software protocol configuration. IPv4 and IPv6 addresses must fall on the correct subnet to function properly. The default gateway, or router, is used to send traffic outside of the LAN; it must be reachable on the LAN.

EXAM TIP You might see at least one diagram-based question testing your knowledge of valid IP addresses, subnet masks, and which router interface your default gateway configuration should point to.

Table 7-4 outlines the reasons for common network issues and potential solutions.

When destination hosts on different networks are unreachable, the IP address, subnet mask, and default gateway must be checked to ensure that their values are correct. If they are correct, the Windows `tracert` or Linux `traceroute` command can be used to determine how far down the line (through routers) transmissions are getting before encountering problems. This is more useful than the `ping` command, which would simply report that the host is unreachable. (Note that Windows machines use the `ping -6`

Network Problem	Possible Cause	Possible Solution
Internet connectivity failure	• Service provider outage • Incorrect IP address for subnet • Incorrect subnet mask • Incorrect default gateway • Incorrect DNS server	• Verify IP address is in correct range for the subnet using `ipconfig` (Windows) or `ifconfig` (Linux) • Ensure that the configured default gateway (router) interface is on the LAN • Ping by IP address instead of name to isolate name-resolution problems • Check your provider SLA to determine support options
LAN connectivity only	• An IPv4 169.254 address is assigned when DHCP is not reachable	• Ensure that DHCP server is running • Ensure that UDP port 67 is not blocked to the DHCP server • For DHCP servers on other subnets, ensure that your LAN's DHCP relay agent is functional
Network service misconfiguration	• DHCP server handing out invalid IP configurations such as incorrect default gateway IP address	• Correct DHCP misconfigurations related to IP range, subnet mask, default gateway, DNS server, etc.
Network resource unreachable	• Name resolution problems • IP misconfiguration • VLAN membership • Incorrect subnet mask • Incorrect route table entry	• Use `nbtstat` (Windows) to troubleshoot NetBIOS name resolution issues; `nslookup` for DNS • Make sure computer is a part of the correct VLAN • View routing table using `route print` (Windows) or `ip route show` (Linux)
Unable to connect to network	• Faulty network cable • Switch port security • NIC speed set incorrectly • RADIUS authentication failure • MAC address filtering	• Replace faulty cables • Configure switch ports to enable device access • Set NIC speed and duplex settings to autodetect • Ensure that proper authentication credentials and methods are used • Add your device MAC address to the filter list to gain network access

Table 7-4 Common Network Issues and Solutions

command to use IPv6, such as when pinging a hostname; Linux systems uses the `ping6` command.)

EXAM TIP The `ping`, `tracert`, and `traceroute` commands use ICMP as their transport mechanism. These commands will not be useful troubleshooting tools if host or network firewalls block ICMP traffic.

IPv6 troubleshooting is not that different from troubleshooting IP4. Similar to how the IPv4 subnet mask is compared to the IPv4 address, devices with the same IPv6 subnet prefix are considered to be on the same network. On a Windows server, `ipconfig` shows both IPv4 and IPv6 information.

The Windows `route` command (`ip route show` in Linux) can be used to display or modify routing table entries on a Windows server. For example, to display routes, you would type `route print`, as shown in Figure 7-14. Take note that the 0.0.0.0 route is the default route; notice the IP address of the default gateway on the same line.

To ensure that network services are listening on a specific TCP or UDP port, use the Windows `netstat` command. For example, if a POP e-mail server is not running and therefore not listening on TCP port 110, clients will be unable to connect to their mailboxes.

Name Resolution Issues

If names are resolving to unexpected IP addresses (the name doesn't match what is in DNS), then there are probably entries in the local HOSTS files on the system. The HOSTS file is checked before DNS servers for name resolution.

Recent answers to DNS queries are cached in the local client DNS memory cache. The Windows `ipconfig` command includes a `/flushdns` parameter that clears out the client DNS cache; use this when the DNS records have changed recently.

For further DNS troubleshooting, use the `nslookup` command. After typing `nslookup` and pressing ENTER, you will be in interactive mode. You can use the server

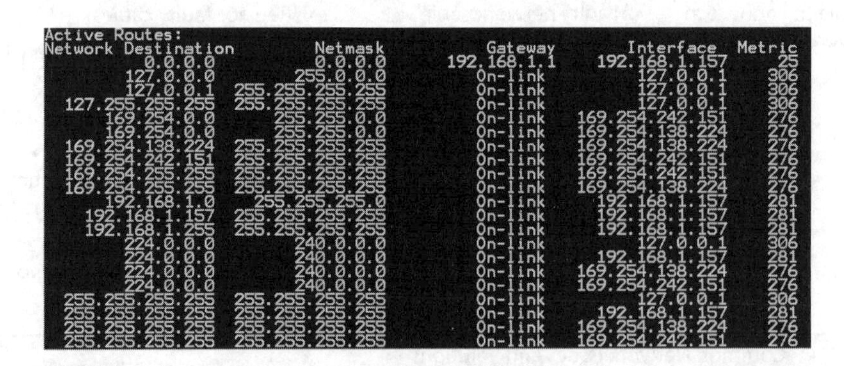

```
Active Routes:
Network Destination        Netmask          Gateway       Interface  Metric
          0.0.0.0          0.0.0.0      192.168.1.1   192.168.1.157     25
        127.0.0.0        255.0.0.0         On-link        127.0.0.1    306
        127.0.0.1  255.255.255.255         On-link        127.0.0.1    306
  127.255.255.255  255.255.255.255         On-link        127.0.0.1    306
      169.254.0.0      255.255.0.0         On-link   169.254.242.151    276
      169.254.0.0      255.255.0.0         On-link   169.254.138.224    276
  169.254.138.224  255.255.255.255         On-link   169.254.138.224    276
  169.254.242.151  255.255.255.255         On-link   169.254.242.151    276
  169.254.255.255  255.255.255.255         On-link   169.254.242.151    276
  169.254.255.255  255.255.255.255         On-link   169.254.138.224    276
      192.168.1.0    255.255.255.0         On-link     192.168.1.157    281
    192.168.1.157  255.255.255.255         On-link     192.168.1.157    281
    192.168.1.255  255.255.255.255         On-link     192.168.1.157    281
        224.0.0.0        240.0.0.0         On-link         127.0.0.1    306
        224.0.0.0        240.0.0.0         On-link     192.168.1.157    281
        224.0.0.0        240.0.0.0         On-link   169.254.138.224    276
        224.0.0.0        240.0.0.0         On-link   169.254.242.151    276
  255.255.255.255  255.255.255.255         On-link         127.0.0.1    306
  255.255.255.255  255.255.255.255         On-link     192.168.1.157    281
  255.255.255.255  255.255.255.255         On-link   169.254.138.224    276
  255.255.255.255  255.255.255.255         On-link   169.254.242.151    276
```

Figure 7-14 Output from the Windows `route print` command

```
C:\>nslookup
Default Server:  google-public-dns-a.google.com
Address:  8.8.8.8

> server 192.168.1.1
Default Server:  [192.168.1.1]
Address:  192.168.1.1

> set type=mx
> whitehouse.gov
Server:  [192.168.1.1]
Address:  192.168.1.1

Non-authoritative answer:
whitehouse.gov  MX preference = 105, mail exchanger = mail3.eop.gov
whitehouse.gov  MX preference = 105, mail exchanger = mail1.eop.gov
whitehouse.gov  MX preference = 110, mail exchanger = mail6.eop.gov
whitehouse.gov  MX preference = 105, mail exchanger = mail2.eop.gov
whitehouse.gov  MX preference = 105, mail exchanger = mail4.eop.gov
whitehouse.gov  MX preference = 110, mail exchanger = mail5.eop.gov
> _
```

Figure 7-15 Using `nslookup` to view mail server information through MX records

directive to connect to a different DNS server. The `set type=` command changes the type of DNS resource record you want to test, as shown in Figure 7-15.

Security Problems and Solutions

Plenty of problems arise from security compromises, from loss of critical business data, to reputation loss and potential lawsuits—the list goes on and on. Many (not all) security problems are preventable, however, and this section will discuss how to troubleshoot security problems and how to prevent them from reoccurring.

Malware Troubleshooting

In addition to malware notifications, symptoms of malware infection include the following:

- Excessive and prolonged hardware resource use
- Inability to reach network resources
- Web browser home page is changed and is not editable
- Web browser opens pages you didn't navigate to
- Rogue processes or services (mystery processes) running
- Missing log entries (cleared by the attacker)
- Encrypted files with a message demanding payment

User awareness and training is the number one defense against most security threats. Chapter 6 discussed social engineering and user awareness regarding network malware attacks.

Servers should never be used as desktop computers. Tasks such as checking e-mail, reading the news, or downloading drivers should never be allowed directly on a server.

When infections are detected, the server or subnet must be isolated immediately; this can be done manually or automated through your antimalware solution. You can specify a script that runs on detection. The script might look at the subnet address and disable routing to and from the subnet, or it might disable the switch port that links that subnet to the rest of the network.

Malware Removal

The removal of malware can be done in many ways:

- Vendor infection removal tool
- Windows system restore point
  - Client OS only, not Windows Server OS
  - Revert to previous configuration, not data
- Reinstall or reimage the server
  - Ensure that you have a working backup
- Boot through alternative means to remove the infection
  - Windows safe mode
  - USB boot to run removal tool
  - PXE boot to run removal tool

Use more than one antimalware product to ensure that remnants of the infection do not remain; however, do not run multiple antimalware products at the same time, because some infections could be missed due to conflicts. Keep in mind that even if multiple scans do not detect an infection, this doesn't mean the system is not infected; a zero-day attack may be the culprit, for example, which will not be detected by a virus scan that isn't looking for it.

This is where antimalware heuristic analysis becomes useful in detecting previously unknown malware by analyzing suspicious behavior, similarly to how IDS and IPS systems watch for abnormal host activities or network traffic. The downside is false positives—the reporting of a problem when one does not exist.

Too Few Permissions

Chapter 6 discussed file system permissions for Windows and Linux systems. Normally, users are added to groups, and groups are added to ACLs and either granted or denied permissions.

Windows

On Windows servers, combining share and NTFS permissions results in the most restrictive permissions being applied, and this is a big part of troubleshooting file system issues in Windows environments. In the GUI, you can view the properties of a file or folder to see the effective permissions for a given user or group if a user is unable to open a file.

Too few permissions can also mean applications won't launch. Windows systems might need User Account Control (UAC) settings loosened up to allow apps to run. Some apps require administrative privileges not only to install, but also to run—it depends on the app and where it reads and writes to and from in the file system and registry.

For Windows machines, local Group Policy executes before Active Directory Site, Domain, and OU Group Policy settings. Group Policy is often used to harden Windows clients and servers, but sometimes it might be a little too restrictive, and it's important that you know how to view effective Group Policy Objects (GPOs) for a server to troubleshoot this type of issue. Where the `gpudate` command forces a Group Policy update, `gpresult /r` shows the resultant set of policy, listing GPOs that are applied to the machine where the command was run. Figure 7-16 shows the output from `gpresult /r`.

Security filtering enables Group Policy administrators to ensure that only specific users or computers get Group Policy settings. This can be done by specifying individual users, computers, or groups, or by using Windows Management Instrumentation (WMI) filters. WMI filters use the WMI Query Language (WQL), as shown in the following example, where Microsoft Hyper-V and VMware virtual machines are being selected:

```
SELECT *
FROM SMS_R_System AS Sys
INNER JOIN SMS_G_System_Computer_System AS CompSys ON
CompSys.ResourceId = Sys.ResourceId
 WHERE
(CompSys.Manufacturer = 'Microsoft Corporation'
OR CompSys.Manufacturer = 'VMware, Inc.')
```

EXAM TIP Exam questions may imply that central configuration changes (Group Policy) have been made and that they have affected some or all users or computers. Remember that "some" computers or users could be very specific, as shown in the preceding WQL example. WQL can query any hardware or software attribute related to users or computers.

```
Microsoft Windows [Version 6.3.9600]
(c) 2013 Microsoft Corporation. All rights reserved.

C:\Users\Administrator>gpresult /r

Microsoft (R) Windows (R) Operating System Group Policy Result tool v2.0
c 2013 Microsoft Corporation. All rights reserved.

Created on 8/1/2016 at 7:42:28 AM

RSOP data for FAKEDOMAIN\Administrator on SRV2012-1 : Logging Mode
------------------------------------------------------------------

OS Configuration:            Primary Domain Controller
OS Version:                  6.3.9600
Site Name:                   Default-First-Site-Name
Roaming Profile:             N/A
Local Profile:               C:\Users\Administrator
Connected over a slow link?: No

COMPUTER SETTINGS
------------------
    CN=SRV2012-1,OU=Domain Controllers,DC=fakedomain,DC=local
    Last time Group Policy was applied: 8/1/2016 at 7:39:43 AM
    Group Policy was applied from:      Srv2012-1.fakedomain.local
    Group Policy slow link threshold:   500 kbps
    Domain Name:                        FAKEDOMAIN
    Domain Type:                        Windows 2008 or later

    Applied Group Policy Objects
    -----------------------------
        Default Domain Controllers Policy
        Default Domain Policy
```

Figure 7-16 Output from the Windows `gpresult /r` command

Linux

Linux administrators can use the sudo command prefix in front of a command that requires elevated privilege—of course, sudo has to be configured in the first place to allow this. The following command enables a regular user to set the password for bjones using sudo:

```
sudo passwd bjones
```

Another consideration in Linux is the SetUID special bit, which allows an executed script or binary to run not as the invoker, but as the file owner (which could be root). This warrants very careful attention, but it can solve the problem of a regular user not being able to run a script or program. The following example adds the SetUID bit to a file called /backupscript.sh. If someone can execute the script, it will run with the permissions of whoever the file owner is (find this out by typing `ls -l`).

```
chmod u+s /file.txt
```

Restoring File System ACLs

You can save file system ACLs and restore them if you run into trouble later. The `icacls` command works well for this on Windows servers; `getfacl` and `setfacl` work well in Linux.

Windows ACLs The first command displays ACL entries for user DLachance in and under E:\Projects. The second command saves the ACL entries to a file, and the third command restores ACLs to the file system from the Project_ACLs_Server1 file.

```
icacls E:\Projects /T | find "DLachance"
icacls E:\Projects\ /save {Projects_ACLs_Server1} /T
icacls E:\Projects /restore {Project_ACLs_Server1}
```

If users were once able to open files and now cannot, ACLs might have been changed, so you can use `icacls` in this case.

Linux ACLs The Linux `getfacl` and `setfacl` commands work well for saving and restoring ACLs. In the following examples, the first command recursively gets file system ACLs from /budgets and saves to a file called /budget_acls; the second command restores ACLs from the saved file.

```
getfacl -R /budgets >/budget_acls
setfacl --restore=/budget_acls
```

Too Many Permissions

When someone needs permissions quickly to do something in Windows, it's tempting to add the user to the Administrators (local) or Domain Admins (Active Directory) group to expedite the request—but this is blatant disregard for the principle of least privilege!

Users must be granted only those permissions required to complete a job task and nothing more. Of course, this might take a bit of research and testing on your part, and it's inconvenient—just like doing the right thing always is in real day-to-day life! It's worth the up-front time investment to grant permissions correctly.

A security audit can reveal this problem, or you can proactively check into it, perhaps by using commands such as `icacls` or `getfacl`, or by using a third-party security auditing tool.

Too Much Running

Modern server OSs are bare-bones, meaning they don't have many extra software components installed by default, so you have to install them. This is a good thing, because having too many services running simultaneously on a single server can negatively affect performance.

Port-scanning tools (such as the one shown in Figure 7-17) should be used periodically as a proactive measure to determine what ports are open on hosts. This gives you a picture of which network services are running, which is related to which firewall ports should be open on both host-based and network-based firewalls.

Of course, having many services running also increases the attack surface and increases the amount of time required to patch the server—so keep it minimal when possible!

Confidentiality and Integrity

Encryption provides confidentiality. A *cipher* is an algorithm that is used to scramble, or encrypt, and decrypt data. Use of an incorrect cipher can cause problems. Some hardware appliances and software configurations require the use of certain ciphers. For example, server file encryption software might be able to decrypt AES 128-bit files but not AES 256-bit messages, so cipher strength can be a problem.

The same type of situation could occur at the network level. You might be using an older web browser that does not support the encryption required by the web server. Yet another web browser problem might be PKI certificate trust; when connecting to an HTTP web server, your browser checks the signer of the server's PKI certificate. If the

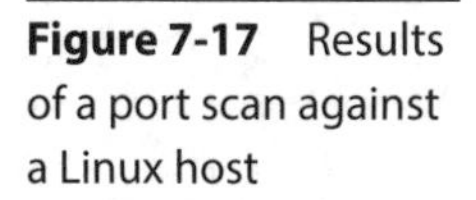

Figure 7-17 Results of a port scan against a Linux host

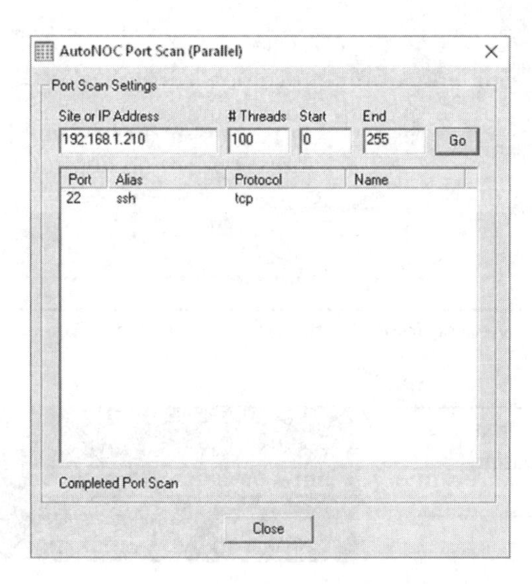

web browser does not trust the signer, it does not trust the PKI certificate used by the web site. This is solved by adding a new trusted certificate signer to the web browser device.

Integrity ensures the trustworthiness of data, in that it is authentic and has not been tampered with. Authentication can occur at the network packet level or at the file level. You can use packet sniffing (capturing) tools such as Wireshark to analyze packets on the network as well as bad packet checksums. Packet checksums are used to ensure that what is received is what was sent—and, if not, a retransmission might occur (which depends on the protocol being used). Packet sniffing can also reveal the use of insecure tools such as Telnet (Figure 7-18), which transmits data in clear text. The use of insecure tools can introduce malware or could serve as an attack vector for malicious uses—more trouble that we don't need!

Files can be hashed using various tools. A *file hash* is a unique value that represents the state of a file. If anything about the file changes, when we generate a new hash, it won't match the old one; this tells us that something has changed.

Window PowerShell supports file hashing using the `get-filehash` cmdlet:

```
get-filehash .\Project1.txt
```

The Linux `md5sum` command, as shown in Figure 7-19, can be used to generate and verify file hashes.

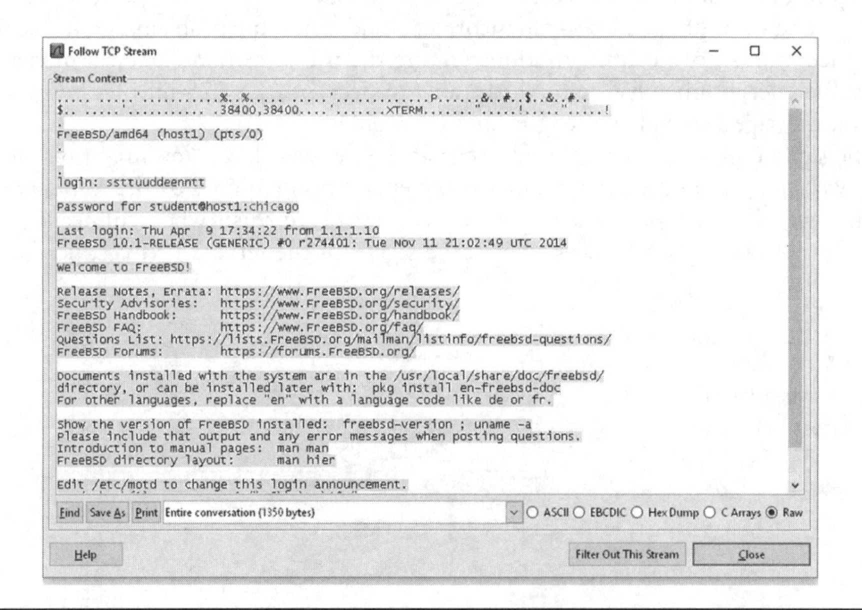

Figure 7-18 Viewing Telnet captured network traffic in Wireshark

Figure 7-19 Hashing files in Linux using `md5sum`

```
[root@rhel7-1 projects]# md5sum project_c.txt
f7605655a833cc8f445ba2ccaf0f8b73  project_c.txt
[root@rhel7-1 projects]#
```

Performance Optimization

Performance optimization applies to hardware, software, and specific implementation settings. It's important that you always monitor your environment for any changes in performance so that you can take action before you end up troubleshooting major issues.

Plenty of enterprise-class network and server monitoring tools are available, such as Spiceworks and Microsoft System Center Operations Manager, to name a few.

The Windows Performance Monitor tool (Figure 7-20) is built into the Windows OS. It enables you to add items to monitor such as network components, specific software components, hardware items such as CPUs and physical memory, and more. You can also use Performance Monitor to reach out over the network to monitor servers.

Linux administrators commonly use tools such as `ps`, `top`, and `iostat` for performance monitoring.

Hardware Optimization

Naturally, getting the fastest and most reliable hardware is always desired. More CPU cores and more RAM (especially for hypervisor servers) all make a difference in performance.

Since disk I/O often tends to be the performance bottleneck, it warrants our attention when it comes to optimizing performance. As discussed in Chapter 3, SSDs perform better than magnetic HDDs, and you can configure them both in storage tiers so that frequently accessed data is stored on the faster SSDs.

Whether server storage is local or accessed via a SAN, hardware RAID levels designed for performance (disk striping, or RAID 0, for example) should be used.

Software Optimization

Having fast hardware is important, but so is the software configuration that uses it. For example, adding more RAM to a hypervisor server makes sense, because it will host multiple virtual machines, but at the software level, each virtual machine might be configured with dynamic memory. This means virtual machines currently needing RAM can "borrow" it from those virtual machines that do not currently need it.

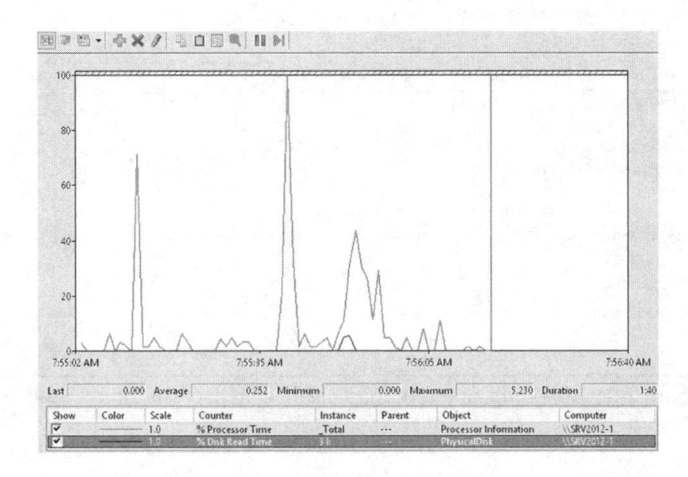

Figure 7-20 Windows Performance Monitor

Less is more. Keep your server OS clean, and install only the components that are needed. Not only will this keep your server running quickly, but it reduces the attack surface, decreases patching time, and reduces the overall amount of troubleshooting. The more stuff you have installed and running, the greater the likelihood of something going wrong.

Network Optimization

In addition to getting faster network equipment (switches, routers, NICs) or Internet connections, you can improve network performance with what you already have.

VLANs can be configured within network switches to group machines that communicate often with one another into smaller networks. Breaking large networks into smaller ones makes network transmissions much more efficient and essentially speeds up the network.

Servers normally have multiple NICs. You might consider configuring NIC teaming to group NICs together for better network throughput into and out of the server. Bear in mind that network switch ports where the server NICs are plugged in must be configured so that inbound server traffic can take advantage of NIC teaming.

Network load balancing (NLB) distributes incoming traffic for network services such as a web site to multiple back-end servers running the same service and holding the same content. For example, you might have four back-end web servers configured the same that replicate web site content to one another. The public IP address of the NLB is what DNS FQDNs would resolve to, not the back-end server IPs. Load balancers can improved the performance of an on-premises application or a cloud application.

One great thing about this in the public cloud is elastically scaling the number of back-end servers as needed behind the NLB, such as in response to increased demand. The end result is that the network service responds quickly.

Notice in Figure 7-21 that load balancers listen on a specific public port—in this case, TCP port 80 for an HTTP application—and that the configuration specifies an internal

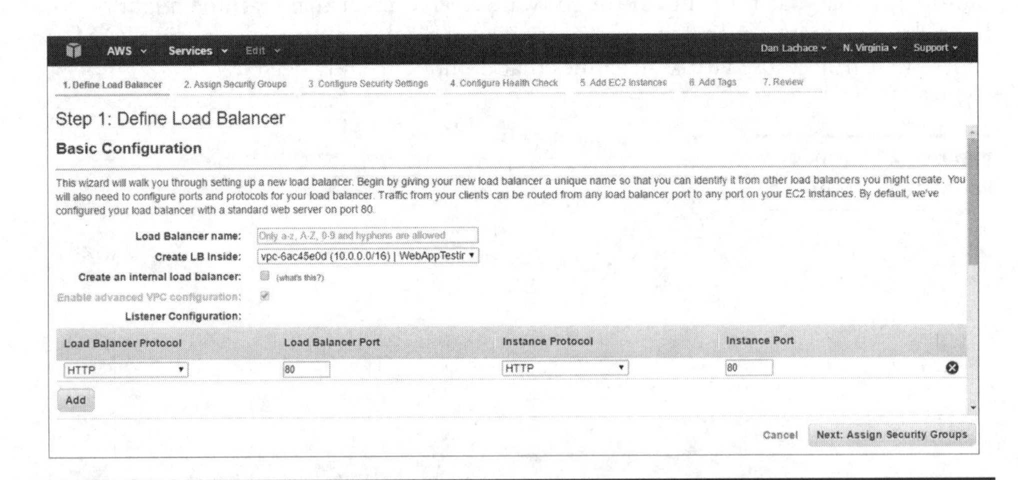

Figure 7-21 Creating an elastic load balancer in the Amazon Web Services cloud

port number that could be different. Also notice in the figure that step 5 of the wizard enables you to add multiple EC2 virtual machine instances (the back-end servers).

You should periodically capture network traffic and examine the capture results to ensure that only required network protocols are in use.

Hands-on Exercises

Exercise 7-1: Explore Windows Performance Monitoring Tools

1. Ensure that the Srv2012-1 virtual machine is running and you are logged on with the domain Administrator account with the password Pa$$w0rd.
2. From the Start menu, type **perfmon.exe** and press ENTER to start Performance Monitor.
3. On the left, expand Monitoring Tools and click Performance Monitor.
4. Click the green plus sign at the top of the screen to add monitored items.
5. Scroll within the list, expand Physical Disk, and choose Avg. Disk Queue Length. At the bottom left, choose C: and click Add. Then click OK. Disk commands that cannot be serviced immediately due to a busy disk are queued up, which is normal in most environments. The specific value that should be of concern here will vary in different environments.
6. Start Windows Explorer. Navigate to C:. Right-click C:\Program Files, choose Copy, and then press CTRL-V to paste.
7. Switch back to Performance Monitor and notice the graph spikes. Click the highest graph spike to display the specific metric that the line represents.
8. Delete the copy of Program Files on C:.
9. On the left, expand Data Collector Sets. Right-click User Defined and choose New, Data Collector Set. Enter **Notify of CPU spikes** for the name.
10. Choose Create Manually (Advanced).
11. Click Next and select Performance Counter Alert. Click Next.
12. Click Add. Scroll down to the Processor category and expand it. Choose %Processor Time, click Add, and then click OK.
13. At the bottom, specify Above 90 and click Next.
14. Choose Open Properties For This Data Collector Set and click Finish. In the Notify Of CPU Spikes Properties dialog box, click the Schedule tab, click Add, and set the beginning date to today's date. Click OK twice.
15. Double-click Notify Of CPU Spikes in the list. Double-click DataCollector01. Set the sampling interval to every 15 minutes.
16. Open the Alert Action tab and check the logging option. Then click OK.

Exercise 7-2: Explore Linux Performance Monitoring Tools

1. Ensure that you are logged into RHEL7-1 with the root account, with a password of Pa$$w0rdLinux. Press ENTER after each command you type in the following steps.
2. Choose Applications | Utilities, and start a terminal session.
3. Type **`df -h`** and notice free disk space on disk devices under the Avail column as well as the Use% column.
4. Type **`iostat`** to view disk read and write information.
5. Type **`ps -aux | grep sshd`** to view SSH daemon process information only. `Grep` is a line-filtering command. Notice the PID (column 2) and the %CPU utilization (column 3).
6. Type **`top`**. Notice that the display changes every few seconds.
7. Press s and enter **`.5`** to increase the update frequency to every half second. Press ENTER.
8. Type **`Q`** to exit.

Exercise 7-3: Use Windows PowerShell to Retrieve Event Log Information

1. Ensure that the Srv2012-1 virtual machine is running and that you are logged on with the Domain Administrator account.
2. Start PowerShell.
3. Enter **`get-eventlog system`**. Notice the long list of event log entries. You can interrupt this if it takes too long by pressing CTRL-C.
4. Enter **`get-eventlog system -newest 5`**.
5. Enter **`get-eventlog system -entrytype warning | more`**. Warning log entries are displayed.
6. Enter **`get-eventlog security -newest 10 -computername Srv2012-1`**. Remote security log entries are displayed from Srv2012-1.

NOTE The `-computername` parameter is used here for demonstration purposes only. It is not needed because we are already at Srv2012-1 issuing the command. You can specify multiple computer names in a comma-separated list.

Exercise 7-4: View Linux Log File Entries

1. Ensure that you are logged into RHEL7-1 with the root account.
2. From the Applications menu, start a terminal session.
3. Type **`dmesg | grep scsi`** to view SCSI disk device startup messages.
4. Type **`cat /var/log/messages | more`** to review the Linux system log file one screen at a time. Press the SPACEBAR to advance one line at a time. Press Q to quit.

NOTE To view real-time log file updates in Linux, use `tail -f`—for example, `tail -f /var/log/messages`. Press CTRL-C to exit the viewing.

Chapter Review

Troubleshooting and performance optimization are linked. Poor performance indicates that you should troubleshoot the case and remedy the issue. Follow a structured approach to solve problems as quickly and efficiently as possible.

Troubleshooting Methodology

Follow the standard troubleshooting steps:

1. Identify the problem.
   - Determine the scope.
   - Question stakeholders.
   - Reproduce the problem.
   - Consult log files and documentation.
2. Establish a theory of probable cause.
   - Check the obvious.
3. Test the theory.
   - Use a test environment.
4. Establish a plan of action.
   - Notify stakeholders.
   - Establish implementation timeline.

5. Implement a solution or escalate.
    - Change one thing at a time.
    - Revert ineffective changes.
6. Verify functionality.
    - Test thoroughly.
    - Satisfy the end user.
7. Perform a root cause analysis.
    - Determine the source of symptoms.
8. Document the solution.
    - Keep a record during all troubleshooting phases.

Hardware Problems and Solutions

Hardware problems are quickly fixed with proper documentation (OEM and implementation) as well as tools such as multimeters to test power and diagnostic tools to test memory and RAID controller configurations. Other hardware issues to watch out for include the following:

- Apply firmware patches.
- Ensure that proper HVAC is in place.
- Determine any hardware incompatibilities.
- Look for component failures (sometimes identified during POST).
- Look for boot failures.
- Check power issues.

Software Problems and Solutions

Software troubleshooting includes the operating system, drivers, and applications. Resolving software issues includes taking actions such as these:

- Apply software patches.
    - Operating system
    - Drivers
    - Applications
- Reset the user password.
- Delete corrupt user profiles.
- Ensure that user permissions are set correctly.
- Run antimalware scans.
- Use monitoring tools to identify memory leaks or runaway processes.

- Boot into safe mode, repair mode, or rescue mode.
- Ensure that dependent services are running.
- Restart problematic services.

Storage Problems and Solutions

Physical storage device and cable issues can sometimes be the source of problems. Hot spare disks in disk arrays provide a quick way to resolve failed disk issues. Other items include the following:

- Disk I/O bus termination
- Failed disk adapters
- Failed disks
- Failed network path to network storage
- Insufficient disk space
- Insufficient user permissions to access storage
- File system corruption
- Slow file access
- Incorrect use of RAID level

Network Problems and Solutions

Physical network components such as NIC, switches, routers, and wireless access points can fail. Firmware and driver updates should be applied for optimal stability and functionality. TDRs and OTDRs can be used to ensure copper-based and fiber-optic cable continuity. Other network issues include the following:

- Incorrect IP address, subnet mask
- Incorrect default gateway, DNS server
- DHCP/DNS server unreachable
- Firewalls (network ACLs) blocking legitimate traffic
- Incorrect VLAN membership
- Mismatched NIC speed settings

Security Problems and Solutions

Documentation regarding the implementation of security controls reduces time spent troubleshooting. Other security issues include the following:

- Malware infections
- Inadequate authentication as required by server
- Untrusted or expired PKI certificate

- Insufficient permissions to access a network resource
- Too many permissions granted beyond what is required
- Incorrectly assigned share, NTFS, or Linux file system permissions
- Group Policy setting applying too little or too much security
- Linux users not using the `sudo` command prefix to run elevated commands
- Unnecessary installed software
- Unneeded running services
- Incorrect configured network firewall ACLs
- Mismatched cryptography ciphers
- Inability to decrypt transmissions or files

Performance Optimization

Performance optimization can result from replaced components, changed configurations, and ongoing monitoring of resource use.

Windows monitoring tools include the following:

- Task Manager
- Resource Monitor
- Performance Monitor
- Reliability history
- Log files

Linux monitoring tools include these:

- `ps`
- `top`
- `iostat`
- `df`

Network optimizations include NIC teaming, VLAN traffic isolation, and network load balancing.

Questions

1. Which troubleshooting step involves questioning stakeholders?
   A. Identify the problem.
   B. Establish a theory of probable cause.
   C. Test the theory.
   D. Establish a plan of action.

2. Which troubleshooting step involves reproducing the problem?
   A. Identify the problem.
   B. Establish a theory of probable cause.
   C. Test the theory.
   D. Establish a plan of action.

3. Which troubleshooting step involves making only a single change at a time?
   A. Identify the problem.
   B. Establish a theory of probable cause.
   C. Test the theory.
   D. Implement the solution.

4. Which troubleshooting item focuses on how and why a problem occurred?
   A. Test the theory.
   B. Identify the problem.
   C. Establish a plan of action.
   D. Perform root cause analysis.

5. Users complain that a database server has slowed down over the last hour despite the fact that no more users have connected. You run an antimalware scan, which comes up clean. The amount of network traffic has not changed. You reboot the server and the problem still persists. What is the most likely cause of the problem?
   A. Malware infection
   B. Boot sector corruption
   C. DDoS attack
   D. Overheating

6. One of your servers, FS1, is configured with a RAID 5 array. The server has 2TB of free disk space and overall CPU and memory utilization is hovering at 40 percent. Over the last hour, file reads from FS1 have been very slow. What is the most likely cause of the performance issue?
   A. Insufficient disk space
   B. File encryption
   C. Runaway process
   D. Failed RAID 5 disk

7. Which tool should be used to test server power supplies?
   A. Multimeter
   B. TDR
   C. OTDR
   D. Compressed air

8. A user station statically configured with IPv4 cannot download Group Policy settings; the error message states that a domain controller could not be found. The station can communicate with other local and remote hosts. Prior to the change from DHCP to static configuration, Group Policy worked. What is the most likely cause of the problem?
   A. Incorrect subnet mask
   B. Incorrect default gateway
   C. Incorrect DNS server
   D. Incorrect IP address

9. You are an Active Directory domain administrator. You attempt to install a server application on a domain-joined server. When you attempt to run the installer, nothing happens. What is the likely cause of the problem?
   A. Lack of administrative privileges
   B. Server needs to be patched
   C. User Account Control
   D. Insufficient disk space

10. A shared network folder contains Linux shell scripts. The folder permissions are set as shown in the following illustration. Technicians in the it_admins group are unable to run scripts from the /scripts folder. What should you do?

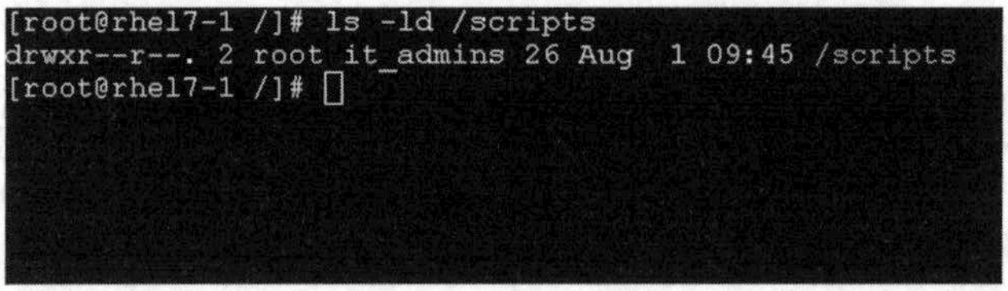

```
[root@rhel7-1 /]# ls -ld /scripts
drwxr--r--. 2 root it_admins 26 Aug  1 09:45 /scripts
[root@rhel7-1 /]# 
```

   A. Grant the it_admins group the execute permission.
   B. Set the UID bit on scripts so that they run as the owner.
   C. Grant the it_admins group the write permission.
   D. Tell technicians to use `sudo`.

11. A newly installed NIC driver on your Windows server has rendered the system unstable. What should you do?

    A. Roll back the driver.

    B. Reimage the server.

    C. Revert the server using a system restore point.

    D. Remove the NIC.

12. Which Linux command can be used to terminate a rogue process?

    A. `terminate`

    B. `remove`

    C. `taskkill`

    D. `kill`

13. Which Linux tool should you use to view disk device read and write statistics?

    A. `df`

    B. `fdisk`

    C. `iostat`

    D. `diskstat`

14. Which Linux tool should you use to troubleshoot CPU resource utilization in real-time?

    A. `iostat`

    B. `kill`

    C. `ps`

    D. `top`

15. Which PowerShell cmdlet can fix corrupt filesystems?

    A. Diskpart

    B. Fdisk

    C. Fix-volume

    D. Repair-volume

16. You have manually configured a route to a remote network on your Windows server. Which command will show this newly added route?

A. `ipconfig`

B. `ifconfig`

C. `ip route show`

D. `route print`

17. Your server IP settings are configured as shown in the following illustration. Which setting is incorrect?

```
Ethernet adapter Internal:

   Connection-specific DNS Suffix  . :
   Link-local IPv6 Address . . . . . : fe80::ca6:9b7d:4cce:f38c%16
   IPv4 Address. . . . . . . . . . . : 192.168.1.200
   Subnet Mask . . . . . . . . . . . : 255.255.255.0
   Default Gateway . . . . . . . . . : 192.168.15.253
```

A. The IPv6 address prefix

B. The IP address

C. The subnet mask

D. The default gateway

18. Which Linux command reports each router crossed when communicating with a remote host?

A. `traceroute`

B. `tracert`

C. `routetrace`

D. `routetr`

19. What is one possible drawback of heuristic host and network analysis?

A. False negatives

B. True negatives

C. True positives

D. False positives

20. Which Windows command can be used to view and troubleshoot file system ACLs?
    - A. `icacls`
    - B. `getfacl`
    - C. `setfacl`
    - D. `cipher`

Questions and Answers

1. Which troubleshooting step involves questioning stakeholders?
    - A. Identify the problem.
    - B. Establish a theory of probable cause.
    - C. Test the theory.
    - D. Establish a plan of action.

    A. Questioning stakeholders is a part of problem identification. B, C, and D are incorrect. Stakeholder questioning falls under problem identification and not the other troubleshooting steps.

2. Which troubleshooting step involves reproducing the problem?
    - A. Identify the problem.
    - B. Establish a theory of probable cause.
    - C. Test the theory.
    - D. Establish a plan of action.

    A. Reproducing the problem relates to problem identification. B, C, and D are incorrect. Reproducing problems is part of problem identification and not the other troubleshooting steps.

3. Which troubleshooting step involves making only a single change at a time?
    - A. Identify the problem.
    - B. Establish a theory of probable cause.
    - C. Test the theory.
    - D. Implement the solution.

    D. Changing one item at a time is part of implementing the solution. A, B, and C are incorrect. These troubleshooting steps do not include changing one item at a time.

4. Which troubleshooting item focuses on how and why a problem occurred?
   - **A.** Test the theory.
   - **B.** Identify the problem.
   - **C.** Establish a plan of action.
   - **D.** Perform root cause analysis.

   D. Root cause analysis deals not with symptoms of problems, but with what caused the symptoms. This can be used to prevent similar future incidents. A, B, and C are incorrect. The listed troubleshooting steps are not as specific as a root cause analysis.

5. Users complain that a database server has slowed down over the last hour despite the fact that no more users have connected. You run an antimalware scan, which comes up clean. The amount of network traffic has not changed. You reboot the server and the problem still persists. What is the most likely cause of the problem?
   - **A.** Malware infection
   - **B.** Boot sector corruption
   - **C.** DDoS attack
   - **D.** Overheating

   D. Overheating can cause CPU cores to throttle themselves (slow down) to reduce heat generated. A, B, and C are incorrect. The question states that a malware scan was performed and there was no infection. Rebooting the server means there are no boot sector corruption issues. A DDoS attack would increase network traffic.

6. One of your servers, FS1, is configured with a RAID 5 array. The server has 2TB of free disk space and overall CPU and memory utilization is hovering at 40 percent. Over the last hour, file reads from FS1 have been very slow. What is the most likely cause of the performance issue?
   - **A.** Insufficient disk space
   - **B.** File encryption
   - **C.** Runaway process
   - **D.** Failed RAID 5 disk

   D. RAID 5 can tolerate a single disk failure. When this happens, requested data is rebuilt on demand from distributed parity information on other disks in the array. A, B, and C are incorrect. There is plenty of free disk space; file encryption is not mentioned in the question; and a runaway process would most likely increase CPU or memory utilization, which is low.

7. Which tool should be used to test server power supplies?

A. Multimeter

B. TDR

C. OTDR

D. Compressed air

A. Multimeters can be used to verify that the correct voltage is delivered from power supplies to components. B, C, and D are incorrect. TDRs and OTDRs are used to test copper and fiber cable continuity. Compressed air is used to clear away accumulated dust.

8. A user station statically configured with IPv4 cannot download Group Policy settings; the error message states that a domain controller could not be found. The station can communicate with other local and remote hosts. Prior to the change from DHCP to static configuration, Group Policy worked. What is the most likely cause of the problem?

A. Incorrect subnet mask

B. Incorrect default gateway

C. Incorrect DNS server

D. Incorrect IP address

C. DNS queries are used to find service location records for domain controllers. Pointing to a different DNS server could mean the required service location records are not present. A, B, and D are incorrect. The subnet mask, default gateway, and IP address cannot be problematic if communication with local and remote hosts is working.

9. You are an Active Directory domain administrator. You attempt to install a server application on a domain-joined server. When you attempt to run the installer, nothing happens. What is the likely cause of the problem?

A. Lack of administrative privileges

B. Server needs to be patched

C. User Account Control

D. Insufficient disk space

C. User Account Control is the most likely problem. Even logged-in administrators may have to right-click an installer and choose Run As Administrator. A, B, and D are incorrect. There is no lack of privileges; the user is a domain administrator. Server patching and insufficient disk space would not cause this symptom.

10. A shared network folder contains Linux shell scripts. The folder permissions are set as shown in the following illustration. Technicians in the it_admins group are unable to run scripts from the /scripts folder. What should you do?

```
[root@rhel7-1 /]# ls -ld /scripts
drwxr--r--. 2 root it_admins 26 Aug  1 09:45 /scripts
[root@rhel7-1 /]#
```

A. Grant the it_admins group the execute permission.

B. Set the UID bit on scripts so that they run as the owner.

C. Grant the it_admins group the write permission.

D. Tell technicians to use `sudo`.

A. The Linux execute permission is missing and is required to run shell scripts. B, C, and D are incorrect. The Linux UID bit runs a script as the owner, not the invoker. This level of access is not needed and violates the principle of least privilege. Write permission is not needed to run a script, and `sudo` is not required to run a script.

11. A newly installed NIC driver on your Windows server has rendered the system unstable. What should you do?

A. Roll back the driver.

B. Reimage the server.

C. Revert the server using a system restore point.

D. Remove the NIC.

A. Driver rollback reverts only the change to the driver. B, C, and D are incorrect. Windows servers cannot use system restore points. Reimaging the server is overkill when only a driver was changed. Removing the NIC is unnecessary since driver rollback will solve the problem.

12. Which Linux command can be used to terminate a rogue process?

A. `terminate`

B. `remove`

C. `taskkill`

D. `kill`

D. Given the Process Identifier (PID), the Linux `kill` command can terminate the process. A, B, and C are incorrect. There is no Linux `terminate`, `remove`, or `taskkill` command, although `taskkill` is a valid Windows command.

13. Which Linux tool should you use to view disk device read and write statistics?

 A. `df`

 B. `fdisk`

 C. `iostat`

 D. `diskstat`

 C. The Linux `iostat` command displays disk device read and write statistics. A, B, and D are incorrect. `df` shows disk free space, `fdisk` is used to work with disk partitions, and `diskstat` is not a valid Linux command.

14. Which Linux tool should you use to troubleshoot CPU resource utilization in real-time?

 A. `iostat`

 B. `kill`

 C. `ps`

 D. `top`

 D. The Linux `top` command shows a changing display of the top resource-consuming processes. The timing interval for the display can be configured. A, B, and C are incorrect. Disk space statistics result from the `iostat` command. Given the PID, `kill` terminates processes. `ps` lists processes and potentially their CPU utilization, but it is a static display (unchanging).

15. Which PowerShell cmdlet can fix corrupt filesystems?

 A. Diskpart

 B. Fdisk

 C. Fix-volume

 D. Repair-volume

 D. The PowerShell repair-volume cmdlet can fix file system problems when the disk volume is not mounted. A, B, and C are incorrect. Diskpart is used to work with disks and file systems, but not to fix corrupt filesystems. Fdisk is no longer used in Windows, and PowerShell implies that Windows is in use. There is no cmdlet called fix-volume.

16. You have manually configured a route to a remote network on your Windows server. Which command will show this newly added route?

    A. `ipconfig`

    B. `ifconfig`

    C. `ip route show`

    D. `route print`

    D. The `route print` command shows Windows routing table entries. A, B, and C are incorrect. The commands `ipconfig` in Windows and `ifconfig` in Linux do not show routing table information, and `ip route show` is a Linux command.

17. Your server IP settings are configured as shown in the following illustration. Which setting is incorrect?

```
Ethernet adapter Internal:

   Connection-specific DNS Suffix  . :
   Link-local IPv6 Address . . . . . : fe80::ca6:9b7d:4cce:f38c%16
   IPv4 Address. . . . . . . . . . . : 192.168.1.200
   Subnet Mask . . . . . . . . . . . : 255.255.255.0
   Default Gateway . . . . . . . . . : 192.168.15.253
```

    A. The IPv6 address prefix

    B. The IP address

    C. The subnet mask

    D. The default gateway

    D. The default gateway must on the same subnet as the device pointing to it. A, B, and C are incorrect. `fe80` is a valid IPv6 link-local address prefix. The IP address and subnet mask are correct.

18. Which Linux command reports each router crossed when communicating with a remote host?

    A. `traceroute`

    B. `tracert`

    C. `routetrace`

    D. `routetr`

    A. The Linux `traceroute` command shows information for each router crossed when communicating with remote hosts. B, C, and D are incorrect. The `tracert` command is a Windows command, and `routetrace` and `routetr` are not valid commands.

19. What is one possible drawback of heuristic host and network analysis?

    A. False negatives

    B. True negatives

    C. True positives

    D. False positives

    D. Heuristic analysis does not use signature comparisons for malware and network attacks; instead, it tracks what appears to be abnormal or suspicious activity. Occasionally false positives occur, where a problem is reported even though one does not exist. A, B, and C are incorrect. They are not drawbacks of heuristic host and network analysis.

20. Which Windows command can be used to view and troubleshoot file system ACLs?

    A. `icacls`

    B. `getfacl`

    C. `setfacl`

    D. `cipher`

    A. The Windows `icacls` command is designed to work with file system ACLS. B, C, and D are incorrect. `getfacl` and `setfacl` are Linux commands, and `cipher` is a Windows command for working with the Encrypting File System (EFS).

CHAPTER 8

Preparing for the Worst

In this chapter, you will

- Learn about disaster recovery
- Identify threat impacts on business operations
- Understand business continuity
- Distinguish various replication types
- Implement appropriate backup techniques

This chapter will help you proactively plan for negative incidents that can affect business operations. Threats have to be mapped to their potential impact to the organization, and server technicians must be aware of the procedures within the disaster recovery plan to return IT systems to a functional state.

Disaster Recovery

IT problems could be as small as a failed drive in a RAID 5 array or as large as an entire office or data center being unavailable. Bouncing back quickly from catastrophic IT incidents results from proactive planning and from technicians who know their roles.

The *recovery time objective* (RTO) is the maximum amount of time that can be tolerated for an IT service to be down before it has a negative impact on the business. As such, the RTO is an important component of a business impact analysis (BIA).

Alternate Sites

Alternate sites enable business operations to continue when a primary site experiences some kind of disruption. For example, suppose a data center experiences region-wide communications link failures. Customers that depend on IT services from the unreachable data center can be redirected to another, alternate, data center, where IT systems are running and customer data has already been replicated from the primary site.

Many things must be done before a site failure occurs:

- An alternate location must be acquired or built.
- High-speed communication links must be in place between the sites.

- The IT infrastructure has to be in place at the alternate site.
  - Hardware
  - Hypervisors up and running
  - Dynamic Host Configuration Protocol (DHCP) and Domain Name Service (DNS)
- Data replication between the two sites must be configured.
  - Varying solutions determine how often data replicates.
  - Communications link speeds determine how much data can be replicated within a given timeframe.

When an alternate site is active and a negative incident occurs, things are set into motion, such as the following:

- Failing over IT services to the alternate site
  - DHCP and DNS
  - Hosted web sites
  - Virtual machines
  - Line of business applications
- Ensuring network addresses changes do not affect IT service consumers
  - Dynamic DNS updates for changed IPv4 and IPv6 addresses
- Ensuring that notifications are sent to affected stakeholders

Individual network services can be made highly available using failover clustering solutions. Multiple servers (cluster nodes) use the same shared storage and have the software installed and configured identically, so that if one server fails, another one can take over.

Some specific services, such as DHCP, can be specifically configured for failover as shown in Figure 8-1. Administrators configure clustered services as either active/active or active/passive. Active/active means the clustered service is actually running simultaneously on multiple cluster nodes. Active/passive means if the node where the service is running fails, the service fails over and starts up on another cluster node.

Clustering solutions use a periodic heartbeat transmission from each cluster node to ensure nodes have not failed. It's best to use a dedicated network adapter for cluster hearbeats.

Hot Site

A *hot site* is an alternate location that can actively continue business operations at a moment's notice when the primary site becomes unavailable. Communication links, network equipment and software, staff, as well as up-to-date data are ready to go so that business operations can continue well within the RTO.

Large organizations and government agencies control their own data centers, and hot sites are entirely under their own control. Smaller organizations and individual consumers indirectly partake in this through IT service provider disaster recovery (DR) sites.

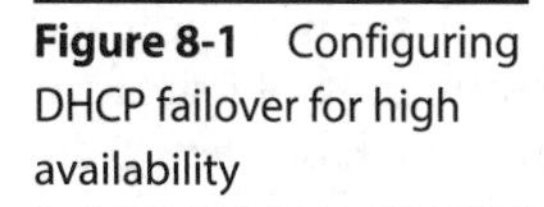
Figure 8-1 Configuring DHCP failover for high availability

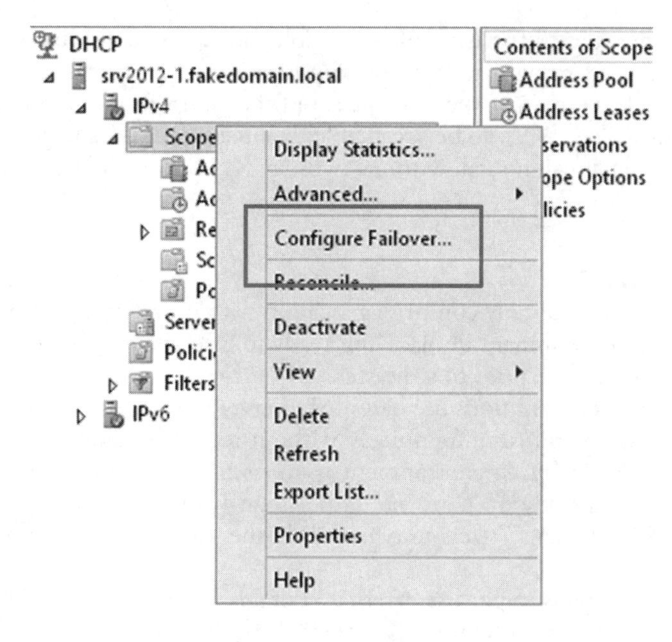

DR sites are commonly used by public cloud providers. These organizations have large data centers located throughout the world that offer cloud IT services to companies and individuals in different regions. The data centers are designed to withstand natural and manmade disasters—for example, large generators can provide power if the power goes out.

Shared DR hot site facilities are used by multiple companies and are less expensive than a DR host site dedicated to a single company. Regulations or organizational security policy might prohibit IT system and data cohabitation with other organizations, however.

Hot sites stay up-to-date with continuous data protection (CDP) replication between sites, so that data is accessible from the hot site should the primary site become inaccessible.

EXAM TIP A hot site is the most expensive type of alternate site to maintain, because it must contain equipment, software, staff, and up-to-date data resulting from replication from the primary site.

Cold Site

Unlike hot sites, cold sites do *not* have IT equipment, software, data, and staff already in place. Essentially, a *cold site* is a location with power and communications links in place. In the event of a disaster, equipment, software, data, and people need to be provided at the cold site.

One common problem with a cold site is software. Getting operating system and application software installed and patched can take time (less than the RTO; otherwise, a cold site would not be used). Not only is time an issue, but version incompatibilities can slow things down even more. The specific software versions used at the primary location also must be available for use at a cold site.

Then there's the issue of data. Cold sites don't continuously replicate with primary sites, so restoring data from backup locations (tape or cloud) is required. Cold sites are much less expensive than hot sites, but they must fit into an organization's business continuity plan (BCP) to be acceptable. If it takes four days to get a cold site functional, for example, it will not fall within a two-day RTO, so a cold site might not be feasible to use in such a case.

Warm Site

Warm sites not only comprise a location with power and communication links, but they also have equipment in place and ready in case of a disaster; software and data, however, are not in place prior to a disaster.

Many organizations use bare-metal server restoration solutions to get server operating systems up and running quickly without requiring manual installations and configurations. A *bare-metal* environment is a system or network in which a virtual machine is installed directly on hardware rather than within the host operating system (OS). The term "bare metal" refers to a hard disk, the usual medium on which a computer's OS is installed.

Technicians might use external bootable USB drives to apply the bare-metal images, or a network PXE boot environment might be first configured to enable multiple simultaneous bare-metal deployments over the network.

Once OS and application software is installed, patched, and configured, data is required. This involves restoration from a chosen backup solution, whether it is on-premises, restoration from the cloud, or a hybrid of both. For example, the Amazon Web Services (AWS) Storage Gateway is a virtual machine that runs on a customer network and can present cloud storage as virtual tapes for on-premises backup software. Figure 8-2 shows the AWS Storage Gateway configuration screen.

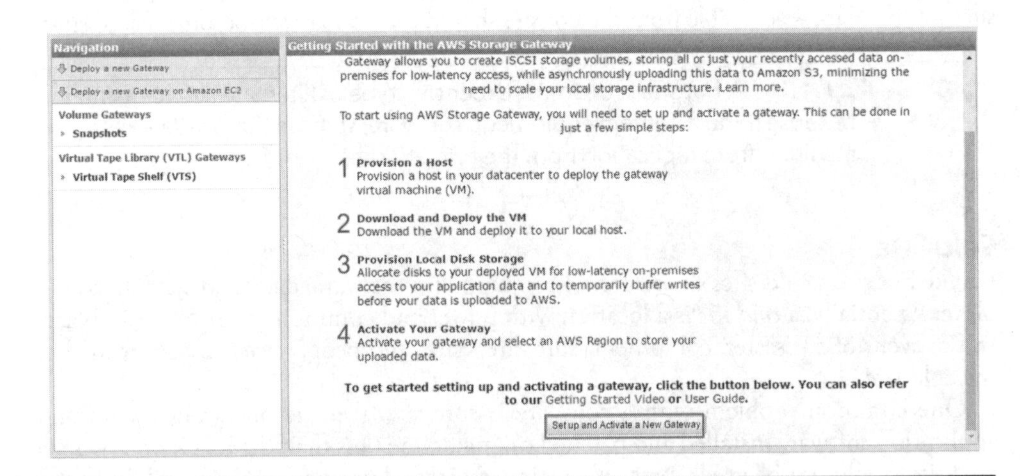

Figure 8-2 Configuring the AWS Storage Gateway

EXAM TIP Make sure you know what distinguishes one type of alternate site from another. Exam questions may test you on this using different wording than presented here, but the concepts are the same. For example, a question could link the recovery time objective (RTO) to a site type.

Data Replication

Having a readily available copy of up-to-date data is crucial with disaster recovery. Backups are still required, but data replication can immediately provide the data without requiring a restoration procedure. Replication can be implemented in plenty of ways, such as at the disk level, server level, and site level.

Synchronous replication writes to the primary and alternate location simultaneously; with *asynchronous* replication, there is a slight delay before the alternate write completes. Naturally, synchronous replication solutions tend to be more expensive than asynchronous ones, but with a short RTO, the cost of synchronous solutions could be justified, especially when you consider the fact that some data could be lost with an asynchronous solution.

Disk-to-Disk

RAID level 1 (disk mirroring) writes a second copy of data to a disk that differs from the primary written copy of data. Should the primary disk fails, the mirrored copy kicks in without missing a beat.

Enterprise-class storage array vendors provide replication solutions for their disk array enclosures. The only issue is incompatibility; most vendor replication solutions work only with their own products.

The Linux tar Command You can also use the Linux `tar` (tape archiver) command to create compressed archives for backup purposes. Commonly used `tar` command line parameters are shown in Table 8-1.

For example, to create a compressed archive called UserFiles.tar.gz under /Backup from the /UserFiles folder, you would use the following:

```
tar -cvzf /Backup/UserFiles.tar.gz /UserFiles
```

Table 8-1 Commonly Used Linux `tar` Command Line Parameters

Parameter	Description
`-c`	Create an archive
`-v`	Display verbose output
`-z`	Compress the archive with gzip
`-f`	Specify the path and filename of the archive file
`-x`	Extract the specified archive
`-C`	Change to directory for extraction of the archive

To decompress the same archive and re-create the folder on /, you would use the following:

```
tar -zxvf /Backup/UserFiles.tar.gz -C /
```

The Linux `dd` (disk dump) command can also be used to back up specific disk blocks or even entire partitions. For example, the following example uses the `dd` command to back up (`if` means input file) the master boot record (MBR) of a bootable Linux disk (/dev/sda) to a backup file (`of` means output file) in /backup called sda_mbr_back. The `bs` means block size for the 512-byte first boot sector that contains the MBR.

```
dd if=/dev/sda of=/backup/sda_mbr_back bs=512 count=1
```

The following example restores the MBR to a disk (/dev/sda) from a backup file. Notice here we use only 446 bytes to retain the current partition table and disk signature on /dev/sda:

```
dd if=/backup/sda_mbr_back of=/dev/sda bs=446 count=1
```

Of course, there are many other file and disk backup solutions for Linux; `tar` and `dd` just happen to be built into most distributions.

Server-to-Server

Also called *host-to-host replication*, this solution uses software within the server operating system to replicate data between two or more servers. The only issue here is that we are introducing more processing work for the server OS that really should be focusing on other tasks.

Windows DFSR Windows Server operating systems provide Distributed File System Replication (DFSR) as a role service that can synchronize folder contents between servers. Only file block changes are synchronized, and changes are compressed before being sent over the network.

Replication can be scheduled, or servers can be set to continuous replication. Bandwidth throttling can also be configured so that replication doesn't consume all of the available bandwidth. Windows DFSR is considered asynchronous replication.

Currently, DFSR in Windows Server 2012 R2 supports only NTFS; FAT32 and Resilient File System (ReFS) are not supported. Server administrators can configure one or more servers in a DFSR replication group as read-only to prevent changes from that host. DFSR could be used to replicate data from branch office servers to a central server where data backups take place. The configuration of a DFSR replication group is shown in Figure 8-3.

Plenty of third-party replication solutions are available for Windows with varying capabilities.

rsync UNIX and Linux admins often use the rsync tool to replicate data between hosts. In addition, other rsync variants work on the Windows platform.

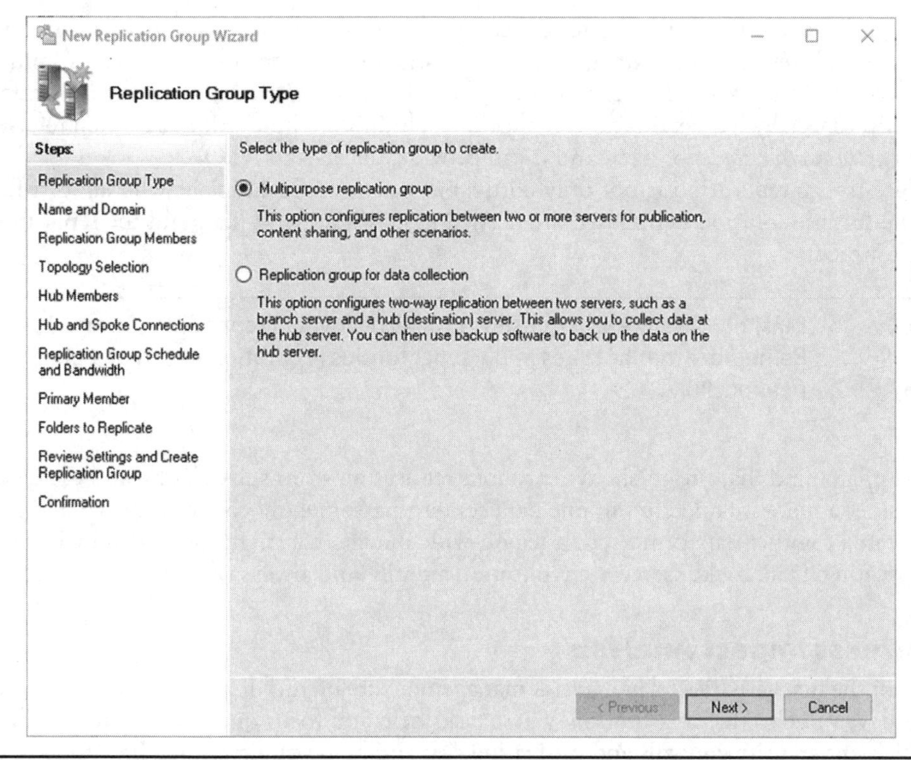

Figure 8-3 Configuring a DFSR replication group in Windows

The rsync tool can be used to synchronize data between two or more local folders over an intranet or over the Internet. Like Windows DFSR, only file changes are synchronized. The following example synchronizes the /budgets/2016 folder from a server named server2 to a local folder called /incoming/rsync. The `-a` preserves extra attributes such as permissions, `-v` is for verbose output, and `-z` compresses the transfer:

```
rsync -avz server2:/budgets/2016/ /incoming/rsync
```

As with Windows, plenty of third-party replication solutions are available for UNIX and Linux, with varying options.

Site-to-Site

Keeping data synced between sites might be required by service providers and emergency-providing organizations, for example, and this is a prime example of a primary and hot site. Instead of host-based replication solutions such as Windows DFSR or the UNIX-based rsync, for serious replication between data centers more advanced (and expensive) solutions from vendors such as HP, IBM, or EMC (and many other vendor solutions are available) would be used.

Cloud providers use site-to-site replication between their data centers to ensure that customer IT services and data are highly available in the event of a data center failure. Network links between data centers must be able to accommodate large data transfers quickly, especially if a synchronous replication solution is employed; this is often referred to as *active-active copies* of data, and it can provide a near-zero RTO.

Site-to-site replication is not only costly, but complex. Technicians who are certified in the specific solution being used are needed to configure and maintain the replication environment.

EXAM TIP Many exam questions will expect you to connect the dots. Remember that hot sites imply synchronous replication over high-speed network links.

Keep in mind that site-to-site synchronous replication won't solve all of your headaches. Consider a malware infection in one data center that somehow goes undetected and gets replicated to other data centers, or a region-wide outage that might be caused by inclement weather. Data backups beyond replication are still (and always will be) very important.

Business Impact Analysis

Two of the first activities related to risk management are identifying and prioritizing assets that have value to the organization. These tasks help you focus on allocating resources to implement security controls and mitigating risk and help you determine how the loss of IT systems or data can negatively impact your organization.

Who and What Are Affected?

Prioritizing the impact of failed systems or data inaccessibility is part of a BIA. Even if a mission-critical database server has failed, if infrastructure services such as DHCP and DNS have also failed, they need to be operational first.

Following is a sample list of DR priorities that will vary from one organization to the next:

- Personnel safety
- Critical organizational data
- Network infrastructure hardware
- Network infrastructure software
- Mission-critical database servers
- Front-end applications (that use the back-end database servers)

The RTO is a big factor in determining what type of failures can be tolerated and for how long. Think of public cloud providers that have service level agreements (SLAs) with their customers that guarantee uptime, such as the SLA pictured in Figure 8-4. Resource allocation to protect critical IT systems is related to the amount of tolerable downtime.

Definitions

- "Monthly Uptime Percentage" is calculated by subtracting from 100% the percentage of minutes during the month in which Amazon EC2 or Amazon EBS, as applicable, was in the state of "Region Unavailable." Monthly Uptime Percentage measurements exclude downtime resulting directly or indirectly from any Amazon EC2 SLA Exclusion (defined below).
- "Region Unavailable" and "Region Unavailability" mean that more than one Availability Zone in which you are running an instance, within the same Region, is "Unavailable" to you.
- "Unavailable" and "Unavailability" mean:
    - For Amazon EC2, when all of your running instances have no external connectivity.
    - For Amazon EBS, when all of your attached volumes perform zero read write IO, with pending IO in the queue.
- A "Service Credit" is a dollar credit, calculated as set forth below, that we may credit back to an eligible account.

Figure 8-4 An example of a public cloud provider SLA

EXAM TIP Don't confuse RTO with recovery point objective (RPO), which is discussed later. RTO is the maximum amount of tolerable downtime, and RPO is the maximum tolerable amount of data loss.

Business Continuity

Business operations must continue even in the face of natural and man-made disasters or technology failures. Preparation is the key. Where a business continuity plan takes a high-level approach to ensuring that the organization keeps running, disaster recovery plans are more specific to a technological solution.

Disaster Recovery Plan

A DR plan prepares an organization for potential negative incidents that can affect IT systems. Imagine a mission-critical database server running in a virtual machine that no longer boots. A plan is needed to get the server up and running again as quickly as possible. Presumably, if the server is that important, it has been made highly available through failover clustering—nonetheless, the failed server still needs to be corrected.

DR plans include step-by-step procedures to recover failed systems such as a mission-critical database. Proper documentation makes this known to technicians who must know their role in the DR plan.

Organizations also outsource IT expertise in some cases, such as with public cloud computing or synchronous replication solution vendors. A comprehensive DR plan will include details about these solutions as well as contact information in the event of a problem.

Failure	Response
Power outage reveals that UPS batteries were not charged	Test UPS batteries and replace if necessary
Server completes POST but will not start operating system	Boot from operating system installation media and perform repair
Old server is replaced with new hardware	Perform bare-metal restore on new hardware
Server operating system is not responsive over the network	Use Integrated Lights Out (iLO) or Integrated Dell Remote Access (iDRAC) to manage server remotely
Network connectivity is unavailable for server management	Use KVM locally
A physical disk in a RAID 5 array fails	Ensure hot spare is plugged in or configure RAID 6

Table 8-2 IT Failures and Solutions

DR plans are effective only if the procedures are known and responsibilities are assigned. When roles and recovery steps are known, RTO is minimized. Table 8-2 lists common failure situations and responses that would be detailed in the DR plan.

Companies should have multiple DR plans for various IT systems. A DR plan document should contains items such as these:

- Table of contents
- Scope of the DR document
- Contact information for escalation and outsourcing
- Recovery procedures
- Document revision history
- Glossary

The mean time to repair (MTTR) is a measure of time that expresses, on average, how long it takes to get failed components back up and running. This helps with planning equipment lifecycle costs and how to quickly recover from failed components. Therefore, a smaller MTTR value is desirable.

Business Continuity Plan

The BCP ensures that business operations can continue or resume quickly during or after an IT failure. It should also include preventative measures that show stakeholders that the organization is committed to being prepared for the worst.

Backups are helpful in recovering from failure. The RPO relates to the amount of tolerable data loss and is normally associated with backup frequency. For example, if the RPO is 10 hours, backups must occur at least every 10 hours.

Creating and using a BCP involves the following steps:

1. Assemble the BCP team.
2. Identify and prioritize critical IT systems and data.
3. Determine whether required skills are available internally or must be outsourced.

4. Determine whether alternate sites (hot, warm, cold) will be used.
5. Create a DR plan for each IT service.
6. Review the BCP with the BCP team.
7. Run periodic drills to ensure effectiveness.

Data Backup

Data replication technologies provide additional copies of data that are readily available, yet backups must still be performed as well. Figure 8-5 shows the backup feature available with the Windows Server 2012 R2 operating system.

The organization's policies may be influenced by laws or regulations that specify how often backups must be performed, how long they must be retained, and in which country the data must reside. Most of today's organizations have additional data backup options including cloud backup solutions, although some types of data might be restricted from this type of backup.

Backup Types

With today's big data requirements, there are limitations to how much data can be backed up within a certain timeframe. For example, in some cases, there just isn't enough time to perform a nightly full backup of all data on an enterprise storage area network (SAN). In such cases, selective backups give server administrators the ability to restore only files that are required.

File systems provide an archive attribute that is turned on whenever a file is modified. Essentially, this flag means "I have been changed and I need to be backed up!" Not every

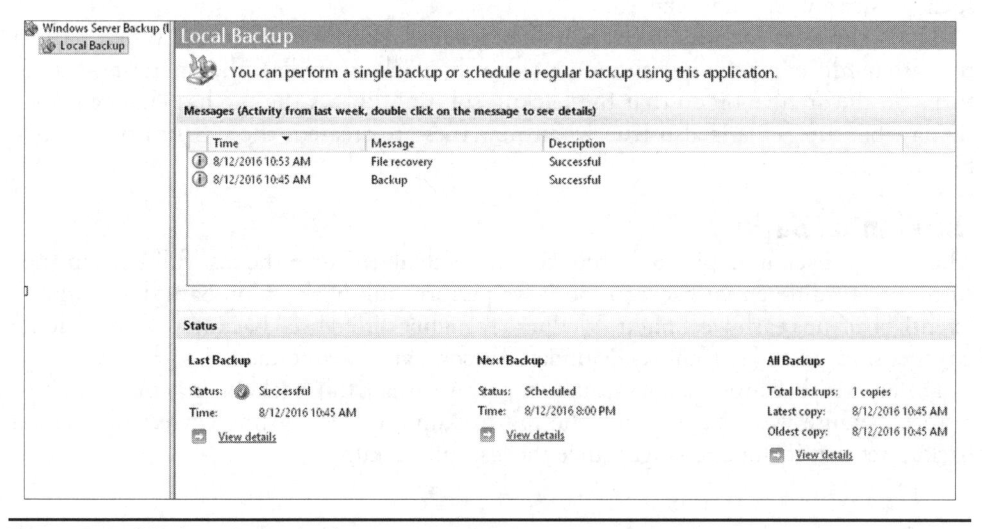

Figure 8-5 Windows Server backup

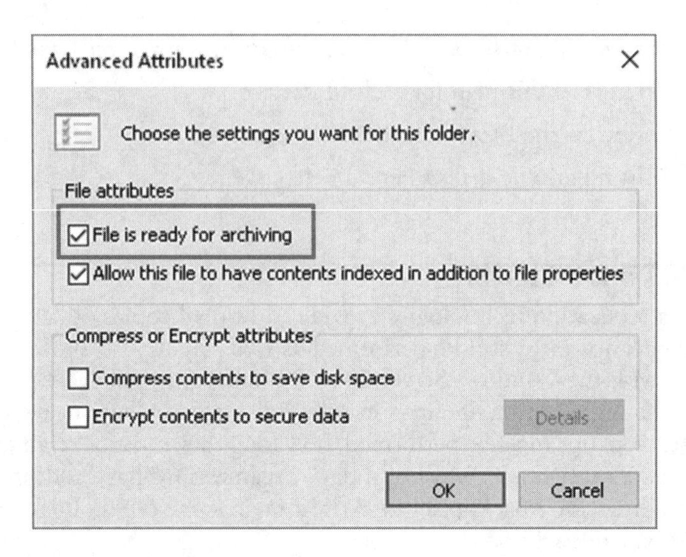

Figure 8-6 The archive bit of a Windows file

backup solution uses the archive bit, but most do (and this can be configured in a GUI such as the Windows dialog shown in Figure 8-6), in addition to file date and time stamps. Different backup types will set the archive bit accordingly, which is explained in the following sections.

Full Backup

As the name implies, a *full backu*p copies all data specified in the backup set. Technicians also call this a normal or copy backup. Full backups take longer than other backup options, but they take the least amount of time to restore, because all data is contained in a single backup set. As a result, full backups are commonly performed only periodically, such as once a week on weekends.

The archive bit for files is cleared when a full backup is performed. When backed files are modified in the live system (not on the backup media), the operating system turns on the archive bit so that the backup solution knows the file has changed since the last backup. This is also true when new files are created; the OS sets the archive bit on.

Differential Backup

This type of backup copies only files that have changed since the last full backup (not since the last differential backup). So if we perform full backups on Saturdays and differential backups each weeknight, Wednesday night's differential backup will copy all file changes since Saturday (Sunday, Monday, Tuesday, and Wednesday).

Differential backups take less time to perform than full backups but more time to restore, because we need not only the full backup set, but also the correct differential backup set that includes changes since the last full backup.

The archive bit is *not* normally cleared with this type of backup, because when the next differential backup runs, we want to copy all changed files since the last full backup (where the archive bit is normally cleared).

Incremental Backup

Where differential backups copy files changes since the last full backup, incremental backups copy only files that have changed since the last incremental *or* full backup. For example, we might perform a full backup each Saturday and an incremental backup each weeknight. Wednesday evening's backup will include only those files changed since Tuesday evening's backup.

The archive bit is normally cleared when this type of backup runs, because we want to capture all changes each time the incremental backup is run. This backup type takes the least amount of time but takes the most time to restore.

Snapshots

Snapshots, also called checkpoints, can be taken of a virtual machine (shown in Figure 8-7) to capture its settings as well as data stored in virtual hard disk files. If problems are encountered with the VM in the future, it can be reverted to a previous snapshot. However, a VM snapshot should not be relied upon as the sole backup. Backup agents can be installed within each VM as would normally be done on physical servers to granular backup and restore options.

EXAM TIP Remember that snapshots do not replace backups. If you are required to restore specific items, such as specific files, VM snapshots will not do the trick; reverting a VM snapshot reverts the VM settings and virtual hard disk contents.

Figure 8-7 Taking a snapshot of a VMware virtual machine

Other than virtual machines, snapshots can also apply to disk volumes, entire storage arrays, logical unit numbers (LUNs), hypervisors, and databases; they are often used in SAN environments, where they're called *storage snapshots*.

Windows servers can have the built-in Volume Shadow Service (VSS) configured for each disk volume to enable scheduled snapshots (called *volume shadow copies*). The snapshots contain only changed disk blocks so they don't consume much space. Many backup agents actually use the snapshots as their backup source, which eliminates the problem of backing up open files. Windows users can also benefit from restoring previous versions of files, or even undeleting files that have been removed from the Windows Recycle Bin.

Bare Metal Backup

When servers will not boot or are not behaving and can't be fixed, they may need to be reinstalled from an OS image. This is also true for virtual machines, although traditionally the term "bare metal" was used for physical servers.

Bare metal indicates that you have only the server (physical or virtual) and must install the OS, applications, configuration settings, and patches. Data can also be included in a bare metal recovery image. The idea is to get servers back up and running as quickly as possible in the event of some kind of problem, and the specific procedures should be a part of a DR plan. The Windows Server 2012 R2 operating system includes bare metal backup options (Figure 8-8).

Some bare metal solutions can also be used to deploy new servers quickly while changing unique identifiers such as server names, IP addresses, and licenses. Most bare metal

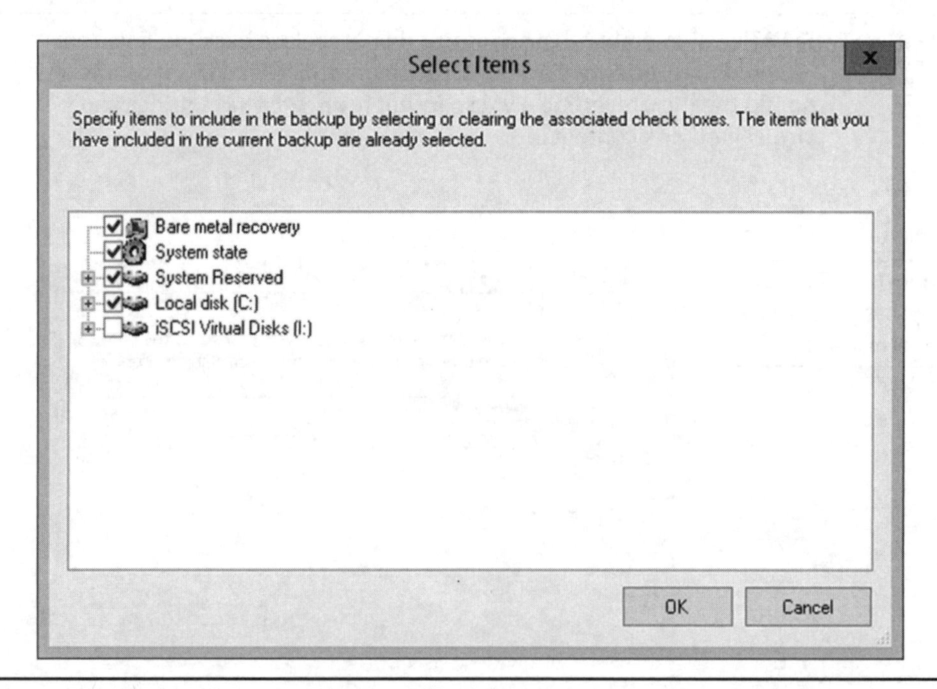

Figure 8-8 Windows Server 2012 bare metal backup option

tools use recovery points, which are essentially snapshots of changes at various points in time. When performing a bare metal recovery, we normally have a choice of snapshots, or *recovery points*.

Bare metal solutions need some kind of a boot device, whether it's USB or PXE network boot. Recovery of the OS, apps, and data can be done from local media or from a network server.

Backup Media

Now that you understand the types of backups and the reasons for doing so, let's consider where the backup data can be stored. You have numerous tape drive and media systems to choose from, depending on your capacity, speed, and archiving needs. Today's standards include Linear Tape-Open (LTO), Advanced Intelligent Tape (AIT), and Digital Linear Tape (DLT), which are discussed in the following sections.

Where most tape media is accessed sequentially, or in linear fashion, standard disk storage, including USB drives and CDs, DVDs, and Blu-rays, supports random data access instead of having to find data at a specific place on tape media.

As with most technology, tape capacities, number of writes, and transfer speeds change frequently. Generally speaking, modern tape media has the ability to store about 2TB of compressed data with transfer rates ranging from 10 to 80 MBps. Depending on the media, you might get from 200 to 1000 writes before the media needs to be replaced.

Consider the following when choosing a backup solution:

- What will be backed up?
  - Files
  - Bare metal recovery images
  - Databases
  - Disk volumes
  - Storage arrays
  - Entire storage appliance
- How much data will be backed up?
- How much time is available to perform backups?
- Which backup types will be used?
  - Full
  - Differential
  - Incremental
  - Snapshot
  - Bare metal
- Are backups being performed over slow network links?

- What type of storage media will be used?
  - Hard disks
  - Cloud storage
  - Magnetic tape
- Must data be archived for the long term?

Linear Access Tape

Linear access tape, often called Linear Tape-Open (LTO), is magnetic storage media that uses the Linear Tape File System (LTFS); it was introduced in 2010 and has since been revised several times. It offers large capacities, fast data seek, and streaming, and it is commonly used with tape backup systems and for archiving. An XML file is used as a catalog of backed-up content on the LTFS and is not stored at the beginning of the tape, which makes access quicker (no need to rewind tape). LTFS can also be used as additional storage media for copying purposes, apart from backup purposes.

Advanced Intelligent Tape

Advanced Intelligent Tape (AIT) was introduced in the 1990s. This magnetic tape storage is used with tape backup and archiving systems and has been revised since its inception.

Each AIT data cartridge contains a chip with metadata, which means that the backup catalog can be accessed quickly, regardless of what part of the tape is currently being accessed.

Digital Linear Tape

The Digital Linear Tape (DLT) standard (*the* industry standard) has been around since the 1980s and has been revised numerous times. Because of its 30-plus–year rating, DLT is often used for long-term archiving. DLT cartridges should be placed in protective cases to ensure long-term data storage.

The SuperDLT (SDLT) standard supports larger capacities and transfer rates. You can use SDLT in older DLT systems, but only with read access.

On-premises Backup

Many organizations continue to use on-premises tape backup solutions instead of, or in addition to, cloud backup solutions.

As mentioned earlier, the AWS Storage Gateway is a virtual appliance that runs on-premises and enables backup solutions to "see" virtual tape devices for cloud backup purposes. Remember that cloud backups are a type of offsite backup solution that is similar to physical backup storage media at another location.

Wherever backup media is stored, it needs to be physically secured. You might choose to encrypt backups for additional security. Backup media storage must be carefully considered—for example, we don't want to discover that high humidity has destroyed our backups or archives when we need to restore data.

Physical and virtual servers can have backup agents installed for granular backup and restore options. Your backup solution may also support the backup of storage arrays and databases. You'll also hear the term *tape library* used on occasion. This refers to a management solution for multiple tape devices and backup media used for backup purposes. Some tape libraries are robotic in that specific tapes can be mounted upon request for access to the backed-up data.

Cloud Backup

Over the last few years, individuals as well as organizations have begun trusting public cloud providers with their data. Cloud backup is basically an extension of your office or data center network hosted on provider equipment and accessed over the Internet.

The biggest showstopper for cloud backup adoption tends to be the perception that cloud security is lacking. Public cloud providers must undergo third-party security audits from various entities to ensure consumer confidence in their services. Because of economies of scale, cloud providers have the resources to secure IT infrastructure properly at a level that often exceeds what we can do in our organizations. Figure 8-9 shows the Microsoft Azure cloud service.

Cloud Backup Security

The first security consideration is how to connect to the cloud provider's data center. The standard is to connect over the Internet, but, from a security perspective, there are two alternatives:

- Connect your network to the cloud provider over the Internet with a site-to-site VPN.
- Connect your network to the cloud provider with a private network connection that bypasses the Internet.

The second issue is whether cloud backups are encrypted. Some cloud providers support server-side encryption; otherwise, you'll have to encrypt data before backing it up to the cloud. Figure 8-10 shows an example of encryption options when uploading files to the cloud.

Backup and Restore Best Practices

After you select a backup solution, you need to use and maintain it properly. Also, you'll need to adopt a backup and tape rotation strategy.

Although we will focus on the Grandfather-Father-Son (GFS) tape rotation scheme, two other schemes warrant a mention:

- Tower of Hanoi
- Incremental rotation

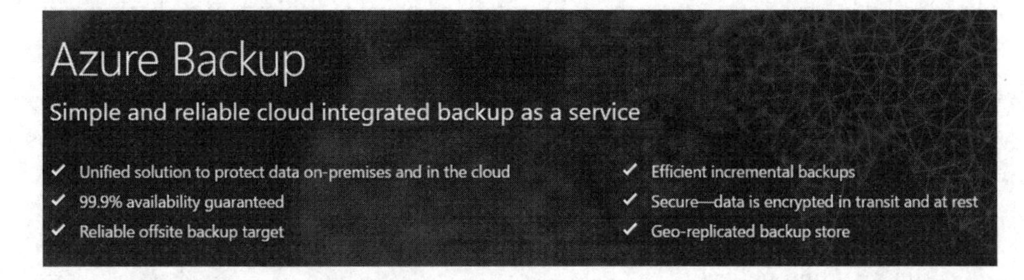

Figure 8-9 One of many cloud backup solutions

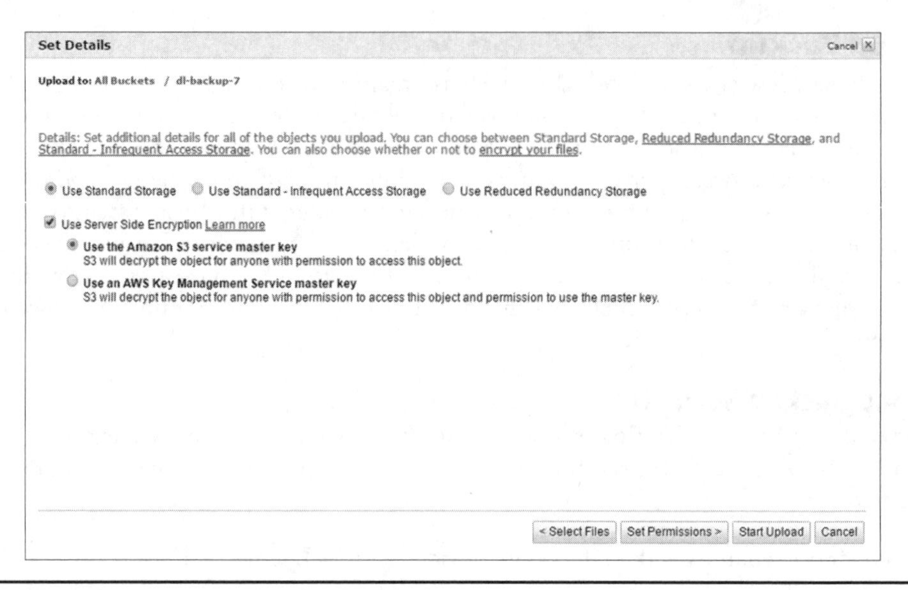

Figure 8-10 Encryption options for cloud backup

Grandfather-Father-Son

GFS is the most common tape rotation strategy. Because the amount of available tape backup media is finite, media reuse in inevitable. Keep in mind that different tape media enable different numbers of writes to be performed.

The GFS rotation method uses three backup sets, such as daily, weekly, and monthly—where each tape gets rotated on a schedule. You could use quarters and years as backup cycles for even longer term archiving. In our example, here's where the nomenclature comes in:

- **Son** Daily backup cycle
- **Father** Weekly backup cycle
- **Grandfather** Monthly backup cycle

This means that on day seven, the Son tape becomes a Father and will be used next for weekly backups. Other daily tapes keep getting reused as the cycle continues. On week four, the Father becomes a Grandfather, and it will be used next for monthly backups. Monthly backups can then be stored offsite.

From a high-level perspective, the GFS rotation scheme enables you to back up file versions that are recent or that are months, or perhaps even years, old.

Other Best Practices

Many simple tasks such as the following can help contribute to a dependable backup solution:

- Clear and concise backup media labeling
- Data retention policy

- Integrity verification (often referred to as read-after-write verification)
- Backup media offsite storage
- Backup media encryption
- Backup media environmental controls
- Period data restoration tests

Hands-on Exercises

Exercise 8-1: Configure the Volume Shadow Service on Windows Server 2012 R2

1. Make sure you are logged into the Srv2012-1 virtual machine with the Administrator account (Fakedomain\Administrator) with a password of Pa$$w0rd (or whatever you have indicated as the password).
2. Start Windows Explorer.
3. In the navigator on the left, click This PC. In the rightmost panel, right-click Local disk (C:) and choose Properties.
4. Open the Shadow Copies tab. Notice each disk volume in the list shows "Disabled" under the Next Run Time column.
5. Select C:\ and then click the Settings button.
6. For the maximum size, set the Use Limit Value to 4000 MB.
7. Click the Schedule button and select the boxes to the left of Sat and Sun to ensure that volume shadow copies are taken at 7:00 A.M. on weekends. Click OK three times to return to Windows Explorer.

Exercise 8-2: Restore Previous Versions of Files in Windows

1. Ensure that you are logged into the Srv2012-1 virtual machine with the Administrator account.
2. Open Windows Explorer.
3. On the left, click This PC.
4. On the right, double-click Local disk (C:).
5. Right-click and select New, Folder. Enter **Contracts** for the folder name and press ENTER.
6. Double-click the Contracts folder. Right-click in the right side of the screen and choose New, Text Document. Enter **Contract_A** for the filename and press ENTER.
7. Double-click the Contract_A file and enter the following text in the file: **Sample Contract Line One**. Close Notepad by clicking the X in the upper-right corner and save the change.

8. Click This PC on the left, and then right-click Local disk (C:) and choose Properties.
9. Open the Shadow Copies tab.
10. Ensure that C:\ is selected and click the Create Now button to manually create a disk volume snapshot of drive C:. Click OK.
11. Double-click Local disk C:\, and then double-click the Contracts folder.
12. Double-click the Contract_A file, enter **New Changes** on a separate line, close Notepad, and save the changes.
13. Right-click the Contract_A file and choose Restore Previous Versions.
14. Notice the version of the file in the snapshot from a minute ago. Click the Open button at the bottom. Notice the text "New Changes" is not displayed because it did not exist when the snapshot was taken. Close Notepad. Close the Contract_A Properties dialog box by clicking the close box.
15. Select the Contract_A file. Press SHIFT-DEL. Choose Yes to delete the file permanently. The file will not be available in the Recycle Bin.
16. In the address bar at the top, click Local disk (C:).
17. On the right, right-click the Contracts folder and choose Restore Previous Versions. Notice the version of the Contracts folder from when the snapshot was manually created earlier in this exercise.
18. Click Open. Notice that the address bar at the top indicates how old the currently viewed folder contents are. Notice that the Contract_A file is listed; it can be undeleted from here.
19. Right-click the Contract_A file and choose Copy. Close the Contracts window. Close the Contract Properties dialog box.
20. Double-click the Contract folder.
21. Right-click in the white space on the right and choose Paste. The Contract_A file is restored. Double-click Contract_A. Notice the "New Changes text" is absent in the file; you have undeleted a version of the file that corresponds to when the snapshot was taken.

Exercise 8-3: Configure and Use Windows Server Backup

1. Ensure that you are logged into the Srv2012-1 virtual machine with the Administrator account.
2. Open PowerShell icon (third icon from the bottom left on the taskbar).
3. Type **`get-windowsfeature *backup*`** to list server components that contain the word "backup." Notice that the Windows Server Backup component is not installed (no X in the box).
4. Type

```
install-windowsfeature windows-server-backup -
includemanagementtools
```

5. Once the installation has completed (if it seems stuck, press ENTER in the PowerShell window), click the Start button at the bottom left of the taskbar. Type **back** and wait for Windows Server Backup to appear; then click it.
6. Click Local Backup on the left. Notice the Backup Schedule, Backup Once, and Recover options on the far right. Click Backup Schedule.
7. On the Backup Schedule Wizard screen, click Next.
8. Choose Custom and click Next.
9. On the Select Items For Backup screen, click Add Items.
10. Click the + symbol to the left of Local disk (C:) and select the checkbox next to the Contracts folder. Click OK and then click Next.
11. Once A Day is currently set to 9:00 P.M.; change this to 8:00 P.M., and then click Next.
12. On the Specify Destination Type screen, choose Back Up To A Volume. Click Next.
13. On the Select Destination Volume screen, click the Add button and choose drive I:, which was created in an earlier lab for iSCSI virtual disk files. Click OK and then click Next.
14. On the Confirmation screen, click Finish and then Close.
15. On the far right in the Actions panel, click Backup Once.
16. On the Backup Options screen, ensure that Schedule Backup Options is selected. Click Next.
17. On the Confirmation screen, click Backup. When the backup Status shows "Completed," click Close. Note the backup status items in the middle of the screen. Leave the wbadmin screen open.
18. Open Windows Explorer. Go to Local disk (C:) and double-click it.
19. Select the Contracts folder. Press SHIFT-DEL. Choose Yes on the confirmation screen.
20. Switch back to the wbadmin screen.
21. In the Actions panel on the right, click Recover.
22. On the Getting Started screen, ensure that This Server (SRV2012-1) is selected and click Next.
23. On the Select Backup Date screen, accept the default and click Next.
24. On the Select Recovery Type screen, ensure that Files And Folders is selected and click Next.
25. Click the + symbol to the left of Srv2012-1. Do the same for Local disk (C:).
26. Select the Contracts folder and click Next.
27. Accept the defaults on the Specify Recovery Options page and click Next.
28. Click Recover.

29. Once the Status shows "Completed," click Close.
30. Start Windows Explorer and verify that C:\Contracts has been restored. If Windows Explorer was already open, press F5 on the keyboard to refresh the screen.

Exercise 8-4: Use the Linux tar Command for Data Backup

1. Make sure you are logged into the RHEL7-1 virtual machine with the root account, with a password of Pa$$w0rdLinux. If you are not logged on as root, you may need to prefix the commands in the exercise with `sudo` to gain elevated privileges. Press ENTER after each command you issue in this exercise.
2. Choose Applications | Utilities. Then (if required) scroll down and choose Terminal.
3. In the Terminal window, type **`mkdir /asia_contracts`**.
4. Enter **`touch /asia_contracts/file{1,2,3,4}.txt`** to create four empty text files (file1.txt, file2.txt, and so on).
5. Enter **`ls /asia_contracts`** to verify that the files have been created.
6. Enter **`mkdir /backup`**.
7. Enter **`tar -cvzf /backup/asia_contracts.tar.gz /asia_contracts`**. The `c` means create, `v` means verbose output, `z` means compress with gzip utility, and `f` means file. (Linux compressed tar filenames normally have a .tar.gz file extension, but this is not required.)
8. Enter **`ls /backup`** to ensure that the compressed tar file was created.
9. Enter **`rm -rf /asia_contracts`** to delete the folder and its contents. Type **`ls`** to verify that there is no longer an /asia_contracts folder.
10. Enter **`cd /backup`**.
11. Enter **`tar -zxvf asia_contracts.tar.gz -C /`**. The `x` means extract, and the `-C` means extract to a specified path.
12. Enter **`ls /`** to verify that the /asia_contracts folder has been restored.
13. Close all windows.

Chapter Review

This chapter focused on the proactive planning of how to deal with negative incidents when they occur. The overarching premise is to restore business operations as soon as possible.

Disaster Recovery Sites

A hot site is a facility that includes power, communications, hardware, software, data, and staff. This is the most expensive type of alternate site to maintain. A warm site provides a location, power, equipment, and communications links, but not up-to-date data.

A cold site consists only of a location, power, and communication links. A cold site is the least expensive type of alternate site.

Data Replication

Synchronous replication ensures that data is written to primary and alternate locations without delay; this results in up-to-date data between a primary and a hot site. Asynchronous replication includes a slight delay before data is written to alternate sites, and as a result this is less expensive than synchronous solutions.

Disk-level replication solutions include disk enclosure (array) and disk mirroring solutions that are used within a site, not between sites. Server replication solutions include commonly used tools such as Windows DFSR and rsync, which can run on Windows and Linux platforms.

Business Impact

An inventory of assets is needed before related threats can be identified. This allows for the prioritization of assets and risks and helps you determine the impact that threats can have on business operations.

Assets include the following:

- IT systems
- IT processes
- Business and manufacturing processes
- Personnel
- Data
- Trademarks

The recovery time objective (RTO) determines the maximum amount of tolerable downtime. Disaster recovery plans must take the RTO into account.

Disaster Recovery Plan

A disaster recovery (DR) plan is used to bring failed systems online as quickly and efficiently as possible. The DR plan must be updated periodically to reflect changing threats.

The DR plan contains step-by-step procedures detailing exactly how systems are to be quickly recovered. All stakeholders must know their roles for the effective recovery of failed systems.

Items found within the DR plan include the following:

- Table of contents
- DR scope
- Contact information
- Recovery procedures

- Document revision history
- Glossary

Business Continuity Plan

Where DR plans are specific to a system, a business continuity plan (BCP) is more comprehensive and is not as specific as a DR plan. The purpose of a BCP is to ensure that overall business operations resume quickly after a negative incident.

BCPs include preventative measures such as backup policies. The recovery point objective (RPO) indicates the maximum tolerable data loss and is related to backup frequency. So, for example, an RPO of 12 hours means backup must never be more than 12 hours old.

BCP activities include these:

- Assemble a team.
- Identify and prioritize assets.
- Identify skill requirements to recovery systems.
- Determine whether alternate sites will be used.
- Create a DR plan for each IT system.
- Review the BCP with the BCP team.
- Conduct periodic BCP drills.

Data Backups

Backups are required even if disk mirroring or data replication solutions are being used. Virtual machine snapshots are a point-in-time picture of virtual machine settings and data. These are useful before making a critical change to a virtual machine, because they serve as a quick way to revert back to a known working configuration, but they should never replace backups.

Take care when choosing a backup type, which can influence the amount of time taken to back up and restore data.

Common backup types include the following:

- **Full** All data is backed up and the archive bit is cleared.
- **Incremental** Data that has changed since the last full or incremental backup is backed up and the archive bit is cleared.
- **Differential** Data that has changed since the last full backup is backed up; the archive bit is *not* cleared.
- **Snapshot** Settings and data stored in virtual hard disk files and volumes are captured.
- **Bare metal** This enables the entire OS and data to be restored.
  Important backup considerations include the following:
  - Amount of time to complete backup (backup window)

- Backup devices and media being used:
  - Media capacity
  - Media lifetime
  - Backup data transfer speed
  - Cloud backup
- Regulatory compliance
- Data retention
- Backup type
- Backup media rotation strategy
- Media labeling
- Verification of backed-up data
- Media encryption
- Media offsite storage including cloud
- Media storage environmental controls
- Periodic restore drills

Backup rotation strategies are designed to retain data for a period of time and to reuse backup media. Common backup rotation strategies include Tower of Hanoi, incremental rotation, and Grandfather-Father-Son. Grandfather-Father-Son is the most common backup rotation type and is used for long-term data archiving.

Questions

1. Which of the following best describes RTO?
   A. The maximum tolerable amount of lost data
   B. The maximum tolerable amount of failed array disks
   C. The maximum amount of tolerable downtime
   D. The maximum tolerable amount of failed services

2. Which type of disaster recovery site provides a facility with power and communications links only?
   A. Cold
   B. Warm
   C. Hot
   D. Basic

3. Which factor enables up-to-date hot site data?
   - **A.** Disk mirroring
   - **B.** Cloud backup
   - **C.** Synchronous replication
   - **D.** Asynchronous replication

4. Which common Linux tool synchronizes file systems between remote hosts?
   - **A.** chmod
   - **B.** CUPS
   - **C.** NFS
   - **D.** rsync

5. Which type of replication provides a near-zero RTO?
   - **A.** rsync
   - **B.** Asynchronous
   - **C.** DFSR
   - **D.** Synchronous

6. After identifying assets in a BIA, what should be done next?
   - **A.** Prioritize assets
   - **B.** Assemble BIA team
   - **C.** Create DR plan
   - **D.** Assess risk

7. How can servers be remotely managed when network connectivity is unavailable?
   - **A.** iLO
   - **B.** iDRAC
   - **C.** RDP
   - **D.** KVM

8. You need to prevent a dual disk failure from bringing down a RAID 5 array. What should you do?
   A. Add two hot spares to the RAID 5 array.
   B. Add one hot spare to the RAID 5 array.
   C. Configure RAID 6.
   D. Configure RAID 1.

9. Which type of backup does not clear the archive bit?
   A. Full
   B. Differential
   C. Incremental
   D. Bare metal

10. Which backup type takes the longest to restore?
    A. Full
    B. Copy
    C. Incremental
    D. Differential

11. Which type of backup takes the longest?
    A. Full
    B. Synchronous
    C. Incremental
    D. Differential

12. Which type of restore should be used for operating system, data, and configuration settings that can be applied to different servers?
    A. Full
    B. Copy
    C. Bare metal
    D. Differential

13. Your company uses an image to repair failed servers. Optical drives are disabled in all server UEFI settings. Which options can be used to boot and apply images? Choose two.
    A. CD
    B. USB
    C. DVD
    D. PXE

14. What type of configuration redirects users from a failed server to another running instance of a network service?
    A. PXE
    B. Failover clustering
    C. NIC teaming
    D. Round-robin

15. Which items would be available at a warm site? Choose two.
    A. Network links
    B. Data
    C. Staff
    D. Power

16. Which requirement justifies the cost of a hot site?
    A. Low RPO
    B. High RPO
    C. Low RTO
    D. High RTO

17. An SLA guarantees that user data will be available in at least one data center. What type of replication is needed between data centers?
    A. Hot
    B. Synchronous
    C. Warm
    D. Asynchronous

18. An organization's BCP stipulates that the RPO is five hours. How often should backups be performed?

A. Less than the RPO

B. Less than the RTO

C. More than the RPO

D. More than the RTO

Questions and Answers

1. Which of the following best describes RTO?

A. The maximum tolerable amount of lost data

B. The maximum tolerable amount of failed array disks

C. The maximum amount of tolerable downtime

D. The maximum tolerable amount of failed services

C. The recovery time objective (RTO) relates to the maximum amount of tolerable downtime. A, B, and D are incorrect. The maximum tolerable amount of lost data relates to the recovery point objective (RPO). Various RAID levels determine how many failed disks can be tolerated. The RTO is not related to the maximum tolerable amount of failed services.

2. Which type of disaster recovery site provides a facility with power and communications links only?

A. Cold

B. Warm

C. Hot

D. Basic

A. Cold sites provide a facility with power and communications links only. B, C, and D are incorrect. Warms sites provide power, communications links, as well as equipment and software, but lack up-to-date data. Hot sites provide a facility with power, communications links, equipment, software, up-to-date data, and staff. A basic site is not a type of disaster recovery site.

3. Which factor enables up-to-date hot site data?
   A. Disk mirroring
   B. Cloud backup
   C. Synchronous replication
   D. Asynchronous replication

   C. Writing up-to-date data simultaneously to multiple locations is called synchronous replication and is often used between a primary and hot disaster recovery site. A, B, and D are incorrect. Disk mirroring is not used to replicate data between sites. Cloud backup normally relies on a schedule. Asynchronous replication introduces a delay before writing to alternate sites.

4. Which common Linux tool synchronizes file systems between remote hosts?
   A. chmod
   B. CUPS
   C. NFS
   D. rsync

   D. rsync is often used in Linux to synchronize file systems between hosts. A, B, and C are incorrect. chmod is used to set Linux file system permissions. Common UNIX Printing System (CUPS) is a Linux print server. Network File System is a Linux network file system standard.

5. Which type of replication provides a near-zero RTO?
   A. rsync
   B. Asynchronous
   C. DFSR
   D. Synchronous

   D. A near-zero recovery time objective (RTO) means very little tolerance for downtime; this is provided by synchronous replication. A, B, and C are incorrect. rsync and DFSR are asynchronous replication and they do not provide near-zero RTO.

6. After identifying assets in a BIA, what should be done next?
   A. Prioritize assets
   B. Assemble BIA team
   C. Create DR plan
   D. Assess risk

   A. After asset identification, prioritization must occur. B, C, and D are incorrect. The business impact analysis (BIA) team would already be assembled if assets have been identified. The disaster recovery (DR) plan and risk assessment do not happen until assets are prioritized.

7. How can servers be remotely managed when network connectivity is unavailable?
   - **A.** iLO
   - **B.** iDRAC
   - **C.** RDP
   - **D.** KVM

   D. Keyboard, video, mouse (KVM) switches can be used to administer servers locally. A, B, and C are incorrect. iLO, iDRAC, and RDP are remote management tools that rely on network connectivity.

8. You need to prevent a dual disk failure from bringing down a RAID 5 array. What should you do?
   - **A.** Add two hot spares to the RAID 5 array.
   - **B.** Add one hot spare to the RAID 5 array.
   - **C.** Configure RAID 6.
   - **D.** Configure RAID 1.

   C. RAID 6 can tolerate two disk failures. A, B, and D are incorrect. RAID 5 can tolerate a single disk failure. RAID 1 can tolerate a single disk failure.

9. Which type of backup does not clear the archive bit?
   - **A.** Full
   - **B.** Differential
   - **C.** Incremental
   - **D.** Bare metal

   B. Differential backup must capture all changes since the last full backup and thus does not clear the archive bit for backed-up files. A, C, and D are incorrect. Full and incremental backups do clear the archive bit when backing up files. Bare metal restores are not related to archive bits.

10. Which backup type takes the longest to restore?
    - **A.** Full
    - **B.** Copy
    - **C.** Incremental
    - **D.** Differential

    C. Restores using incremental backups means restoring the last full backup and each incremental backup to the point of failure. A, B, and D are incorrect. Full and copy backups are the quickest to restore since only a single backup set is needed. Differential backups are the next quickest to restore following full.

11. Which type of backup takes the longest?
    - A. Full
    - B. Synchronous
    - C. Incremental
    - D. Differential

    A. Because everything is being backed up, full backups take the longest to complete. B, C, and D are incorrect. Synchronous, without being discussed in a specific context, is not a backup type. Incremental backups take the least amount of time; only changes since the last full or incremental must be captured. Differential backups capture all changes since the last full backup.

12. Which type of restore should be used for operating system, data, and configuration settings that can be applied to different servers?
    - A. Full
    - B. Copy
    - C. Bare metal
    - D. Differential

    C. Bare metal backups can be used to quickly restore an entire operating system, applications, and data, even to a new server. A, B, and D are incorrect. Full, copy, and differential backups are not designed to restore operating systems, applications, and data to different servers.

13. Your company uses an image to repair failed servers. Optical drives are disabled in all server UEFI settings. Which options can be used to boot and apply images? Choose two.
    - A. CD
    - B. USB
    - C. DVD
    - D. PXE

    B, D. USB local boot and PXE network boot do not rely on optical media. A and C are incorrect. CDs and DVDs are optical media.

14. What type of configuration redirects users from a failed server to another running instance of a network service?

A. PXE

B. Failover clustering

C. NIC teaming

D. Round-robin

B. Failover clustering uses multiple servers (nodes), each having the same network service and access to the same data on shared storage. If a server fails, users get redirected to the network service on a running server. A, C, and D are incorrect. PXE is a network boot standard. NIC teaming groups server NICS together for load balancing or aggregated bandwidth. Round-robin is a term often used with DNS where there are multiple A records with the same name, each pointing to a different IP address.

15. Which items would be available at a warm site? Choose two.

A. Network links

B. Data

C. Staff

D. Power

A, D. Warm sites include network links and power; they are missing only staff and up-to-date data. B and C are incorrect. Data and staff are available at hot sites but not warm sites.

16. Which requirement justifies the cost of a hot site?

A. Low RPO

B. High RPO

C. Low RTO

D. High RTO

C. A low RTO means very little tolerance for downtime. Hot sites align with this requirement. A, B, and D are incorrect. Recovery point objective (RPO) relates to the amount of tolerable data loss and does not align to a hot site as RTO does.

17. An SLA guarantees that user data will be available in at least one data center. What type of replication is needed between data centers?

A. Hot

B. Synchronous

C. Warm

D. Asynchronous

B. Synchronous replication between data centers means there is no delay when writing data. This aligns with SLA guarantees in this context. A, C, and D are incorrect. Hot and warm replication do not exist. Asynchronous replication introduces a delay from the primary write.

18. An organization's BCP stipulates that the RPO is five hours. How often should backups be performed?

A. Less than the RPO

B. Less than the RTO

C. More than the RPO

D. More than the RTO

A. The RPO defines the maximum amount of tolerable data loss. If the RPO is five hours, then backups must occur within this timeframe. B, C, and D are incorrect. The RTO does not apply in this scenario as well as RPO does.

APPENDIX

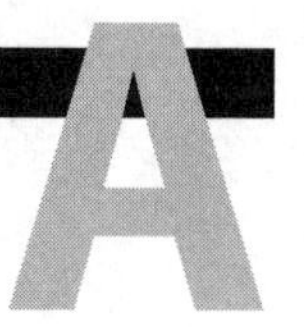

About the Hands-on Exercises and Lab Set-up

Performing tasks hands-on is, for most people, the best way to learn and retain information. Each chapter in this book contains not only text and practice questions that will help you achieve your CompTIA Server+ certification, but also hands-on exercises to reinforce what was covered in each chapter.

Lab Exercise Overview

Figure A-1 shows the three virtual machine servers that you'll create and configure through the exercises.

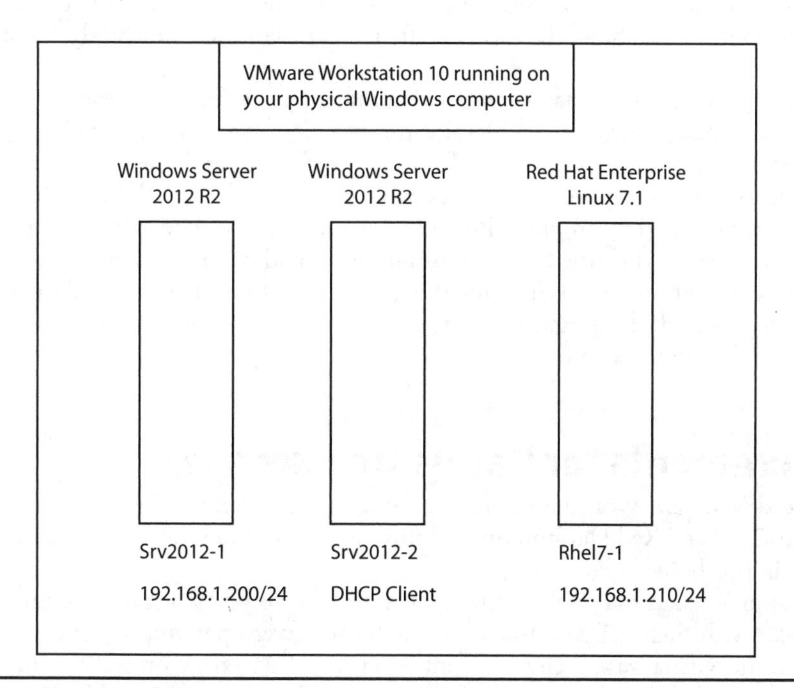

Figure A-1 Virtual machine layout used in lab exercises

Windows

The Windows Server operating system is widely used around the world in numerous industries. The lab exercises in this book are designed to familiarize you with how to configure the operating system to meet specific business needs.

Windows servers can be administered using various graphical tools, either locally on the server or remotely using a remote management solution such as Remote Desktop Protocol (RDP). For many years, administrators have also managed Windows servers from the command line using batch files, Visual Basic scripts, and, more recently, PowerShell.

Command line tools provide a way for you to automate repetitive tasks by creating scripts containing the relevant commands. These scripts can even be scheduled using the Windows Task Scheduler in the Control Panel.

The CompTIA Server+ Certification SK0-004 exam will not test you on many specifics of the Windows operating system, but you will be tested on general server concepts that are reinforced by completing the lab exercises. It's similar to a boxer doing push-ups or skipping rope; those exercises will never be used in the ring during a boxing match, but they help condition the body (and, by extension, the mind) for the real thing.

Linux

Like Windows, Linux is widely used around the world in numerous industries for a variety of network services. According to Microsoft, the Azure cloud platform contains more Linux virtual machines than Microsoft virtual machines—apparently, there is some interest in Linux.

CompTIA Server+ candidates should be comfortable performing basic administrative tasks in the Linux environment. Despite the fact that there are hundreds of different Linux distributions, the vast majority of concepts and command line syntax are the same.

Throughout this book, the lab exercises will have you working with Red Hat Enterprise Linux 7.1, mostly at the command line. Linux commands, unlike Windows commands, are case-sensitive. This is true even with some command parameters, so that `-c` and `-C`, for example, might not mean the same thing (it depends on the command).

If you install Red Hat Enterprise Linux 7.1 as per the instruction in the lab exercise, the labs should run smoothly.

Requirements for Hands-on Exercises

You'll need VMware Workstation 10.x as well as the installation media for Windows Server 2012 R2 and Red Hat Enterprise Linux Server 7 to follow along with the hands-on exercises in this book.

You can download free trials of these software titles so you won't have to buy them to experiment with them. If you decide to install the server operating systems on physical systems or in a virtualization environment other than VMware Workstation 10, the exercise steps will differ slightly from the ones in this book. For example, adding virtual hard disks in VMware takes seconds, but on a physical host you need to acquire and install the physical disks before they can be used by the server operating system.

The lab exercises are written for VMware Workstation 10 running on a Windows computer. You'll need the appropriate access to install software on the computer and it will have to meet hardware requirements listed in the following sections.

Hardware Requirements

To facilitate the installation and configuration of the Windows and Linux operating systems, the lab exercises are written to be used on VMware Workstation 10 virtual machines. Microsoft Hyper-V, Oracle VM VirtualBox, or another virtualization system will work equally as well, but if you don't use VMware Workstation 10, the lab instructions in this book will differ slightly from those you'll need for your environment.

You can run VMware Workstation 10 on any type of machine as long as certain requirements are met. For example, if you have a laptop computer that meets the following requirements, you're good to go! Here are the hardware requirements for your VMware host computer that will run Windows and Linux virtual machines:

- 64-bit computer
- Hardware virtualization (Intel Virtualization Technology or AMD Virtualization)
- At least 8GB of RAM in total
- Enough storage space for both the Windows and Linux ISO files (approximately 8GB of disk space)
- Enough storage space to create Windows and Linux virtual machines (approximately 80GB of disk space)

Note that these are minimum requirements; more RAM and disk space is better!

VMware Workstation 10

You can download VMware Workstation 10 from https://my.vmware.com/web/vmware/info?slug=desktop_end_user_computing/vmware_workstation/10_0, as shown in Figure A-2. You can use VMware Workstation for free for 30 days, but you'll need to create an account at VMware before you can proceed with the download. If you want to follow along with the specific instructions for labs, make sure you download and install VMware Workstation 10 for Windows.

Install VMware Workstation 10

The downloaded installation provides an executable (.exe) file that you can run on your Windows computer. Make sure that you don't have another virtualization product installed because it could interfere with the installation or running of VMware Workstation. Follow these steps to install the product:

1. Double-click the downloaded .exe installer file. Depending on your computer's configuration, you may be prompted to allow the installer to run.

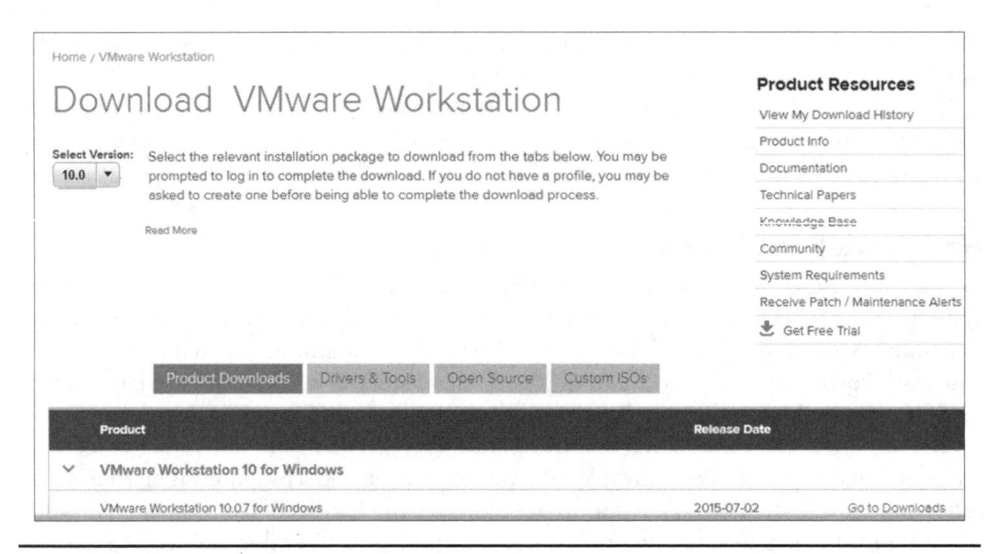

Figure A-2 VMware Workstation 10 download web page

2. On the Welcome screen, click Next.
3. On the License Agreement screen, select I Accept The Terms In The License Agreement, and then click Next.
4. On the Setup Type screen, choose Typical.
5. On the Destination Folder screen, click Next.
6. On the Software Updates screen, deselect Check For Product Updates On Startup, and then click Next.
7. On the User Experience Improvement Program page, uncheck Help Improve VMware Workstation, and then click Next.
8. On the Shortcuts screen, click Next.
9. On the Ready To Perform The Requested Operations screen, click Continue.
10. On the Enter License Key screen, click the Skip button.
11. Once the installation completes and you've closed any installation windows, go to your computer's Start menu and start the VMware Workstation application to ensure that it launches.
12. On the Welcome To VMware Workstation 10 screen, select I Want To Try VMware Workstation 10 For 30 Days. Enter a valid e-mail address, and then click Continue and then Finish.
13. On the Thank You For Evaluating VMware Workstation! screen, click Close.
14. Close the VMware Workstation application.

Acquiring Windows and Linux Installation Media

Since URLs change, you may need to use your favorite search engine to find these downloads; however, URL links are provided in the following sections for convenience.

Windows

Visit the TechNet Evaluation Center at microsoft.com/en-us/evalcenter/evaluate-windows-server-2012-r2, as shown in Figure A-3, to download the Windows Server 2012 R2 installation ISO file. If you don't already have an account, you'll need to register before you can download the ISO file for a free 180-day evaluation.

Save the ISO file in a place that you can access from the machine on which you install VMware Workstation 10.x. You'll need approximately 4GB of disk space to store this Windows Server ISO file.

Linux

Visit the Red Hat Customer Portal at access.redhat.com/downloads and click Start Evaluation next to Red Hat Enterprise Linux, as shown in Figure A-4, to download the Red Hat Linux Enterprise Server 7.1 installation ISO file for x86 and x64 architectures. Like VMware Workstation, you can use the product for free for 30 days. If you don't already have an account, you'll need to create one before you can download the software.

The machine on which you plan to run VMware Workstation 10.x must have access to the ISO file. You can even store the ISOs on a USB flash drive with enough space if you choose. You'll need approximately 3.8GB of disk space to store this Linux ISO file.

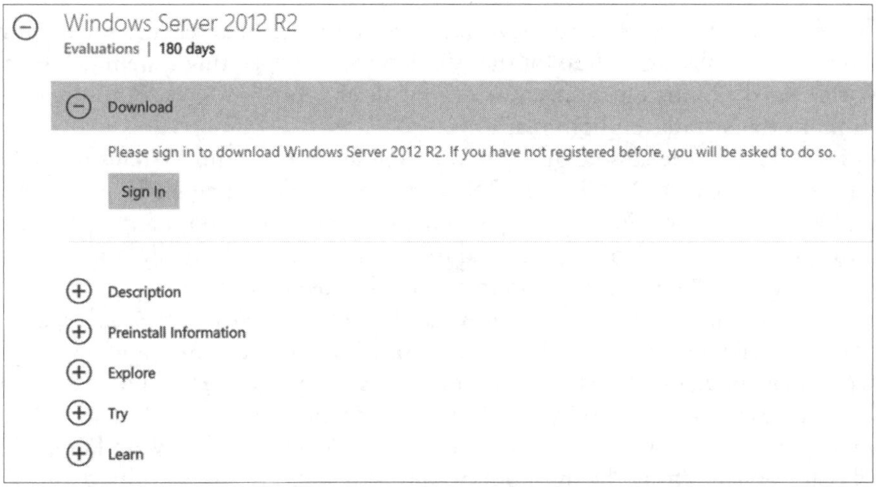

Figure A-3 Windows Server 2012 R2 download web page

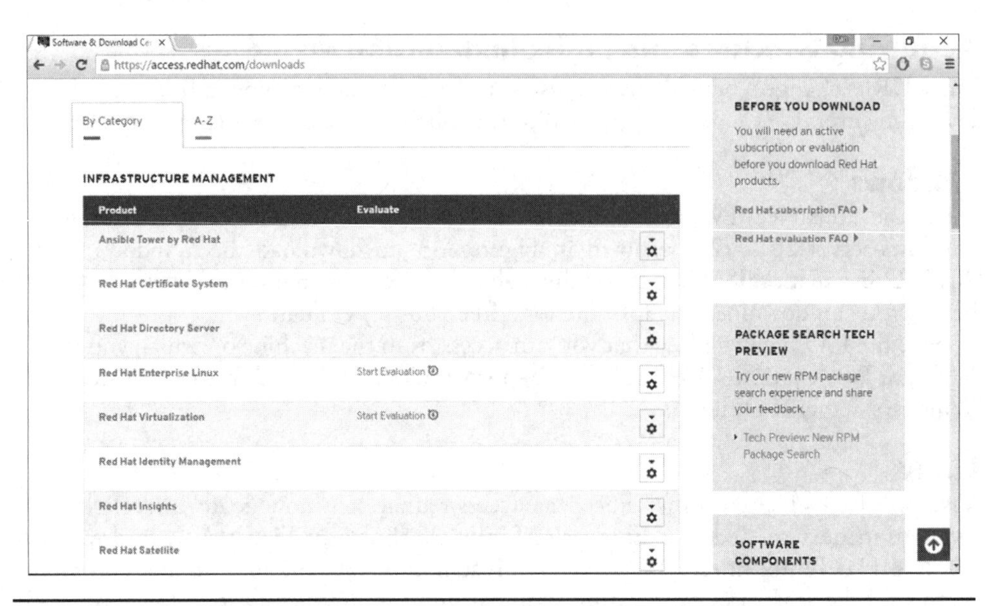

Figure A-4 Red Hat Enterprise Linux 7.1 download web page

Lab Exercise Miscellany

When installing both the Windows and Linux operating systems in VMware Workstation during the lab exercises, you'll be prompted to specify a password. Passwords expire, so if you must change your password, take careful note of it. The lab exercises provide the original installation password, but if you changed the password, you'll have to enter it instead.

The lab exercises correspond to the topics covered in each chapter, and the interesting thing is that some labs are written for the Windows Server operating system, while others are written for the Linux operating system. This means you'll get great exposure to common administrative tasks on both platforms.

Topics covered in the labs range from installing server operating systems to configuring server roles such as DHCP and DNS, encrypting files using EFS and OpenSSL, setting file system permissions, using performance monitoring tools, and using backup tools, to name a few. The labs are designed to be performed sequentially from Chapter 1 through Chapter 8; failure to do them in order will cause confusion.

Even though every lab may not mention it, if you have plenty of free disk space, you might want to take a virtual machine snapshot of each virtual machine after you successfully complete the lab exercises in each chapter. This way you can easily revert back to the original configuration if something goes wrong in a future lab.

As you perform each step in a lab exercise, always ask yourself, "Why am I doing this?" to make sure you're getting the most out of the exercise. Learn lots, and have fun!

APPENDIX B

URL Reference

The CompTIA Server+ exam covers a broad range of topics. While you won't need to be an expert in every topic covered in this book, you can't be sure exactly what you'll be tested on, so it's best to cover all bases. Also, if you're looking for more detailed information on topics touched upon in this book, this URL reference is for you!

The following URL reference comes not only from URLs referenced throughout this book, but also includes references for more in-depth coverage of topics such as IPv6, configuring network ACL firewall rules on a Cisco router, and configuring network PXE boot. Remember that URLs change, so some of the items listed below may not work exactly as listed, but luckily search engines make this a non-issue.

www.mheducation.com Learning titles including higher-education IT topics.

www.submarinecablemap.com Shows global layout of undersea communications cables.

www.whatismyip.com Shows your public IPv4 address as seen by the Internet.

www.wireshark.org Network protocol analyzer.

https://my.vmware.com/web/vmware/info?slug=desktop_end_user_computing/vmware_workstation/10_0 Download page for VMware Workstation 10.

https://www.microsoft.com/en-us/evalcenter/evaluate-windows-server-2012-r2 Download page for Windows Server 2012 R2.

http://access.redhat.com/downloads Download page for Red Hat Enterprise Linux.

https://www.microsoft.com/en-us/evalcenter/evaluate-hyper-v-server-2012-r2 Download page for Microsoft Hyper-V Server 2012 R2.

https://www.virtualbox.org Download page for VirtualBox.

http://test-ipv6.com/ Shows your IPv4 and IPv6 configuration as viewed from the Internet.

www.ipv6forum.com IPv6 information.

https://tools.ietf.org/html/rfc2460 IPv6 specification.

https://tools.ietf.org/html/rfc3904 IPv6 transition technologies.

https://aws.amazon.com/ Amazon Web Services public cloud solutions.

http://azure.microsoft.com Microsoft Azure public cloud solutions.

www.rackspace.com Rackspace public cloud solutions.

www.kali.org Kali Linux penetration testing distribution.

http://ieee.org Institute of Electrical and Electronics Engineers. Many standards stem from here including 802.1x, 802.11, and so on.

www.rfc-editor.org Requests for comments; used to define networking standards implementation.

https://certification.comptia.org/docs/default-source/exam-objectives/comptia-server-(sk0-004)-objectives.pdf?sfvrsn=2 CompTIA SK0-004 Server+ exam objectives.

https://certification.comptia.org/certifications/server CompTIA SK0-004 Server+ certification information.

https://www.sans.org/security-resources/policies/ Sample security policy templates.

www.subnet-calculator.com IPv4 subnet calculator.

www.iana.org/assignments/service-names-port-numbers/service-names-port-numbers.xhtml Service Name and Transport Protocol Port Number Registry.

https://www.microsoft.com/en-ca/cloud-platform/system-center-configuration-manager Microsoft System Center Configuration Manager, otherwise called SCCM. SCCM is an enterprise-class inventory and change management system.

https://www.symantec.com/products/information-protection/managed-pki-service Cloud-based managed PKI service.

www.openssl.org Open source SSL and TLS tools.

www.defaultpassword.com List of default usernames and passwords used for network devices.

https://www.youtube.com/watch?v=0uRR72b_qvc Microsoft data center video tour.

https://www.youtube.com/watch?v=zDAYZU4A3w0 Google data center video tour.

www.speedtest.net Tests your Internet connection speed.

www.howtogeek.com/177621/the-beginners-guide-to-iptables-the-linux-firewall Guide for working with the UNIX and Linux iptables command to configure firewall rules.

www.cisco.com/c/en/us/support/docs/security/ios-firewall/23602-confaccesslists.html Cisco network ACL reference.

http://nvlpubs.nist.gov/nistpubs/Legacy/SP/nistspecialpublication800-123.pdf National Institute of Standards and Technology (NIST) guide to general server security.

https://technet.microsoft.com/en-us/library/jj648426(v=ws.11).aspx Windows Server 2012 WDS deployment guide. WDS provides PXE network boot services.

https://www.sans.org/reading-room/whitepapers/standards/osi-model-overview-543 OSI model reference.

https://gallery.technet.microsoft.com/windows-server-2012-r2-nic-85aa1318 Windows Server 2012 R2 NIC teaming reference.

http://shabaztech.com/sccm-2012-r2-quickstart-installation-guide/ Microsoft System Center Configuration Manager 2012 R2 installation guide.

http://shibboleth.net Open source Single Sign-On identify provider solution.

https://www.emc.com/en-us/storage/data-storage.htm Dell EMC storage solutions.

www8.hp.com/ca/en/products/disk-storage/product-detail.html?oid=5386548 Hewlett Packard SAN storage.

www-03.ibm.com/systems/storage/san IBM SAN solutions.

https://technet.microsoft.com/en-ca/library/hh825176.aspx Deployment image servicing and management (DISM) command line usage.

https://www.youtube.com/watch?v=uOQcpVIUPzc Tech support social engineering scam.

https://technet.microsoft.com/en-us/library/dn408191(v=ws.11).aspx Windows Server 2012 dynamic access control.

APPENDIX

Real-World Best Practices

Certified CompTIA Server+ technicians are expected to understand not only concepts, but how they are applicable in real network environments. A small sampling of the server-related body of knowledge includes the following:

- Servers
- Virtualization
- Cloud computing
- Storage
- Networks
- Security

This book not only addresses the official CompTIA Server+ SK0-004 exam objectives, but it also adds some tips and extra information that is relevant whether you work in a tiny server room or a large data center. This appendix serves as a convenient quick reference for best practices related to servers.

Server Installation

Up-front planning can save considerable time down the road; this definitely applies to server installations. Table C-1 lists tips that can help make server installations smooth, but remember that organizations use servers for different purposes; this serves as a generic list of reminders.

Details to Consider	Why It Is Relevant
Plan physical server hardware.	Go beyond minimum requirements to get the best performance.
Plan virtual server hardware.	Virtual servers have virtual hardware; consider how many virtual machines might be running concurrently on a single physical host.
Plan server roles.	Know beforehand what the server will be used for; this can sometimes dictate installation choices as well as hardware requirements.

Table C-1 Server Installation Best Practices (*Continued*)

Details to Consider	Why It Is Relevant
Plan cloud-based virtual machine template use.	Determine which virtual machine template you will use. Cloud providers offer plenty of templates so that you can have a server virtual machine, even one preconfigured with additional software, up and running in minutes.
Plan server IP configuration settings.	Ask your network team about IP addresses that you can use, the subnet mask, default gateway, and, if needed, DNS server IP addresses. If your server will be a member of a specific VLAN, you may have to use a specific IP address or be plugged into a specific switch port.
Cluster virtualization servers.	If you're running on-premises hypervisors, make sure they are clustered so that if one cluster node fails, virtual machines can still run on the remaining cluster node(s). Running five virtual machines on a single server that goes down is not good; you'd be better off with five physical servers in that case!
Get the fastest disk subsystem your budget allows for.	Don't get cheap here; disks are often the slowest component in a server.
Acquire the installation media for your chosen server operating system.	You won't need this if you're deploying a cloud-based virtual machine or an image. Keep the installation media for rescue purposes in case the server can't boot.
Document the server configuration settings.	This will facilitate troubleshooting.

Table C-1 Server Installation Best Practices

Virtualization

Virtual servers can run on-premises or in the public cloud. Once a virtualization solution is chosen, further details need to be determined, as you'll see in Table C-2.

Cloud Computing

Many organizations and individuals are using, to some degree, some type of cloud computing. The great thing is that somebody else deals with the underlying hardware; you can use your cloud service right away and, in some cases, pay only for what you use. All you need is an Internet connection and some kind of app—in many cases, just a web browser. Table C-3 will give you things to think about before jumping into a commitment with a public cloud provider.

Details to Consider	Why It Is Relevant
Potential virtual machine density on the hypervisor	If, for example, one cluster node fails and three new virtual machines will start up on another cluster node, it has to have the physical hardware resources to accommodate the three failed-over virtual machines.
Virtual network switches	Each virtual machine has one or more virtual NICs connected to a virtual network switch. The virtual switch may allow communication only between virtual machines on the hypervisor or it may allow access to the real network. If clustering, make sure all cluster nodes have the same virtual network switch configuration; otherwise, failed-over virtual machines will be inaccessible over the network.
Virtual NICs	You can control MAC addresses if required as well as VLAN tagging options for virtual machine VLAN membership.
Dynamic memory	Consider better memory usage; virtual machines needing more RAM can get it from those virtual machines not currently needing much.
Storage location of virtual hard disks	For hypervisor clustering, virtual machine hard disks and configuration files should reside on shared storage that is visible to all cluster nodes.
Storage location of snapshots	Snapshots, or checkpoints, can consume large amounts of disk space.
Virtual machine live migration	Administrators can essentially move a virtual machine from one hypervisor to another with zero downtime, but only if shared storage is used, and in some cases, similar CPUs exist in the source and target hypervisor.

Table C-2 Virtualization Best Practices

Details to Consider	Why It Is Relevant
Is cloud computing the right choice for your company?	Not every business will benefit from cloud computing. Laws and regulations can prevent some aspects of IT systems or data from residing in the cloud.
Cloud computing is not necessarily cheaper than an on-premises solution.	Cloud providers charge a subscription fee in addition to usage charges. Yes, you don't have the capital investment in hardware and in software licenses, but on the other hand, you will be paying monthly over the long term.
Avoid vendor lock-in.	Try to use apps, tools, and file formats that are standardized. This way, if needed, you can switch to a different provider or even use an on-premises solution with data generated in the cloud.

Table C-3 Cloud Computing Best Practices (*Continued*)

Details to Consider	Why It Is Relevant
Read the service level agreement!	The SLA is a contract between you (or your company) and the cloud provider, and it often cites details about expected service uptime, how quickly tech support will respond to you, and so on. SLA details can sometimes be negotiated.
Turn off, disable, or delete cloud resources when you are not using them!	With many cloud services, you get charged for what you use while you're using it. For example, leaving a database virtual machine running in the cloud could cost hundreds or even thousands of dollars per month.
Be sure about the deletion of cloud data.	Ask your cloud provider if deleted cloud data really is deleted. Could another cloud tenant potentially undelete your data?
Check into data replication.	Check into replicating your cloud systems and data to other data centers or regions if supported.

Table C-3 Cloud Computing Best Practices

Storage

Server storage is often the slowest subsystem in a physical or virtual server. For an on-premises network, you need to determine whether server storage will be local to the server or accessed over the network. Table C-4 addresses further storage considerations.

Details to Consider	Why It Is Relevant
Hardware RAID	If you have the choice, use hardware RAID every time over software RAID. If you want the best performance, get the fastest disks you can afford and configure a RAID 0 striped array, for example. If fault tolerance is important, configure RAID 1 or RAID 5.
Backup frequency	Your company may have a very low tolerance for downtime and data loss. For important data, always have three backups: one stored on-premises on backup tapes, another set of tapes stored in a different physical location, and a third set in the public cloud if acceptable.
Backup testing	If you don't test, how can you be sure data can be restored when it is needed?
LUN masking/zoning	You should limit which network storage is visible to certain servers to avoid data corruption and data leakage.
Volume shadow copies	For Windows servers, this enables users to retrieve deleted files as well as previous versions of files.
Bare-metal image	You need a quick and easy way to get at least the server OS running in case the server won't start.

Table C-4 Server Storage Best Practices (*Continued*)

Details to Consider	Why It Is Relevant
Hot spares	This type of disk can be used automatically when another disk fails.
User disk space quotas	This prevents users from using all of the server disk space.
Thin provisioning	This enables disk volumes to grow as needed; disk space requirements cannot always be accurately predicted upon volume creation.
iSCSI dedicated VLAN	This is good for security and performance.
Multiple paths to network storage	Remove single points of failure—for example, FC HBAs could link to multiple FC switches.

Table C-4 Server Storage Best Practices

Networks

Some servers are connected to internal protected networks, while others might offer a public web site on a DMZ. There are plenty of network options for physical and virtual servers, and Table C-5 discusses them.

Details to Consider	Why It Is Relevant
Static IP configuration	Servers are infrastructure and should not have dynamically changing IP settings.
Multiple NICs	Depending on the server role, multiple NICs might be required—for example, when using a server as a firewall appliance connected to multiple networks.
VLAN membership	Determine whether a specific IP address or physical switch port determines VLAN membership.
NIC teaming	Grouping two or more NICs together can be used for NIC load balancing or aggregated bandwidth; talk to your switch administrator if you will be doing this.
IP routing	For servers with two or more NICs, determine whether routing should be enabled. For example, on a PAT appliance, routing must be enabled, but on a forward proxy server, routing should be disabled.
Network protocol analyzer	Run periodic network scans to see what kind of traffic is flying around the network. You may need your switch administrator to configure a monitoring port for this purpose so that your machine can see all network traffic.

Table C-5 Network Best Practices

Security

Not every reader will agree on what constitutes a secure computing environment. The idea is to minimize the risk of threats occurring. You'll find more in Table C-6.

Details to Consider	Why It Is Relevant
Mobile device corporate partition	This enables selective wipe of corporate apps, settings, and data if the mobile device is lost or stolen.
Network-based firewall	This must exist at every network entry and exit point, so it makes sense to configure packet-filtering rules on routers. Start by denying all traffic, and then add only allowances for required traffic.
Host-based firewall	Every device (including smartphones), where possible, should be running a host-based firewall to control inbound and outbound traffic for that device.
Log forwarding	For critical servers and devices visible to public networks, configure log forwarding to a secured host on a secured network.
Assigning permissions to groups, not users	Managing permissions for individual users doesn't scale well and can present a security risk for forgotten user permissions.
802.1x	Use 802.1x-compliant devices such as network switches and wireless access points to require authentication before being allowed on the network; use a central RADIUS server for authentication.
Multifactor authentication	Usernames and passwords are single-factor authentication and can be guessed or brute-forced from anywhere over a network. For example, compromising a hardware VPN security token and a username and password is much more difficult over a network.
Do not use WEP or WPA	For Wi-Fi networks, don't use WEP or WPA because they have been proven to be hackable using freely available tools such as Kali Linux. For even better security, don't use Wi-Fi at all!
Do not use a descriptive name for a wireless network	The wireless network name, or SSID, is easily viewable even if you disable SSID broadcasting. Naming the wireless network Acme_Bank_Security_Cameras is a bad idea if it really is used for that purpose.
Wireless MAC filtering	Use defense in depth; a collection of hurdles will keep most of the bad guys out.
Patch hardware and software	This is continuous and needs to be monitored to ensure that patching completes successfully. Test updates first in a controlled environment before deploying to production environments.
Periodic network and host vulnerability scans	IT changes quickly and so do new threats; run scans frequently to identify weaknesses.
Period penetration testing	Taking a vulnerability scan a step further, pen tests actively exploit weaknesses. Be careful with this in production environments because systems can be disrupted and sensitive data disclosed.
Disable/uninstall anything that is not absolutely required	The more stuff on servers, the more a malicious user could potentially tap into. Turn off and uninstall software that is not in use, disable or delete inactive user accounts, and disable server GUIs.

Table C-6 Security Best Practices (*Continued*)

Details to Consider	Why It Is Relevant
Encrypt data in motion	All network traffic should be encrypted, including internally on a private LAN. IPSec can be used to encrypt all network traffic without having to configure it for each network service or application.
Encrypt data at rest	Protect stored data with encryption on all types of storage media including, but not limited to, USB thumb drives, storage arrays, cloud storage, and smartphones.
IDS/IPS	Use intrusion detection and prevention solutions on networks and hosts where appropriate.
Antimalware	Where possible, every device (including smartphones) should have an up-to-date antimalware solution. Larger companies should use a solution that can send a centralized alert when malware is detected. Always leave real-time monitoring turned on, unless it prevents the proper installation of trusted software.
Reduce the list of trusted root authorizes on all devices	There are way too many trusted certificate sources on today's devices that are rarely used. The compromise of one trusted root means devices will gladly trust its certificates.
Protect the true identify of servers	Even public web sites should sit behind a reverse-proxy server.
Use strong passwords	Enable password complexity requirements in your environment.
Limit the use of USB removable media	This can prevent data leakage and malware infections.
Train users about security, especially social engineering scams	All other security controls can be defeated if users are easily fooled.
Managed service accounts	On Windows servers, this type of account can be used by a service. The account automatically changes its password based on the Active Directory domain's password policy. This prevents service accounts from either having no password or keeping the same password for extended periods of time.
sudo	UNIX and Linux technicians can prefix commands requiring elevated permissions with sudo instead of logging in as root.
Do not use Telnet remote administration	Use SSH instead; SSH encrypts network traffic, while Telnet is clear text.
Use separate administrative accounts	Accountability and auditing are made easy when each administrator has his or her own account.
For developers and script writers, use secure coding guidelines	This prevents many security problems, including escalation attacks, SQL injection attacks, cross-site scripting attacks, and so on.
Keep up with the latest security issues related to hardware and software used in your environment	Take proactive steps to address discovered vulnerabilities.

Table C-6 Security Best Practices

APPENDIX D

CompTIA Server+ Certification Exam Objectives (SK0-004)

Domain Name	Percent of Examination
Server Architecture	12%
Server Administration	24%
Storage	12%
Security	13%
Networking	10%
Disaster Recovery	9%
Troubleshooting	20%

1.0 Server Architecture

1.1 Explain the purpose and function of server form factors

- Rack mount
  - Dimensions
    - 1U, 2U, 4U
  - Cable management arms
  - Rail kits
- Tower
- Blade technology
  - Blade enclosure
    - Backplane/midplane
    - Power supply sockets
    - Network modules / switches
    - Management modules
  - Blade server

1.2 Given a scenario, install, configure and maintain server components

- CPU
  - Multiprocessor vs. multicore
  - Socket type
  - Cache levels: L1, L2, L3
  - Speeds
    - Core
    - Bus
    - Multiplier
  - CPU stepping
  - Architecture
    - x86
    - x64
    - ARM
- RAM
  - ECC vs. non-ECC
  - DDR2, DDR3
  - Number of pins
  - Static vs. dynamic
  - Module placement
  - CAS latency
  - Timing
  - Memory pairing
- Bus types, bus channels, and expansion slots
  - Height differences and bit rate differences
  - PCI
  - PCIe
  - PCI-X
- NICs
- Hard drives
- Riser cards
- RAID controllers
- BIOS/UEFI
  - CMOS battery

- Firmware
- USB interface/port
- Hotswap vs. non-hotswap components

1.3 Compare and contrast power and cooling components

- Power
  - Voltage
    - 110v vs. 220v vs. −48v
    - 208v vs. 440v/460v/480v
- Wattage
- Consumption
- Redundancy
- 1-phase vs. 3-phase power
- Plug types
  - NEMA
  - Edison
  - Twist lock
- Cooling
  - Airflow
  - Thermal dissipation
  - Baffles/shrouds
  - Fans
  - Liquid cooling

2.0 Server Administration

2.1 Install and configure server operating systems

- Determine server role/purpose
- Update firmware
- BIOS/UEFI configuration
  - Boot order
- Disk preparation
  - RAID setup
  - Partitioning
  - Formatting

- File system type
  - Ext 2, 3, 4
  - NTFS
  - FAT32
  - ReiserFS
  - UFS
  - VMFS
  - ZFS
- Swap

- Configure hostname
- Local account setup
- Connect to network
- Join domain/directory
- Address security concerns
  - Patching
  - OS hardening
  - Compliance to company procedures/standards
- Enable services
- Install features/roles/applications/drivers
- Performance baseline
  - Server optimization
  - Swap or pagefile optimization
- Unattended/remote installations
  - Deploying images and cloning
  - Scripted installs
    - PXE boot
    - TFTP

2.2 Compare and contrast server roles and requirements for each

- Web server
- Application server
- Directory server
- Database server

- File server
- Print server
- Messaging server
- Mail server
- Routing and remote access server
- Network services server
    - DHCP
    - DNS/WINS
    - NTP

2.3 Given a scenario, use access and control methods to administer a server

- Local hardware administration
    - KVM
    - Serial
    - Virtual Administration console
- Network-based hardware administration
    - KVM over IP
    - ILO
    - iDRAC
- Network-based operating system administration
    - RDP
    - SSH
    - VNC
    - Command line / shell

2.4 Given a scenario, perform proper server maintenance techniques

- Change management
- Patch management
    - Operating System updates
    - Application updates
    - Security software updates
    - Firmware updates
    - Device drivers updates

    - Compatibility lists
        - Operating systems
        - Hardware
        - Applications
    - Testing and validation
- Outages and service level agreements
    - Scheduled downtime
    - Unscheduled downtime
    - Impact analysis
    - Client notification
    - MTTR
- Performance monitoring
    - CPU utilization
    - Memory utilization
    - Network utilization
    - Disk utilization
        - Disk IOPS
        - Storage capacity
    - Comparison against performance baseline
    - Processes and services monitoring
    - Log monitoring
- Hardware maintenance
    - Check system health indicators
        - LEDs
        - Error codes
        - Beep codes
        - LCD messages
    - Replace failed components
        - Fans
        - Hard drives
        - RAM
        - Backplanes
        - Batteries

- Preventative maintenance
  - Clearing dust
  - Check proper air flow
- Proper shutdown procedures
  - Fault tolerance and high availability techniques
- Clustering
  - Active/active
  - Active/passive
- Load balancing
  - Round robin
  - Heartbeat

2.5 Explain the importance of asset management and documentation

- Asset management
  - Licensing
  - Labeling
  - Warranty
  - Life cycle management
    - Procurement
    - Usage
    - End of life
    - Disposal/recycling
  - Inventory
    - Make
    - Model
    - Serial number
    - Asset tag
- Documentation
  - Service manuals
  - Network diagrams
  - Architecture diagrams
  - Dataflow diagrams
  - Recovery documentation

    - Baseline documentation
    - Change management policies
    - Service level agreement
    - Server configuration
- Secure storage of sensitive documentation

2.6 Explain the purpose and operation of virtualization components

- Hosts and guests
- Management interface for virtual machines
- Hypervisor
    - Type I
    - Type II
    - Hybrid
- Hardware compatibility list
    - BIOS/UEFI compatibility and support
    - CPU compatibility support
    - AMD-V/Intel VT
- Resource allocation between guest and host
    - CPU
    - Storage
    - Memory
    - Network connectivity
        - Direct Access (Bridging) vs. NAT
        - Virtual NICs
        - Virtual switches
    - Video

3.0 Storage

3.1 Given a scenario, install and deploy primary storage devices based on given specifications and interfaces

- Disk specifications
    - RPM
    - Dimensions/form factor
    - Capacity
    - Bus width

    - IOPS
    - Seek time and latency
    - Hotswap vs. non-hotswap components
- Interfaces
    - SAS
    - SATA
    - SCSI
    - USB
    - Fibre Channel
- Hard drive vs. SSD

3.2 Given a scenario, configure RAID using best practices

- RAID levels and performance considerations
    - 0
    - 1
    - 5
    - 6
    - 10
- Software vs. hardware RAID
    - Performance considerations
- Configuration specifications
    - Capacity
    - Bus types
    - Drive RPM
- Hotswap support and ramifications
- Hot spare vs. cold spare
- Array controller
    - Memory
    - Battery-backed cache
    - Redundant controller

3.3 Summarize hardware and features of various storage technologies

- DAS
- NAS
    - iSCSI
    - FCoE

- SAN
  - Fibre Channel
  - LUN and LUN masking
  - HBAs and fabric switches
- JBOD
- Tape
  - Drive
  - Libraries
- Optical drive
- Flash, CompactFlash, and USB drive

3.4 Given a scenario, calculate appropriate storage capacity and plan for future growth

- Base10 vs. Base2 disk size calculation (1000 vs. 1024)
- Disk quotas
- Compression
- Capacity planning considerations:
  - Operating system growth
    - Patches
    - Service packs
    - Log files
  - Temporary directories
  - Databases
  - Application servers
  - File servers
  - Archival

4.0 Security

4.1 Compare and contrast physical security methods and concepts

- Multifactor authentication
  - Something you have
  - Something you know
  - Something you are

- Security concepts
  - Mantrap
  - RFID chip
  - ID card
  - Biometric
  - Keypad
  - Access list
  - Security guard
  - Security camera
  - Keys and locks
    - Cabinet
    - Rack mount
    - Server
  - Safe

4.2 Given a scenario, apply server hardening techniques

- OS hardening
  - Stopping unneeded services / closing unneeded ports
  - Install only required software
  - Install latest operating system patches
- Application hardening
  - Install latest patches
  - Disabling unneeded services/roles/features
- Endpoint security
  - HIDS
  - Antimalware
- Remediate security issues based on a vulnerability scan
- Hardware hardening
  - Disabling unneeded hardware and physical ports/devices
  - BIOS password
  - Disable WOL (Wake-on-LAN)
  - Setup boot order
  - Chassis locks / intrusion detection

4.3 Explain basic network security systems and protocols

- Firewall
  - Network-based
  - Host-based
- Port security / 802.1x / NAC
- Router access list
- NIDS
- Authentication protocols
  - LDAP
  - RADIUS
  - TACACS
  - TACACS+
- PKI
  - Private key
  - Public key
  - Certificate authority
  - SSL/TLS
- VPN
- IPSec
- VLAN
- Security zones
  - DMZ
  - Public and private
  - Intranet and extranet

4.4 Implement logical access control methods based on company policy

- Access control lists
  - Users
  - Groups
    - Roles
  - Resources
    - File system
    - Network ACLs

        - Peripheral devices
        - Administrative rights
        - Distribution lists
- Permissions
    - Read
    - Write/Modify
    - Execute
    - Delete
    - Full control/Superuser
    - File vs. share

4.5 Implement data security methods and secure storage disposal techniques

- Storage encryption
    - File level encryption
    - Disk encryption
    - Tape encryption
- Storage media
    - Soft wipe
        - File deletion
    - Hard wipe
        - Zero out all sectors
    - Physical destruction
    - Remote wipe

4.6 Given a scenario, implement proper environmental controls and techniques

- Power concepts and best practices
    - UPS
        - Runtime vs. capacity
        - Automated graceful shutdown of attached devices
        - Periodic testing of batteries
        - Maximum load
        - Bypass procedures
        - Remote management

- PDU
  - Connect redundant rack PDUs to separate circuits
- Capacity planning
  - PDU ratings
  - UPS ratings
  - Total potential power draw
- Multiple circuits
  - Connect redundant power supplies to separate PDUs
- Safety
  - ESD procedures
  - Fire suppression
  - Proper lifting techniques
  - Rack stability
  - Floor load limitations
  - Sharp edges and pinch points
- HVAC
  - Room and rack temperature and humidity
    - Monitoring and alert notifications
  - Air flow
    - Rack filler/baffle/blanking panels
  - Hot aisle and cold aisle

5.0 Networking

5.1 Given a scenario, configure servers to use IP addressing and network infrastructure services

- IPv4 vs. IPv6
- Default gateway
- CIDR notation and subnetting
- Public and private IP addressing
- Static IP assignment vs. DHCP
- DNS
  - FQDN
  - Default domain suffix / search domain
- WINS

- NetBIOS
- NAT/PAT
- MAC addresses
- Network Interface Card configuration
  - NIC teaming
  - Duplexing
    - Full
    - Half
    - Auto
  - Speeds
    - 10/100/1000 Mbps
    - 10 Gbps

5.2 Compare and contrast various ports and protocols

- TCP vs. UDP
- SNMP 161
- SMTP 25
- FTP 20/21
- SFTP 22
- SSH 22
- SCP 22
- NTP 123
- HTTP 80
- HTTPS 443
- TELNET 23
- IMAP 143
- POP3 110
- RDP 3389
- FTPS 989/990
- LDAP 389/3268
- DNS 53
- DHCP 68

5.3 Given a scenario, install cables and implement proper cable management procedures

- Copper
  - Patch cables
    - Crossover
    - Straight through
    - Rollover
  - CAT5
  - CAT5e
  - CAT6
- Fiber
  - Single-mode
  - Multi-mode
- Connectors
  - ST
  - LC
  - SC
  - SFP
  - RJ-45
  - RJ-11
- Cable placement and routing
  - Cable channels
  - Cable management trays
    - Vertical
    - Horizontal
- Labeling
- Bend radius
- Cable ties

6.0 Disaster Recovery

6.1 Explain the importance of disaster recovery principles

- Site types
  - Hot site
  - Cold site
  - Warm site

- Replication methods
  - Disk to disk
  - Server to server
  - Site to site
- Continuity of Operations
  - Disaster recovery plan
  - Business continuity plan
  - Business impact analysis
    - Who is affected
    - What is affected
    - Severity of impact

6.2 Given a scenario, implement appropriate backup techniques

- Methodology
  - Full/Normal
    - Copy
  - Incremental
  - Differential
  - Snapshot
  - Selective
  - Bare metal
  - Open file
  - Data vs. OS restore
- Backup media
  - Linear Access
    - Tape
  - Random Access
    - Disk
    - Removable media
    - Optical media
- Media and restore best practices
  - Labeling
  - Integrity verification
  - Test restorability

- Tape rotation and retention
  - Media storage location
- Offsite
- Onsite
- Security considerations
- Environmental considerations

7.0 Troubleshooting

7.1 Explain troubleshooting theory and methodologies

- Identify the problem and determine the scope
  - Question users/stakeholders and identify changes to the server/environment
  - Collect additional documentation/logs
  - If possible, replicate the problem as appropriate
  - If possible, perform backups before making changes
- Establish a theory of probable cause (question the obvious)
  - Determine whether there is a common element of symptom causing multiple problems
- Test the theory to determine cause
  - Once theory is confirmed, determine next steps to resolve problem
  - If theory is not confirmed, establish new theory or escalate
- Establish a plan of action to resolve the problem and notify impacted users
- Implement the solution or escalate as appropriate
  - Make one change at a time and test/confirm the change has resolved the problem
  - If the problem is not resolved, reverse the change if appropriate and implement new change
- Verify full system functionality and if applicable implement preventative measures
- Perform a root cause analysis
- Document findings, actions, and outcomes throughout the process

7.2 Given a scenario, effectively troubleshoot hardware problems, selecting the appropriate tools and methods

- Common problems
  - Failed POST
  - Overheating

- Memory failure
- Onboard component failure
- Processor failure
- Incorrect boot sequence
- Expansion card failure
- Operating system not found
- Drive failure
- Power supply failure
- I/O failure
- Causes of common problems
  - Third-party components or incompatible components
  - Incompatible or incorrect BIOS
  - Cooling failure
  - Mismatched components
  - Backplane failure
- Environmental issues
  - Dust
  - Humidity
  - Temperature
  - Power surge/failure
- Hardware tools
  - Power supply tester (multimeter)
  - Hardware diagnostics
  - Compressed air
  - ESD equipment

7.3 Given a scenario, effectively troubleshoot software problems, selecting the appropriate tools and methods

- Common problems
  - User unable to log on
  - User cannot access resources
  - Memory leak
  - BSOD/stop
  - OS boot failure

    - Driver issues
    - Runaway process
    - Cannot mount drive
    - Cannot write to system log
    - Slow OS performance
    - Patch update failure
    - Service failure
    - Hangs no shut down
    - Users cannot print
- Cause of common problems
    - User Account Control (UAC/sudo)
    - Corrupted files
    - Lack of hard drive space
    - Lack of system resources
    - Virtual memory (misconfigured, corrupt)
    - Fragmentation
    - Print server drivers/services
    - Print spooler
- Software tools
    - System logs
    - Monitoring tools (resource monitor, performance monitor)
    - Defragmentation tools
    - Disk property tools (usage, free space, volume or drive mapping)

7.4 Given a scenario, effectively diagnose network problems, selecting the appropriate tools and methods

- Common problems
    - Internet connectivity failure
    - Email failure
    - Resource unavailable
    - DHCP server misconfigured
    - Non-functional or unreachable
    - Destination host unreachable
    - Unknown host

    - Default gateway misconfigured
    - Failure of service provider
    - Cannot reach by hostname/FQDN
- Causes of common problems
    - Improper IP configuration
    - VLAN configuration
    - Port security
    - Improper subnetting
    - Component failure
    - Incorrect OS route tables
    - Bad cables
    - Firewall (misconfiguration, hardware failure, software failure)
    - Misconfigured NIC, routing/switch issues
    - DNS and/or DHCP failure
    - Misconfigured hosts file
    - IPv4 vs. IPv6 misconfigurations
- Networking tools
    - ping
    - tracert/traceroute
    - ipconfig/ifconfig
    - nslookup
    - net use/mount
    - route
    - nbtstat
    - netstat

7.5 Given a scenario, effectively troubleshoot storage problems, selecting the appropriate tools and methods

- Common problems
    - Slow file access
    - OS not found
    - Data not available
    - Unsuccessful backup
    - Error lights

    - Unable to mount the device
    - Drive not available
    - Cannot access logical drive
    - Data corruption
    - Slow I/O performance
    - Restore failure
    - Cache failure
    - Multiple drive failure
- Causes of common problems
    - Media failure
    - Drive failure
    - Controller failure
    - HBA failure
    - Loose connectors
    - Cable problems
    - Misconfiguration
    - Improper termination
    - Corrupt boot sector
    - Corrupt file system table
    - Array rebuild
    - Improper disk partition
    - Bad sectors
    - Cache battery failure
    - Cache turned off
    - Insufficient space
    - Improper RAID configuration
    - Mismatched drives
    - Backplane failure
- Storage tools
    - Partitioning tools
    - Disk management
    - RAID array management
    - Array management
    - System logs

- Net use/mount command
- Monitoring tools

7.6 Given a scenario, effectively diagnose security issues, selecting the appropriate tools and methods

- Common problems
  - File integrity issue
  - Privilege escalation
  - Applications will not load
  - Can't access network file/shares
  - Unable to open files
  - Excessive access
  - Excessive memory utilization
- Causes of common problems
  - Open ports
  - Active services
  - Inactive services
  - Intrusion detection configurations
  - Antimalware configurations
  - Local/group policies
  - Firewall rules
  - Misconfigured permissions
  - Virus infection
  - Rogue processes/services
- Security tools
  - Port scanners
  - Sniffers
  - Cipher
  - Checksums
  - Telnet client
  - Antimalware

APPENDIX E

About the CD-ROM

The CD-ROM included with this book comes complete with Total Tester customizable practice exam software with 200 practice exam questions and a secured PDF copy of the book.

System Requirements

The software requires Windows Vista or higher and 30MB of hard disk space for full installation, in addition to a current or prior major release of Chrome, Firefox, Internet Explorer, or Safari. To run, the screen resolution must be set to 1024 × 768 or higher. The secured book PDF requires Adobe Acrobat, Adobe Reader, or Adobe Digital Editions to view.

Installing and Running Total Tester Premium Practice Exam Software

From the main screen you may install the Total Tester by clicking the Total Tester Practice Exams button. This will begin the installation process and place an icon on your desktop and in your Start menu. To run Total Tester, navigate to Start | (All) Programs | Total Seminars, or double-click the icon on your desktop.

To uninstall the Total Tester software, go to Start | Control Panel | Programs And Features, and then select the Total Tester program. Select Remove, and Windows will completely uninstall the software.

Total Tester Premium Practice Exam Software

Total Tester provides you with a simulation of the CompTIA Server+ (SK0-004) exam. Exams can be taken in Practice Mode, Exam Mode, or Custom Mode. Practice Mode provides an assistance window with hints, references to the book, explanations of the correct and incorrect answers, and the option to check your answer as you take the test. Exam Mode provides a simulation of the actual exam. The number of questions, the types of questions, and the time allowed are intended to be an accurate representation of the exam environment. Custom Mode allows you to create custom exams from selected domains or chapters, and you can further customize the number of questions and time allowed.

To take a test, launch the program and select CompTIA Server+ (SK0-004) from the Installed Question Packs list. You can then select Practice Mode, Exam Mode, or Custom Mode. All exams provide an overall grade and a grade broken down by domain.

Secured Book PDF

The entire contents of the book are provided in secured PDF format on the CD-ROM. This file is viewable on your computer and many portable devices. Adobe Acrobat, Adobe Reader, or Adobe Digital Editions is required to view the file on your computer. A link to Adobe's web site, where you can download and install Adobe Reader, has been included on the CD-ROM.

NOTE For more information on Adobe Reader and to check for the most recent version of the software, visit Adobe's web site at www.adobe.com and search for the free Adobe Reader or look for Adobe Reader on the product page. Adobe Digital Editions can also be downloaded from the Adobe web site.

To view the book PDF on a portable device, copy the PDF file to your computer from the CD-ROM and then copy the file to your portable device using a USB or other connection. Adobe offers a mobile version of Adobe Reader, the Adobe Reader mobile app, which currently supports iOS and Android. For customers using Adobe Digital Editions and an iPad, you may have to download and install a separate reader program on your device. The Adobe web site has a list of recommended applications, and McGraw-Hill Education recommends the Bluefire Reader.

Technical Support

For questions regarding the Total Tester software or operation of the CD-ROM, visit www.totalsem.com or e-mail support@totalsem.com.

For questions regarding the secured book PDF, e-mail techsolutions@mhedu.com or visit http://mhp.softwareassist.com.

For questions about book content, e-mail hep_customer-service@mheducation.com. For customers outside the United States, e-mail international_cs@mheducation.com.

1-phase power Designed for moderate power requirements, this is normally used in households.

1U Unit of measurement of height for racks and rack-mounted equipment. 1U equals 1 3/4 inch.

3G Third-generation wireless telecommunications network.

3-phase power Designed for demanding power requirements; normally used in industrial environments as well as for data centers.

4G Fourth-generation wireless telecommunications network; speeds are faster than 3G, which supports more broadband applications.

6to4 An IPv6 transition technology that allows IPv6 traffic over the IPv4 Internet. Routers on both ends must support IPv6 and must have an IPv6 address configured on their internal interface.

A Domain Name Service (DNS) record type that resolves fully qualified domain names (FQDNs) to IPv4 addresses.

AAAA DNS record type that resolves FQDNs to IPv6 addresses.

access control list (ACL) List of entities such as users and groups that are granted or denied permissions to a resource such as a file.

Active Directory Domain Services (AD DS) Microsoft's Lightweight Directory Access Protocol (LDAP)–compliant network database containing objects such as users, groups, and computers. The database is replicated between domain controller servers and is used for authentication, centralized Group Policy settings, and storage of some network application configurations including DNS and activation keys.

Active Directory Federation Services (ADFS) Microsoft's Identify Federation solution used for web Single Sign-On (SSO). ADFS can be configured with user and device claim types that are consumed by trusting applications. Claims are digitally signed by ADFS using a private key; trusting applications verify the signature with the related public key.

Advanced Encryption Standard (AES) Supersedes DES as an encryption standard. This symmetric block cipher comes in 128-bit, 192-bit, and 256-bit cipher strengths.

Advanced Intelligent Tape (AIT) A magnetic tape storage medium used with tape backup and archiving systems.

Advanced RISC Machine (ARM) A 32-bit and 64-bit multicore processor type used in small computing devices such as smartphones.

air-gapped Air-gapped networks do not have a connection to the Internet either wirelessly or using a wired connection. This isolation can be used for testing purposes or highly sensitive networks.

alternating current (AC) This type of power uses small variations in voltage and current and is available from power outlets and consumed by power supplies.

AMD Virtualization (AMD-V) AMD's virtualization firmware support that is required by some Type 1 and Type 2 hypervisors.

anycast Similar to multicasting, this IPv6 transmission method attempts to find the nearest receiver of a multicast group.

application server A server configured to serve a specific business need beyond core functionality, such as a generic file server or database server.

asynchronous replication Data replication method in which a delay occurs after the initial data write before the secondary write takes place.

Automatic Private IP Address (APIPA) Self-assigned unique LAN IPv4 addresses that Windows devices use when the Dynamic Host Configuration Protocol (DHCP) server is unreachable. APIPA devices can communicate only with other APIPA devices on the LAN.

bare metal This term is often used to describe installation or disaster recovery scenarios where a computer system has no operating system installed.

baseboard management controller (BMC) An interface between server management tools and the physical server hardware being managed. The BMC also monitors the state of servers and is often used with blade servers.

battery-backed write caching Used with disk array controllers upon restart for data not yet written to disk. Because it is cached (it is not lost during a power cycle), data gets written to disk.

binary Numeric system consisting of 0's and 1's.

biometric authentication Uses a personal identifying characteristic for proof of identity, such as a fingerprint or retinal scan.

BIOS Basic input-output system; the firmware instructions embedded on a motherboard that provide basic hardware functionality including the initial power on self test (POST) sequence when the machine is powered on.

BitLocker Microsoft's disk volume encryption tool. Although it can be used without the Trusted Platform Module (TPM), it is designed to use TPM functionality.

blade enclosure Blade servers (essentially server motherboards) are placed into a blade enclosure, which is mounted into a rack. Since each blade does not have its own cooling, networking, and power, this is supplied through the enclosure.

blade server A thin server that is placed into a blade enclosure that provides cooling, networking, and power. Blade servers increase server density in data centers compared to rack-mounted and tower servers.

botnet A group of infected computers under centralized malicious user control. The malicious user can provide instructions for the group of computers, much like an army general ordering soldiers to perform a task.

bring your own device (BYOD) A policy that allows people to bring their own personal computing devices into a business environment. In corporate environments using mobile devices, the company often exercises control over business apps, settings, and data on the device in a separate logical device partition that can be selectively wiped while leaving personal apps, settings, and data intact.

British thermal units (BTUs) BTUs provide a standard way to measure the heat output of computing equipment, which can be then used to determine cooling requirements from the HVAC system.

broadcast Network broadcasts can apply at the hardware or software level. Broadcasts are transmissions that are received by all network nodes on the LAN. Routers do not forward broadcasts by default.

buffer overflow An exploit that provides more data than the programmer intended in memory. This can lead to remote escalation attacks. Secure coding practices can prevent this from happening.

bus width Buses are sets of conductors that carry data (bits) around the computer, and a computer consists of various buses. The bus width, or size, is commonly 32 or 64 bits.

business continuity plan (BCP) This proactive planning ensures that business operations continue when negative incidents occur; this plan is not as detailed or specific as a disaster recovery plan.

business impact analysis (BIA) Identifies the degree and scope of impact on a business when negative incidents occur. The BIA enables easier prioritization of assets that require protection from threats.

cable management arm In equipment racks, a folding arm that holds cables. When rack equipment is slid out on rack rails, the arm extends to provide longer cable lengths.

cache A small amount of high-speed memory used to fetch recent instructions or data.

CAT3 Category 3 copper-wire network cabling that is designed to support up to 10 Mbps.

CAT5 Category 5 copper-wire network cabling that is designed to support up to 100 Mbps; also called 100Base-T or Fast Ethernet.

CAT5e Category 5 copper-wire network cabling that is designed to support up to 1000 Mbps (1 Gbps); also called 1000Base-T or Gigabit Ethernet.

CAT6 Category 6 copper-wire network cabling that is designed to support up to 10 Gbps. It is more resistant to interference than CAT5 and has more twists per foot in the cable. Also called 10GBase-T. Longer cable distances (approximately 60–100 meters) can be run at 1 Gbps.

CAT7 Category 7 copper-wire network cabling that is designed to support up to 10 Gbps; uses individual wire pair shielding, which makes it useful in environments with high electromagnetic interference (EMI).

central processing unit (CPU) A microprocessor chip on a motherboard that carries out instructions within the system. Modern CPU chips consist of multiple logical CPU cores within a single physical chip.

certificate authority (CA) Issuer of digital security certificates in a Public Key Infrastructure (PKI). Companies can create their own CAs or use certificates issued from trusted third-party CAs.

checkpoint Also called a snapshot, a checkpoint takes a point-in-time picture of virtual machine settings and data disks. This can also refer to disk volume snapshots, which copy only disk blocks changed since the previous snapshot.

cipher An algorithm used for encryption, decryption, or hashing mathematical operations.

Classless Inter-Domain Routing (CIDR) A shorthand way of referring to the number of bits in a network mask. For example, /24 can be used to represent 255.255.255.0.

clock multiplier Defines a relationship between the external CPU bus speed (MHz) versus the internal CPU speed (GHz).

cloud Pooled computing resources that can be self-provisioned rapidly, usually over the Internet. IT resource usage is metered so that consumers pay only for what they use. Cloud computing resources must be available from anywhere, at any time, using any type of device.

CMOS Complementary metal oxide semiconductor; battery-powered firmware used to retain hardware settings available in the BIOS.

cold aisle Used in data centers to manage airflow for equipment and cost optimization. Cold aisles feed cool air to equipment intake fans.

cold site An alternate site used for disaster recovery. The site has power and communications links but no computing equipment, staff, or data.

column access strobe (CAS) latency A memory characteristic that defines how long it takes for requested memory content to leave the actual memory chip on its way to the bus.

Common UNIX Printing System (CUPS) The standard UNIX print server software components.

Complex Instruction Set Computing (CISC) A microprocessor design used in larger non-mobile computing devices such as desktops and servers. This type of chip is not designed for energy efficiency but rather for performance.

confidentiality Prevent disclosure of sensitive information to unauthorized users; provided by encryption.

continuous data protection (CDP) Real-time replication (synchronous) often used for data between data centers.

converged network adapter (CNA) Server expansion card that combines Ethernet and Fibre Channel functionality.

CPU cache High-speed memory used to keep recently executed data or CPU instructions readily available for subsequent use.

cross-over cable Cable in which receive and transmit wires are reversed on either end of the cable; used to link two network computing devices directly together. This type of cable can also be required by older network equipment—to link two old Ethernet switches together, for example.

crosstalk Interference caused by electronic signals on adjacent wires. This can be reduced with wire shielding and by twisting wire pairs together a specific amount of times per foot. The more twists per foot, the less crosstalk, which means transmissions at higher frequencies are possible.

customer replaceable units (CRUs) Components provided under warranty by a vendor that get installed by the customer.

daemon A background process on a UNIX or Linux system not tied to a user session. Examples include the sshd daemon for remote management or the syslogd daemon for logging.

data center A facility dedicated to housing computing equipment. Special designs enforce security; control HVAC; improve resistance to floods, fire, and earthquakes; and have backup power and communications solutions.

data deduplication A storage mechanism designed to save storage space by removing redundant data blocks to conserve space.

daughter card An expansion circuit board that gets plugged into a motherboard. Unlike a normal expansion card, daughter cards have direct access to CPU and memory resources.

DDR3 Double data rate 3 memory; a type of dynamic RAM supported by some motherboards. DDR transmits data on the rise and fall of computer clock signals.

DDR4 Double data rate 4 memory; a type of dynamic RAM supported by some motherboards where speeds are faster than DDR3. DDR transmits data on the rise and fall of computer clock signals.

deep packet inspection Ability to access data beyond packet header fields for application-specific data. Packet payloads can be examined, often for the purposes of security or performance. Also called OSI Layer 7 inspection.

default gateway IP address of a router interface on the LAN; used by nodes to transmit data to remote networks.

demilitarized zone (DMZ) A network whose hosts are exposed to the Internet with controlled access to an internal network. Services that must be reached from the Internet such as VPNs and public web sites should be placed in the DMZ. An alternative is to use a reverse proxy in the DMZ that listens for requests and forwards them to the actual servers located on a protected internal network.

denial-of-service (DoS) attack An attack that prevents the legitimate use of a computing resource—for example, flooding a host with specially crafted packets could cause the host to crash.

Desired State Configuration (DSC) A Microsoft PowerShell method of centrally configuring and hardening Windows and Linux hosts.

differential backup Backup method in which changed items since the last full or differential backup get copied. The archive bit is not modified with this type of backup.

Digital Linear Tape (DLT) The industry standard for tape backup media, DLT is often used for long-term archiving. DLT cartridges should be placed in protective cases to ensure long-term data storage.

digital signature A unique value generated by a private key along with data such as an e-mail message. Signatures are verified on the receiving end with the mathematically related public key. This can be used to assure the recipient that the sender is who they say they are and that the transmission has not been tampered with.

direct-attached storage (DAS) Local storage available to a server. As long as the server does not have to communicate with storage over some kind of network, it is DAS.

direct current (DC) As opposed to alternating current (AC) from power outlets, DC provides a consistent voltage and amperage to sensitive digital components. Batteries and power supplies provide DC.

disaster recovery (DR) plan A plan that is specific to an IT system with a step-by-step procedure to recover an IT system as quickly and efficiently as possible.

disk mirroring Also called RAID 1, data written to one disk is also written to a second disk in case the first disk fails. RAID 1 means 50 percent of the storage capacity is usable, and it is considered a fault-tolerant disk solution.

disk scrubbing A method of removing data from a disk to ensure that data remnants cannot be resurrected and data reconstructed. This method normally uses multiple passes to write useless random data to the hard disk.

disk striping Also called RAID 0, this distributes written data across multiple disks with the result being improved performance. Other RAID variations use different forms of striping along with parity, or recovery information, to gain the additional benefit of fault tolerance; an example of this is RAID 5.

distributed denial-of-service (DDoS) Very similar to a DoS, this attack prevents the legitimate use of a computing resource. For example, flooding a host with specially crafted packets could cause the host to crash, but what makes this different from a DoS attack is that multiple hosts under malicious user control are involved in executing the attack against the victim host or network.

DNS forward lookup The most common type of lookup. Queries for the IP address given a FQDN (such as www.fakesite.com) are received by the DNS server, and the IP address is returned to the query originator.

DNS reverse lookup Queries for the FQDN given the IP address are received by the DNS server and the FQDN is returned to the query originator.

domain controller (DC) A Windows server that holds a replica of the Active Directory database. The server is discovered in DNS through service location records and performs authentication and replication with other domain controllers, and it provides Group Policy settings.

Domain Name Service (DNS) A network service that listens on UDP port 53 for client queries. Forward DNS lookups are the most common type of query, in which the client has a FQDN but needs the corresponding IP address. Multiple DNS servers can be used for high availability and better performance. Microsoft Active Directory requires DNS.

double data rate (DDR) Refers to memory chips; data is transmitted on the rise and fall of a timing signal.

Dual Inline Memory Module (DIMM) Common type of memory circuit board with multiple memory chips that plugs into sockets on a motherboard. DIMMs can have 168, 184, or 240 pins.

Dynamic Access Control (DAC) Permissions are granted to a resource if conditions are met. Conditions can be expression-based, such as only full-time employees, or users must be members of two specific groups and be based in Chicago, for example, as opposed to users simply being members of a group and thus receiving group permissions.

Dynamic Host Configuration Protocol (DHCP) Centralized IPv4 and IPv6 settings deployed to DHCP clients. Clients initially discover DHCP servers using software broadcasts that cannot traverse routers, in which case a DHCP relay agent would be required.

Dynamic Random Access Memory (DRAM) A classification for memory that requires constant electricity to retain data stored in memory cells. This is the most common type of main system memory.

Edison plug A type of electrical plug that is standard in American households and is more rounded than NEMA (National Electrical Manufacturers Association) plugs—but like NEMA, it has three prongs.

electromagnetic interference (EMI) Also called radiofrequency interference. Some equipment, or even adjacent wires within a cable, can emit electrical noise that can interfere with other electronic transmissions in close proximity.

electrostatic discharge (ESD) Differences in electrical potential between two items result in electrons flowing to the lesser charge in an attempt to equalize voltage. This exchange can damage sensitive electronic circuits and can be reduced with ESD wrist straps or mats.

Encrypting File System (EFS) Microsoft file and folder encryption. Unlike BitLocker, EFS does not rely on TPM. EFS decryption is dependent upon the user being successfully authenticated. BitLocker disk volume encryption is in no way related to user accounts.

encryption Scrambling of data. A mathematical algorithm is used with a key to change plain text into cipher text (encrypted data). The purpose is to ensure that only authorized users (those with the decryption key) can access private data.

error correcting code (ECC) A type of memory chip often used in servers that can not only detect but also correct certain types of data corruption errors in memory.

Ethernet switch A network device with multiple physical ports where network nodes such as servers, desktops, and routers can be plugged in. Multiple switches can be linked together with a straight-through cable, although older switches may require a cross-over cable. Layer 3 switches add routing capabilities. Most switches are manageable over the network using Telnet, SSH, HTTP, or HTTPS.

exabyte One quintillion, or 10^{18}, bytes.

Extended File Allocation Table (exFAT) A Microsoft file system often used with Secure Digital (SD) cards and USB flash drives.

EXT3 The Extended File System, a UNIX and Linux file system. This journaled file system is used with many Linux distributions.

EXT4 A journaled UNIX and Linux file system. Compared to EXT3, EXT4 supports larger files and file system sizes, and journaling can be disabled.

failover cluster Two or more servers offering the same IT service that keep in constant communication with each other. When a cluster node fails, users are redirected to a remaining node that offers the same network service.

fiber-optic cable A type of cable that transmits pulses of light rather than electrical signals through tiny glass or plastic tubes. Signals can travel much farther than copper wires before degrading, and additional security is provided because it is difficult to wiretap fiber-optic cables. Single-mode fiber is often used for longer distances, while multimode fiber is used for shorter distances.

Fibre Channel (FC) Enterprise-class high-speed network connecting servers to storage. FC uses special equipment such as FC host bus adapter cards in servers and FC switches, to name a few. FC does not require that fiber-optic cables are used, although it is common.

Fibre Channel host bus adapter (FC HBA) Servers that access storage over a Fibre Channel storage network require at least one FC HBA. Multiple FC HBAs allow multiple paths from the server to network storage and provide fault tolerance.

Fibre Channel over Ethernet (FCoE) A standard designed to place disk commands into Ethernet frames as opposed to using higher level IP packets, which introduce more overhead. Special equipment is required.

field replaceable units (FRUs) A computer component that can be quickly and easily removed from a computer or other piece of electronic equipment and replaced by the user or a technician without having to send the entire product or system to a repair facility. Certified technicians follow proper procedures when replacing failed components such as Fibre Channel HBAs or motherboards.

File Allocation Table 32 (FAT32) A Microsoft file system stemming from the 1990s. Although rarely used for hard disks, it is still used occasionally for smaller USB flash drives.

file encryption key (FEK) A bulk encryption key used with Microsoft EFS. User private keys (after successful authentication) are used to decrypt the FEK, which is then used to decrypt EFS-encrypted files or folders.

file integrity *See* hashing.

File Transfer Protocol (FTP) A network protocol used to transfer files between servers and clients on a network. FTP servers normally listen on TCP ports 20 and 21.

firewall A hardware or software solution that controls network traffic into or out of an individual host or an entire network.

firmware Software stored in a chip.

form factor An aspect that defines the physical size and shape of components.

front side bus (FSB) A communications interface that carries data between the CPU and the northbridge.

FTPS An extension of FTP that supports the Secure Sockets Layer (SSL) and Transport Layer Security (TLS) cryptographic protocols.

full backup A backup in which all selected files and folders are backed up. The archive bit is normally cleared.

full-duplex Transmission of data in two directions; information can be sent and received simultaneously.

full wipe All information on the system is completely deleted.

fully qualified domain name (FQDN) The complete domain name of a specific computer/host on the Internet, such as www.mheducation.com.

geofencing A virtual barrier of geographic boundaries created by a feature in a program using GPS. This is often used to control mobile device apps or web sites.

gigabit (Gb) A unit of digital information equivalent to 125 megabytes.

gigabyte (GB) A unit of digital information equivalent to about 1 billion bytes, or 1000 megabytes.

Grandfather-Father-Son (GFS) Backup rotation method that uses three backup sets such as daily, weekly, and monthly, where each tape gets rotated on a schedule. You could use quarters and years as backup cycles for even longer term archiving

Group Policy A Windows feature that defines user, security, and network policies. Group policy can be configured locally on a single host or centrally through Group Policy Objects (GPOs).

Group Policy Object (GPO) An Active Directory object that contains specific policy settings for defined groups of users or computers.

guest A virtualized OS running on a hypervisor host.

GUID Partition Table (GPT) A layout of the partition table on a storage device such as a hard disk drive or a solid state drive that uses globally unique identifiers (GUID). GPT provides up to 128 disk partitions compared to MBR's maximum of 4.

half-duplex A system in which information can be both sent and received, but not at the same time.

hard disk drive (HDD) A magnetic data storage device that stores information on rigid, rotating platters.

hardening Securing a system by reducing its attack surface, usually by removing unneeded services or programs and applying patches.

hardware compatibility list (HCL) A list of hardware that is compatible with a specific operating system.

hashing Mathematical algorithms are used with data to result in a unique value, or hash. This can be done in the future as well to detect whether or not a file or transmission was modified since the last hash. Modifications result in a different hash.

Health Insurance and Portability and Accountability Act (HIPAA) A piece of legislation passed in the United States in 1996. Title II of this legislation deals with how digital healthcare/patient information should be stored, as well as privacy and security rules regarding this digital information.

heating, ventilation, air conditioning (HVAC) Provides comfort and acceptable air quality indoors and in vehicles including heat, ventilation, and air conditioning as well as humidity control. This is especially critical in data centers that house hundreds or thousands of computing devices.

hexadecimal A numerical system made up of 16 symbols (base 16) from 0 to 9, A to F, where A = 10 and F = 15.

high availability Continuous access to data or IT systems. Disk mirroring, backups, and failover clustering provide high availability.

host The software that is installed on a system that interfaces with the underlying hardware directly. This term is often used to refer to a virtualization server.

host bus adapter (HBA) A circuit board that connects a host to other storage and network devices.

host intrusion detection system (HIDS) A system that monitors a computer system, logs suspicious activity, and alerts administrators. A HIDS must be tweaked for a specific environment and can be configured against a baseline of normal activity.

host intrusion prevention system (HIPS) A system that monitors a computer system and logs suspicious activity and alerts administrators, but it also has the ability to stop the activity from continuing. A HIPS must be tweaked for a specific environment and can be configured against a baseline of normal activity.

HOSTS file A file on network devices used to map hostnames to IP addresses. The HOSTS file is checked before DNS servers.

hot aisle A row in which the exhaust fans of server racks are facing one another. Cool air from the cold aisle is supplied to equipment intake fans. The goal is to keep equipment cool and energy costs down.

hot site A duplicate of the original network equipment site that would allow a business to continue computer and network operations in case of a disaster. Power, communications, equipment, software, data, and staff are ready to go. This relies on data replication from the original site to the hot site.

hot spare An extra component that can be used immediately when a primary component fails.

human interface device (HID) A computer device that interfaces directly and takes input from people, such as a stylus, mouse, or keyboard.

Hypertext Markup Language (HTML) A set of markup tags that are used to create web documents.

Hypertext Transfer Protocol (HTTP) An application protocol for distributed information systems. Web servers use HTTP to deliver HTML content to web browser and normally listen on TCP port 80 or 443 for secured connections.

Hypertext Transfer Protocol Secure (HTTPS) HTTP communication that is encrypted with Transport Later Security (TLS) or Secure Sockets Layer (SSL), which requires the web server to be configured with a PKI certificate. The server normally listens on TCP port 443 for this type of connection.

hypervisor A program that lets multiple guest operating systems running in virtual machines share the resources of a single host. Type 1 hypervisors interact directly with underlying hardware, whereas Type 2 hypervisors require an existing operating system and do not interact directly with hardware.

IEEE 802.1x An Institute of Electrical and Electronics Engineers (IEEE) standard used to define port-based network access control, which controls device access to a network. Wireless access points, network switches, and VPN devices are examples of devices that can be 802.1x-compliant.

incremental backup A backup of files that have changed since the last full or incremental backup. This type of backup clears the archive bit and takes the least amount of time to back up but the most amount of time to restore.

Information Technology Infrastructure Library (ITIL) A suite of practices used to align IT services with business needs.

Infrastructure as a Service (IaaS) A cloud service model in which providers offer infrastructure such as virtual machines and storage as a self-provisioned service to subscribers. Subscribers can rapidly provision and deprovision these services and pay only for what they use.

input/output operations per second (IOPS) A unit of measurement for the maximum number of reads and writes a storage device can perform per second.

Integrated Dell Remote Access (iDRAC) Administrators can connect to remote servers at the hardware level, even using a friendly web browser interface. This requires an additional IP configuration because the server OS does not have to be running.

Integrated Lights Out (ILO) management ILO offers secure remote management capabilities as well as server monitoring and alerting capabilities.

Intel VT Intel's hardware virtualization support required by some hypervisors.

Intelligent Platform Management Interface (IPMI) A remote server management solution commonly used with various vendors' blade enclosures. IPMI also provides server monitoring and inventory functionality.

Internet Control Message Protocol (ICMP) A protocol of the TCP/IP suite used to check for network connectivity issues. Tools such as ping and tracert use ICMP.

Internet Message Access Protocol (IMAP) An e-mail protocol that stores e-mails while also enabling the end user to view and change the e-mails from multiple devices. IMAP normally listens on TCP port 143 or 993 if enabled for SSL or TLS.

Internet Protocol (IP) The primary communications protocol for relaying datagrams between networks. This protocol maps to Layer 3 (the network layer) of the OSI model.

Intra-Site Automatic Tunnel Addressing Protocol (ISATAP) Allows IPv6 traffic on an internal IPv4 network. The IPv4 address is embedded within the IPv6 address.

intrusion detection (ID) A device or program that monitors a network or system for security violations or malicious activity.

intrusion prevention (IP) A device or program that monitors network traffic for security violations or malicious activity and can prevent the activity from continuing.

IPSec Network security that works with IPv4 and IPv6; it allows encrypting and authentication of network packets without application-specific configurations.

IPv4 The fourth revision of the Internet Protocol. Still used by the majority of networks today, although all free addresses have been exhausted. IPv4 uses a 32-bit address space where addresses are expressed in decimal form, such as 192.168.1.1.

IPv6 The sixth revision of the Internet Protocol. Gaining traction, it is a 128-bit address space where addresses are expressed in hexadecimal form, such as 2000:1:234::1.

iSCSI Internet Small Computer Systems Interface; SCSI disk commands are placed into IP packets, which enables servers to connect to network storage using standard network equipment. iSCSI initiators consume disk space over the network from iSCSI targets.

Kerberos A network authentication protocol that uses tickets to identify computers over a nonsecure network; used by Active Directory.

keyboard video mouse (KVM) Used to connect a single keyboard, video, and mouse to multiple servers. Newer solutions enable KVM over IP.

kilobyte (KB) A unit of digital information equivalent to about 1000 bytes.

kilowatt (kW) Equals 1000 watts, often used for UPS power ratings, although sometimes the rating is in volt-amperes (VA).

L1 cache The fastest cache available to the CPU. Located on the CPU die.

L2 cache The next fastest cache available to the CPU after L1 cache. Located on the CPU die.

L3 cache The next fastest cache available to the CPU after L2 cache. Located on the CPU die.

large form factor (LFF) A 3 1/2-inch hard disk drive.

Layer 2 Tunneling Protocol with Internet Protocol Security (L2TP/IPSec) A VPN solution in which IPSec encrypts data using a variety of sources for keys, including a symmetric key, PKI certificates, Kerberos, and so on.

lights-out management (LOM) The use of a dedicated management channel that enables administrators to monitor servers even when they are powered off.

Lightweight Directory Access Protocol (LDAP) A protocol for using and maintaining a distributed directory information service over a network. Microsoft Active Directory is LDAP-compliant.

Linear Tape-Open (LTO) Magnetic storage media that uses the Linear Tape File System (LTFS).

Linux A UNIX-like operating system that was created and is maintained under the free and open-source software development and distribution model.

logical unit number (LUN) A number that identifies available storage on a storage area network (SAN).

LT connector Fiber-optic snap-in connector commonly used with single-mode fiber.

mail exchanger (MX) record A resource record in DNS that specifies a mail server responsible for a specific domain.

malware Malicious software such as a virus, worm, and spyware.

management information base (MIB) A database of configuration settings and statistics present on most network devices; queries from an SNMP management console.

mantrap A room with two sets of interlocking doors; the first set of doors must be closed and locked before the second set will open to allow a person through.

master boot record (MBR) A type of boot sector at the beginning of PC partitioned storage devices.

megabit (Mb) A unit of digital information equivalent to 125 kilobytes.

megabyte (MB) A unit of digital information equivalent to about 1 million bytes, or 1000 kilobytes.

midplane A printed circuit board (PCB) with server blades that connect on one side (the front) and other components accessible on the other side (the back).

mobile device management (MDM) The administration of mobiles devices, such as tablets or smartphones, using a centralized tool.

multicast A method of sending IP datagrams to all interested listeners in a single transmission. Interested listeners must be registered with the multicast group address to receive transmissions.

multifactor authentication (MFA) A method of computer access authentication that relies on at least two of the following: something you know, something you have, or something you are.

multihoming A host with two or more network interfaces.

multi-mode fiber A type of optical fiber used to communicate over short distances.

Nano Server A version of Microsoft Windows Server with a small footprint that is optimized for remote access and cloud services.

near-field communication (NFC) A set of protocols that enables two devices to communicate when within approximately 4 centimeters (2 inches) of each other.

NEMA connector The standard two-prong (or three-prong with ground) electrical plug used in North America.

network address translation (NAT) A way of remapping one IP address space into another. The most common use is to allow internal hosts to gain Internet access where the source IP address for outgoing transmissions is translated to the NAT router's public interface IP address.

Network File System (NFS) A UNIX file sharing protocol that allows a computer to access files over a network.

network interface card (NIC) A device that connects a computing device to a network. NICs have a unique hardware, or MAC, address.

network intrusion detection (NID) A system that is placed at a point in a network to monitor traffic on the network for attacks.

network intrusion prevention (NIP) A system used to detect and prevent exploits or attacks.

network load balancing (NLB) A process that takes inbound traffic for a network service and distributes it to the least busy and running back-end server hosting the service. The end user perception is better performance when accessing the network service in busy environments.

Network Time Protocol (NTP) A protocol for clock synchronization between computers on a network over UDP port 123.

NIC balancing *See* NIC teaming.

NIC bonding *See* NIC teaming.

NIC teaming Combining multiple network cards together for redundancy or performance.

northbridge Also known as a host bridge; communicates with the CPU directly through the front side bus. This chipset connects the southbridge and other performance-sensitive components of the motherboard to the CPU.

NTFS NT File System; the file system that Windows NT operating systems use to store files on a storage device. NTFS supports auditing, compression, local file system permissions, encryption, and disk space quotas.

Open Shortest Path First (OSPF) A router protocol that finds the best path for packets as they pass through a series of connected networks.

Open Systems Interconnection (OSI) model An effort to standardize computer networking as with the seven-layer OSI model.

optical time domain reflectometer (OTDR) A device used to certify the performance of fiber-optic links.

OS X The current operating system used on Macintosh computers.

out-of-band management The use of a dedicated channel for managing devices outside of normal communication methods.

Payment Card Industry Data Security Standard (PCI DSS) A proprietary security standard for companies that handle cardholder information.

PCI Express (PCIe) The serial transmission–based PCI Express standard supersedes both PCI and PCI eXtended (PCI-X) with more bandwidth, which is especially useful with video, storage, and network cards. The bandwidth will vary depending upon the specific version of PCIe and how many lanes (channel of communication) are used.

PCI eXtended (PCI-X) A 64-bit parallel transmission standard that runs at various frequencies (often the case with expansion slots and cards), which influences the data transmission speed.

Peripheral Component Interconnect (PCI) A standard parallel-based bus that is used to attach hardware devices to a computer.

Platform as a Service (PaaS) A cloud computing service that allows subscribers to run and manage applications without dealing with the difficulties of creating and maintaining the underlying infrastructure; often used by developers to quickly deploy database platforms used by applications.

plug-and-play (PnP) A device that can be automatically discovered and used when installed while the computer is still powered on. The BIOS, operating system, and device must all support PnP.

Point-to-Point Tunneling Protocol (PPTP) Microsoft's standard VPN solution that uses Microsoft Point-to-Point Encryption (MPPE) for encryption. Unlike other VPN solutions, limited configuration options for encryption are available.

Port Address Translation (PAT) An extension of NAT that enables the mapping of multiple internal IP addresses to a single public IP address.

port aggregation A network switch port configuration that groups ports together, often for the purpose of server NIC teaming.

Post Office Protocol (POP) A protocol used by e-mail clients to retrieve messages from a server over TCP port 110 or 995 if secured with SSL or TLS.

power on self test (POST) A process run by firmware immediately after a computer is powered on, which verifies basic power and hardware functionality.

power supply unit (PSU) A computer component that transforms AC power supplied by the power company to lower voltage DC power for internal components.

Preboot Execution Environment (PXE) Enables a computer to boot from a server prior to booting the OS; requires DHCP, a PXE boot server, and a PXE-enabled NIC.

principle of least privilege A policy that every user, process, or program is granted access only to resources that are necessary to complete a specific task, and nothing more.

printed circuit board (PCB) An insulating sheet of material on which conductive leads of conducting materials are placed to create electric circuits.

private branch exchange (PBX) A telephone system used to switch calls between users on local lines while enabling users to share a limited number of external phone lines. This is how a single phone number can have multiple extensions internally.

PTR record A record that resolves an IP address to a domain; used for reverse DNS lookups.

public key authentication Authentication that uses a related public key and private key pair instead of the standard username and password. The public key is normally stored on the device (usually a server), while the private key is stored by the user.

Public Key Infrastructure (PKI) A hierarchy of security certificates issued by a certificate authority to users, devices, and services. Each certificate contains many items, including a unique public and private key pair as well as an expiry date.

quality of service (QoS) A defined measure of performance used to prioritize different types of network traffic over others. For example, VoIP traffic is normally given a higher priority than SMTP traffic on a network.

rack-mounted server A server designed to be placed in a rack with other servers and equipment in a server room or data center; takes less space than tower servers.

radio-frequency identification (RFID) A way of using radio frequencies to identify and track tags attached to objects.

Random Access Memory (RAM) Computer memory; it retains information only when connected to a power source and thus is considered volatile. Hard disks are considered nonvolatile memory because they retain information even with no power.

recovery point objective (RPO) Maximum tolerable amount of data loss normally expressed in time, such as four hours. This would mean backups must occur at least every four hours.

recovery time objective (RTO) Maximum amount of time that can be tolerated for an IT service to be down before it has a negative impact on the business.

Reduced Instruction Set Computing (RISC) A CPU with a simplified instruction set. The few instructions that are available can be executed quickly.

Redundant Array of Inexpensive Disks (RAID) Combines multiple physical disks into a single unit for redundancy and/or performance purposes. RAID can be configured within an operating system or using the more reliable hardware RAID controller solution. There are many RAID levels, and each uses a different disk configuration to achieve fault tolerance and optimal performance.

ReiserFS A journaled file system that is supported on Linux.

Remote Authentication Dial-In User Service (RADIUS) A protocol that provides authentication, authorization, and accounting management to users who use a network service. Edge devices such as VPN appliances and wireless access points can be configured to forward authentication requests to a central RADIUS server.

Remote Desktop Protocol (RDP) A Microsoft protocol used to provide a GUI to connect to another computer over a network; uses TCP port 3389.

Remote Installation Service (RIS) A service that enables computers with PXE to install Microsoft operating systems remotely; superseded by Windows Deployment Services (WDS, or WinDS).

Remote Server Administration Tool (RSAT) A Windows Server feature that enables remote management of other computers running the Windows Server OS.

Resilient File System (ReFS) A Microsoft file system designed to succeed NTFS eventually. ReFS allows disk volume corruption repair even while the volume is mounted.

reverse proxy A server that listens for client connections to a target network service such as a web server. The reverse proxy forwards these requests to a different host where the network service actually resides.

revolutions per minute (RPM) Used to determine access time and read/write speed of spinning physical media such as CDs, DVDs, and hard disk drives.

RJ-11 A standard connector for twisted-wire pairs that is commonly used in telephony. Also used by modems.

RJ-45 A standard connector for twisted-wire pairs that is used in Ethernet networks.

rollover cable A cable used to connect a computer directly to a router's console port.

rotational latency The amount of time it takes for the desired part of the disk to pass under the read/write heads of a hard disk drive.

Routing and Remote Access Service (RRAS) A Microsoft Server service that enables the configuration of routing protocols, NAT, and VPNs.

Routing Information Protocol (RIP) A protocol that uses hop counts as a routing metric. Packets going through a router constitute a hop count.

RSA token Used for VPN authentication, this device is synchronized with the VPN device and has a small display showing a numeric value that changes periodically, every 90 seconds for instance.

runaway process Processes that keep consuming resources.

Samba The term "Samba" stems from Microsoft's Server Message Block (SMB) protocol; it is an open source product that provides Windows file and print services on various UNIX and Linux platforms.

sandbox A tightly controlled area and set of resources in which a program can be run without risking harm to the host operating system or computer.

SC connector Subscriber connector; a snap-in fiber-optic cable connector that is somewhat square in shape.

scale out To add more nodes to a system.

scale up To add more resources to a single node.

secure boot A technology that checks the system boot loader's cryptographic key against a list of authorized keys that are stored in firmware.

Secure Copy Protocol (SCP) A network protocol that uses Secure Shell (SSH) for data transfers between hosts on a network.

Secure File Transfer Protocol (SFTP) FTP over SSH, which provides file access, transfer, and management over a secured connection.

Secure Shell (SSH) A network protocol that provides administrators a secure way to access remote systems; uses TCP port 22.

Secure Sockets Layer (SSL) An application-specific security technology for providing an encrypted link between a server and a client; requires a PKI certificate for the server.

Security as a Service (SECaaS) A business model in which a large service provider integrates its security services with a corporate infrastructure on a subscription basis.

seek time The time it takes for a disk drive to locate where the data that is to be read is stored.

selective wipe A technique in which application data on mobile devices is wiped if access to the data has been revoked, while leaving personal apps, settings, and data untouched.

serial-attached SCSI (SAS) A serial protocol that moves data between computer storage devices and tape drives. SAS supersedes older SCSI standards that use parallel transmission.

server A computer designed and configured to be accessed concurrently by multiple users.

server core A minimal server installation of a Windows Server OS that does not include GUI components.

Server Message Block (SMB) A protocol implemented in Windows for network file sharing.

service level agreement (SLA) A contract between the end user and the service provider that dictates what is expected of both parties.

SFP connector Small Form Factor Pluggable; this network connector is most often used with fiber-optic networks but can be used with copper cable networks.

shielded twisted pair (STP) A type of twisted-pair cable that has an additional outer covering to protect against outside interference.

Simple Mail Transfer Protocol (SMTP) An Internet standard for e-mail transmission between servers; uses TCP port 25 or 465 if secured with SSL or TLS.

Simple Network Management Protocol (SNMP) A protocol for collecting and analyzing information about devices and configuring this information to affect their behaviors over a network. SNMP management tools can access MIBs on devices over UDP port 161. An SNMP agent must be running on network devices.

single data rate (SDR) memory A computer bus that transfers data only once every clock cycle.

single-mode fiber Optical fiber designed to transmit light over long distances.

Single Sign-On (SSO) An authentication process that enables a user to enter a single username/password combination to access multiple applications.

small form factor (SFF) A computer form factor designed to reduce the size of a desktop computer; also a smaller hard disk size than a large form factor at 2 1/2 inches.

snapshot *See* checkpoint.

Software as a Service (SaaS) A software licensing and delivery model in which the software is hosted at a central location and provided on a subscription basis.

solid-state drive (SSD) A storage device that stores data in flash memory, as opposed to storing data on magnetic rotating disk platters.

solid-state hybrid drive (SSHD) A combination of hard disk and solid-state technology in the same package.

southbridge The second chip of the chipset on a computer motherboard. It generally handles buses or interfaces that do not need direct access to the CPU or that do not need much bandwidth, such as PCI.

ST connector Straight tip, a fiber-optic connector that is rounded and elongated, and commonly used with multi-mode fiber.

start of authority (SOA) A type of DNS record that contains information about a DNS zone such as the serial number, zone refresh interval, and so on.

Static Random Access Memory (SRAM) A type of volatile memory. Unlike DRAM, the information in memory does not need to be constantly refreshed. It is both faster and more expensive than DRAM and is typically used for CPU cache.

storage area network (SAN) A network that provides access to block-level data storage as opposed to servers having the own dedicated local storage.

storage tier Two or more types of storage that are differentiated by various attributes such as frequency of access. Frequently accessed data is often stored on faster media.

straight-through cable The type of cable used when RJ-45 connectors at each end have the same pinout; normally used to connect computing devices to network switches.

subnet mask A mask that is used to determine what subnet an IP address is from. When compared against an IP address, it separates the network portion of the IP address from the host portion. The mask can be expressed in decimal, such as 255.255.0.0, or in CIDR format, such as /16.

SuperDLT Supports larger capacities and transfer rates than DLT.

symmetric multiprocessing (SMP) Where two or more identical physical processors with centralized memory operate under a single operating system. The motherboard must have multiple CPU sockets.

synchronous replication Data is written to a primary location and another location without delay.

Telnet A protocol used to access a computer system remotely. Its only form of security is a password that is sent in clear text over the network. Telnet listens on TCP port 23.

terabyte (TB) A unit of digital information equivalent to 1 million million (10^{12}) bytes, or 1000 gigabytes.

Teredo A technology that enables IPv6 traffic to pass over the IPv4 Internet through NAT. The Teredo server must reside on the IPv4 Internet. Public Teredo servers and relays are available.

Terminal Access Controller Access-Control System (TACACS) A protocol that enables a remote access server to forward a user password to an authentication server.

thin provisioning Enables storage to be configured without knowing the size required. Disk volumes grow over time as needed.

time-domain reflectometer (TDR) A device that determines the quality of metallic cables by observing reflected waveforms.

top-level domain (TLD) A domain at the highest level of the domain name system of the Internet, such as .com or .uk.

tower server A computer intended to be a server in an upright case that can stand alone.

transfer rate The speed at which data can be transmitted from one device to another. Usually measured in Mbps or Gbps.

Transmission Control Protocol (TCP) A TCP/IP suite transport protocol that establishes a connection between two hosts before transmitting. TCP requires an acknowledgment from the recipient for every sent packet.

Transmission Control Protocol/Internet Protocol (TCP/IP) A suite of protocols that map to different layers of the OSI model.

Transport Layer Security (TLS) A cryptographic protocol that provides secure communications over a computer network. TLS supersedes SSL.

Trivial File Transfer Protocol (TFTP) A protocol that is a simple version of FTP used when user authentication is not required, such as with PXE boot.

Trusted Platform Module (TPM) A firmware standard for a secure cryptoprocessor that is used to secure hardware by integrating cryptographic keys into devices.

unicast Communication on a network between a single sender and a single receiver.

unified extensible firmware interface (UEFI) A replacement for the BIOS. A specification that defines an interface between an OS and the platform's firmware.

uninterruptible power supply (UPS) A device that provides emergency battery power when the input power source fails. The purpose is not long-term power but rather enough power to enable equipment to shut down properly.

Universal Serial Bus (USB) A standard serial bus that is used as a connector between computer peripherals and computers.

UNIX A family of multitasking, multiuser operating systems derived from the original AT&T Unix.

unshielded twisted pair (UTP) A type of twisted-pair cable that has no additional protection or shielding against outside interference.

User Account Control (UAC) A security feature in versions of Windows from Vista onward. When a program requires administrative privileges, a prompt appears asking whether you do or do not agree to give the program administrative privileges; this prevents scripts and programs from executing without user consent.

User Datagram Protocol (UDP) An alternate transport protocol to TCP that is used for establishing low-latency and loss-tolerant connections, such as online video gaming. Unlike TCP, there is no session establishment or acknowledgment of sent packets.

virtual CPU (vCPU) A physical CPU that is assigned to a virtual machine.

virtual hard disk (VHD) A file format that contains the disk partitions and file system of a virtual machine.

virtual local area network (VLAN) A broadcast domain that is isolated at the data link layer. VLANs are configured within switches and are used to create multiple networks for the purposes of security or network performance.

virtual network interface card (vNIC) A NIC used by a virtual machine as its network interface.

virtual private network (VPN) A private network that extends over a public network or the Internet using an encrypted tunnel.

virtual server A server operating system running within a virtual machine on a hypervisor.

virtualization The ability to create a virtual version of something, such as an operating system, hard disk, or application.

Voice over Internet Protocol (VoIP) A group of technologies used to deliver voice communications and multimedia sessions over IP networks.

volt-ampere (VA) The "apparent power" that is the product of the voltage applied to the equipment multiplied by the current drawn by the equipment.

Wake-on-LAN (WoL) A standard that enables a computer to be turned on over a network when it receives a specially formed packet.

warm site An alternate site that is stocked with hardware that can run business operations in the event of a disaster. All that is needed to make it fully functional is the last backups of the original site, along with personnel.

Wi-Fi A technology that enables computing devices to connect wirelessly using the IEEE 802.11 standard.

Wi-Fi Protected Access (WPA) A security protocol used to secure IEEE 802.11 networks. There are two versions: WPA and WPA2. They are the successors to WEP.

Windows A line of client operating systems developed and supported by Microsoft.

Windows Imaging Format (WIM) A file-based disk imaging format developed by Microsoft to help deploy versions of Windows from Vista onward.

Windows Internet Name Service (WINS) An implementation of the NetBIOS Name Service by Microsoft that enables computers to map hostnames to IP addresses using a centralized service.

Windows Server Update Services (WSUS) A program developed by Microsoft that enables administrators to deploy updates selectively to computers in a corporate environment.

Wired Equivalent Privacy (WEP) A security algorithm for IEEE 802.11 wireless networks that is superseded by WPA and WPA2, which provide better security.

World Wide Name (WWN) A unique identifier used in Fibre Channel, ATA, and SAS as well as other storage technologies.

Write Once Read Many (WORM) A data storage device that can be written to only once.

X.509 A standard that specifies formats for public key certificates, certificate revocation lists, attribute certificates, and a certification path validation algorithm.

XFS A 64-bit journaling file system created by SGI and used in Linux.

zero-day A vulnerability in a program that is unknown to the vendor.

ZFS A file system and logical volume manager developed by Sun Microsystems and used by Solaris, OpenSolaris, and FreeBSD, among others.

zombie net *See* botnet.

zone transfer DNS servers can replicate DNS zone records using TCP port 53. Microsoft Active Directory–integrated zones replicate with Active Directory and do not use zone transfers.

INDEX

O

P

LICENSE AGREEMENT

THIS PRODUCT (THE "PRODUCT") CONTAINS PROPRIETARY SOFTWARE, DATA AND INFORMATION (INCLUDING DOCUMENTATION) OWNED BY McGRAW-HILL EDUCATION AND ITS LICENSORS. YOUR RIGHT TO USE THE PRODUCT IS GOVERNED BY THE TERMS AND CONDITIONS OF THIS AGREEMENT.

LICENSE: Throughout this License Agreement, "you" shall mean either the individual or the entity whose agent opens this package. You are granted a non-exclusive and non-transferable license to use the Product subject to the following terms:
(i) If you have licensed a single user version of the Product, the Product may only be used on a single computer (i.e., a single CPU). If you licensed and paid the fee applicable to a local area network or wide area network version of the Product, you are subject to the terms of the following subparagraph (ii).
(ii) If you have licensed a local area network version, you may use the Product on unlimited workstations located in one single building selected by you that is served by such local area network. If you have licensed a wide area network version, you may use the Product on unlimited workstations located in multiple buildings on the same site selected by you that is served by such wide area network; provided, however, that any building will not be considered located in the same site if it is more than five (5) miles away from any building included in such site. In addition, you may only use a local area or wide area network version of the Product on one single server. If you wish to use the Product on more than one server, you must obtain written authorization from McGraw-Hill Education and pay additional fees.
(iii) You may make one copy of the Product for back-up purposes only and you must maintain an accurate record as to the location of the back-up at all times.

COPYRIGHT; RESTRICTIONS ON USE AND TRANSFER: All rights (including copyright) in and to the Product are owned by McGraw-Hill Education and its licensors. You are the owner of the enclosed disc on which the Product is recorded. You may not use, copy, decompile, disassemble, reverse engineer, modify, reproduce, create derivative works, transmit, distribute, sublicense, store in a database or retrieval system of any kind, rent or transfer the Product, or any portion thereof, in any form or by any means (including electronically or otherwise) except as expressly provided for in this License Agreement. You must reproduce the copyright notices, trademark notices, legends and logos of McGraw-Hill Education and its licensors that appear on the Product on the back-up copy of the Product which you are permitted to make hereunder. All rights in the Product not expressly granted herein are reserved by McGraw-Hill Education and its licensors.

TERM: This License Agreement is effective until terminated. It will terminate if you fail to comply with any term or condition of this License Agreement. Upon termination, you are obligated to return to McGraw-Hill Education the Product together with all copies thereof and to purge all copies of the Product included in any and all servers and computer facilities.

DISCLAIMER OF WARRANTY: THE PRODUCT AND THE BACK-UP COPY ARE LICENSED "AS IS." McGRAW-HILL EDUCATION, ITS LICENSORS AND THE AUTHORS MAKE NO WARRANTIES, EXPRESS OR IMPLIED, AS TO THE RESULTS TO BE OBTAINED BY ANY PERSON OR ENTITY FROM USE OF THE PRODUCT, ANY INFORMATION OR DATA INCLUDED THEREIN AND/OR ANY TECHNICAL SUPPORT SERVICES PROVIDED HEREUNDER, IF ANY ("TECHNICAL SUPPORT SERVICES"). McGRAW-HILL EDUCATION, ITS LICENSORS AND THE AUTHORS MAKE NO EXPRESS OR IMPLIED WARRANTIES OF MERCHANTABILITY OR FITNESS FOR A PARTICULAR PURPOSE OR USE WITH RESPECT TO THE PRODUCT. McGRAW-HILL EDUCATION, ITS LICENSORS, AND THE AUTHORS MAKE NO GUARANTEE THAT YOU WILL PASS ANY CERTIFICATION EXAM WHATSOEVER BY USING THIS PRODUCT. NEITHER McGRAW-HILL EDUCATION, ANY OF ITS LICENSORS NOR THE AUTHORS WARRANT THAT THE FUNCTIONS CONTAINED IN THE PRODUCT WILL MEET YOUR REQUIREMENTS OR THAT THE OPERATION OF THE PRODUCT WILL BE UNINTERRUPTED OR ERROR FREE. YOU ASSUME THE ENTIRE RISK WITH RESPECT TO THE QUALITY AND PERFORMANCE OF THE PRODUCT.

LIMITED WARRANTY FOR DISC: To the original licensee only, McGraw-Hill Education warrants that the enclosed disc on which the Product is recorded is free from defects in materials and workmanship under normal use and service for a period of ninety (90) days from the date of purchase. In the event of a defect in the disc covered by the foregoing warranty, McGraw-Hill Education will replace the disc.

LIMITATION OF LIABILITY: NEITHER McGRAW-HILL EDUCATION, ITS LICENSORS NOR THE AUTHORS SHALL BE LIABLE FOR ANY INDIRECT, SPECIAL OR CONSEQUENTIAL DAMAGES, SUCH AS BUT NOT LIMITED TO, LOSS OF ANTICIPATED PROFITS OR BENEFITS, RESULTING FROM THE USE OR INABILITY TO USE THE PRODUCT EVEN IF ANY OF THEM HAS BEEN ADVISED OF THE POSSIBILITY OF SUCH DAMAGES. THIS LIMITATION OF LIABILITY SHALL APPLY TO ANY CLAIM OR CAUSE WHATSOEVER WHETHER SUCH CLAIM OR CAUSE ARISES IN CONTRACT, TORT, OR OTHERWISE. Some states do not allow the exclusion or limitation of indirect, special or consequential damages, so the above limitation may not apply to you.

U.S. GOVERNMENT RESTRICTED RIGHTS: Any software included in the Product is provided with restricted rights subject to subparagraphs (c), (1) and (2) of the Commercial Computer Software-Restricted Rights clause at 48 C.F.R. 52.227-19. The terms of this Agreement applicable to the use of the data in the Product are those under which the data are generally made available to the general public by McGraw-Hill Education. Except as provided herein, no reproduction, use, or disclosure rights are granted with respect to the data included in the Product and no right to modify or create derivative works from any such data is hereby granted.

GENERAL: This License Agreement constitutes the entire agreement between the parties relating to the Product. The terms of any Purchase Order shall have no effect on the terms of this License Agreement. Failure of McGraw-Hill Education to insist at any time on strict compliance with this License Agreement shall not constitute a waiver of any rights under this License Agreement. This License Agreement shall be construed and governed in accordance with the laws of the State of New York. If any provision of this License Agreement is held to be contrary to law, that provision will be enforced to the maximum extent permissible and the remaining provisions will remain in full force and effect.